EVENTS
management

an international approach

Nicole Ferdinand & Paul J. Kitchin

EVENTS
management
an international approach

⑤SAGE

Los Angeles | London | New Delhi
Singapore | Washington DC

2011004 250

SAGE Publications Ltd
1 Oliver's Yard
55 City Road
London EC1Y 1SP

SAGE Publications Inc.
2455 Teller Road
Thousand Oaks, California 91320

SAGE Publications India Pvt Ltd
B 1/I 1 Mohan Cooperative Industrial Area
Mathura Road
New Delhi 110 044

SAGE Publications Asia-Pacific Pte Ltd
3 Church Street
#10–04 Samsung Hub
Singapore 049483

Library of Congress Control Number: 2011937425

British Library Cataloguing in Publication data

A catalogue record for this book is available from the British Library

ISBN 978-0-85702-240-0
ISBN 978-0-85702-241-7 (pbk)

Typeset by C&M Digitals (P) Ltd, Chennai, India
Printed by MPG Books Group, Bodmin, Cornwall
Printed on paper from sustainable resources

FSC
MIX
Paper from responsible sources
FSC® C018575
www.fsc.org

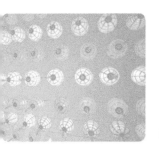

Contents

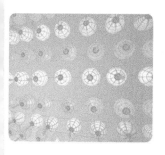

Notes on Contributors

Editors

Nicole Ferdinand has been a senior lecturer in events management at the London Metropolitan Business School since September 2006 and also leads its post-graduate event management programmes. She currently serves as Editor of the *London Journal of Tourism, Sport and Creative Industries* and visiting lecturer for the Stenden University of Applied Sciences in the Netherlands. Following a successful event management career that spans over ten years in her native country of Trinidad and Tobago, Nicole still continues to serve as an Event Management consultant to public and private sector organizations as well as community-based groups.

Paul J. Kitchin has been a lecturer in sport management at the University of Ulster since September 2009 and is responsible for the delivery of the sport business modules on the MSc Sport Management course. He is an editorial board member of the *International Journal of Sports Marketing and Sponsorship* and the *International Journal of Sports Management and Marketing*. Paul has over ten years experience working with UK third-sector sporting organizations in the provision of research, planning and consultancy services. Prior to this work Paul was employed as an Events Officer at the Melbourne Sports and Aquatic Centre in Victoria, Australia.

Contributors

Dr Nazia Ali, Lecturer in Tourism and Events Management, Faculty of Education, Sport and Tourism Division of Tourism and Leisure, University of Bedfordshire, United Kingdom.

Dr Elena Cavagnaro, Professor, Service Studies, School of Hospitality, International Hospitality Management, Stenden University of Applied Sciences, The Netherlands.

Sarah Edwards, Lecturer, School of Hospitality, Food and Events Management, University College Birmingham, United Kingdom.

Nicole Ferdinand, Senior Lecturer, Events Management and Programme Director, Post-graduate Event Management Courses, Department of Tourism, Sport and the Creative Industries, London Metropolitan Business School, United Kingdom.

Dr Alain Ferrand, Professor, Faculty of Sport Sciences, University of Poitiers, France.

Dr Rumen Vassilev Gechev, Professor in Economics and Business, University of National and World Economy (UNWE), Bulgaria.

Dr Stephen Henderson, Senior Lecturer, UK Centre for Events Management, Leeds Metropolitan University, United Kingdom.

Bruce Johnson, Senior Lecturer in Human Resource Management, Department of Human Resource Management, London Metropolitan Business School, United Kingdom.

Paul J. Kitchin, Lecturer in Sport Management, School of Sport Studies, University of Ulster, United Kingdom.

Polly Larner, Senior Lecturer and Course Director at London College of Communication, University of the Arts London, United Kingdom.

Dr Marc Mazodier, Lecturer, Ehrenberg-Bass Institute for Marketing Science, University of South Australia.

Thomas Neese, Senior Project Manager at GRAVITY, Germany.

Dr Stephen Page, Professor, School of Tourism, Bournemouth University.

Dr Ioannis S. Pantelidis, Senior Lecturer in Hospitality and Culinary Arts, School of Service Management, University of Brighton, United Kingdom.

Albert Postma, Professor, Scenario Planning, European Tourism Futures Institute, Stenden University of Applied Sciences, The Netherlands.

Ivna Reic, Senior Lecturer in Events and Creative Industries Management and Programme Director, Undergraduate Event Management Courses, Department of Tourism, Sport and the Creative Industries, London Metropolitan Business School, United Kingdom.

Dr Sacha Reid, Lecturer, Department of Tourism, Leisure, Hotel and Sport Management, Griffith Business School, Australia.

Dr Brent W. Ritchie, Associate Professor, Deputy Head, School of Tourism, University of Queensland, Australia.

Tariq Saed Al-Abdulla, Head of Technical Affairs Section, Qatar Olympic Committee, Qatar.

Maher N. Safi, Marketing Expert, Qatar Olympic Committee, Qatar.

Dr Stephen J. Shaw, Reader in Regeneration and City Management, Cities Institute, London Metropolitan University, United Kingdom.

Liander Taylor, Adjunct Faculty, ACC, Cedar Park, Texas.

Dr Jo-anne Tull, Lecturer and Academic Co-ordinator, BA Carnival Studies, Department of Creative and Festival Arts, The University of the West Indies, Trinidad and Tobago.

Dr Simone Wesner, Senior Lecturer in Cultural Industries Management, Department of Tourism, Sport and the Creative Industries, London Metropolitan Business School, United Kingdom.

Dr Nigel L. Williams, PMP, Prince2, Senior Lecturer Project Management, Department of Business Systems, Business School, University of Bedfordshire, United Kingdom.

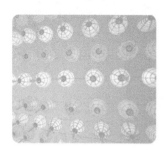

Foreword

The field of events has seen nothing short of a dramatic growth in intellectual interest in the last decade and my own academic interest in events has evolved over a number of years since my involvement in the first journal in the field – *Event Management* – and my own subsequent research on different facets of events. These have been interesting years as a researcher to see a wave of development – that has overtaken the boom of the 1980s and 1990s in Tourism Studies – with the rise of Event Studies and its more specialized educational focus on Event Management and Marketing. This book is part of this new wave of growth in events research as a new generation of texts seek to map out where the educational landscape of event education is now heading as well as synthesizing the rapidly growing literature base.

So how does it fit with other books in the field? There are clearly a number of texts in the field which seek to cover all of the fundamentals of event management. This text is somewhat different to those as it has a principal focus on current global issues and the principles of management associated with these emerging themes, so it extends the educational interface with events education by focusing on these themes. In this respect it is a very useful introduction to the field which brings together a wide range of international contributors with different expertise and knowledge of this area of study.

In many ways, events education and research addresses many of the now well-known concepts and ideas that emerged with the growth in Tourism Studies. There is a similar pattern of development evident where wider developments in social science contributed to the emerging knowledge base and evolution of concepts. Yet what is distinctive in the events field is that much of the curriculum and literature splits very markedly into two distinct camps – the *academic* and the *practitioner* field. The latter is a key feature of much of the growth in events education – it is vocational and aligned to employment opportunities in a rapidly expanding sector of employment. In the UK alone, it is estimated that the event sector employs around 530,000 people and is worth around £36 billion. In addition, it has benefited from one important feature of the postmodern society – leisure consumption, which in this case is reflected in the growing consumption associated with festivals and events as generators of economic activity.

Whilst we see wide-ranging debates around this very theme, the contents of this book demonstrate that the creation of an event focus in many areas of social science and business and management follow many changes in society and the economy. We now have very large and well funded organizations in some countries that are charged with attracting and promoting mega-events because of their major contribution to the livelihoods of people and localities. Sometimes such organizations work with tourism organizations and in other cases as stand-alone bodies. Where tourism was a key contributor to the redevelopment of places that had seen the effects of de-industrialization and structural changes in their local economies in the 1980s and 1990s, events have become a more specialist and visible element of these redevelopment and regeneration projects. However, this trend also raises many debates on who are the beneficiaries of this type of place-building and reimaging through regeneration schemes in the case of mega-events where social, economic and environmental changes occur.

So how does this book address these emerging debates and other contemporary themes in events research and education? First and foremost, this is a book with a global focus reflecting the theoretical debates on the changing nature of production and consumption in an increasingly globalized world. It highlights many of the important principles associated with event management and the contemporary debates now facing the sector.

I commend this new book to its readers as a fresh and stimulating new perspective on event management that addresses many of the current issues that managers and students need to understand in pursuit of the fulfilling event experience in a global world. I hope you will find this book a significant help in your studies and future careers.

Stephen Page
Professor, School of Tourism, Bournemouth University

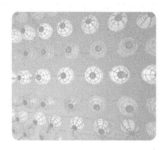

Companion Website

Be sure to visit the companion website at www.sagepub.co.uk/ferdinand to find a range of teaching and learning materials for both lecturers and students, including the following:

For lecturers:

Instructor's manual: Contains a range of teaching materials for each section of the book, including:

- Overviews of each section
- Teaching notes
- Additional case studies
- Quizzes
- Video clips

PowerPoint slides: PowerPoint slides for each chapter for use in class are also provided. These slides can be edited by instructors to suit teaching styles and needs.

For students:

Online readings: Full access to selected SAGE journal articles related to each chapter, providing students with a deeper understanding of the topics covered in each chapter.

PART 1

INTRODUCING AN INTERNATIONAL APPROACH TO EVENTS MANAGEMENT

Events form an integral part of all societies. Historically, they have provided meaning and structure to daily life and over time they have assumed increased dominance in other spheres of leisure activity, such as sport, cultural pursuits and tourism and also in the activities of business, political and charitable organizations. As Richards (2010) observes, contemporary communities and organizations throughout the world now all seem to share a common compulsion to organize events. In some instances the hosting of events, especially large-scale ones, is seen as a pre-text for fast tracking urban regeneration and stimulating economic growth (Chalkley and Essex, 1999). In others, events are seen as a means of building and/or reviving the brands of cities (Robertson and Guerrier, 1998; Waitt, 1999, 2003), organizations (Javalgi et al., 1994; Pope and Voges, 2000) and products (Gorse et al., 2010). For others still, events are a way to raise money and awareness for charitable causes (Webber, 2004).

There are numerous reasons for events to be organized, just as there is great diversity in *how* they are organized. Often this diversity is rooted in the socio-cultural milieus of host communities. The political, economic and technological situations of different countries will also account for variations in the form and function of events. At the same time, global issues such as rising migration, ageing populations, terrorism concerns and climate change have led to a great deal of convergence in event management practices throughout the world. Many metropolitan cities, for example, Sydney, London and New York, boast a host of ethnic festivals dedicated to celebrating the cultures of migrant populations, as well as music concerts and other types of entertainment which cater to older attendees, mirroring current population trends. Increasingly, high levels of security and the implementation of sustainable event management principles are synonymous with hosting events which are described as being of 'international standard', regardless of the country in which they are staged.

This first section of *Events Management: An International Approach*, examines the dual tensions at work in international events management – an engagement with the global issues impacting the events industry and an understanding of the specific local factors, which account for the differences in how events are staged from country to country. The chapters in this section of the text seek to provide the background for the approach taken throughout by introducing the issues and challenges that characterize the contemporary events landscape.

Chapter 1 by Ferdinand and Shaw examines the ways in which events have shaped the lives of individuals, communities, organizations, cities and also countries across the globe. It compares and contrasts the meanings and functions of events in countries such as the United States, Canada, Indonesia, Germany, the Netherlands, Singapore and the United Kingdom by exploring the diverse reasons cities and communities in these countries have undertaken the hosting of events. The authors highlight how events have been used to respond to global issues, including excessive consumerism, racial, ethnic and class divisions and an increasingly competitive trading environment. They also outline the unintended consequences of events, such as the redistribution of public funds away from local communities (in the case of large-scale events), the perpetuation of ethnic stereotypes (which can occur within ethnic festivals) and the acquisition of significant long-term debt (especially when international sporting events are involved).

In Chapter 2, Ferdinand and Wesner shift from a global perspective to a focus on the specific factors which shape events management in host communities – which include political, economic, socio-cultural and technological conditions; stakeholder relationships; resource availability; competition and intercultural differences. By outlining a model of the international events environment, these authors demonstrate how global and local forces interact to shape the staging of events and create significant challenges for event organizations operating both at home and outside their countries of origin.

This first section introduces key concepts such as globalization, event/experiential marketing and event tourism, which are built upon in the succeeding sections. It also strives to provide a balanced view of international events, highlighting their benefits as wells as drawbacks. In summary, Part 1 seeks to provide a foundation on which a deeper understanding of international events management practice and the critical issues involved in international events management can be established.

References

Chalkley, B.S. and Essex, S.J. (1999) 'Urban development through hosting international events: A history of the Olympic Games', *Planning Perspectives*, 14(4): 369–394.

Gorse, S., Chadwick, S. and Burton, N. (2010) 'Entrepreneurship through sports marketing: A case analysis of Red Bull in sport', *Journal of Sponsorship*, 3(4): 348–357.

Javalgi, R.G., Traylor, R.B., Gross, A.C. and Lampman, E. (1994) 'Awareness of sponsorship and corporate image: An empirical investigation', *Journal of Advertising*, 23(4): 47–58.

Pope, N.K.L. and Voges, K.E. (2000) 'The impact of sport sponsorship activities, corporate image, and prior use on consumer purchase intention', *Sport Marketing Quarterly*, 9(2): 96–102.

Richards, G. (2010) 'Leisure in the Network Society: From pseudo events to hyperfestivity', inaugural address given at the public acceptance of the appointment of Professor in Leisure Studies at Tilburg University, 8 October.

Robertson, M. and Guerrier, Y. (1998) 'Events as entrepreneurial displays: Seville, Barcelona and Madrid', in D. Tyler, Y. Guerrier and M. Robertson (eds), *Managing Tourism in Cities*. Chichester: John Wiley and Sons. pp. 215–228.

Waitt, G. (1999) 'Playing games with Sydney: Marketing Sydney for the 2000 Olympics', *Urban Studies*, 36(7): 1005–1077.

Waitt, G. (2003) 'Social impacts of the Sydney Olympics', *Annals of Tourism Research*, 30(1): 194–215.

Webber, D. (2004) 'Understanding charity fundraising events', *International Journal of Nonprofit and Voluntary Sector Marketing*, 9(2): 122–134.

1

Events in Our Changing World

Nicole Ferdinand and Stephen J. Shaw

Learning Objectives

By reading this chapter students should be able to:

- Reflect on the meaning of events for individuals in different societies.
- Identify the practices of business, communities and countries which have been influenced by the popularity of events.
- List and evaluate the positive and negative impacts that events have had on communities and the urban environment.
- Understand the key criticisms that are made of events.
- Critically discuss the potential of events to achieve long-term, sustainable economic development.

Introduction

Events have been a part of human civilizations since ancient times. They have marked changing seasons, heralded the appointment of new leaders, celebrated religious rites and rituals and also signified births and deaths. In modern societies they continue to serve these functions but they have become significantly more complex and elaborate and their audiences have grown exponentially. The 2009 inauguration of the 44th American President, Barack Obama, set records for being the most popular presidential inauguration by attracting a live viewing audience of over 2 million and an online audience of over 45.5 million viewers (Heussner, 2009). It was an elaborate production costing over US$170 million (£104 million) to stage (Mayerowitz, 2009). The 2008 Beijing Olympics was viewed by a record 4.7 billion television viewers (Neilsen, 2008) and cost over US$40billion (£25 billion) to stage, making it the most expensive Olympic Games event of all time (CBC News, 2008). Both these examples demonstrate how drastically the roles of events in societies have changed and how integral they have become to daily life.

Like other leisure/symbolic/experience goods, events now have an ever-increasing value for individuals (see Lash and Urry, 1994; Nazreth, 2007; Pine and Gilmore,

1999). Toffler's (1970: 226) prediction that in the future individuals would 'begin to collect experiences as consciously and passionately as they once collected things' seems to have come true. For communities as well, events have taken on new meanings. Whereas once community events marked the details of local life, in contemporary migrant communities, which are often comprised of immigrants from many different countries, events have become a way of re-connecting with homelands and heritage. Many communities also host what have been described as 'placeless festivals' (MacLeod, 2006) which are not associated with any particular community or country, but rather represent shared interests and ideals or are staged purely for commercial reasons. In the realm of business the impact of events on organizations can be seen in the contemporary strategies of marketers. Event or experiential marketing has emerged as a central feature of the marketing mix for organizations around the world and continues to dominate marketing budgets. As organizations become bigger and bigger and cross national boundaries, international meetings and conferences have emerged as a vital tool for keeping employees in touch with one another. In cities, mega-events have been used as catalysts for major regeneration projects by city governments that aspire to 'world city' status. Many countries have also promoted and continue to promote events as a means of impacting positively on long-term economic development.

Despite the current ubiquity enjoyed by events and the state of 'hyperfestivity' (Richards, 2010) that now dominates the twenty-first century, events are not without their critics or drawbacks. For example, the proliferation of placeless festivals has been criticized for transforming formerly meaningful celebrations into largely meaningless tourist spectacles (MacLeod, 2006), much in the way Boorstin (1961) condemned 'pseudo events' for being media creations and irrelevant to real life. Globally, the 2008 financial crisis has heightened concerns from corporations as to whether there is adequate return on investment to justify spending on events. Meeting planners are now being pressed to provide detailed proof of return on investment for corporate meetings and the ability to do so has been highlighted as vital to their business' future success (MPI, 2010).

In cities, the claims and pronouncements of civic leaders of the benefits of events have often been proven to be overly extravagant (Gold and Gold, 2005). The unintended social, economic and fiscal consequences of events have even triggered political dissent and regime change, when outcomes fail to meet expectations, or where adverse impacts on particular communities, especially at the local and neighbourhood level, outweigh the promised benefits (Shaw, 2003). The hosting of large-scale events has also left countries facing substantial long-term debt due to cost-overruns or losing face internationally due to poor organization and planning.

This chapter seeks to provide students with a comprehensive overview of the ways in which events are currently shaping the lives of individuals, organizations, communities and economies, highlighting their potential to be forces of positive change and transformation as well as sources of negative consequences and outcomes. It strives to give a balanced, critical appraisal of events and their role in societies across the globe.

What Do Events Mean to Us?

For most people events are an integral part of daily life. They represent critical milestones and are among the most memorable experiences individuals can have. The persistence of wedding, birthday, graduation and farewell celebrations demonstrate the enduring relevance of events to human life. At the same time, as we as human beings have changed so has the meanings events have for us. For many in consumption-driven Western societies, events are no longer a time of rest or recuperation from labour or times to reflect on religious values and beliefs or even to mark the changing seasons and rhythms of life. They are instead sites in which individuals seek to connect with each other and find meaning, as opportunities for both are now in short supply.

Indeed, the emergence of modern day music festivals and sporting events as forms of alternative spirituality has been observed by a number of commentators as a feature of postmodern life (Kommers, 2011; Parry, 2007; Partridge, 2006). One such event is the Burning Man Festival which has been staged annually since 1986. It is a celebration of self-expression, survival, sharing and radical self-reliance which features interactive art-making, gift-giving, performance and costuming. For regular attendees, known as 'burners', the festival site – the desert of Black Rock City, Nevada – is a place of pilgrimage where authentic, spontaneous expressions of spirituality can be experienced by all attendees regardless of faith. It also represents a stark contrast to the consumerism of modern life as attendees are required to participate in a 'gift-economy', relying on gifts given to them by others to survive for the duration of the festival. Burning Man culminates in the burning of a 50-foot effigy of a man, which has various meanings for attendees. Sherry and Kozinets (2007) highlight some of these meanings in an ethnographic study of the festival. See Table 1.1 below.

Sporting events such as the Olympic Games and the FIFA World Cup are also, for sports fans, sites of pilgrimage. The venues where great sporting feats have taken place are for some comparable to shrines in which they can walk in the footsteps of their sporting heroes (Gammon, 2004).

In non-western societies, yet to be dominated by modern capitalism, events have also taken on new meanings for individuals. Thanks to the spread of cultural tourism, communities previously untouched by the outside world are now sought out by tourists searching for new cultural experiences. For the practitioners of indigenous cultural art forms, staging events for visitors can be a source of pride, empowerment and additional income. For example, Cole's (2007) study, which features cultural tourism in Eastern Indonesia, demonstrates how villagers use the cultural events they stage for visitors to achieve a sense of enhanced identity. However, at the same time, staging events in this manner can also change their meanings and significance, turning once sacred rites and rituals into 'commodities to be traded in the global cause of tourism development' (Clarke, 2000: 23). Greenwood's (1989) often cited seminal essay on Spain's Alarde of Fuenterrabia illustrates how a once important historic ritual has been rendered inauthentic by its development for the tourism market. Events in such cases can become performances

Table 1.1 *Symbolism of the 'burn' at the Burning Man Festival*

• Profound loss	• A stripping of the self
• Pure wonderment	• Purification
• A combustion of the id	• A loss of direction
• Release from restraint	• Crucifixion
• Sacrifice	• Adrenalized joy

which rob individuals 'of the very meanings by which they organize their lives' (Greenwood, 1989: 179).

The meaning of events can also change over time as societies evolve. Gay Pride celebrations, in cities such as San Francisco, London and Sydney, for example, were once highly politicized events where gays came together to assert their rights as individuals. Nowadays these parades are fun, festive days for the entire family. There is now much less of a stigma surrounding homosexuality in many societies, so these events have become mainstream tourist attractions endorsed by politicians and local businesses for the publicity and other benefits that can be derived from their staging. Likewise Carnival, which is celebrated in the Caribbean island of Trinidad, was once a commemoration of the end of slavery in which participants heavily criticized and satirized former slave masters and government officials. The modern festival, although still bearing some resemblance to the post-slavery celebrations, has evolved into an event which has a wider, far more universal message of freedom and self-expression which transcends race, class or economic classifications. Events like these can demonstrate to individuals how their societies have evolved over time, reflecting profound changes in social attitudes, political and economic circumstances or even how a society sees itself.

Events in Organizations

One of the key ways that events are used by organizations is in event and/or experiential marketing. The popularity of these practices has been linked in large part to increasing media fragmentation and competition amongst firms which have led to consumers being bombarded with an endless array of choices and thus less responsive to traditional methods of advertising.

The terms event and experiential marketing are often used interchangeably but they are defined quite differently in the literature. Event marketing generally refers to the process planned by an organization of integrating a variety of communication elements behind an event theme – most often through the sponsorship of another organization's event (Tuckwell, 1991). Experiential marketing in contrast is most often associated with the promotion of brands. It seeks to create an on-going, emotional attachment between a brand and its customers by bringing it to life in the form of an event, experience or interaction (McCole, 2004). (Chapter 6 in this volume discusses this topic in greater detail.)

The other key ways in which organizations utilize events are as ways of communicating with and motivating its staff or members. Perhaps the most common of these types of events are meetings. They can be used to inform staff of changes, initiate projects or keep employees on track and working towards a goal. Many organizations will also have events which are not specifically related to the organization's work but are instead meant to be activities which give employees or members an opportunity to relax or be entertained. These can come in the form of awards ceremonies, office parties or elaborate incentive programmes. These types of events form a major component of the MICE (meetings, incentive travel, conferences and exhibitions) sector which is where the relationship between events and organizations is perhaps most visible.

Conferences and exhibitions can also bring together colleagues from similar industries, professions or interest groups in forums to meet and share ideas and information. The exuberance of the sector has been somewhat curbed by the 2008 financial crisis as in many organizations events are now being viewed as unnecessary extras in times of austerity. Event managers in this sector are now under pressure to prove the value of hosting these events, bringing a new level of scrutiny to claims of events being able to enhance organizational performance. (See Chapter 14 in this volume where a more detailed overview of the MICE sector and its current issues and challenges is given.)

Events – Engines of Social Integration for Communities?

In large cities that are gateways to immigration, events such as street festivals and carnivals bring together members of ethnic and cultural minorities, some of whom may be recent arrivals, while others may have settled for several generations. As with food, music and other traditions, religious and secular festivals can play an important role in uniting those communities and reinforcing their shared identities. In some cases the event evolves over time and takes on new forms and meanings through fusion with other cultural influences. Thus, the bigger picture or mosaic of many festivals at different times in the annual events calendar may confer a 'cosmopolitan' character to a city as a whole that can be promoted to external audiences as a positive feature.

In Putnam's (2000) terminology, the process of staging such festivals may help to build *bonding capital* within a network of people with common cultural or ethnic origins. The timing of traditional festivals may connect community members with their countries of origin, for example, New Year and spring festivals. Further, to transnational communities as well as members of the majority culture, their enactment may confirm associations between a particular minority and the urban spaces where the festival takes place. In some circumstances, the event may connect favourably with the majority community of the city concerned, and provide an enjoyable opportunity for the latter to gain a better understanding of the lives of immigrants within their own city. Thus festivals may help create bridges between communities: *bridging capital*. Nevertheless, there is a rather thin line between expression of elements of cultural identity to visiting 'tourists' and the reinforcement of cultural or ethnic stereotypes: a simplification that commercial sponsors may tend to reinforce to promote products such as exotic food and drink.

In their study of ethnically diverse neighbourhoods in Montreal, Germain and Radice (2006: 113) observe that few authors have related the concept of 'cosmopolitanism' explicitly to street-level encounters in public spaces such as those facilitated through festivals, but amongst those authors there are two camps. On the one hand, there are 'idealists' who emphasize 'the potential to unite citizens and/or political movements and institutions across national and other boundaries', including Hannerz (1996: 103) who defines cosmopolitanism as a 'willingness to engage with the Other' that encourages individuals to develop abilities to make their way in other cultures, building upon active listening, observation and reflection. Bloomfield and Bianchini (2004: 88–9) comment that some festivals, carnivals and community events can be seen both as cultural expressions of specific ethnic minorities and as civic celebrations belonging to the whole city, notable examples being Berlin's annual Karnivale der Kulturen (carnival of cultures) which offers a showcase for African, Latin American, Asian, Turkish and Indian music and dance, and Rotterdam's Caribbean Carnival, an inter-cultural event that has evolved and interacted with contemporary Dutch culture.

In contrast to this somewhat upbeat and optimistic reading of 'cosmopolitan' festivals, a more cynical interpretation emphasizes a trend towards commodification of events and other 'exotic products' that trades upon ethnic and cultural difference as a commercial opportunity. With particular reference to 'Disneyfied Latin Quarters' in North American cities, critics have characterized the process as top-down homogenization. Global competition impels cities to create 'cosmopolitan' spaces in which to entertain the desirable target market of affluent, footloose cosmopolites. Judd (1999: 36) describes Greektown in Baltimore as 'a two-block-square renovated district' that envelops the traveller 'so that he/she only moves inside secured, protected and normalized environments'. He concedes to the possibility that cultural events may 'help foster community solidarity and spirit', such as the St Patrick's Day parades. Nevertheless, he concludes that tourist bubbles are 'more likely to contribute to racial, ethnic, and class tensions than an impulse toward local community' (Judd, 1999: 52–3). More recently, Hannigan (2007) has highlighted the sophisticated 'controlled edge' that satisfies the desire of young professionals for a visibly gritty street panorama without the danger: a safe adventure in neo-bohemia (see Table 1.2).

Table 1.2   *Positive and negative impacts of ethnic festivals*

POSITIVE IMPACTS	NEGATIVE IMPACTS
• Bringing together of cultural and ethnic minorities • Providing a 'cosmopolitan' image for cities • Connecting immigrants with their countries of origin • Fostering of inter-cultural understanding • Providing enjoyable leisure opportunities for local and external audiences	• Reinforcing of cultural and ethnic stereotypes • Commodifying of culture • Highlighting of cultural differences which can increase cultural/ethnic/racial tensions • 'Disneyfying' of community landscapes • Reducing cultural events to 'exotic products' to be bought and sold

Case Study 1.1   Ethnic Festivals of Historic 'Neighbourhoods' in Canadian Cities

In Toronto, Vancouver, Ottawa, Montreal and other Canadian gateway cities, minority 'neighbourhoods' are conspicuous features of the historic urban landscape. Until the 1950s, the cities were settled mainly by people of British, and (in Quebec Province) of French ancestry, but nowadays their populations are highly diverse. Annual festivals and other events that are performed in the streets of urban and inner suburban neighbourhoods provide a significant means for identity-building. As in other North American gateway cities, communities that have largely moved away to more distant suburbs or other cities, maintain an attachment to localities that in former times provided places of initial settlement. In many cases, some religious, cultural and commercial institutions remain, and the re-enactment of religious and secular festivals each year – by descendants of Canadians who migrated from Southern and Eastern Europe, Africa, Asia, Latin America, the Caribbean and other world regions – continues to provide the focus for community gatherings that facilitate occasional contact between dispersed families, friends and other former compatriots, as well as nostalgic connection with the neighbourhood.

Since the 1970s, in Toronto and other cities in Ontario Province, an increasing number of neighbourhood festivals have been organized and/or sponsored by 'Business Improvement Areas' (BIAs) – not-for-profit agencies that are empowered to promote their localities with special purpose funds raised from additional local taxes levied on commercial property (Shaw, 2007). Where restaurateurs and bar owners are strongly represented on their boards, it is understandable that cultural and ethnic identities are linked with food and drink. For example, in early August, the main thoroughfare is closed to traffic to accommodate the Pilaros Taste of the Danforth festival celebrating Greek cuisine. Toronto's Greektown is further embellished by Greek as well as English street signs (Hackworth and Rekers, 2005). Likewise, the Corso Italia BIA has an Italian food and wine festival, Italianate streetlights, banners and floral displays. In both cases, the 'original' residential population is declining, and fewer remaining descendants continue to speak Italian at home. Nevertheless, the streets have continuing significance to Canadians of Greek and Italian origin, and their bars are popular venues to watch sporting events on television when their national teams are playing.

In contrast, the festivalization and rejuvenation of Montreal's Chinatown was guided by a formal plan, formulated by a panel on which residents, faith and community organizations, as well as traders were represented (Shaw, 2007). The Chinatown Development Plan, endorsed by Mayor Borque (Ville de Montreal, 1998: 11), acknowledges that its historic landscape 'is the most potent symbol of the Chinese community's roots in Montreal and Quebec society ... where Chinese in Quebec can meet those from other areas in the north-eastern part of North

(Continued)

(Continued)

America'. This rejuvenation targeted a locality that suffered lack of investment and visible neglect until the early 2000s and sought to strike an appropriate balance between commercial development as a tourism attraction, and the social integration of Chinese Quebecers. A key achievement was the creation of Sun-Yat-Sen Park on a former vacant lot. On summer weekends this space provides an important meeting area for Chinese Canadians from across the Province of Quebec and further afield, who celebrate religious and cultural ceremonies, and gather for family occasions such as weddings.

Figure 1.1   *Sun-Yat-Sen Park, Montreal*

'Eventscapes' – Place Marketing Tools to Position Cities and Localities on the World Map?

As Richards and Palmer (2010: 27–31) observe, the 'eventful' city has become a vast stage on which festivals, sporting activities such as marathons, parades, carnivals and other high-profile happenings are organized and promoted for the (assumed) benefit of local people as well as visitors. Throughout the world, 'festivalization' – the temporary transformation of a place into symbolic space in which the public domain is claimed for particular forms of consumption (see Van Elderen, 1997) – is now a critical feature of strategies for place-making that combine destination marketing to enhance urban competitiveness with spectacular achievements of the city-building professions that include urban design, architecture and planning that convert ephemeral features of city life and urbanity into fixed cultural capital. These may include: iconic buildings for exhibitions and conventions; sports stadia; museums and galleries; and concert halls. There may also be the creation or upgrading of public spaces to accommodate major events in the open air.

In this context, festivals and other events – together with impressive urban landscapes on which they can be staged and promoted – have become 'a means of improving the image of cities, adding life to city streets and giving citizens renewed pride in their city' (Richards and Palmer, 2010: 27–31). Looking back over the last half-century, as many industrial economies climbed out of the economic restrictions and austerity in the aftermath of the Second World War, the 1960s and 1970s brought greater prosperity, and a more competitive trading environment. Increasing recognition was given to the prestige and potential commercial advantages of hosting large-scale events, especially international trade expositions (Expos), Olympic Games and world class festivals of the arts.

Through media-oriented festivalization, the city could be presented as a backdrop for events that had the potential to attract the attention of the global business, sporting and cultural elite. In general, the aesthetics of such events celebrated universal as opposed to place-specific references, with an understandable tendency to emulate successful formulae. Further, in an inspiring era of innovation that included wide-bodied jets, satellite and space technology, the staging of global spectacles was often ultra-modern if not futuristic. Contemporary observer Relph (1976) argued that the global and future-orientation of such events, like the 'placelessness' of the corporate architecture of shopping malls, theme parks and airports, was destroying any remaining sense of spatial and cultural identity. Musing on the Ontario Place Exhibition complex in Toronto, Relph explained the underlying logic of events that are 'deliberately intended as points of innovation as trend-setters in design and style and taste: they are meant to be copied' (1976: 105). Since the 1980s, however, there has been a marked 'cultural turn' away from serial 'me-too' replication towards the nurturing of events that are more strongly connected with the place and its communities.

Nearly 20 years ago, Kotler et al. (1993) chronicled a broader shift in the principles and practices of place marketing, especially in North America; an abandoning of the crude and undifferentiated 'smokestack-chasing' of former times. Instead, from the early 1990s, astute place marketers adopted more sophisticated 'product development and competitive niche thinking … seeking to define themselves as distinctive places with competitive advantages for target industries' (Kotler et al., 1993: 78). Public sector agencies form strategic partnerships with commercial and voluntary sector organizations in coalitions for growth, as post-industrial cities/localities adapt to new economic conditions, and reimage themselves as centres for culture and entertainment of every kind from classical music to casinos. An important differentiation strategy for effecting lasting change is the staging of events, a notable example being the 1996 Olympic Games, and Atlanta's aspiration to emerge from the international sporting event as a model of racial harmony, southern hospitality and corporate-government collaboration, consolidating its position as capital of the New South (Holcomb, 1999).

Over the first decade of the twenty-first century, events-led marketing of cities/localities attained new levels of sophistication and intensity, as cities work hard to enhance their international appeal, especially from the perspective of Florida's (2002) highly mobile 'creative classes': the hard-to-define but 'rising' elite that civic leaders continue to regard as prime movers of the post-industrial global economy, and thus the critical target markets to ensure future success. Florida's model places a premium on social cohesion and 'tolerance' as key ingredients in the place-marketing mix. Thus, it is acknowledged in principle that events programmes ought to reflect rooted identities, and that events can play a role that helps to reinforce the unique sense of place that is meaningful and beneficial to residents and visitors alike.

In practice, however, civic leaders and place marketers may well struggle to strike an acceptable balance in organizing events that simultaneously enthuse all sections of the resident population and appeal to external audiences, especially the highly mobile and elusive creative classes. Further, events must present the city/locality itself in ways that attract the attention of footloose globe-trotters whose engagement with the place in question may be temporary and somewhat superficial. Chang (2000) and Jayne (2006) draw attention to Singapore's events programme to support the city-state's Renaissance City branding that targeted international conventions, conferences and other business-related tourism. Criticism was levelled at its dual effect. Not only did it redistribute arts funding away from local cultural production, but the focus of the events programme on internationally oriented 'high culture' engaged only a very small minority of the host population.

With the attention of global media audiences, a city/locality or indeed a whole country can be 'located' on the world map through the successful hosting of a large-scale event. A notable example of the former is the 2010 Ryder Cup golfing championship held in Newport, Wales, and positive positioning of nations through events includes the 2010 FIFA World Cup in South Africa. In a few instances, home-grown festivals and carnivals – as opposed to major sporting events secured through international competition between rival hosts – have also developed into globally recognized event-brands. Initially, at least, these may provide the showcase for distinctive national, regional or urban (sub-) cultures that are likewise exposed to international audiences.

With regard to home-grown events there is, however, a strong possibility that global celebrity status may change the whole ethos of the event. In time, the event may be severed from its roots: the locality that nurtured it. MacLeod (2006: 232) has commented that, despite aspirations to express cultural distinctiveness, over time many large-scale events have become 'world parties', to some degree disconnected with the place and its 'hosts'. On the one hand, the celebrations bring international fame, but on the other, local communities may feel a loss of 'ownership' and control, a phenomenon that critics have observed in Edinburgh's International Festival and in London's Notting Hill Carnival (Smith, 2009). Moreover, an event that fails to deliver the intended benefits to local electors and businesses may be the subject of public disaffection that may bring significant problems for the re-election of civic leaders who stake their political careers on a positive outcome.

Events – Engines of Sustainable Economic Recovery and Growth for Countries?

Events may play a significant role in attracting higher-spending visitors to areas of a city that hitherto have not been regarded as safe or desirable destinations for leisure and tourism. Thus, they are important catalysts to reimage localities that have been avoided by all but the most adventurous of sightseers, because of their associations with the poverty and disadvantage of immigrant communities and concerns over personal security, especially after dark. As emphasized above, the temporary or permanent festivalization of local streets and public spaces may support social integration, with outcomes that are hard-to-measure, but which are generally assumed to be beneficial for transnational communities, inter-culturalism and creativity. At the same time, festivalization may serve an explicitly economic role through area-based initiatives that are designed to regenerate localities where more established industries such as manufacturing and distribution are in serious decline, unemployment is high, and where investment is badly needed to revitalize neglected inner-city streetscapes and infrastructure.

Events may therefore be expected to contribute to economic outcomes that can be quantified, not only by headcounts to estimate the number of visitors to the area concerned, but also through assessment of the number of business start-ups, as well as jobs created and retained through stimulation of an emerging visitor economy. It has been argued that place marketing and place making to support regeneration at the micro-scale of streets and public spaces within an inner-city or inner suburban district should be conceptualized in a similar way to strategies for the economic recovery and growth of nations and city-regions. The use of local festivals and other events to support the restructuring of local economies through a shift from production to consumption-based industries may therefore be considered. In particular, local events that attract the attention of outsiders can challenge preconceptions and prejudices of external audiences, as well as create wealth for the locality through increased expenditure on local goods and services.

There is a considerable debate over the extent to which agencies of state, especially local authorities, should regulate market forces and intervene through land use planning, and other powers and duties, to harmonize economic regeneration with longer-term social and environmental objectives. As highlighted in the discussion of social integration, the 'place-product' has complex and heterogeneous functions and meanings. However, it may be the case that particular commercial streets and enclaves are visited by members of the majority culture and by tourists with varied demands for 'exotic' goods and services, while the area continues to serve as a commercial, cultural and social hub for members of a minority group. These issues have important ramifications for local authorities and their place-making responsibilities to promote local wellbeing: a role that has to be balanced with the desire to capture local economic benefits as opportunities arise from the often volatile ebbs and flows of globalization.

Case Study 1.2   International Events and Montreal

Geographically and economically marginalized from the commercial heartland of North America, and understandably defensive of the Francophone culture of its majority population within a mainly English-speaking continent, events have featured strongly in Montreal's 'World City' aspirations (Shaw, 2003). Over the past half-century, successive city governments have put considerable faith in the power of events to support this global ambition, through bidding for prestigious international business, sporting and cultural events, as well as by facilitating and promoting a year-round programme of festivals that originated in the city itself, and whose reputation has spread beyond Canada. Observers have identified two distinct phases in this events-led marketing strategy: the 'modernist' period from the 1960s through to the mid-1980s; and a 'postmodern' period from the mid-1980s through to the present day. In Montreal, the cultural turn of large-scale events in the 1980s reflected not only a deep shift in the base of civic power and its ideology, but also the high-profile instigation by politicians of 'world parties' and their consequences played its own role in the civic regime change.

The staging of prestigious events was critical to the political strategy and initial success of the charismatic Mayor Jean Drapeau (in office 1954 to 1957 and 1960 to 1986) to promote his modernist vision of Montreal as an international city. The Civic Party that he led was supported by the interests of the establishment, especially developers, builders and merchants while avoiding alienation of small businesses and property owners (Hamel and Jouve, 2008). The structure and style of urban governance were highly centralized and paternalistic. The World Fair or 'Expo' in 1967, during which 50 million people visited the city, brought international acclaim. The Olympic Games in 1976 attracted positive media attention abroad, but brought criticism by residents' groups and urban social movements, especially because of the demolition of low-rent housing to make way for the Olympic Stadium. Political opponents denounced a staggering cost overrun that necessitated debt repayments that continued into the twenty-first century, and dismissed the Olympics as 'bread and circuses' to divert public attention away from economic decline (Germain and Rose, 2000).

The adverse response by the Montreal electorate to the Olympics was a factor that contributed to the end of Drapeau's long reign as mayor and to regime change in city government, while at provincial level profound changes were effected in the 'Quiet Revolution' and in the assertion of francophone nationalism with the rise of Parti Quebecois (PQ). The Montreal Citizens' Movement (RCM), a coalition of social movements led by Mayor Dore, eventually gained control of the city in 1986 with public support for its emphatic rejection of grandiose and extravagant public projects and its commitment to democratization and decentralization.

(Continued)

(Continued)

Figure 1.2   *Olympic Tower, Montreal*

However, by 1994 the RCM were out of office again, and the subsequent coun-cil led by Mayor Pierre Borque gained support from a pro-growth coalition of the new francophone capitalist class in its drive to 're-internationalize' the city; its new vision reflected the rise of a new kind of francophone nationalism in the Quebec Province of Canada, 'one interested in taking on all the trappings and responsi-bilities of the modern nation and state, [which] pressed both city and provincial elites to look for external validation and identity' (Paul, 2004: 579).

Critical to this global 'imagineering' strategy was to stage spectacular events in the downtown area and the rebranding of Montreal as a 'City of Festivals'. Major ones include the Montreal World Film Festival, Franco-Folies Francophone pop music festival and Just for Laughs international comedy festival. Canada's largest tourism event, the Montreal Jazz Festival, was first staged in 1980 with concerts spread over the summer and mainly in the more counter-cultural atmosphere of the city's 'Latin Quarter' of Eastside. From 1987 it was moved to Place des Arts adjacent to the Central Business District, and by 2004 it had become an 11-day programme, with over CN\$1 million (over £650,000) sponsorship from all three levels of government, along with major commercial sponsors such as Alcan Aluminium (Paul, 2004). Although to a lesser extent than the example of Singapore (above), in more recent years city government has been criticized for its

(Continued)

(Continued)

overriding desire to attract and impress the internally oriented elite; for many residents the events programmes are decreasingly in tune with popular tastes and with the true creative producers of the bohemian fringe.

Furthermore, the lessons of the Montreal Olympics and the prevailing neo-liberal ideology suggest that events should recover their costs. Nevertheless, the completion in 2009/10 of the new Quartier des Spectacles – a showpiece all-weather platform to accommodate major events – raises important questions of priority in an era of austerity and unprecedented fiscal restraint.

Figure 1.3   *Quartier des Spectacles, Montreal*

Case Study Questions

1 What reasons have been put forward in the case for successive Canadian governments pursuing an international events strategy?
2 What have been the benefits and drawbacks of pursuing this strategy?
3 What can politicians do to avoid becoming subjects of criticism due to the negative consequences associated with international events?
4 What meanings do events such as the World's Fair and the Olympic Games have for the ordinary citizens of a country?

Chapter Summary

Events are a vital part of the human experience. They provide cherished memories, mark critical milestones and reinforce beliefs, values and cultures. In postmodern societies events have become a source of spirituality in and of themselves, as the fast-paced march of the modern world has left many individuals isolated and trapped by consumer-driven culture. The staging of cultural events for tourists is also a source of income and pride for the practitioners of indigenous cultural forms without access to other resources. However, if care is not taken in exploiting cultural events for their commercial benefits, economic motivations can rob people of the meanings these events have for them. Events can also demonstrate to individuals how their societies have changed.

For organizations, events provide opportunities to make personal connections with their customers, to communicate with stakeholders and to motivate employees. At the same time, the 2008 financial crisis has caused many to question whether these benefits can be realized and many organizations are now viewing events as unnecessary costs.

In communities comprised of large immigrant populations, ethnic festivals can be vehicles for social integration and opportunities for immigrants to display aspects of their culture to the host community. Cynics also point out these types of events make commodities out of the cultures of immigrants and reduce their neighbourhoods into 'Disneyfied', tourist bubbles which heighten race, class and cultural tensions.

Place-marketing strategies, which utilize large-scale events, are integral to the development strategies of many cities and countries. Events and the infrastructure that is established to support their staging, such as new sporting stadia, concert halls and other iconic buildings, are used to enhance the image and competiveness of destinations. Benefits of such strategies include increased tourist visitors, new job creation and business opportunities. The hosting of large-scale events is also a major undertaking that requires a tremendous amount of resources which are often paid for with public funds. Thus, it is hardly surprising these types of events attract a great deal of scrutiny and criticism, especially when they appear to be enriching a minority of citizens. Moreover badly managed events can lead to the downfall of governments due to the severity of their unintended outcomes, which include negative publicity, financial loss and substantial long-term debt.

Review Questions

1   How do personal circumstances shape the meanings events have for individuals?
2   What are the arguments for and against staging ethnic festivals in communities?
3   What benefits do events have for organizations?
4   What are the characteristics of the 'eventful' city?
5   How does Canada's experience compare with the staging of large-scale events in your own country?

Additional Resources

Books, book chapters, journal articles

Ali-Knight, J., Robertson, M., Fyall, A. and Ladkin, A. (2009) *International Perspectives of Festivals and Events: Paradigms of Analysis*. London: Elsevier.
A contemporary look at the issues involved in staging festivals and events for economic, social, cultural and community benefit.

Connell, J. and Page, S. (2011) *The Routledge Handbook of Events*. Abingdon: Routledge.
An exploration of the debates and controversies inherent to this rapidly expanding discipline.

Schmidt, D. and Rogers, L. (2008) *Handbook on Brand and Experience Management*. Cheltenham: Edward Elgar Publishing.
A useful guide through the latest research and theory on brand and experience management.

Smith, A. (2007) 'Large-scale events and sustainable urban regeneration: Key principles for host cities', *Journal of Urban Regeneration and Renewal*, 1(2): 178–190.
Provides recommendations for future event host cities about how best to maximize opportunities for sustainable event-driven regeneration.

Tassiopoulos, D. and Johnson, D. (2009) 'Social impacts of events', in R. Razack and J. Musgrave (eds), *Event Management and Sustainability*. Wallingford: CABI. pp. 76–89.
An exploration into the social impacts of events on host communities.

Useful websites

http://www.eventmagazine.co.uk/
Provides free online access to feature articles, news and jobs from the printed *Event Magazine* – a guide to key trends and insights in the event industry.

http://www.event-solutions.com/
Allows access to useful resources for corporate, association and independent event and meeting professionals.

http://www.worldofevents.net/
Links users to relevant information for event industry professionals, educators, students and researchers.

References

Bloomfield, J. and Bianchini, F. (2004) *Planning for the Intercultural City*. Stroud: Comedia.
Boorstin, D. (1961) *The Image: A Guide to Pseudo-Events in America*. New York: Vintage.
CBC News (2008) *Beijing and the Olympics: By the Numbers*. CBC News [online]. Available from http://www.cbc.ca /news/world/story/2008/08/08/f-beijing-by numbers.html.

Chang, T.C. (2000) Renaissance revisited: Singapore as a 'Global City of the Arts'. *International Journal of Urban and Regional Research*, 2(4), 818–831.

Clarke, A. (2000) 'The power to define: Meanings and values in tourism', in M. Robinson, P. Long, N. Evans, R. Sharpley and J. Swarbrooke (eds), *Expressions of Culture, Identity and Meaning in Tourism*. Sunderland: The Centre for Travel and Tourism. pp. 23–36.

Cole, S. (2007) 'Beyond authenticity and commodification', *Annals of Tourism Research*, 34(4): 43–960.

Florida, R. (2002) 'The economic geography of talent', *Annals of the Association of American Geographers*, 92(4): 743–755.

Gammon, S. (2004) 'Secular pilgrimage and sport tourism', in B.W. Ritchie and D. Adair (eds), *Sport Tourism: Interrelationships, Impacts and Issues*. Clevedon: Channel View Publications. pp. 30–45.

Germain, A. and Radice, M. (2006) 'Cosmopolitanism by default: Public sociability in Montreal', in J. Binnie, J. Holloway, S. Millington and C. Young (eds), *Cosmopolitan Urbanism*. London and New York: Routledge. pp. 112–129.

Germain, A. and Rose, D. (2000) *Montreal: Quest for a Metropolis*. Chichester: Wiley.

Gold, J.R. and Gold, M. (2005) *Cities of Culture: Staging International Festivals and the Urban Agenda 1851–2000*. Aldershot: Ashgate Publishing Ltd.

Greenwood, D.J. (1989) 'Culture by the pound: An anthropological perspective on tourism as cultural commoditization', in V.L. Smith (ed.), *Hosts and Guests: The Anthropology of Tourism* (2nd edn). Philadelphia: University of Pennsylvania Press. pp. 171–185.

Hackworth, J. and Rekers, J. (2005) 'Ethnic packaging and gentrification: The case of four neighbourhoods in Toronto', *Urban Affairs Review*, 41(2): 211–266.

Hamel, P. and Jouve, B. (2008) 'In search of a stable urban regime for Montreal: Issues and challenges in metropolitan development', *Urban Research and Practice*, 1(1): 18–35.

Hannerz, U. (1996) *Transnational Connections: Culture, People, Places*. London: Routledge.

Hannigan, J. (2007) 'From fantasy city to creative city', in G. Richards and J. Wilson (eds), *Tourism, Creativity and Development*. London and New York: Routledge. pp. 48–56.

Heussner, K.M. (2009) *Obama Makes Internet History: Inauguration Sets Record for Streaming Online Video*. ABC News [Online]. Available from http://abcnews.go.com/Technology/president-obama-inauguration-sets-record-video-views-online/story?id=6699048.

Holcomb, B. (1999) 'Marketing cities for tourism', in D.R. Judd and S. Fainstein (eds), *The Tourist City*. New Haven: Yale University Press. pp. 54–70.

Jayne, M. (2006) *Cities and Consumption*. London: Routledge.

Judd, D. (1999) 'Constructing the tourist bubble', in D. Judd and S. Fainstein (eds), *The Tourist City*. New Haven: Yale University Press. pp. 35–53.

Kommers, H. (2011) 'Hidden in music: Religious experience and popular culture', *Journal of Religion and Popular Culture*, 23(1): 14–26.

Kotler, P., Haider, D. and Rein, I. (1993) *Marketing Places: Attracting Investment, Industry and Tourism to Cities, States and Regions*. New York: The Free Press.

Lash, S. and Urry, J. (1994) *Economies of Signs and Space*. London: Sage Publications Ltd.

MacLeod, N. (2006) 'The placeless festival: Identity and place in the post-modern festival', in D. Picard and M. Robinson (eds), *Festivals, Tourism and Social Change: Remaking Worlds*. Clevedon: Chanel View Publications. pp. 222–237.

Mayerowitz, S. (2009) *What Recession? The $170 Million Inauguration*. ABC News [Online]. Available from http://abcnews.go.com/Business/Inauguration/president-obama-inauguration-cost-170-million/story?id=6665946.

McCole, P. (2004) 'Refocusing marketing to reflect practice: The changing role of marketing for business', *Marketing Intelligence and Planning*, 22(5): 531–539.

Meetings Planners International (MPI) (2010) *Future Watch 2010*. Chicago: RR Donnelly and Sons Company.

Nazreth, L. (2007) *The Leisure Economy: How Changing Demographics, Economics, and Generational Attitudes Will Reshape Our Lives and Our Industries*. Ontario: John Wiley and Sons Canada, Ltd.

Neilsen (2008) *The Final Tally – 4.7 Billion Tunes in to Beijing 2008 – More Than Two in Three People Worldwide: Nielsen*. The Nielsen Company [Online]. Available from http://www.nielsen.com/us/en/insights/press-room/2008/the_final_tally_-.html.

Parry, J. (2007) *Sport and Spirituality: An Introduction*. Oxon: Routledge.

Partridge, C. (2006) 'The spiritual and the revolutionary: Alternative spirituality, British free festivals, and the emergence of rave culture', *Culture and Religion: An Interdisciplinary Journal*, 7(1): 41–60.

Paul, D.E. (2004) 'World cities as hegemonic projects: The politics of global imagineering in Montreal', *Political Geography*, 23: 571–596.

Pine, B. and Gilmore, J. (1999) *The Experience Economy: Work is Theatre and Every Business a Stage*. Boston: Harvard Business School Press.

Putnam, R.D. (2000) *Bowling Alone: The Collapse and Revival of American Community*. New York: Simon and Schuster.

Relph, E. (1976) *Place and Placelessness*. London: Pion.

Richards, G. (2010) 'Leisure in the Network Society: From pseudo events to hyperfestivity', inaugural address given at the public acceptance of the appointment of Professor in Leisure Studies at Tilburg University, 8 October.

Richards, G. and Palmer, R. (2010) *Eventful Cities: Cultural Management and Urban Revitalization*. Amsterdam: Elsevier.

Shaw, S. (2003) 'The Canadian world city and sustainable downtown revitalisation: Messages from Montreal 1962–2002', *British Journal of Canadian Studies*, 16(2): 363–377.

Shaw, S. (2007) 'Inner city ethnoscapes as cultural attractions: Micro-place marketing in Canada', in M. Smith (ed.), *Tourism, Culture and Regeneration*. Wallingford: CABI. pp. 49–58.

Sherry, J.F. and Kozinets, R.V. (2007) 'Nomadic spirituality and the burning man festival', *Research in Consumer Behavior*, 11: 119–147.

Smith, M.K. (2009) *Issues in Cultural Tourism Studies* (2nd edn). London: Routledge.

Toffler, A. (1970) *Future Shock*. New York: Random House Inc.

Tuckwell, K.J. (1991) *Canadian Marketing in Action*. Scarborough: Prentice Hall.

Van Elderen, P.L. (1997) *Suddenly One Summer: A Sociological Portrait of the Joensuu Festival*. Joensuu: University Press.

Ville de Montreal (1998) *Chinatown Development Plan*. Ville de Montreal: Service de l'Urbanisme.

2
The International Events Environment

Nicole Ferdinand and Simone Wesner

Learning Objectives

By reading this chapter students should be able to:

- Describe what it means to take an international approach to events management.
- Identify key changes in the global environment, which are impacting events and event organizations.
- Use strategic planning tools to identify and analyse the environment in which international events take place.
- Understand how event organizations can formulate strategic responses to global changes.
- Appreciate how culture and customs can dictate how event organizations operate.

Introduction

Exactly what constitutes international events management is still yet to be defined in events management literature. However, recently published events management texts which profess an international focus or approach to the subject (see, for example, Yeoman et al., 2004; Ali-Knight et al., 2008; Page and Connell, 2011) share a focus on international activities, such as tourism and international sponsorship, and are concerned with differences between cultures and countries. Additionally, they engage with a number of global issues affecting people and organizations throughout the world, such as terrorism and sustainability. In essence they suggest international events management or an international approach to events management requires an engagement with international activities, cultural differences and global issues. There is also a distinct focus on 'international events', which are becoming increasingly common place in the events marketplace.

This chapter strives to highlight the growing international dimensions of events management, whilst recognizing the differences in events management practices that occur country to country. It starts by briefly outlining the characteristics and origins of international events. It then seeks to provide an understanding of the international events environment, which is the focus of the chapter. It divides the international events environment into global and local/community factors and outlines how they impact international events management practice.

International Events

What are they?

Although the term 'international event' is widely used to describe a variety of events, it is not part of most event typologies (see, for example, Falassi, 1987 and Getz, 2005). Within academic literature the terms major, mega or hallmark event are used to describe events which would commonly also be referred to as international events. For instance, Bowdin et al. (2006: 16) describe major events as events that are capable of attracting 'significant visitor numbers, media coverage and economic benefits', noting that many international sporting events fall into this category. Additionally, Jago and Shaw (1998: 29) define mega-events as 'one-time major events[s]' which are 'of an international scale', such as the New York World's Fair (1939) and the Festival of Britain (1951). Moreover, Ritchie (1984: 2) describes hallmark events as those which 'were developed primarily to enhance awareness, appeal and profitability of a tourism destination'. The Edinburgh International Festival is perhaps a classic example of a hallmark event.

In the absence of an exact definition, some key characteristics of international events are apparent. Perhaps first and foremost is their explicit focus on attracting international audiences. Secondly, they are large-scale events which have significant impacts on their host communities. Thirdly, they attract international or global media attention. Finally, these events have specific economic imperatives such as increasing tourism visitors, job creation and providing new business opportunities. Thus, international events may be described as large-scale events which attract international audiences and media attention and meet a variety of economic objectives for the destinations in which they are hosted.

The origins of international events

International events can be traced as far back as the beginnings of leisure and tourism, to Mesopotamia (situated approximately in modern-day Iraq) which is known as the 'Cradle of Civilization'. It was there, for the first time in human history, that the surplus production of food and the formation of wealth led to the emergence of a small 'leisure-class' of priests, warriors and others that did not have to worry continually about its day-to-day survival. This elite class that inhabited the early cities found them 'overcrowded and uncomfortable' and tried to escape whenever possible (Weaver and Lawton, 2006: 57). They escaped to other countries to visit historic sites, buy artefacts and also attend events. For example, the ancient Olympic Games held between 776 and 261 BC, provides one of the first examples of an event with an international character and it is described as one of the first recorded examples of sport event tourism (Weaver and Lawton, 2006).

Early modern events which attracted international audiences were visited by travellers undertaking the classical 'Grand Tours', which first became popular during the mid-sixteenth century (Withey, 1997). 'Grand Tour' was a term used to describe the extended travel of young men from the aristocratic classes of the United Kingdom and other parts of northern Europe to continental Europe for educational and cultural purposes (Towner, 1996). These tours were not regarded as strictly leisure pursuits as they were seen as educational and cultural experiences that were vital for anyone seeking to join the ranks of the elite. They eventually gave way to simple sightseeing and began to include aspiring members of the middle classes as well as aristocrats (Weaver and Lawton, 2006). For these travellers, attending cultural events and religious festivals were important features of Grand Tours and accounted in some part for the seasonal variations of visits to certain city centres. Rome, for instance, was particularly popular during Christmas, Easter and Carnival celebrations (Towner, 1985). These events, although rooted within the communities in which they were staged, became international because of the presence of these travellers on Grand Tours. It should be noted, however, that at this point, events attracting international audiences and tourism generally would not have been widespread. The cost of travel, along with the lack of tourism infrastructure made travelling to other countries an expensive, difficult and often dangerous affair.

Thomas Cook, a former preacher turned tour operator, has been credited with revolutionizing tourism travel by pioneering packaged tours. In so doing he democratized and also dramatically expanded tourism opportunities by making it much easier and cheaper for those wishing to travel by charging fixed prices for accommodation, travel and even food for a given route. He and later his company Thomas Cook and Sons (officially established in 1871) negotiated much cheaper rates in block than would be possible for individuals to do on their own. Thomas Cook was also responsible for taking British tourists to some of the early modern international events such as the Great Exhibition hosted in London's Hyde Park in 1851 (the first ever World's Fair or exhibition) and the International Exhibition hosted in 1855 in Paris (Thomas Cook Retail Limited, n/d).

World's Fairs and international exhibitions were among the first examples of international events as they are contemporarily understood. Britain and France were the principle sponsors of these events which were established between the late nineteenth and early twentieth centuries as these countries were the dominant colonial powers at the time. These events served to display their colonies, or their internally colonized peoples, to their home population, to their rivals and to the world at large (Benedict, 1991). The United States also hosted some of these early fairs and exhibitions, such as Chicago's World Columbian Exhibition in 1893 (Trennert, 1993) and the Louisiana Purchase Exposition (also known as the Saint Louis World's Fair) in 1904 (Benedict, 1991). Other notable international events established during this early period include the modern Olympic Games held in Athens in 1896 and Test Cricket, which was first played in 1877 (ESPN EMEA Limited, n/d).

The International Events Environment

It is evident that the origins and later establishment of modern international events can be linked to a number of factors. Perhaps most crucial was the emergence of leisure, as without a leisure class there could not be an international event audience. Innovations such as those pioneered by Thomas Cook and Sons were also very important because they provided the foundation for widespread event tourism which continues to be a key driver of the international events market. Global politics greatly influenced the form and function of the first international events, such as international exhibitions, which were focused on demonstrating the political and economic dominance of their sponsors – the governments of the leading colonial powers at the time. Getz (2005) describes these types of factors as 'global forces' which impact the planning and management of events. He suggests that all events are part of a system of interacting elements which consist of organizational factors (human, physical and financial resources), the local or community context (key stakeholders, resource availability and competition) and global forces (forces impacting on events, event organizations and event tourism).

International events, in particular, are also heavily influenced by 'globalization' – a term which refers to a number of processes that have enabled companies, products, people, money and information to move more freely and quickly around the world (Morrison, 2006).

Event managers need to be aware of not only the global forces in the international events environment, but also the particular local situations in which they find themselves. They must recognize the specific requirements of international events management, whilst also paying due attention to the differences in events management practices that occur country to country and also amongst different cultures within countries. International events management requires an understanding of the elements which constitute the international events environment and the formulation of appropriate responses.

By adapting Getz's (2005) events management system, it is possible to develop a model of the international events environment. Important additions to Getz's (2005) system are issues surrounding globalization, the local forces as opposed to global forces which affect events, event organizations and event tourism and also cultural differences (see Figure 2.1).

Globalization

At the heart of globalization is a deeper level integration amongst economies throughout the world, which has been in large part driven by the increase in multinational and transnational corporations (MNCs and TNCs). The former are businesses which own divisions and offices in multiple countries whereas the latter are companies which coordinate different aspects of their business activities across countries without necessarily taking ownership of the organizations performing these activities.

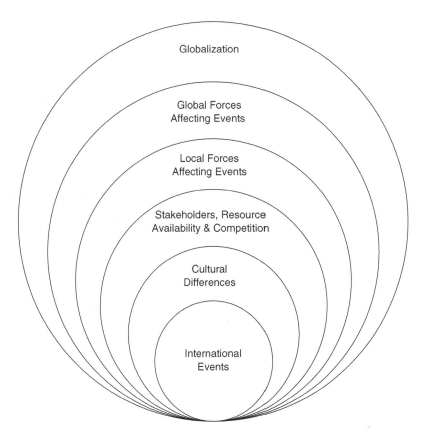

Figure 2.1   *The international events environment*

The proliferation of MNCs and TNCs has resulted in an unprecedented level of competition amongst manufacturers. This situation has been extremely beneficial for the growth of events and event organizations, as countries throughout the world, particularly the most developed societies, have been moving away from traditional production activities to economic development strategies involving tourism, leisure and sport (Burbank et al., 2001).

Event and festival tourism which was regarded as 'an emerging giant' (Getz and Frisby, 1988: 22) two decades ago now occupies 'significant status' in both domestic and international mass tourism markets (Picard and Robinson, 2006: 2). Increasingly, festivals and special events are consciously being developed as tourist attractions (Getz, 1998) by festival and event organizers, local communities and governments. Throughout the world there have been unprecedented investments into event infra-structure, such as convention and performing arts centres, stadia and festival malls. The following highlight some of the ways in which aspects of globalization have facilitated the growth of events and event organizations:

The increase in air travel and the cultural tourist market for events

Reductions in the cost of air travel and the convenience and ease of finding information about previously remote locals provided by the internet means that more and more people are travelling than ever before. The growth of the international tourism industry has been particularly striking in the last decade. From 2000 to 2009 international tourist arrivals have grown from 683 million to 880 million, after reaching its highest ever level of 919 million in 2008 (UNWTO, 2010). A significant number of these tourists would have been travellers going to a country for the specific purpose of attending cultural events. These tourists, also known as cultural tourists, are typically described as 'well-educated people with high status occupations and good incomes' that have travelled to a destination for the expressed purpose of experiencing culture (Richards, 2007: 18–19). In the last two decades cultural tourism has become a particularly important source of income for cultural facilities, festival and event organizers and also destinations.

In the past cultural tourism was associated with 'high culture' and the relatively wealthy as air travel and knowledge of foreign cultures was restricted to those who had the income and the education to acquire a lifestyle which included learning about rituals and practices of people in faraway places. Today cultural tourism is commonplace, so much so that it is beginning to lose all meaning as a distinct category of tourism (Richards, 2001). This dramatic shift was unthinkable just a few decades ago.

The development of file-trading and file-sharing technologies and live music events

File-trading and file-sharing technologies have made it very easy for music to be shared and traded across the globe, particularly illegally. Whereas these innovations have severely depressed sales of recorded music, it has led to the unprecedented growth in live music events throughout the last decade, as artists are now keener to tour as their incomes from recorded music have drastically fallen (Keynote, 2010). In fact, live music in the last decade has come to be regarded somewhat as the saviour for music companies and artists alike (Mintel, 2010a).

The increase in international organizations and the demand for international meetings, incentive travel, conferences and exhibitions (MICE)

The rise of MNCs and TNCs has also been accompanied by the internationalization of other organizations such as trade associations, charitable organizations and special interest groups. The increase in the numbers of international organizations throughout the world has led to a dramatic increase in the demand for events which cater to providing opportunities for organizations to bring colleagues scattered across the globe to meet to exchange ideas and information. The rapid expansion of the conference sector in the latter half of the twentieth century, in particular, can be directly linked to the proliferation of international organizations (Lawson, 2000). Today international meetings, incentive travel, conferences and exhibitions (MICE) have now become an established part of the events industry (Davidson and Rogers, 2006). In fact the worldwide MICE market is now estimated to be worth about US$650 million (£400 million) (Mintel, 2010b).

Global forces impacting events, events organizations and tourism

Outside of globalization there are a number of other forces which affect the way in which events are staged across the world. These forces can be studied using strategic planning tools such as a PEST or PESTEL analysis. PEST includes **p**olitical and legal changes, **e**conomic conditions, **s**ocio-cultural trends and innovations in **t**echnology. In a PESTEL analysis, changes in **l**egislation are treated separately as are **e**nvironmental concerns, such as global warming and climate change. Event managers can use PEST or PESTEL analyses to continually scan the global environment and adjust their events and organizational plans to either avoid or minimize threats and capitalize on opportunities. These can be discovered by asking key questions. These can include:

- Have there been any recent changes in global politics that can impact events?
- What new international laws and regulations have recently been introduced that event managers should be aware of?
- What are current economic conditions like?
- Have there been any critical events affecting global financial markets?
- What are the key global socio-demographic trends impacting event audiences?
- Are there any other trends that event managers can take advantage of when designing event activities (for example, popular music trends and sporting activities)?
- What new technological developments can event managers take advantage of to improve the quality, efficiency and/or lower the costs of their events?

Figure 2.2 is an illustrative PEST analysis which demonstrates the implications that global forces have for the staging of events.

Local/community context

Local forces affecting events, events organizations and event tourism

The local/community context in which events are staged impacts every aspect of an event organization's operations. Event organizations wishing to stage events outside of their country of origin need to research the local/community context in which they are organizing events carefully as it has fundamental implications for strategy and planning decisions. For instance, the ease and the cost at which visas and work permits can be acquired will determine how much of the event organization's personnel travel to staff an event overseas and how many local temporary members of staff are hired. Similarly, wage levels and general living standards will affect the prices that can be charged for event tickets. Likewise, the ethnic mix of the population in

Political	• **Terrorism** The events of 9/11 and the more recent attacks on the Sri Lankan cricket team in Lahore, India in 2009 have intensified concerns about terrorist attacks, particularly at sporting events. The main implication of these concerns has been the phenomenal increase in the costs of security for sporting events in particular, as there is a need not only to secure stadia and other sporting venues but individual athletes as well. Costs of securing the Vancouver 2010 Olympics, for example, exceeded US$1 billion (Farrell, 2010).
Economic	• **Global recession** The 2008 financial crisis, which plunged many of the world's economies into recession, has had dire impacts for many events. Many international events are reporting fewer visitors and participants from overseas. Competitive pricing, back-to-basics no-frill events and the hosting of events closer to home were among the key future trends for the industry identified in Future Watch 2010, a survey undertaken of event planners in 39 countries across the globe (Meeting Planners International, 2010).
Social	• **Ageing populations** Many countries throughout the developed world now have ageing populations, as a result of increased life expectancy and decreased birth rates. Moreover, older people are enjoying greater levels of vitality as they get older, and as a result are attending events in larger numbers than ever. Among the impacts that have been visible at events is the resurgence in popularity of music concerts featuring older bands and reunion tours such as the Police's 2007 tour, which was recognized by Billboard as having the top-grossing and top-ticket selling tour of that year (Peters, 2007).
Technological	• **The development of virtual and web-based technologies** The development of more reliable and increasingly cheaper technologies that can be harnessed for the hosting of events such as meetings and conferences is of greater interest to event planners now more than ever before. In the 2010 Future Watch survey event managers indicated that providing good alternatives to live meetings were among their key concerns for the future, ranking fifth out of a possible 16 items (Meeting Planners International, 2010).

Figure 2.2   *Global forces impacting events*

a particular event location may mean that marketing materials, food and drink served and the event programme may have to be changed to suit local tastes. Moreover, political unrest and instability may result in some event organizations choosing not to bid to host some events as the costs to secure the company's property and staff in some countries may simply be too high. Event organizations in their enthusiasm to expand their operations overseas may not pay enough attention to the implications that local conditions will have on event operations, often with disastrous consequences. Underestimating the significance of these forces can ultimately be the source of event failure.

It is perhaps taken for granted that event organizations staging events in their own countries will be mindful of their local/community context. However, when local or community events are developed for tourism audiences, event organizers, in anticipating tourist revenues, can focus too much on international visitors, whilst neglecting the community that hosts the event. This situation can generate a great deal of local resentment towards visitors and the event itself, especially if the event receives public funds. International events management requires the careful balancing of the needs of local and international audiences.

PEST or PESTEL analyses should be done for the country/city/community in which an event takes place to reveal local conditions which can impact an event, event organizations and event tourism, especially those affecting local attendees or

Table 2.1 *Local political, economic, social, technological, environmental and legal factors*

Political Conditions	• The presence of political unrest
	• Recent changes in political administrations
Economic Circumstances	• Cost of labour
	• Currency exchange rates
	• Wage levels
	• Interest rates
	• Reliability of the local banking systems
	• General living standards
Social Trends	• Dominance of particular cultural practices or beliefs
	• Racial and ethnic make-up of local populations
	• Openness to outside influences
Technology Levels	• Availability of telecommunications infrastructure
	• Availability of electricity and indoor plumbing
	• Level of internet penetration amongst local populations
Environmental Issues	• Level of environmental consciousness amongst local populations
	• Local weather patterns
	• Potential for extreme weather conditions due to seasonal fluctuations
Legal Requirements	• Visa and work permit requirements
	• Health and safety laws
	• Labour laws
	• Insurance requirements
	• Regulations governing alcohol, cigarette and drug consumption at indoor and outdoor event venues
	• Licences and certification required by event staff

stakeholders. Table 2.1 provides a checklist of political, economic, social, technological, environmental and legal factors that are applicable in a local context. Environmental and legal factors are especially relevant within a local context, as there is such variation in these factors amongst different countries.

Case Study 2.1   The International Cricket Council versus the West Indies

West Indians are renowned throughout the cricket world for their love of cricket and for the exuberant, carnivalesque atmosphere that they bring to matches. Indeed, in the West Indies cricket is much more than a game, it is a statement about Caribbean pride and also post-colonial aspirations. From the 1930s to the late 1980s, the cricket ground provided an avenue for freedom of expression, giving voice to anti-colonial sentiments which could not yet be expressed by most West Indians in other spheres of life. The International Cricket Council's 2007 World Cup which was hosted in the West Indies represented for many West Indians an opportunity to show the world their love for cricket, and also to demonstrate that nine small island nations with a population of a mere six million people combined could pull off the remarkable feat of co-hosting a major international sporting event.

Instead West Indians found themselves hosting a heavily commercialized, tightly regulated series of matches which bore little resemblance to the bacchanalian celebrations which characterize West Indian cricket. Ticket prices were set between US$10 (£6.13) for warm-up matches to US$300 (£184.02) for the finals, which effectively priced many Caribbean people out of the market (McKenzie, 2007). The banning of outside foodstuff and the requirement for a written request to be made to take musical instruments such as steel and kettle drums and conch shells to matches (Bhola, 2007), robbed the West Indies World Cup of its island flavour. Critics, including legendary former West Indian team captain Sir Vivian Richards, accused the ICC and the local organizing committee of stifling the true spirit of the game in the Caribbean (BBC, 2007). The early exits of both the West Indies team and other Caribbean crowd favourites India and Pakistan did little to help matters. The end result was half-empty stands devoid of any atmosphere throughout the preliminary and early qualifying matches. Prolific cricket writer Tony Becca blamed the organizers for focusing too much on a tourist market, which, in the end, largely failed to materialize and ignoring the needs of the Caribbean people (Soni and Gough, 2007).

In a last ditch attempt to rescue a world cup that had become an embarrassment, a marketing campaign called 'Ram-de-Dance' was launched to focus on local spectators to ensure that the remaining 12 qualifying matches in Grenada and the semi-final and final matches in Barbados were well attended (*Guyana Chronicle*, 2007). The Grenadian and Barbadian tourist boards teamed up to slash cruise ship prices to make trips between both islands affordable. The

(Continued)

(Continued)

ICC also relaxed restrictions on re-entry at stadia and on the bringing in of outside food and beverages and musical instruments (BBC, 2007). There was also a steady distribution of free tickets to Caribbean residents. In the end these efforts would yield results. The semi-final and final matches were packed with lively spectators. However, for many, it was a case of too little too late as the damage had already been done. Many islanders felt the ICC and local organizers simply sought to engage the West Indian people as a last resort and that the World Cup had never really been about the local fans (ESPN EMEA Limited, 2007).

Case Study 2.1 illustrates how failing to recognize the economic, social and cultural aspects of host countries can adversely affect the outcomes of events. As Horne (2010) observes, the ICC Cricket World Cup 2007 staged in the Caribbean reveals several of the underlying tensions that arise when an international sporting event is staged outside the advanced urban centres of the northern hemisphere. It highlights the problems that arise when a 'one-size-fits-all' approach is taken to delivering an event. The pricing and security measures implemented, whilst unproblematic in the developed world, were not appropriate in a Caribbean context. The ICC, perhaps too late, learned an important lesson about the need to accommodate the wishes of host communities.

Stakeholders

Event stakeholders consist of a variety of individuals, groups and organizations which are impacted by or can influence the outcome of an event. Bowdin et al. (2006), for example, identify participants and spectators, host organizations, host communities, co-workers, media and sponsors as key event stakeholders. Getz (2007), citing a number of research studies, demonstrates how stakeholder theory can be used to analyse how different types of stakeholders can influence the outcome of events (see Figure 2.3).

For event organizers staging events outside of their home countries, understanding stakeholder power relationships, networks and the potential for collaboration amongst stakeholder groups in their events' host communities is particularly important. For example, identification and accessing of gate keepers (those who allow or deny entry to the local market) is an important first step for event organizations wishing to operate outside their country of origin. However, gate keepers can include a diverse group of individuals such as politicians, public sector workers, event managers and community group leaders, so identifying these individuals can be a difficult task. Working through local stakeholder networks and/or forming local collaborations are useful strategies that event organizations can adopt to enter new markets.

Stakeholder management is also important for event organizations staging international events in their own countries. The staging of large-scale events often involves entire communities, cities and also countries and requires the collaboration

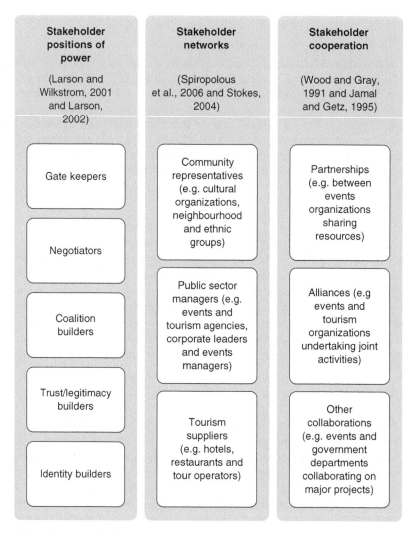

Figure 2.3   *Event stakeholder types*

of stakeholders at multiple levels, especially when these events receive significant amounts of public sector funding (Ferdinand and Williams, 2011).

Resource availability

Events organizations, just like other organizations, need rare and valuable resources to build and sustain (in the case of repeated events) a competitive advantage. Signature venues, cutting-edge lighting systems, highly skilled crews and technical personnel are all examples of resources that can make an event stand out from its

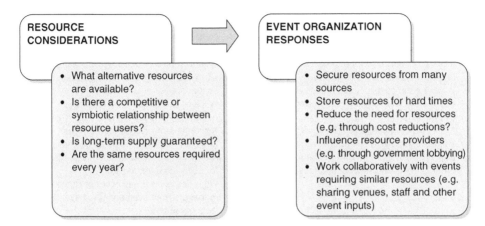

Figure 2.4   *Resource considerations and event organization responses*

competitors. International events, in particular, require significant resources which are difficult to estimate in advance and the supply of these resources is subject to seasonal variations. Getz (2007) suggests that event organizations need to consider their positions in relation to the scarcity of resources and take appropriate action (see Figure 2.4).

Event managers staging events outside of their home countries – for example, the organizers of international music tours – must carefully consider which resources they will carry with them from home and which they will trust overseas providers to supply. These decisions will be driven by a variety of factors which differ from country to country. A good tour manager will want to minimize costs, whilst ensuring the quality of a tour from country to country is maintained. Though it may seem cheaper to use local suppliers rather than travelling with a huge entourage and loads of equipment, if local crews are inexperienced and local equipment poorly maintained, the tour may end up incurring many unforeseen costs due to inefficient use of labour and equipment breakdowns (Vasey, 1998).

In some cases, the choice of whether or not to hire local contractors may not be a choice the event manager can make. For example, in the United States, many states may require event managers staging events within their jurisdiction, to hire unionized labour (Goldblatt, 2005). Table 2.2 provides a list of local considerations for event managers working outside their home countries thinking about using local resources.

Competition

For event managers unfamiliar with a country, local competitors can be valuable sources of information – such as local trends, fee and pricing structures and the availability of materials and resources. However, event managers should by no means try to duplicate the efforts of local competitors but 'take their best ideas and make them

Table 2.2   *Considerations for using local resources*

• Are the resources required for the event all available locally? • If there are resources that aren't available locally, are there any alternatives? • What are the costs of local resources versus the costs of transporting resources from overseas? • Are local resources (e.g. lighting, rigging and staging equipment) compatible with resources that will be brought in from the home country? • What is the quality of local resources?	• Do the practices of local suppliers comply or conflict with the event's/event organization's values (e.g. Do local suppliers share the event organization's sustainable or ethical values?)? • Will a failure to use local resources negatively impact the event (e.g. Will local residents protest or boycott an event which does not hire local labour or businesses?)? • Are there any financial incentives offered for using local resources? • What has been the experience of the event managers from overseas who have used local resources?

better' (Nuntsu and Shukla, 2005: 183). Competing events within a destination also provide event managers with the opportunity to undertake cross-promotions and strengthen the offering of their individual events. For example, an international conference or exhibition organizer can publicize nearby arts and cultural events happening at the same time, thereby allowing attendees to combine a business trip with some interesting leisure opportunities. Event managers organizing similar or related events can also collaborate to target international audiences as through collaboration they can offer attendees a package of complementary events. This allows attendees to make the most of the money spent on travel.

Conversely, the absence of local competing competitors in the off-peak tourist season of a destination can also present several opportunities for events which target international event audiences. In off-peak tourist seasons, the cost of many critical event inputs such as labour, catering and venues tend to be lower. Additionally, events may benefit from the support of local governments and communities for boosting tourism during these low periods. Likewise, hosting events in lesser known towns or cities, which do not have many competing events, also provides the hosts of international events with many benefits. Lesser known destinations can provide publicity and focus on an event which more popular ones cannot (Catherwood et al., 1992).

Cultural differences

In a world that is becoming increasingly interconnected, there is a need for event organizations to understand everyday cultural customs and practices which distinguish one country from another. Cultural sensitivity is increasingly relevant in a climate in which many event organizations are bidding for events overseas and more and more event organizations are beginning to resemble MNCs and TNCs, which have operations that span countries across the globe. For example, event organizations which have employees of varying nationalities and ethnicities need to be aware of the potential pitfalls that can arise from language differences. They must also be mindful of languages spoken by event attendees and ensure that these are translated correctly and accurately. For example, in preparation for the Beijing Olympics there was a huge drive to stamp out 'Chinglish' on signs at public tourist attractions, which could potentially cause embarrassment. However, aside from the misunderstandings that can arise when language is translated, there can also be difficulties when individuals speak the same language but do not have the same communication style. Hall and Hall (1990) highlight four dimensions along which communication patterns amongst societies can be compared (see Table 2.3).

Table 2.3 *Dimensions of communication styles*

Context	The amount of information that must be explicitly stated if a message or communication is to be successful. North Americans are perhaps the most famous examples of a cultural group which is low context in communication (very explicit in their communication), whereas Asian societies such as Japan and China are noted for high context communication (much of their communication is implicit or unsaid).
Space	The personal space that must be maintained between individuals whilst communicating. South Americans are known for being particularly close to each other whilst communicating as opposed to the British who generally maintain a greater level of personal space.
Time	How time is interpreted, whether as monochronic or polychronic. In monochronic cultures, tasks tend to be tightly scheduled and sequenced one at a time. In polychronic cultures, time is more flexible and multiple tasks are performed at the same time. Germany is renowned for having a culture which is monochronic, as timeliness is highly valued by Germans; whereas their European neighbours France are known for being polychronic. For French people human interaction and relationship building are valued more highly than sticking to schedules.
Information Flow	The structure and speed at which messages move between individuals and/or organizations and how action chains work – whether they are geared more towards communication or task completion. The Spanish are known for the speed at which they share information whereas in countries like the United States information is highly focused and compartmentalized, and information flow is much slower.

Source: Adapted from Hall and Hall (1990)

These differences have real implications for the planning and organization of events. For example, it is not uncommon in high context cultures for agreements to be struck for the staging of events without contracts or with very simple contracts, whereas in low context cultures, contracts are likely to be highly detailed and descriptive. Likewise in monochronic cultures, clients are likely to be insistent on a timely start to a business meeting or conference and look unfavourably upon attendees that are late, whereas in polychronic cultures, a meeting scheduled for a 9:00am start may see attendees arriving up until 9:30am and expecting that others will be waiting for them. Event managers working with clients from cultural backgrounds different from their own need to be sensitive to these differences and be careful not to let personal value judgements affect the fulfilment of clients' requests. It is not up to the event manager to decide when an event should start and end and what should be its outcome.

In addition to language and communication differences, cultural values are becoming more important to event organizations. Perhaps the most influential study of cultural values is Hofstede's (1991) study of IBM employees, in which he developed empirical profiles of different countries based on five dimensions of basic cultural values (see Table 2.4).

Table 2.4   *Dimensions of basic cultural values*

Power Distance	This is the degree to which a culture accepts a hierarchical or unequal distribution of power in organizations and society.
Uncertainty Avoidance	This is the degree to which cultures accept or avoid risks in everyday life.
Individualism	This is the degree to which individuals see themselves as integrated or separated from social groups and free of or restricted by social pressure.
Masculinity/Femininity	This is the degree to which masculine and feminine roles are separated and how un/favourably society looks upon aggressive and materialistic behaviour.
Time Horizon	This is the degree to which a society is prepared to put off immediate gratification in favour of long-term goals.

Source: Adapted from Hofstede (1991)

As is the case with communication styles, an awareness of differences in cultural values is very important for event managers, especially when negotiating contracts. Event managers can run the risk of offending potential clients by failing to recognize and observe the protocol involved in very hierarchical organizations. In pitching concepts to clients, the degree of uncertainty avoidance will be an important cultural dimension to consider, as organizations within cultures which are more prone to taking risks will be more open to or perhaps expect concepts which are highly experimental and unusual. Table 2.5 provides a list of some other cultural factors to be considered by event managers.

Table 2.5   *Other cultural factors*

• Religion	• Humour
• Early socialization and family structures	• Food and eating behaviour
• Small-group behaviour	• Work ethic
• Public behaviour	• Education system
• Leisure pursuits and interests	• Traditions
• Holidays and ceremonies	• History
	• Social class structure

Case Study 2.2 Second Life: Training the Next Generation of International Event Managers

Background

London Metropolitan University is one of Europe's largest universities boasting 190 nationalities from almost every country in the world (London Metropolitan University, 2008), making it one of the most culturally diverse campuses in the United Kingdom (UK). It offers a range of programmes focused on the events industry, including Events Marketing Management, International Sports Management, Tourism Management and Arts and Heritage Management. Teaching and learning tends to be very interactive and hands-on, which some students find very challenging, particularly those from countries whose education systems are quite different. Second Life (SL) was harnessed as a teaching tool by Dr Simone Wesner, Senior Lecturer in Arts and Heritage Management, to give students the experience of organizing an exhibition for an international audience. Project-based learning experiences have long been considered to be one of the most effective tools in Events Management education. However, exercised in real-life, they require long-term involvement and field experience. They are also often not cost-effective and carry a high risk of failure. Many courses therefore opt for placement-oriented practical experience instead (Bric, 2009). In SL all of the above-mentioned obstacles are overcome as event projects are implemented within the semester schedule, with a minimal budget and without the need for prior experience.

What is Second Life?

SL is a software programme catering for the virtual world which provides a platform that enables participants to create their own virtual content. It is part of a wider group of multi-user online virtual environments (MUVEs) that operate in real time via the motional use of personalized avatars (see Figure 2.6 for examples). This open and easily accessible software has attracted many higher education institutions since its launch in 2003 by Linden Research Inc. (also known as Linden Lab), with the majority of universities in the UK purchasing or renting spaces or islands in order to facilitate their learning and teaching practice. Linden Lab allocates server capacity to buyers and provides a virtual space that is sectored into regions, which are then divided into islands (Molka-Danielsen and Deutschmann, 2009). SL operates without geographical borders and anyone with a computer and reliable internet access can join in.

(Continued)

(Continued)

The assignment

As with a real-life event, students worked according to an event brief. They had to develop an event mission and objectives, as well as a strategy (including resource allocation, staffing, marketing and financial management). Students designed their events independently but were advised to work within the parameters of the 'Experimental Learning Framework' which follows four stages: foundation, participation, creation and multiplication. During the foundation stage, students familiarized themselves with SL while creating an avatar and finding their way around. Typically they set up their accounts in SL, chose a name, body and clothing for their avatar and learned to walk and fly while either attending generic SL tutorials or studying the self-explanatory introduction tools provided in SL. During the participation stage, emphasis was placed on communication and participation within a set environment. Students attended seminars, lectures and workshops at the London Metropolitan SL campus. After this point, the planning of most events was nearly complete and some students also started hosting their events. The majority of event projects involved extensive communication with other event organizers, audiences and artists. These communications included initial contact, commissioning of art work and staff recruitment. Next, the students went into the creation phase where event projects were set into motion. Towards the end of the student event projects, an event evaluation, including a self-reflective exercise, was carried out that led to multiplication, the final stage of the ELF, where experiences and data were exchanged and analysed.

Challenges and opportunities

The Collyer, one of London Metropolitan University's islands, houses the Nordstar gallery (see Figure 2.5) where the students staged their exhibitions. One of the

Figure 2.5   *Nordstar gallery in SL*

(Continued)

(Continued)

key challenges that students faced was targeting attendees, as SL has no geographical restrictions as far as audience attendance is concerned. Thus, when designing their exhibition programmes, one of the key considerations was timing, since SL operates as a real-time application. One student working from Cyprus scheduled an exhibition opening for a Saturday afternoon which translated into a Saturday night for the UK. This arrangement excluded most fellow UK students, since they were engaged in real-life social activities at that time, whilst a number of academics from North America joined during their lunch time and some Australian visual arts enthusiasts stayed up until early morning to attend.

Learning from this experience, other students paid particular attention to targeting the right group of people for their events. The exhibitions that were staged early on in the semester, in particular, could not rely on SL box office data sets from the gallery to target attendees, and therefore tended to rely on word-of-mouth and friend networks. However, a less targeted advertising campaign with banners on the main opening page of SL produced a new audience (newcomers, not normally gallery goers in real life) that would have not initially been targeted by the students, but developed into a reliable group of interested visitors to the gallery (see Figure 2.6).

Figure 2.6   *Avatars in the Nordstar gallery*

An unexpected benefit of SL was that it succeeded in engaging students that did not normally participate in class discussions. The anonymity of SL, along with the opportunity to visualize objects in three dimensions, facilitated some lively debates. The box-like shape of the gallery became associated with the Chinese interpretation of space and resulted in a discussion about cultural stereotypes and their use in exhibition design and urban planning. Students also discussed

(Continued)

(Continued)

the cultural context and symbolic meaning of buildings in different parts of the world. As a lecturer, Dr Wesner was pleased to discover that SL seemed to help students to engage in group projects and overcome initial barriers related to their own cultural backgrounds (see Figure 2.7).

Figure 2.7   *Student avatars in discussion*

Additionally, students indicated that SL helped in their understanding of dimensions in real-world design processes and gave them confidence in their abilities. For example, one student organized an exhibition that showed art works by artists who exclusively produced art work in SL and placed them in the Nordstar gallery. The sculptures were amended in size and proportion to the location built for the exhibition, which would of course have been impossible to achieve in a real-world situation. However, later the same student successfully applied her understanding of dimensions while on placement in a London gallery.

Conclusion

It is evident that SL can provide a valuable learning alternative in International Arts Events Management training. It offers a close match to real-life experiences while operating purely in the virtual world. Projects can be planned, implemented and evaluated from start to finish with very little impact on the environment, limited funding and from any location in the world that provides internet access. Learners are able to transfer their experiences into non-virtual work applications. The building capacity of SL offers a creative environment that encourages learners to experiment within a changeable space.

(Continued)

(Continued)

Case Study Questions

1 What global forces should the students planning their exhibitions in SL have considered when formulating their marketing strategies?
2 Other than the issue of time zones, how could local country conditions impact the attendance of the student exhibitions by members of the public located in different parts of the world?
3 What sorts of features should students incorporate into their exhibitions to signal that they are catering to an international audience?
4 What are the most important benefits that can be derived from undertaking events management training in SL? What are the limitations of the approach?

Chapter Summary

This chapter highlighted the need for event managers to take an international approach to events management. The increase in air travel, the proliferation of multinational and transnational organizations and the increasing importance of live music events has created unprecedented opportunities for event organizations to expand their operations to meet new demands. These new opportunities come with the challenges of serving an increasingly international events audience. To make the most of these opportunities and to minimize any new threats, event managers need to be constantly scanning the environment for global forces that may impact their events, whilst at the same time being conscious of the local conditions within different countries. PEST and PESTEL analyses are valuable tools that can be used for this purpose.

Event managers taking a 'one-size-fits-all' approach may find themselves hosting events which offend local communities and fail to meet client requirements, leading ultimately to event failure. The cultures and customs of societies can have a profound effect on the day-to-day business operations of event organizations with employees of different nationalities. During contract negotiation and event conceptualization, cultural traits such as those described by Hall and Hall (1990) and Hofstede (1991) should be carefully considered by event organizations so that cultural misunderstandings are minimized.

Review Questions

1 How has globalization expanded the market for international events?
2 What global forces should an event manager staging an international conference for business owners consider?

3   What are some key local conditions event managers coming to your country should be aware of?
4   How does language differ from communication?
5   Using your own country as an example, highlight how communication styles impact the staging of events.

Additional Resources

Books, book chapters and journal articles

Gannon, M.J. and Pillai, R. (2010) *Understanding Global Cultures: Metaphorical Journeys Through 29 Nations, Clusters of Nations, Continents and Diversity* (4th edn). Thousand Oaks, CA: Sage Publications Inc.
A guide to cultural metaphors which helps outsiders make sense of what particular cultures consider important.

Morrison, T. and Conaway, W.A. (2006) *Kiss, Bow or Shake Hands* (2nd edn). Avon: Adam Media.
A comprehensive guide to doing business in more than 60 countries.

Page, S. and Connell, J. (2011) *The Routledge Handbook of Events*. Abingdon: Routledge.
An exploration into the diversity that constitutes the events sector.

Povey, G. and van Wyk, J.A. (2010) 'Culture and the event experience', in P. Robinson, G. Dickson and D. Wale (eds), *Events Management*. Oxford: CAB International. pp. 1–18.
This chapter investigates cultural, political and societal influences that have shaped the events industry since the 1960s.

Silvers, J.R., Bowdin, G.A.J., O'Toole, W.J. and Nelson, K. (2006) 'Towards an international Event Management Body of Knowledge (EMBOK)', *Events Management*, 9(4): 184–198.
A framework of skills and competencies for international events management.

Useful websites

http://www.euromonitor.com/
Euromonitor International is the world's leading independent provider of business intelligence on industries, countries and consumers.

http://www.ises.com/
ISES is the International Special Event Society, which through its chapters throughout the world provides a range of resources for event managers.

http://oxygen.mintel.com/
Mintel Oxygen hosts a wide range of market intelligence reports from across the globe including a wide range of leisure activities such as spectator sports, the performing arts, the MICE industry and music concerts and festivals.

References

Ali-Knight, J., Robertson, M. and Fyall, A. (2008) *International Perspectives of Festivals and Events: Paradigms of Analysis.* London: Elsevier.

BBC (2007) *ICC Chief Defends Ticket Pricing.* BBC [Online]. Available from http://news.bbc.co.uk/sport1/hi/cricket/6537791.stm.

Benedict, B. (1991) 'International exhibitions and national identity', *Anthropology Today*, 7(3): 5–9.

Bhola, R. (2007) *World Cup Ban Stump Grenada Fans.* BBC [Online]. Available from http://news.bbc.co.uk/1/hi/world/americas/6537511.stm.

Bowdin, G., Allen, J., O'Toole, W., Harris, R. and McDonnell, I. (2006) *Events Management* (2nd edn). Oxford: Butterworth-Heinemann.

Bric, A. (2009) 'Teaching arts management: Where did we lose the core ideas?', *Journal of Arts Management, Law and Society*, 38(4): 270–280.

Burbank, M.J., Andranovich, G.D. and Heying, C.H. (2001) *Olympic Dreams: The Impact of Mega-events on Local Politics.* Boulder: Reinner Publishers.

Catherwood, D.W., Ernst & Young and Van Kirk, R.L. (1992) *The Complete Guide to Special Event Management: Business Insights, Financial Advice, and Successful Strategies from Ernst & Young, Advisors to the Olympics, the Emmy Awards, and the PGA Tour.* Hoboken: John Wiley and Sons.

Davidson, R. and Rogers, T. (2006) *Marketing Destinations and Venues for Conferences, Conventions and Business Events.* Oxford: Butterworth-Heinemann.

ESPN EMEA Limited (n/d) *England/photos.* ESPN EMEA Limited [Online]. Available from http://www.espncricinfo.com/england/content/image/387609.html?object=62396;page=1.

ESPN EMEA Limited (2007) *A Volunteer's Viewpoint: Crushing the Essence of the Caribbean.* ESPN EMEA Limited [Online]. Available from http://www.espncricinfo.com/wc2007/content/story/288885.html.

Falassi, A. (1987) 'Festival: Definition and morphology', in A. Falassi (ed.), *Time out of Time: Essays on the Festival.* Albuquerque: University of New Mexico Press. pp. 1–10.

Farrell, C. (2010) *Terror at the Munich Olympics.* Minnesota: Abdo Consulting Group Inc.

Ferdinand, N. and Williams, N. (2011) 'Event staging', in S. Page and J. Connell (eds), *The Routledge Handbook of Events.* Abingdon: Routledge. pp. 234–247.

Getz, D. (1998) 'Event tourism and the authenticity dilemma', in W.F. Theobald (ed.), *Global Tourism* (2nd edn). Oxford: Butterworth-Heinemann. pp. 409–427.

Getz, D. (2005) *Event Management and Event Tourism* (2nd edn). New York: Cognizant Communication Corporation.

Getz, D. (2007) *Event Studies: Theory, Research and Policy for Planned Events.* Oxford: Butterworth-Heinemann.

Getz, D. and Frisby, W. (1988) 'Evaluating management effectiveness in community-run festivals', *Journal of Travel Research*, 2: 22–29.

Goldblatt, J.J. (2005) *Special Events: Event Leadership for a New York.* New York: John and Wiley and Sons.

Guyana Chronicle (2007) *Dehring Declares 'Ram-De-Dance' Campaign. Guyana Chronicle*, 9 April [Online]. Available from http://www.landofsixpeoples.com/gytoday0704js.htm.

Hall, E. and Hall, M. (1990) *Understanding Cultural Differences.* Yarmouth: Intercultural Press.

Hofstede, G. (1991) *Cultures and Organizations: Software of the Mind.* New York: McGraw-Hill.

Horne, J.D. (2010) 'Cricket in consumer culture: Notes on the 2007 Cricket World Cup', *American Behavioral Scientist*, 53(10): 1549–1568.

Jago, L. and Shaw, R. (1998) 'Special events: a conceptual and differential framework', *Festival and Event Tourism*, 5(1/2): 21–32.

Jamal, T. and Getz, D. (1995) 'Collaboration theory and community tourism planning', *Annals of Tourism Research*, 22(1): 186–204.

Keynote (2010) *Music Industry.* Keynote [Online]. Available from https://www.keynote.co.uk/market-intelligence/view/product/2324/music-industry?highlight=music&utm_source=kn.reports.search.

Larson, M. (2002) 'A political approach to relationship marketing: Case study of the Storsjoyran festival', *International Journal of Tourism Research*, 4(2): 119–143.

Larson, M. and Wilkstrom, E. (2001) 'Organising events: Managing conflict and consensus in a political market square', *Event Management*, 7(1): 51–65.

Lawson, F. (2000) *Conference, Congress and Exhibition Facilities: Planning, Design and Management.* Oxford: Architectural Press.

London Metropolitan University (2008) *Guide for International Students.* London Metropolitan University [Online]. Available from www.londonmet.ac.uk/international.

McKenzie, A. (2007) *Twenty20 Avoids World Cup Errors.* BBC [Online]. Available from http://news.bbc.co.uk/sport1/hi/cricket/other_international/6970745.stm.

Meetings Planners International (2010) *Future Watch 2010.* Chicago: RR Donnelly and Sons Company.

Mintel (2010a) *Music Concerts and Festivals – UK.* Mintel [Online]. Available from http://0academic.mintel.com.emu.londonmet.ac.uk/sinatra/oxygen_academic/search_results/show&/display/id=479850.

Mintel (2010b) *Business Travel World Wide – International.* Mintel [Online]. Available from http://0academic.mintel.com.emu.londonmet.ac.uk/sinatra/oxygen_academic/search_results/show&/display/id=483944.

Molka-Danielsen, J. and Deutschmann, M. (2009) *Learning and Teaching in the Virtual World of Second Life.* Trondheim: Tapir Academic Press.

Morrison, J. (2006) *The International Business Environment: Global and Local Market Places in a Changing World* (2nd edn). New York: Palgrave Macmillan.

Nuntsu, N. and Shukla, N. (2005) 'Sponsorship', in G. Damster, D. Tassipoulos, P. de Tolly, W. Dry, J. Gasche, D. Johnson and J. Knocker (eds), *Event Management: A Professional Development Approach.* Lansdowne: Juta Academic. pp. 173–204.

Page, S. and Connell, J. (2011) *The Routledge Handbook of Events.* Abingdon: Routledge.

Peters, M. (2007) 'Growth on the road', *Billboard*, 24 November: 12.

Picard, D. and Robinson, M. (2006) 'Remaking worlds: Festivals, tourism and change', in D. Picard and M. Robinson (eds), *Festivals, Tourism and Social Change: Remaking Worlds.* Clevedon: Chanel View Publications. pp. 1–31.

Richards, G. (2001) *Cultural Attractions and European Tourism.* Oxon: CABI Publishing.

Richards, G. (2007) 'Introduction: Global trends in cultural tourism', in G. Richards (ed.), *Cultural Tourism: Global and Local Perspectives*. New York: The Haworth Hospitality Press. pp. 1–24.

Ritchie, J.R.B. (1984) 'Assessing the impact of hall mark events: Concepts and research issues', *Journal of Travel Research*, 23(1): 2–11.

Soni, P. and Gough, M. (2007) *Cup Bosses Blamed For Poor Crowds*. BBC [Online]. Available from http://news.bbc.co.uk/sport1/hi/cricket/other_international/west_indies/6513159. stm.

Spiropolous, S., Garagalianos, D. and Sotiriadou, K. (2006) 'The Greek Festival of Sydney: A stakeholder analysis', *Event Management*, 9(4): 169–183.

Stokes, R. (2004) 'A framework for the analysis of events: Tourism knowledge networks', *Journal of Hospitality and Tourism*, 11(2): 108–123.

Thomas Cook Retail Limited (n/d) *Key Dates*. Thomas Cook Retail Limited [Online]. Available from http://www.thomascook.com/about-us/thomas-cook-history/key-dates/.

Towner, J. (1985) 'The grand tour: A key phase in the history of tourism', *Annals of Tourism Research*, 12(3): 297–333.

Towner, J. (1996) *An Historical Geography of Recreation and Tourism in the Western World 1540– 1940*. Chichester: John Wiley.

Trennert, R.A. (1993) 'Selling Indian education at world's fairs and expositions, 1893–1904', *American Indian Quarterly*, 11(3): 203–220.

UNWTO (2010) *UNWTO World Tourism Barometer*, 8(3): 1–64.

Vasey, J. (1998) *Concert Tour Production Management: How to Take Your Show on the Road*. Burlington: Focal Press.

Weaver, D. and Lawton, L. (2006) *Tourism Management* (3rd edn). Milton: John Wiley and Sons Australia, Ltd.

Withey, L. (1997) *Grand Tours and Cook's Tours: A History of Leisure Travel 1750 to 1915*. London: Autumn Press.

Wood, D. and Gray, B. (1991) Toward a competitive theory of collaboration. *Journal of Applied Behavioural Science*, 27(1): 3–22.

Yeoman, I., Robertson, M., Ali-Knight, J., Drummond, S. and McMahon-Beattie, U. (2004) *Festival and Events Management: An International Arts and Culture Perspective*. Oxford: Butterworth-Heinemann.

PART 2

INTERNATIONAL EVENTS MANAGEMENT IN PRACTICE

The first part of this book makes the case for an international approach in events management. The impacts of globalization, which include changes in financial systems, improvements in communications technologies and cheaper air travel, have made it easier for event organizations to operate in multiple countries. Increasingly, events incorporate international inputs such as staging technologies, ticketing and accreditation systems, sponsors and participants. Audiences have undergone a similar evolution and are participating in events outside of their home countries in larger numbers – in person, online or through virtual reality. Thus the conceptualization, delivery and evaluation of events need to be similarly adapted to meet these realities.

Part 2 applies an international approach to events management by identifying how particular elements of the event management process are internationalized. It begins with Chapter 3, in which Ali examines the challenges of designing unique event experiences in an international environment. Event managers need to cater for a heterogeneous audience that may include local and international attendees. This requires the identification of themes that both differentiate and integrate. Differentiated themes distinguish the event against competition and shape attendee expectations. Themes also act as an integrator, synthesizing disparate event elements into a cohesive whole (Pine and Gilmore, 1999; Silvers, 2004).

In Chapter 4, Williams provides guidance for managing the event realization process using a project management approach. Using examples drawn from Africa, India and the United Kingdom (UK), this chapter shows how project management tools and techniques can be used to support event planning and delivery. Closely related to event execution is the building of event teams. Chapter 5 examines key considerations for managing human resources in an international, multi-cultural environment. Johnson also explains that event teams change size or 'pulsate' over time (Hanlon and Jago, 2009; Toffler, 1990) and event managers need to create human

resource systems that are flexible enough to cope. He also highlights that event organizations, unlike traditional organizations, incorporate significant numbers of volunteers. Human resource management practices thus need to be adapted for events to
maximize the contribution of these personnel.

Events can be promoted as experiences on their own or as a way to position products, organizations or brands. Gechev in Chapter 6 examines both of these aspects
and provides useful guidance for event organizers. Financing events is a challenge for
organizers as both costs and returns can vary. Financial planning is therefore critical
and Chapter 7 examines aspects of pricing and cost management for events. Kitchin,
using a worked example from the New Mardi Gras Limited, also demonstrates the
importance of financial reporting and analysis.

As the events industry has developed over time, the need to manage risks has
become a more prominent issue. Chapter 8 identifies the importance of following
legal and ethical guidelines. Ritchie and Reid also detail similarities and differences
in health and safety legislation in different countries, along with the process of risk
management. All of these processes are underpinned by performance tools and measures which form part of event evaluation. Using diverse examples, Tull in Chapter
9 describes the identification, planning and implementation of evaluation processes
for events in an international environment.

Part 2, by focusing on the core competencies of events management and providing
a range of examples from Africa, the Americas, Asia, Australia and Europe, concretizes
international events management and its application in a variety of contexts. It demonstrates the relevance of an international approach not only for event managers
working on high-profile events such as the Olympic Games, the Sydney Mardi Gras
and the St Lucia Jazz Festival but also for those managing national, local and community events such as local exhibitions, religious festivals and weddings. This section
also introduces some of the emerging issues in international events management,
such as new sources of competition and sustainability, which are explored in greater
detail in Part 3.

References

Hanlon, C. and Jago, L. (2009) 'Managing pulsating major sport events organizations', in
    T. Baum, M. Deery, C. Hanlon, L. Lockstone and K. Smith (eds), *People and Work in Events
    and Conventions: A Research Perspective*. Oxford: CABI.
Pine, J.H. and Gilmore, J. (1999) *The Experience Economy: Work is Theatre and Every Business a
    Stage*. Boston: Harvard Business Press.
Silvers, J.R. (2004) *Professional Event Coordination*. New York: John Wiley & Sons.
Toffler, A. (1990) *Power Shift: Knowledge, Wealth and Violence at the Edge of the 21st Century*. New
    York: Bantam Books.

3
Event Design

Nazia Ali

Learning Objectives

By reading this chapter students should be able to:

- Comprehend the various aspects of developing an event theme in view of principles, creativity and cultural sensitivity involved in theme design.
- Recognize key theme elements associated with event design by focusing on venue, catering, entertainment and décor.
- Identify international design trends and current trends in event design for consideration in the events management process.
- Appreciate the importance of events design in the context of theming in events management.

Introduction

This chapter demonstrates the key principles of event design which include theme development and creativity. The basic elements of theme development are described and the process by which these elements are integrated to build a unified event concept is analysed. The chapter also illustrates how cultural sensitivity and keeping up with global trends are necessary in taking an international approach when undertaking event design. The chapter closes with a case study on a modern Hindu wedding, which highlights the importance of an international events management approach for wedding planners, trying to meet the needs of diverse clientele.

Events Design and Events Management

Design features as a key activity component in the planning, development and management of events (Berridge, 2010a; Goldblatt and Nelson, 2001; O' Toole, 2011; Silvers, 2007a). In the event management process, Goldblatt and Nelson

(2001) note design as a main activity, in addition to research, planning, coordinating and evaluating events. Silvers (2007a) conceptualizes design as a core 'domain' or function within events management, which consists of seven facets: (i) catering; (ii) content; (iii) entertainment; (iv) environment; (v) production; (vi) programme; and (vii) theme. These seven facets should not be considered as singular entities or in isolation, but rather as interrelated and interdependent domains, which drive events design. In terms of definition, event design, according to Adema and Roehl (2010), is a two-fold concept, which focuses on (i) aesthetics of the look and feel of an event; and (ii) functional qualities associated with event success. O'Toole defines event design as 'a purposeful arrangement of elements of an event to maximize the positive impression on the attendees and other key stakeholders' (2011: 183).

Event design as a stimulus activates the five senses of hearing, sight, smell, touch and taste embedded in the event experience. The design of an event is both an experience-maker and experience-enhancer, which provides ample opportunity for the attendee to engage in sensory and emotional interaction with the event. Thus, event design is not simply a matter of production but participation to create memorable and unique happenings. In today's experience economy, events design management should move beyond the ordinary to the extraordinary. According to Brown and James (2004: 53), the design of an event is 'the very heart and soul, the *raison d'être* of any truly great event'. However, despite the central role of design in events 'the job description for the typical event manager, fails to include the "design" component' (Brown and James, 2004: 54). Thus it is imperative for international events teams to link theory (knowledge of design) with practice (professional conduct) to 'design management in events' (Berridge, 2010a) or 'theme design management' (Silvers, 2007b), the latter being of relevance to this chapter.

Developing an Event Theme

The emergence of themes in event design has added a dynamic and innovative dimension to events management. Today, theming is playing a critical role in the staging and marketing of events. Event Management Companies (EMC) are involved in generating themes for their customers and specializing in theming for special occasions (for example, birthday, Christmas and wedding parties). Bowdin et al. (2011: 507) observe that themed parties are a significant part of the event industry. In the United Kingdom, EMCs such as Office Christmas (2011) are involved in theming and event production for Christmas Parties. Office Christmas, for example, has hosted the themed event 'The Chocolate Factory' – a design inspired by the British children's author Roald Dahl's book *Charlie and the Chocolate Factory*. As Figure 3.1 illustrates, The Chocolate Factory theme is reflective of Silvers' (2007a) seven facets of design. On a more individual level, private or personal events are organized with themes reflected in, for example, colour, costumes, menu selection and music genres.

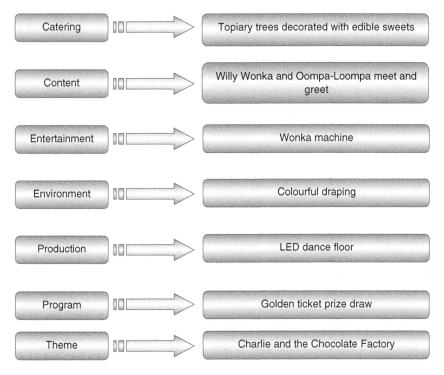

Figure 3.1 *Seven facets of design applied to 'The chocolate factory' themed Christmas party*

Source: Adapted from Silvers (2007a) and Office Christmas (2011)

Principles

As theming is a characteristic of design, principles of design are applied to developing event themes. There is no consensus amongst event management practitioners about principles of theme design. Brown and James (2004) identify five principles which can be applied to event theme design management: (i) scale – size of event utilizing venue space; (ii) shape – layout of event; (iii) focus – directing attendee gaze to physical elements such as colour or movement; (iv) timing – the event programme/schedule/agenda; and, (v) build – ebbs and peaks in an event. Principles of design according to Monroe (2006) 'should have a focus', 'must consider the use of space' and 'must consider and reflect the flow of movement' (cited in Berridge, 2007: 97; and Berridge, 2010a: 190).

Theme ideas

It is difficult to capture and present the kaleidoscopic array of theme ideas. The aim here is to identify theme ideas that are an embodiment of international diversity and

which are a reflection of globalized event product and service. Many EMCs special-
ize in event theme management and their event themes, as presented in Table 3.1, are
inspired by cultural/national identity, dance, food and drink, film, literature, music,
nature, the past, sport or travel, to mention but a few categories. There are also companies selling event 'theme kits', such as the American-based supplier Stumps selling
to event planners and individuals wanting to host a theme party. Popular event
themes identified by Stumps are Arabian, Casino, City, Hollywood and Tropical event
themes (Stumps Party, 2011). Themes create what Bowdin et al. (2011: 493) refer to
as 'unique and unforgettable events'. This is essential in terms of creating an experience, generating the 'wow' factor, and marketing an event to ensure it is successful in
terms of the transition from the intangible to the tangible.

Table 3.1   *Theme examples*

Theme Areas	Ideas
Cultural/National Identity	• African • Egyptian • Moroccan
Dance	• Line Dance • Barn Dance • Salsa
Food and Drink	• British Pub • Boston Tea Party • Cadillac Diner
Film	• Film Legends • Bollywood • James Bond
Literature	• Ali Baba • Narnia • Harry Potter
Music	• Jazz and Blues • Rock 'n' Roll • Boogie Nights
Nature	• Fire and Ice • Fire • Tropical
The Past	• Legends of the 20th Century • Medieval • Titanic
Sport	• Cricket • Rugby • Sporting Heroes
Travel	• Orient Express • Out of Africa • Around the World

Source: Adapted from Amazing Party (2011)

Creativity

Developing an event theme is an act of creativity – a skill – and being creative is a prerequisite for a memorable and successful event. Moreover, event design and creativity are inseparable, in view of themes, because together they 'give something a visual identity and recognition' (Berridge, 2010b: 210). This visual communicative role of creativity is reinforced by another statement by Berridge – he states 'creativity is the one thing that really can make an event stand out from others of a similar kind' (2010a: 192). The act of creativity in event theme design management should, according to Silvers (2007b):

- Use a broad spectrum of stimuli.
- Conduct brainstorming and other idea-generating exercises.
- Remove restrictions of assumptions and traditions.
- Combine ideas in new ways and make connections between unrelated ideas.

For creative inventions in event theme design, it is vital that conceptions are unique, original and authentic. The uniqueness, originality and authenticity of a theme adds value to the 'wow' factor, but also presents a means of escapism to an imaginary or dream-like world. The notion of escapism is well developed in the context of travel and tourism, whereby tourism frees the tourist from her/his daily alienated life (Cohen, 1979; Cohen and Taylor, 1976; Wearing, 2002). Thus, event themes are articulated to represent a form of temporary escapism, which are beyond the reality of the everyday and produce a new experience from a previous or similar event. Therefore, event theme design requires the event planner and her/his team to adopt a 'blank canvas' approach to creativity. Berridge (2010a) advises against the use of past event design templates as these prohibit creative thinking. He urges event teams to forget about past events when crafting the next memorable experience. However, it may prove difficult to fully implement the 'blank canvas' technique as theme design may be constrained by attendees' desire to 're-live' or 're-visit' various elements of previous events. Therefore, to avoid compromising customer loyalty and retention, the 'blank canvas' approach can be applied to various operative areas of a themed event, rather than the entire theme. For example, with reference to Berridge's (2010a: 196–197) work, the functional parts of a themed event which can be creatively adjusted, are seen in Box 3.1.

Box 3.1 Functional Parts of a Themed Event

- Sound
- Decorations
- Timeline

- Edible displays
- Interactive décor
- Parades and float design

Cultural sensitivity in theme design

Events are international in form and content, which brings people and populations of different cultures together. As the global and local cultures meet, it is important that cultural sensitivity is shown in terms of catering, content, entertainment, environment, production, programming and theming because what is acceptable in one culture may not be the case in another culture. Despite culture being a significant theme in events design and considering the international reach of the events industry, cultural sensitivity is not well documented or researched in events management. Cultural sensitivity is defined as 'a matter of understanding the international customers, the context and how the international customers will respond to the context' (Clarke and Chen, 2007: 164).

Although event themes can be transferred from one place to another, the way they are staged will differ depending upon the international customers for whom the event is hosted and the country in which the event is taking place. Event planners should be aware of culturally sensitive matters such as attitudes and values within one society, use of body language, religious beliefs and legal requirements relating to observance of cultural or religious laws. Krugman and Wright (2007), for example, highlight a number of considerations for event managers working in the Middle East:

- Key religious observances (for example, the month of Ramadan which prohibits the consumption of alcohol).
- The high value placed on reputation and personal connections as opposed to contracts.
- The need to have name badges which refrain from using nicknames and that do not make holes in the garments of female attendees (for example, which are worn with a lanyard).
- Many parts of the Middle East use SECAM video systems, which is incompatible with the NTSC and PAL systems (used in the United States and Europe respectively).

Allen (2003) also draws attention to the problems that arise when a female event planner goes to an Islamic country which does not allow a woman on business to move around unescorted.

Event planners should not shy away from cultural diversity and differences, but rather understand and address the cultural sensitivities they encounter. There are many benefits in accommodating, responding and valuing cultural diversity and difference in view of theme design in the events management process. The advantage of having knowledge of international cultures gives an event theme a positive image, and a competitive and creative edge in the global events market.

 Diary of an Event Manager – Anonymous, Event Manager, Brazil

This event manager works for an engineering-based firm which sells complex, customized equipment to the oil and gas sector in the Caribbean. Whilst the

(Continued)

(Continued)

employees attend a lot of industry events, they do not host them very often. However, the company expanded to Brazil in 2010 and needed to find a way to introduce both the company and its products to Brazil.

The event manager remembers: 'While most multinational companies are familiar with our products, the largest potential customers in Brazil are not. After examining existing marketing channels, we found that there were very few ways of reaching a geographically distributed audience in our industry. We decided on an event as a way of introducing the company and providing interaction with its products.'

It was crucial to find the right theme for the event. The event manager spoke to the local staff since she didn't want the company to be seen as foreign, noting that Brazilian culture is fiercely nationalistic. The staff suggested a 'home grown' idea in which the company was presented as a local company, using foreign technology and expertise. This theme was critical in selecting the location and it was decided to hold the event in the company's factory, so that customers could see its local staff. Since the venue was critical to making the theme work, the event manager had a big challenge, as production facilities are designed for technical workers and not for executives in suits.

The event manager also recalls: 'To make sure that visitors had a good experience, we stopped production for the day, but kept staff around to talk to visitors. This was a bit risky since our members of staff have differing educational levels, but we felt it was important to show that our products were made in Brazil by Brazilians. We needed to train the staff to ensure that they would be able to answer questions or direct visitors to where the information could be found. In the middle of the factory, we placed a locally made unit, painted in the colours of the Brazil national flag.'

Paying attention to Brazilian nationalism served this company very well and the event was very successful in introducing the company as a new local provider in the Brazilian market.

Theme Elements

Theme elements (for example, venue, catering, entertainment and décor) must be aligned with the event taking place (Bowdin et al., 2011). However, the importance of theme elements, in addition to the creation of experiences, should consider the creation of emotional connections with an event (Nelson, 2009). After all, being 'wowed' and constantly being reminded of the unforgettable is an emotional response to a significant occurrence in one's life. There are several ways event theme design elements can be exploited to bridge experiences and emotions for both host and guests. It is achieved through drama, atmosphere and service delivery. Nelson (2009), using Goffman's (1959) theory of dramaturgy, Kotler's (1973) conceptualizations of atmospherics, and Bitner's (1992) practices of servicescapes, presents a framework for studying theme elements as stimulants of experience and emotional connections in the context of design. Goffman's (1959) dramaturgy links to emotional connections formed through experiences with the event settings. Kotler's (1973) atmospherics draw upon emotions active through sensory experiences; and Bitner's (1992) servicescapes emotionally attach the attendee to a themed event through interactive experiences.

Venue

A venue is an essential ingredient in the management of planned event environments and is noted by Bowdin et al. (2011: 495) as an 'obvious part of the theme of the event'. Furthermore, O'Toole (2011: 193) states venue location and layout are 'essential elements in event success'. The venue selected provides the scaffolding in which to stage the themed event around and within, consequently dictating the spatial layout. Venue layout has a bearing on the social interactions that take place between the hosts and guests (Nelson, 2009). The objective is to match the scale of the themed event to the venue, which subsequently influences the design principles by ordering the movement, experiences and emotions of audiences once they are encapsulated in the theme (Brown and James, 2004). There are many search techniques available to the event planners to ensure the right venue is selected because location is core to event design and experience. Lindsey (2009) identifies five key avenues to explore during the pre-production stage when venue selection takes place:

- Trade books/CD ROMs
- Tourist boards
- The internet
- Word of mouth
- Head/Sales Offices

Venues can be transformed or used in their original form to complement an event theme. The Ice Hotel (Quebec, Canada) is a venue which is built entirely from ice and is a perfect backdrop for a fairytale-themed wedding. There is a wedding package put together by the Ice Hotel for potential customers wishing to stage a unique experience such as a 'magical' fairytale wedding, which comprises of, for example, the use of the ice chapel and a stay in the Ice Hotel's theme suite with a fireplace (Hôtel de Glace, n/d). Many EMCs plan Christmas parties for corporate clientele, which requires a link between venue and theme that often requires considerable transformation. The Ultimate Experience event organizers transform The Pavilion at the Tower of London to host the 'Bejewelled' theme (The Ultimate Experience Ltd, 2007).

Catering

Bowdin et al. (2011: 507) recognize catering as a 'major element in staging, depending on the theme and nature of an event'. The choice of catering is as important as venue selection because the quality of food and beverage is a vital ingredient in visitor experience (Shone and Parry, 2010). Thus, as a sensory stimulator, the smell or aroma and taste or flavour of cuisine is critical in enhancing the thematic design and experience of an event. Catering design consists of such facets as menu selection, service style, alcohol management and catering operations (Silvers, 2007a). Food and drink provisions and functions in an event could be directed by a given theme, which interrelates with other aspects of design such as content, entertainment, environment, production and programme. The catering design may be unconsciously and/or consciously driven by the sacred or profane character of an event theme. A Bollywood-themed celebration could consist of servings of Asian-inspired gastronomy such as vegetable samosa for starters, curry and rice for main course and a selection of sweetmeats for dessert.

Catering design influenced by a certain event theme is evident in the following examples:

- Arabian Night/Harem-themed party: filled vine leaves, Matbuha (Moroccan cooked salad with grilled peppers and tomatoes), couscous with chicken and vegetables, and sahlab for dessert (Harem Nights, n/d).
- Retro-themed party: 'retro crisps' (space invaders, wotsits and monster munch), pots of baked beans and toasted fingers, tea cups of prawn and salmon cocktail, mini iced fairy cakes, pots of candyfloss and jelly and cream (Purple Grape Catering, 2011).
- Medieval-themed event: duck liver and wild mushroom pate with spiced fruit chutney and melba toast, luxury game pie (venison, pheasant, rabbit and pork), cabbage sautéed with apple and cider, steamed morello cherry pudding with fresh custard, hot mulled wine spiced with cinnamon, nutmeg, cloves and ginger (The Bonafide Food Company, n/d).

Entertainment

Another essential prerequisite, in addition to venue and catering choice, is entertainment for a themed event. No event, whether themed or not, would be complete without some form of entertainment for attendees. Entertainment is a communicative device in an event, which captivates the feelings and emotions of a guest, and cultivates the memories of the attendee (Matthews, 2008). The entertainment domain can be, for example, formal or informal, have appearances by celebrity look-a-likes, roving street entertainers, performances by magicians or stand-up comedians (Berridge, 2010a). Entertainment in events, according to Matthews (2008), has evolved around four genres: (i) singing or music; (ii) storytelling/theatre; (iii) dance; and (iv) athletes or athletic pursuits. The reasons for entertainment in an event are wide and varied, but fall into eight distinct categories: (i) education; (ii) physically moving people; (iii) emotionally moving people; (iv) motivating and inspiring people; (v) decorations; (vi) announcing, introducing or advertising; (vii) creating ambience; and (viii) rewarding performance and for image purposes (Matthews, 2008). In the context of atmospherics and servicescapes, entertainment can be utilized to manipulate emotions and memories as a means of creating experiences at a themed event (Nelson, 2009). Table 3.2 presents some themed events where entertainment plays a central role.

Table 3.2 *Themed events featuring entertainment*

Theme	Entertainment
African	Adungu (acoustic traditional African instrument), bass guitar, saxophone, African drums, Tube Fiddle, calabash, singers and dancers.
Bollywood	Sitar and Tabla players, Bollywood bands, Bollywood dancers, Bollywood karaoke, DJ and roadshows, Bollywood props, Bhangra dancers and Bollywood solo artists and duos.
Murder Mystery	Jolly jesters and plague victims, medieval props, fire eaters and performers, medieval-themed side stalls, caricaturists, medieval inflatable games, minstrels, medieval-themed stilt walkers, and DJ.
Las Vegas	Las Vegas showgirls, Las Vegas casino tables with professional croupiers, Elvis, Rat Pack tributes and swing bands, Las Vegas props, eight-lane giant scalextric, fireworks, DJ and disco.

Source: Adapted from Theme My Party (2010)

Décor

When staging a themed event, décor, as an act of creativity and ambience maker, has a bearing on the success of an event environment. Décor is reflective of theming because it involves transforming ordinary mundane spaces into innovatively 'wowing' settings. Types of décor available to an event planner are vast, which can be utilized to construct an event theme. Some examples of décor are backdrops, themed sets, props, fabrics and soft goods, banners and signs, tension fabric structures, people or creatures, floral displays, inflatable materials and elements of nature (Matthews, 2008). Matthews also draws attention to the 'escape' characteristic of décor in any event:

> People attend events to be transported into an environment that is different from their everyday life, whether it is a concert, a championship football game, or a formal dinner. (2008: 59)

The escapist or imaginary function of themed events in the context of décor requires both the host and guest to enter the world of make-believe. At a themed event, for example a Wild West setting, audiences may be requested to dress up as cowboys or sheriffs to reflect the design of the event and to play an integral part in the entertainment (Bowdin et al., 2011).

Décor can be inspired by many thematic preferences, such as the traditional or modern, classic or chic styles, choice of flowers and floral arrangements, plain or patterned drapes and backdrops, special effects and sculptures. For an Asian wedding some main decorative areas are table centre-pieces, chair decorations and table décor. Asian wedding planners Exclusive Events, based in the United Kingdom, Dubai, India and the United States of America, provide such decorations and props as stage sets, swings, sofas and stools; mandap backdrops and stage drapes; red carpet and aisle runners; LED and uplighting; mandap stage pillars and pedestals; aisle arches; pillars and pedestals; and aisle/foyer decoration and props (Exclusive Events, 2009/2010). The following images,

Table centre-piece

Chair décor

Table décor

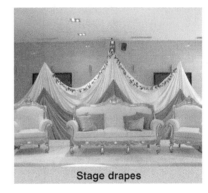
Stage drapes

Figure 3.2   *Theming with a pink colour scheme*

in Figure 3.2, taken at an Asian wedding are designed in the colour theme of pink, which is reflected in one of the table centre-pieces, chair decorations, table décor and stage drapes. Pink, according to Colour Wheel Pro, a colour scheme software tool, 'signifies romance, love and friendship' (cited in Matthews, 2008: 64).

Design Trends

The events industry's operations stretch beyond the local to the global, thus the events sector is affected by international happenings and developments. As event theme design indicates, it doesn't matter where in the world an event is taking place it can be created to reflect people, places and populations elsewhere. Thus, the events industry is a globalized product and service, which requires the events sector to keep up with international trends and current developments in event design in order to continue to create unforgettable and unique experiences. The global trends examined in this section are based upon an external environmental scan, which comprises of an analysis of political, economic, social and technological trends, as described in Chapter 1. The environmental scanning of future event design conducted by Adema and Roehl (2010) informs event design management in keeping up with global trends. Current trends in event design focus upon issues of sustainability in the context of natural environments. As a consequence of climate change and the need to reduce the negative environmental impacts of events, it has been necessary, as part of the events management process, to respond to such environmental concerns.

Keeping up with global trends

Events design will need to keep up with global trends in political, economic, social and technological changes. Moreover, these developments will have an impact upon

Table 3.3   *Global trends in events design*

Trend	Events Industry Perspective	Influence on Theming of Events
Social	'The actual world system will move so we're watching an evolution and I think events encapsulate that. They (events) are the opportunity where large groups of people come together to exchange emotions and feelings that is after all what drives the world.'	To keep up with global happenings, which are of importance to different people and populations, and expose these in themed event settings. This will entail focusing on the 'non-business' element of the events industry as core in delivering the themed service encounter.
Technological	'I think you are going to see a huge integration of digital media online. You have already seen the capabilities of systems like Vivien design, the next step would be to take Vivien and if you could project it on the walls ... creating an event design backdrop in the room by either rear projection or front projection so that it creates a dimensional feel as well of the room but it is all produced by visual media.'	To keep up with the ever-evolving technological advancements at both national and international levels. Technology can be utilized to create virtual themed event settings inside (and outside) of venues and with the power of 3D transport attendees to different themed worlds. Also, theme elements, such as décor, can be easily created and adjusted to suit the needs of customers through the use of digital media.
Economic	'I think controlling costs and finding more value for less money is going to be the link into a lot of people's success.'	To keep up with design trends with limited budgets is a challenge. Cost can be controlled by sourcing local suppliers and forming EMC partnerships on both a national and international scale.
Political	'What I think we are seeing right now is that there is a change in government as there has been here (US) and a change in government in the UK and I think we are moving into an area where there is going to be more caring in the world at a higher social agenda and we are going to use all our resources and skills to try to make the world a better place than just turn a profit.'	To keep up with current political affairs, especially those promoting corporate socio-political responsibility. As national and international government agendas are driven by the concept of 'change', this needs to be embedded in the event theme design. Themed events could take on a political value and by asking themselves – how after this event is the world a better or 'changed' place?

Source: Adapted from Adema and Roehl, 2010: 202

the choice, design and management of future themed events. The environmental scan conducted by Adema and Roehl (2010) to study the future of event design offers an insight into the global trends that the events sector has to take note of. Adema and Roehl (2010) conducted their research with eight (event) industry leaders who held influential positions in event production, event professional associations and event education. Table 3.4 shows a selection of informant responses to how the identified environmental forces design can keep up with the trends.

Current trends in event design

The critical current trend identified to have an impact upon event design is environmental sustainability, which extends the analysis of external factors discussed in the previous section. Sustainable event management has emerged as a response to climate change and reducing the carbon footprint of global citizens. The BS 8901 – the British Standard for Sustainable Event Management – came into force in Britain to ensure the planning, development and management of events did not comprise environmental resources. Although no separate guidelines for 'greener' themed events can be found, the principles and checklists for events in general can be applied to ensure BS 8901 Sustainable Event Management is implemented. Many leading organizations and venues in the United Kingdom have sought to be compliant with BS 8901, for example Lords Cricket Ground, Seventeen Events, Live Nation and London Olympics 2012. Evidence suggests that the London Olympic Games 2012 prompted the creation of BS 8901:

> It's no secret that the creation of BS 8901 was promoted by the Olympic Games coming to London in 2012. Yet for every community, social, sporting or business event, the implications of using the standard reach far beyond a specific date in the calendar. At its heart, BS 8901 is a **whole new way of doing business**, building communities and managing enduring meaningful legacies. No matter how hard the present circumstances might seem, it offers a completely new way of planning a **practical** sustainable future by realising direct benefits in the present. (The Sustainable Events Group, 2010, emphases in original)

For event theme design management, much can be learnt and put into practice in the following theme elements: venue, catering, entertainment and décor. With reference to various guidelines and publications, event theme design can be sustainable, without compromising the uniqueness and 'wow' factor associated with experience, in the following ways:

- Venue: use venues with environmental certification to a national or international standard, such as ISO 14001, BS 8901 or BS 8555; or provide well advertised and clearly labelled recycling facilities (DEFRA, 2007).
- Catering: serve fair trade products, such as coffee, tea and chocolate; or fresh food rather than prepared desserts (DEFRA, 2007).

- Entertainment: supply of sustainable lighting and audio visual equipment (Seventeen Events, 2011); or use of venue which provides in-house audio equipment as this reduces the need for transportation (DEFRA, 2007).
- Décor: hire rather than purchase equipment or materials; or use of reusable display materials and presentation of material in a re-usable format (Government Office for the South West, 2010).

Case Study 3.1   A Modern British Hindu Wedding (by Neta Tailor)

Traditionally, a Hindu wedding is paid for by the bride's parents and the ceremony would only take place in the bride's hometown. Many Hindus would also only marry someone that the family has chosen. The family members would consult a priest and choose a date that would be considered auspicious and there are certain days in the Indian calendar that one would not have a wedding on, as it would be deemed unlucky for the bride and groom. The wedding would only be organized by family members and wedding planners would not be considered. The main wedding ceremony would last for about two hours. The bride would wear a red and white sari that has been given to her by her maternal uncles. The ceremony would consist of the following:

- *Hasta Melap* – The bride's right hand is placed in the groom's right hand and the priest would read out holy chants. A white cloth would then be tied to the bride and groom's outfits.
- *Lawan Phere* – A fire is lit in the middle of a mandap to witness the union of the bride and groom. Together, they would go round the fire four times to symbolize faith, financial stability, procreation and liberation of the soul.
- *Saptapadi* – This is the most important part of the ceremony as you take the seven steps together representing strength, food, progeny, family, prosperity, happiness and life-long friendship.
- *Saubhagya Chinya* – This is the red holy powder that is placed on the bride's forehead by the groom and then he places a mangulsutra (a necklace made of black beads) around her neck to symbolize the welcome of her into his life.
- *Ashirwaad* – This is a blessing that is taken by the bride and groom from the priest, the parents and close family.
- *Vidaai* – The bride is now part of the groom's family and says goodbye to her friends and family. This can be a very emotional time for the bride.

Today, the traditional British Hindu wedding has been embraced by many modern elements. The above-listed ritualistic activities still take place but in a shorter time and these are sometimes considered more as a formality. It is no longer necessary that a priest would need to be formally trained as long as he knew the main ceremony of the wedding. The mandaps are much grander now and are seen as

(Continued)

(Continued)

the main feature of the wedding. The bride may choose her own outfit and may not necessarily wear the red and white colours. In recent years, the scale of wedding and financial expenditure plays a key role in designing the event, which was not/is not the case for a more traditionally orientated wedding.

However, a vital consideration is that the groom's guests appear to have more importance than the bride's guests, whether it is a traditional or a modern wedding. The bride's parents must treat the groom's family with great respect and honour. This is a very sensitive matter and it is always a priority not to upset or offend anyone.

The modern wedding may take place in 5-star hotels, manors and stately homes, unlike in the past when the tradition was to host weddings in school halls and local community centres. Wedding planners are also hired to take care of all the arrangements, which includes the design, staging and management of the modern Hindu wedding. The main design features for a Hindu wedding that would be used are:

- A foyer display which can be simple or elaborate according to the requirements. Fresh flowers, water arrangements and religious statues are often used for foyer displays.
- Aisle displays, again using matching arrangements to the foyer set-up.
- Mandap is a four-pillar canopy, under which a Hindu wedding would take place, which can be simple or elaborate. It can be decorated with fresh flowers and other accessories and is the main focus of the religious ceremony. Traditionally the mandap would be made out of wood but now mandaps are made of all different types of materials to make them as modern and contemporary as possible.
- Seating arrangements for dinner would be made for the bride and groom, the parents and close family and friends, using fresh flowers and draping on all the tables.

An individual would choose the colours for the wedding, and normally all the decorations would match the colour of the bride's outfit. Some brides and grooms would choose to have some 'soft' background music whilst the ceremony is taking place. Some choose to have tabla players (traditional Indian drummers). A DJ or a live band is normally booked for the reception when Bangra and Bollywood dancing takes place, another modern British addition.

The venue selection is vital; the function room must allow the *havan kunj* (the ceremonial ritualistic fire), which requires the organizer to ensure all health and safety rules and regulations are in place at the venue. The venue must have enough capacity for the large number of invited guests. It must have ample parking as Hindu weddings are typically quite large, catering to hundreds of guests. In a modern wedding, it seems to also be important how grand the venue is as in some cases this is a status symbol.

(Continued)

(Continued)

At Hindu weddings it's essential that any type of food that is being served on the day is vegetarian, even within modern ceremonies. In some Hindu communities there are other special dietary requirements such as no garlic and onion to be used in the cooking or one may have a religious day and find that some guests will only eat potato curry made without salt and specific spices. If any errors are made in the kitchen, this could cause guests to complain, with some becoming distressed by this disregard for their religious beliefs.

Case Study Questions

1 What are the main differences between the traditional Hindu wedding and the modern British Hindu wedding?
2 Identify the key cultural and religious provisions which need to be adhered to when organizing a modern Hindu wedding.
3 Why do you think there has been an emerging trend for the use of event planners in designing, staging and managing a modern Hindu wedding?
4 Catering for dietary requirements is an essential consideration at a Hindu wedding – is this determined by culture and/or religion? Can you think of any other cultures and/or religions where dietary requirements need to be observed?
5 You have been asked to design a Hindu wedding which merges both tradition and modernity. List the main design principles and theme elements.

Chapter Summary

This chapter on event design has considered matters relevant to the theming of events, such as developing an event theme, theme elements and design trends. A variety of case examples have been included to highlight the international reach of event theme design management in staging various celebrations. Although much of the practice of theming events is skewed towards North America and Europe, the developmental and professional aspects can be applied to international events management. Event educators, planners and students should embrace global diversity and difference in their teaching, management and study of theming in events. There is an opportunity for intercultural dialogue through theming, which can contribute to alleviating cultural misunderstandings. This intercultural communication and recognition of culturally sensitive issues can enhance an event's design and experience, and continue to create unique, unforgettable and memorable encounters through theming. Theming compels the international events management educator, planner and student to consider the two worlds of events – the business (experience economy) and non-business (emotion-making) dimensions – when reaching out to event audiences.

Review Questions

1 What are the opportunities and challenges facing event managers in developing event themes for culturally diverse attendees?
2 Why do you think it is important to include the 'design' component in job descriptions for event managers?
3 How will global social, technological, economic, political and environmental changes affect event design in the future?
4 You have been asked to design a theme for an event entitled *Fast-Forward – Life in the Year 2112*. Consider the following theme elements: the venue, catering, entertainment and décor.

Additional Resources

Books, book chapters and journal articles

Berridge, G. (2010) 'Design management of events', in D. Tassiopoulous (ed.), *Events Management: A Developmental and Managerial Approach* (3rd edn). Claremont, SA: Jutta. pp. 185–206.
An informative chapter which demonstrates how a design-centric approach can be taken to events.

Bowdin, G., Allen, J., O'Toole, W., Harris, R. and McDonnell, I. (2011) *Events Management* (3rd edn). Oxford: Butterworth-Heinemann.
This text includes chapters which focus on several of the key areas of event design, such as event conceptualization and staging.

Nelson, K.B. (2009) 'Enhancing the attendee's experience through creative design of the event environment: Applying Goffman's dramaturgical perspective', *Journal of Convention and Event Tourism*, 10: 120–133.
This article demonstrates that theatrical principles can be applied in event design.

Reisinger, Y. (2009) *International Tourism: Cultures and Behavior.* Oxford: Butterworth-Heinemann.
Provides comprehensive coverage of cross-cultural issues and behaviour in tourism which includes cultural events and festivals.

Shone, A. and Parry, B. (2010) *Successful Event Management* (3rd edn). Hampshire: Cengage Learning.
A text which takes a practical approach to event design.

Useful websites

http://www.aeme.org
A resource for event management educators which includes articles on the latest developments in the subject area.

http://www.juliasilvers.com
A website which features articles on the core areas of EMBOK, including a specific focus on event design.

http://www.thesustainableeventsgroup.com
Features resources to help the public and private sector design, develop and implement sustainable event management systems.

References

Adema, K.L. and Roehl, W.S. (2010) 'Environmental scanning the future of event design', *International Journal of Hospitality Management*, 29: 199–207.

Allen, J. (2003) *Event Planning Ethics and Etiquette: A Principled Approach to the Business of Special Event Planning*. Mississauga: John Wiley & Sons Canada Limited.

Amazing Party (2011) *Themed Party, Party Themes and Themed Events*. Amazing Party Themes [Online]. Available from http://www.amazingpartythemes.com/themes/THEMES.HTM.

Berridge, G. (2007) *Events Design and Experience*. Oxford: Butterworth-Heinemann.

Berridge, G. (2010a) 'Design management of events', in D. Tassiopoulous (ed.), *Events Management: A Developmental and Managerial Approach* (3rd edn). Claremont, SA: Jutta. pp. 185–206.

Berridge, G. (2010b) 'Event pitching: the role of design and creativity', *International Journal of Hospitality Management*, 29: 208–215.

Bitner, M.J. (1992) Servicescapes: The impact of physical surroundings on customers and employees. *Journal of Marketing*, 56(2): 57–71.

Bowdin, G., Allen, J., O'Toole, W., Harris, R. and McDonnell, I. (2011) *Events Management* (3rd edn). Oxford: Butterworth-Heinemann.

Brown, S. and James, J. (2004) 'Event design and management: Ritual or sacrifice?', in I. Yeoman, M. Robertson, J. Ali-Knight, S. Drummond and U. McMahon-Beattie (eds), *Festival and Events Management: An International Arts and Culture Perspective*. Oxford: Elsevier Butterworth-Heinemann. pp. 53–64.

Clarke, A. and Chen, W. (2007) *International Hospitality Management: Concepts and Cases*. Oxford: Butterworth-Heinemann.

Cohen, E. (1979) 'A phenomenology of tourist experiences', *Sociology*, 13: 179–201.

Cohen, E. and Taylor, L. (1976) *Escape Attempts: The Theory and Practice of Resistance of Everyday Life*. London: Allen Lane.

DEFRA/Department for Environment, Food and Rural Affairs (2007) *Sustainable Events Guide*. London: DEFRA.

Exclusive Events (2009/2010) *Asian Weddings*. Exclusive Events [Online]. Available from http://www.exclusiveevents.com/mandaps/asian-wedding-decorations.asp.

Goffman, E. (1959) *The Presentation of Self in Everyday Life*. New York: Doubleday.

Goldblatt, J. and Nelson, K.S. (2001) *The International Dictionary of Event Management*. New York: John Wiley & Sons.

Government Office for the South West (2010) *Greener Events: A Guide to Reducing the Environmental Impacts of Conferences and Seminars*. Our South West [Online]. Available from http://www.oursouthwest.com.

Harem Nights (n/d) *Arabian Night Parties*. Harem Nights [Online]. Available from http://www.haremnights.co.uk/party_themes.htm.

Hôtel de Glace (n/d) *A Magical Wedding*. Ice Hotel Canada [Online]. Available from http://www.icehotel-canada.com/hotel.php?action=mariage3.

Kotler, P. (1973) Atmospherics as a marketing tool. *Journal of Retailing,* 49(4): 48–64.

Krugman, C. and Wright, R.R. (2007) *Global Meetings and Exhibitions.* Hoboken: John Wiley and Sons Inc.

Lindsey, K. (2009) *Happiness is a Ticked Off List! The Comprehensive Guide on How to Organise and Manage a Perfect Corporate Event.* Leicester: Matador.

Matthews, D. (2008) *Special Event Production: The Resources.* Oxford: Butterworth-Heinemann.

Nelson, K.B. (2009) 'Enhancing the attendee's experience through creative design of the event environment: Applying Goffman's dramaturgical perspective', *Journal of Convention and Event Tourism,* 10: 120–133.

Office Christmas (2011) *Theming and Event Production.* Office Christmas [Online]. Available from http://www.officechristmas.co.uk/theming-and-production.

O'Toole, W. (2011) *Events Feasibility and Development: From Strategy to Operations.* Oxford: Butterworth-Heinemann.

Purple Grape Catering (2011) *Our Menus.* Purple Grape Catering [Online]. Available from http://www.purplegrapecatering.co.uk/site/menu.html.

Seventeen Events (2011) *Our Services.* Seventeen Events [Online]. Available from http://www.seventeenevents.co.uk/about-seventeen/our-services/.

Shone, A. and Parry, B. (2010) *Successful Event Management* (3rd edn). Hampshire: Cengage Learning.

Silvers, J.R. (2007a) *EMBOK Facets and Applications.* Julia Silvers [Online]. Available from http://www.juliasilvers.com/embok/Facets_Aps.htm.

Silvers, J.R. (2007b) *Design Case Study.* Julia Silvers [Online]. Available from http://www.juliasilvers.com/embok/design_case_study.htm#Theme_Design_Overview.

Stumps Party (2011) *Event Party Themes.* Stumps Party [Online]. Available from http://www.stumpspart.com/catalog.cfm?cat=47431.

The Bonafide Food Company (n/d) *Themed Catering: Something a Little Different.* Bonafide Food Company [Online]. Available from http://www.thebonafidefoodcompany.com/themed.htm.

The Sustainable Events Group (2010) *Welcome to the Future of Events – Make BS8901 Work for You.* Sustainable Events Group [Online]. Available from http://www.thesustainableevents-group.com/.

The Ultimate Experience Ltd (2007) *London Christmas Parties 2011.* Ultimate Experience Ltd [Online]. Available from http://www.the-ultimate.co.uk/html/christmas-parties/.

Theme My Party (2010) *Theme My Party* [Online]. Available from http://www.thememyp-arty.co.uk/.

Wearing, S. (2002) 'Re-centring the self in volunteer tourism', in G. Dann (ed.), *The Tourist as Metaphor of the Social World.* Wallingford: CAB International. pp. 237–262.

Acknowledgement

The author would like to thank Neta Tailor (University of Bedfordshire) for kindly providing the case study for this chapter.

4

Event Project Management

Nigel L. Williams

Learning Objectives

By reading this chapter students should be able to:

- Understand the benefits and limitations of applying project management concepts to events.
- Understand the characteristics of a successful event from a project management perspective.
- Evaluate project management techniques and issues, and recommend appropriate applications to event management.
- Select and implement the most effective solution to manage an event project.
- Review the management of past events to learn lessons for future work.

Introduction

The central task of event management is to create a unique experience for a target audience within resource constraints. Successful events therefore require a complex alignment of creative and commercial goals. In an international environment, this challenge is increased as stakeholders may be distributed geographically, making communication and coordination difficult. In order to meet the performance and accountability demands of the international environment, formal mechanisms are needed to support the event design and delivery process. Since events share some characteristics with projects, the discipline of project management may provide some useful tools. However, they need to be adapted to meet the unique characteristics of event management. This chapter presents tools that can be utilized to support the entire event realization process from initiation to closure by:

- Presenting an overview of the similarities and differences between events and projects
- Highlighting the areas in which project management tools can assist event management
- Using an example, developing and presenting a framework for event project management

Events and Project Management

Events have been defined as 'a specific ritual, presentation, performance or celebration' (Allen, 2000). Events arise from a variety of circumstances and have been categorized using a number of methods. Researchers have used purpose (Goldblatt, 2002), scale (Bowdin et al., 2001) and circumstances (Shone and Parry, 2004) as means of categorizing event activities.

Goldblatt (2002) has categorized four purposes of events: *celebration, education, marketing* and *reunion*. Celebration events are linked to particular occasions in a person's, organization's or institution's life and commemorate times of historical significance. Formal education has grown in importance in the last century and linked to this growth are events that may be social or professional. Events are also used for marketing promotion, to encourage interest or grow sales. Marketers are faced with a huge variety of media options and a similarly diverse customer base. Marketing events have been employed as a means of reaching and encouraging purchases. Finally, reunion events gather people to celebrate particular occasions.

Events also occur at a wide variety of scales (Bowdin et al., 2001). Small-scale local or community events serve audiences in the immediate area. Major events, by contrast, serve a greater audience and may even attract international visitors. Events known as hallmark events may emerge from local circumstances and become identified with a particular region. They may also grow to the point where they attract international attention. Entire countries or regions vie to host international scale mega-events such as the Olympics. Table 4.1 shows the diversity of events as conceptualized by previous research.

The demand for events has continued to grow as groups, organizations and institutions increasingly adopt them for a wide range of purposes, as seen in Table 4.1. At the same time, with experience, clients' expectations have increased, raising the level of complexity. Both of these trends have encouraged the adoption of formal mechanisms in order to properly manage events. Since they are both involved in the

Table 4.1 *Events categorized by type*

Getz, 1997	Bowdin et al., 2006	Shone and Parry, 2004	Goldblatt, 2002
Cultural	Cultural	Leisure (Leisure, Sport, Recreation)	Civic Events
Art	Sports	Personal (Weddings, Birthdays, Anniversaries)	Exposition
Entertainment	Business	Cultural (Ceremonial, sacred, art, heritage)	Fairs and Festivals
Sport		Organizational (commercial, political, sales, charitable)	Hallmark Events
Educational			Hospitality
Recreational			Meetings and Conferences
Political			Retail
Personal			Social Life Cycle
Celebration			

creation of intangible outcomes (Heineke and Davis, 2007), events share some similarities with services. However, traditional service operations management techniques are unable to support event planning and delivery as their goal is the optimization of an ongoing process (Bitran and Lojo, 1993), not the management of a time-limited activity. Project management, in contrast, may offer more useful tools for event management. Emerging from a military and engineering background, project management tools have been applied in an increasing range of organizations. Projects have been defined similarly to events – 'a temporary endeavour undertaken to create a unique product or service' (PMI, 2008). Both events and projects have common characteristics: they are temporary in nature, have a unique output, are planned and executed by teams and are goal directed. These similarities are detailed below:

- *Temporary* Unlike other organizational processes, both projects and events are temporary in nature. They begin when authorization is granted and end once objectives are achieved.
- *Unique outputs* Each project and event requires a particular combination of factors: location, date, resources and personnel. As such, the experience of planning and managing both projects and events will be different each time.
- *Executed by teams* Both projects and events are executed by teams formed for that specific purpose (Matthews, 2008).
- *Outcome based evaluation* Since projects and events are unique, they are difficult to evaluate. As such, they are measured by their outcomes or the objectives to be achieved (Jugdev and Mœller, 2005).

While projects possess the above similarities, they also possess key differences that can influence planning and execution. A key difference between events and projects is that in events execution and consumption are simultaneous (Salem et al., 2004) while in projects they may be separate. Additionally, event experiences are co-created with participants, and adjustments during execution require processes that can operate quickly (Tum et al., 2006), whereas projects do not. Moreover dates for celebratory and reunion events generally cannot be adjusted, unlike projects where end dates may be negotiable. Where project management can contribute to events management is in formalizing processes such as planning, scheduling, resource allocation, communication and documentation. This can bring the following benefits to event managers operating in the current international events environment:

Coordination and communication

Events require the coordination of a group of stakeholders, each with distinct needs (Ali-Knight et al., 2009). As events grow in complexity, these stakeholders have progressively increased in number and diversity. Event professionals need to incorporate and manage these inputs to ensure successful execution. Project management can provide a robust set of tools for integrating and disseminating event information and supporting coordination processes.

Improving accountability and external audit

Current trends of sustainability and corporate governance mean that event managers are increasingly called upon to account for their activities (Adema and Roehl, 2009). Increasingly, stakeholders are requesting that event managers minimize the impact of activities using guidelines provided by the sponsor or a standard such as the British Standard 8901 for sustainable events management. The weak global economy following the financial market crisis of 2008 has resulted in additional demands for monitoring of budgets, as organizations seek to shed non-essential spending (Crowther, 2010). By adopting formal processes for event realization, documentation can be generated that record actions taken and their rationale. Project management possesses an array of tools that can generate traceable documents, improving the transparency of planning and execution processes.

Building an internal event knowledge base

Whilst events are unique, lessons learned from previous experience can be invaluable when designing future events. Since events are made up of dynamic and pulsating teams, much of this knowledge can be lost as individuals may leave the organization (see Johnson, in the following chapter for more on 'pulsating organizations'). Project management processes can capture this information, supporting the development of an internal database of event management knowledge. Once compiled, this information forms a valuable input into the planning and delivery of future events, enabling, for example, more efficient selection of volunteers and suppliers.

Recognizing the value that formal processes can bring to the event management field, a group of researchers and professionals have created the EMBOK or Event Management Body of Knowledge (Robson, 2009). While it is still being developed, even in its current form, it can form a useful resource for managers seeking to implement formal management processes in their event organizations (Silvers and Nelson, 2009).

Case Study 4.1   Festival Management in Rural India

Introduction

The tribal people of Purulia, West Bengal in Eastern India have a rich heritage of folk dance, drama and music. This plateau area is endowed with natural beauty and ancient rock and terracotta temples. It is also rich in folk art and traditions. Art and cultural traditions of rural and tribal communities offer tremendous potential for economic development of people who lack formal education and thereby marketable skills for employment generation in conventional sectors. Cultural

(Continued)

(Continued)

tourism or the movement of persons to attractions outside of their normal place of residence can support the development of rural art. By showcasing the traditions of indigenous cultural communities, festivals, rituals, their values and lifestyle to new audiences, it is possible to generate an income for artists and performers, providing an avenue to regional development.

From trails to events

The first step in this process was identifying all of the natural beauty, forests, tribal villages, natural heritages, temple sites, crafts, museums and other interesting and diverse places. Trails were drawn up so that tourists can enjoy tribal dance, drama and songs and also get an opportunity to live among tribal communities and participate in their festivals. In 2009 and 2010, as part of developing these cultural tourism trails, Banglanatak.com organized events during the Hindu time of Holi, the celebration of colours. Set in rural areas, the surrounding trees are laden with red blooms of Palash (flame of the forest), providing an ideal backdrop for folk performances.

Before the event

Planning starts at least two months before the festival and the event team work together with local NGOs and folk artists, mobilizing them to take the lead role in organizing the festivals. Since folk performances are an integral part of the festival, the team confirms artists' availability for the dates allotted. Necessary permissions from the designated authorities are obtained and partnerships with government departments, tourism organizations, travel agents and tour operators are arranged.

Site preparation and staging

A month before the festival, a team of four to five people goes to the site comprising of the manager, two coordinators, a sound and light expert and a food expert. During this initial three to four days, the team stays at the festival site, talks with local villagers in order to understand their expectations from the festival and also encourage them to take active participation. The team also checks the availability of supplies such as food and water at the event site. Since the festival is a three-day event, it is important to plan the programmes so that a tourist staying for two days can also have a glimpse of almost all folk forms. Promotion and publicity of the festival is important as it is imperative to generate interest among the potential visitors. The promotion material includes posters, invitation cards, letters, announcements and social media. As part of promotion and publicity the team tries to involve tourism departments. In 2009, the tourism department of the government of West Bengal promoted the event and sent a tourist bus taking tourists from Kolkata to West Bengal. Both audio/visual

(Continued)

(Continued)

and print media are also used to promote the event. *The Telegraph*, a highly regarded daily in Kolkata, printed a column in the travel section featuring the 2009 Palash Parban at Deulghata.

Event staging

As the festival starts, the day before the holiday, tourists start coming in from the morning. The Banglanatak.com events team provides cars and sets up an information kiosk at the train station in West Bengal. After the cars bring the tourists to the festival site, tourists are registered at the festival venue and given their tent numbers. Arrangements for accommodation are also made for the folk artists who travel from Nadia, Malda and Bankura. The local artists come during the festival time and leave after their performances. The festival starts with an inauguration, the veteran Chau, Jhumur and Baul artists lighting up a camp fire. The Jhumur dancers dance round the campfire. For the next three days the evenings reverberate with the music of Baul, Jhumur and the beatings of Dhamsa, Dhol and Madol. Local people gather around the festival site offering various food and snack items for sale. In the morning of the day of Holi, all tourists congregate together at the temple premises. Everyone showers coloured dye on each other and the folk artists sing and dance. Local liquor, Mahua, is enjoyed by all as they make merriment throughout the morning.

Cars are arranged in the afternoon for the tourists to get a chance to go around and visit the other heritage sites that are present nearby. This is an opportunity for the tourists to interact with the local residents and learn to understand their ways of life. The social isolation and exclusion from which these communities have long suffered is also overcome in the process. As the festival ends on the third day, cars are provided to take the tourists back to the station.

Results

The initiative has created new markets for the folk artists. The folk artists are getting more respect and recognition and the community as a whole is taking more pride in their own culture and heritage. The tourists who visited Deulghata in 2009 did not miss the chance of enjoying the festival in 2010 and almost 60 per cent of tourists were seen again that year. The festival has even been able to attract international tourists, with visitors from Italy attending in 2010.

Event closure

The entire festival arena is packed up by the third day/night and the Banglanatak. com events team leaves the same night or the next morning. The team then reviews the event to determine the lessons for future events. For example, in 2009 the events were scheduled from 6:00pm to 3:00am. But after midnight the number of people reduces drastically. Thus, learning from the previous experience in 2010 the programmes were scheduled from 6:00pm to midnight for all three days.

The Event Project Management Model

Increasingly stakeholders demand that event managers need to stage experiences of greater complexity within resource constraints and under external scrutiny. These requirements dictate that not only must the event experience meet expectations, but that the delivery processes enable efficiency and transparency. For organizers in the current environment of increasing accountability, two areas are assessed to determine whether an event has been successful: the achievement of event objectives and the efficiency and effectiveness of event management processes (Baccarini, 1999).

Event objectives

Events are staged to attain predetermined objectives. These may range from building market awareness for a product to celebrating an occasion to regional economic development. As such, they shape all subsequent event activities (Allen et al., 2002; Bowdin et al., 2001) such as type, scale, location and audience. Refining these event objectives into actionable goals for managers generally requires the management of particular event characteristics. Generally, these are stated as cost, time and quality. However, for events, the second characteristic is frequently not negotiable. A more applicable framework will encompass four main elements. See Figure 4.2 for this framework of feasibility, viability, desirability and stakeholder expectations.

Feasibility

The feasibility component describes all the components of the event to be delivered, their desired level of performance and the means of supply. Events managers need to determine the tangible (stage equipment, décor) and intangible (licences, skills) inputs required to deliver event outcomes. Based on the demands that these inputs need to meet, managers also need to determine the appropriate level of performance or quality for these inputs. Finally, the event team needs to assess the source for these inputs, either internally or from suppliers.

Viability

Events need to achieve financial goals and the viability component assesses the business case for a proposed event. Personal or hospitality events generally need to fit within organizational financial constraints or budgets. Other types of events may be required to generate an expected return or profit.

Desirability

Event concepts need to be desirable to both internal and external stakeholders and these criteria measure the attractiveness. A distinctive event theme provides several benefits to event organizers (Berridge, 2009). The first is that an exciting concept serves to interest planners and encourage active support. The second is that it differentiates the event from competing offerings, allowing event promoters to build anticipation of a unique or distinctive experience to a potential audience. Chapter 3, by Ali in this volume, includes a detailed discussion on the benefits of themes.

Stakeholder expectations

Planning and executing an event is a learning process for both event managers and stakeholders, defined as parties with an interest or affected by event outcomes. Early conceptualizations of project management sought to separate changes in stakeholder expectations from project deliverables, referring to them as an external factor known as 'scope creep' (Melton and Iles-Smith, 2009). This approach frequently resulted in outcomes that did not meet changing stakeholder demands. Event managers need to incorporate these changing expectations, updating plans as necessary.

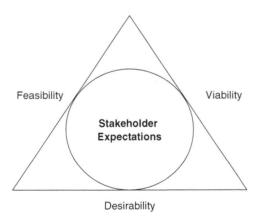

Figure 4.1   *Event objectives*

These components aid both the event planning and delivery process. At the planning level, they enable the conversion of objectives into actionable items. During delivery, event stakeholders also need to determine which criteria take precedence (see Box 4.1).

Box 4.1   Managing Tradeoffs

When problems arise in the event delivery process, the use of clear criteria that are specified in advance helps to make decisions in an objective manner. Key stakeholders need to agree in advance what is the key constraint: feasibility, viability or desirability. The event team's first task is to determine if any issue that arises is a real problem. If it is one that may affect the outcome of the event, the team needs to determine how resources will be allocated from areas other than the key constraint. This process needs to be properly documented as event managers will be called upon to explain their decisions either at periodic planning meetings or during evaluation.

Source: O'Toole and Mikolaitis (2002: 71)

Event processes

Once initial objectives have been agreed and accepted by stakeholders, detailed planning of resources, time and services can then be initiated. Once resources are committed, the team needs to work to non-negotiable deadlines to execute and monitor event activities simultaneously. According to the EMBOK, these actions can be arranged in a cycle of initiation, planning, implementing, event staging and closing (Silvers and Nelson, 2009) as seen in Figure 4.2. The following is a brief overview:

- *Phase 1 – Initiating;* The goal of this phase is to identify all potential ideas and determine which one is best suited to meeting event objectives.
- *Phase 2 – Planning;* This stage elaborates the selected idea and determines the resources required to deliver.
- *Phase 3 – Mobilizing;* In this phase, event setup activities are performed.
- *Phase 4 – Staging;* The event is staged or performed.
- *Phase 5 – Closing;* Evaluation of entire process, and capture the learning from event activities.

Phase 1: Initiating Process Phase

The initiating phase confirms the need for the event, examines alternative event concepts and decides on the concept that best meets the overall event objectives. While the temptation exists for event managers to ignore this phase in order to focus on planning and implementation, it is critical to devote sufficient time to initiation. At this point, few resources are committed and event managers therefore have the greatest opportunity to influence the outcome at the lowest possible cost (PMI, 2008).

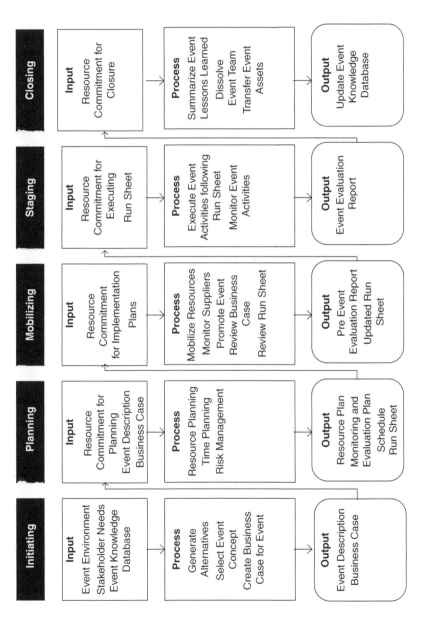

Initiating

Input
Event Environment
Stakeholder Needs
Event Knowledge
Database

Process
Generate
Alternatives
Select Event
Concept
Create Business
Case for Event

Output
Event Description
Business Case

Planning

Input
Resource
Commitment for
Planning
Event Description
Business Case

Process
Resource Planning
Time Planning
Risk Management

Output
Resource Plan
Monitoring and
Evaluation Plan
Schedule
Run Sheet

Mobilizing

Input
Resource
Commitment
for Implementation
Plans

Process
Mobilize Resources
Monitor Suppliers
Promote Event
Review Business
Case
Review Run Sheet

Output
Pre Event
Evaluation Report
Updated Run
Sheet

Staging

Input
Resource
Commitment for
Executing
Run Sheet

Process
Execute Event
Activities following
Run Sheet
Monitor Event
Activities

Output
Event Evaluation
Report

Closing

Input
Resource
Commitment for
Closure

Process
Summarize Event
Lessons Learned
Dissolve
Event Team
Transfer Event
Assets

Output
Update Event
Knowledge
Database

Figure 4.2   *Event project cycle*

Initiation inputs

As described by Ferdinand and Wesner in Chapter 2 of this volume, external environmental forces influence the event industry as a whole. Event managers therefore need to examine the likely effect of these forces and ensure that they are able to manage potential threats and maximize possible opportunities. Once this macro analysis is complete, organizers then need to identify stakeholders and understand their particular interests. For most events, they will include the following (Getz et al., 2007): sponsors, the media, attendees, communities and the event organization.

Sponsors provide resources to execute event activities in exchange for benefits such as building awareness with a particular audience, sales or access to decision makers (Tum et al., 2006). For public events, media is another key stakeholder. For a large-scale event such as the Olympics, television viewership is significantly larger than physical attendees, and is a key influence on staging and delivery. Even with smaller events, such as the religious festival described in the case study, media helps to build anticipation and set expectations for the customer experience. The emergence of the interactive media facilitated by the internet may further shape how events are delivered in the near future (Adema and Roehl, 2009). Both public and private events are staged for the benefit of a particular audience. Event managers need to anticipate, manage, meet and if possible exceed these stakeholder expectations in order for an event to be viewed as successful.

Events can impact the community in which they are staged (Robertson et al., 2009). As seen in the case example, event organizers need to consult these stakeholders in order to ensure that possible benefits are maximized and negative impacts minimized. Finally, the event team is responsible for the achievement of objectives by managing design and delivery and, as such, are important stakeholders.

Initiation activities

For any given event objective, different types of events may be staged. The initiation process explores these options and selects the one that best provides the desired outcome. When developing event concepts, the 5 W's framework from Goldblatt (2005) is a useful structuring device:

1 Why? or the purpose of the event
2 Who? or the specific stakeholders that will be affected by the outcomes
3 When? or the date(s) on which the event is held
4 Where? or the location of the event
5 What? or the details of the event

Within this framework, it is possible to brainstorm or generate a range of ideas that will meet event objectives. For small events, the event team may be sufficient. In the case of large public events, it is necessary to involve external stakeholders to contribute and evaluate ideas.

After options have been generated, they are assessed using the criteria of feasibility, viability and desirability to determine the best possible design that meets event objectives (Lawson, 2005).

- *Feasibility* The feasibility review assesses the resources along with the performance level required to deliver the event and determines if they can be provided directly from event team members, through volunteers or from suppliers. Event organizers will also consider external requirements such as permits or licences. In the Holi festival described above, the event team not only needed to source sufficient accommodation (quantity) for tourists at the site, they would also need to ensure that tents were comfortable (performance level).
- *Viability* This screen establishes the business case for the event, determining if it meets cost or revenue generation criteria. Once the resource needs of a concept are determined, it is possible to generate a cost estimate. At this stage, an accurate estimate may not be possible but an acceptable range is plus or minus 20 per cent (Van der Wagen, 2007). The event team can then determine if proposed means of funding these options either internally or externally (for example, through ticket sales and donations) are sufficient. For events that are required to earn revenue, expected profitability for each option can be forecasted in a similar manner and the results evaluated.
- *Desirability* Each event concept should be assessed and ranked on their desirability. While this is a subjective criterion, assessment of desirability can take the form of an internal and external scan. Internally, event concepts can be evaluated based on the attractiveness to the event team. Externally, the concepts should be compared to events that are planned during the same time frame.

All ideas generated during brainstorming should be ranked according to the above criteria, using either a quantitative (1–5) or qualitative (High-Medium-Low) scale. The highest ranked proposal should be selected for development. For the above case study, a three-day weekend festival incorporating art, performances and food best fit the objective of encouraging cultural tourism in a rural Indian village.

Initiation outputs

For the selected event, the team should convert the event description into a detailed description or scope of works to be used in the next phase, planning. At the same time, the team should also identify critical internal and external constraints in this scope that should be monitored as the event is developed. *Internal constraints* are related directly to the event and can be monitored using the feasibility, viability and desirability dimensions. Working with stakeholders, event managers need to identify which of these elements are non-negotiable and which can be adjusted. For example, Banglanatak.com identified feasibility as the key constraint for their event. As such, the team was willing to acquire additional resources at further cost if necessary, which would reduce viability. *External constraints* are factors imposed on the event such as legal requirements, suppliers and competitors.

Phase 2: Planning Process Phase

The planning phase converts the description into detailed working procedures that enable execution of event activities. These include:

- Work breakdown structure
- Work schedules and deadlines
- Budgets and cash flow
- Areas of high risk, uncertainty and contingency plans
- Personnel plans and resource utilization plans
- Procurement plans
- Documentation management plans

It is important to note that planning is an iterative process due to the complexity of events and the need to incorporate stakeholder input. Individual documents also need to incorporate some element of flexibility in order to respond to changing circumstances. Before detailed planning can begin, the event team may consult with stakeholders to ensure that resources are still available, especially if time has passed between concept selection and detailed planning.

Define event deliverables

Event initiation activities produce a description of an event concept that best meets stakeholder requirements. In the planning stage, this concept is refined into action-able components. A tool that supports this process is a product breakdown structure (PBS), a diagram that represents the activities required to deliver the event as a hier-archical structure. Figure 4.3 shows an example based on the case study.

As seen in Figure 4.3, the highest level of the PBS refers to the event. The second level generally refers to major event components such as venue, décor or entertainment. These major components are further decomposed into lower levels depending on the scale and complexity of the event. To support this process, each PBS element will have

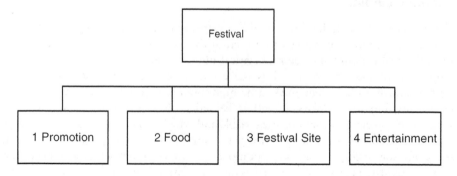

Figure 4.3   *PBS overview for Holi Festival elements*

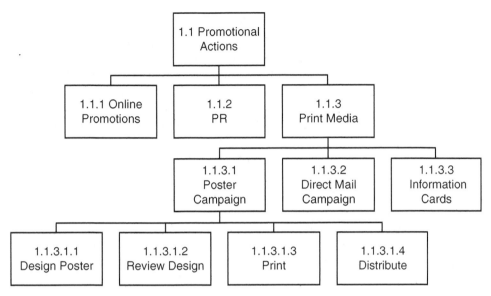

Figure 4.4   *WBS segment for Holi Festival*

a unique code or identifier to enable resource assignment and tracking. The PBS is then converted into a work breakdown structure or WBS, which identifies the activities required to deliver the event components. The format is similar to the PBS and the numbering scheme will be maintained, but each element focuses on activity, not deliverables. Figure 4.4 shows an expanded branch of the promotion element of the WBS.

The lowest level of any WBS is known as the work package and is the point at which time and resources can be properly estimated by the event team (Lester, 2007). For any given event, an experienced team can adequately define the event with a few levels while a less experienced team would need a WBS with more levels to ensure that details are not missed. A WBS simplifies communication among various stakeholders by providing a standard representation of event components in a graphical form. It also aids the project team in refining these components into actionable items known as work packages that can be completed by team members or suppliers. Once a draft WBS has been created by team members, it should be reviewed by stakeholders to ensure that all event elements are accounted for. As the event progresses, the WBS will be further refined and updated to reflect any changes.

Determine resource requirements

Once an initial WBS has been completed, it is possible to determine the resources required to stage the event. The type and amount of resources can be obtained by compiling data from individual work packages. Once the event resource requirements have been collected, event managers can plan how to acquire them, either internally or from suppliers.

Estimate duration and effort for event

Once the requirements and sources of resources are known, it is possible to determine the duration of each activity. Using the WBS, the party responsible should provide an estimate for each work package based on available historical information or expert judgement. A good guideline is that estimates for work packages should be less than the reporting period for the event, in order to support later control activities. If they are, consider decomposing the work package into lower levels.

Sequence work packages

After the duration step is completed, the event team should work out the order or sequence of work packages. While some packages can be executed independently or in parallel, others are dependent on previous activities. The event team needs to identify the sequence of dependent work packages in order to determine the overall time required.

Schedule

Once the relationships, duration and responsibilities for work packages are determined, it is possible to create a draft event schedule. This is commonly done in the form of a Gantt chart, which displays activities using a vertical and horizontal axis (Wilson, 2003). On the horizontal axis, columns are used to display duration and person responsible for each work package. The bottom row shows the duration of the event. Work packages are listed from top to bottom on the vertical axis in the order they will be executed. Work packages are displayed in graphical form as horizontal lines or columns, each line with the length showing the start and end date. This process can be done manually or using software. Once a draft schedule is created, it can be circulated for evaluation. After evaluation, the schedule can be finalized. See Figure 4.5 for a Gantt chart based on the case study.

Create function or run sheet

While Gantt charts are a useful tool in event planning, they are not sufficient to support event delivery. A function or run sheet should be used to show the sequence of activities during event staging (Tum et al., 2006). For small or less complex events, managers may generate a chart showing the key elements of the event, their exact timing along with any critical decisions to be made. Larger, more complex events may incorporate a customer processing chart that anticipates how event attendees will enter and move during the event. See Figure 4.6 for an example of a run sheet. Box 4.2 also has some tips on how run sheets are implemented.

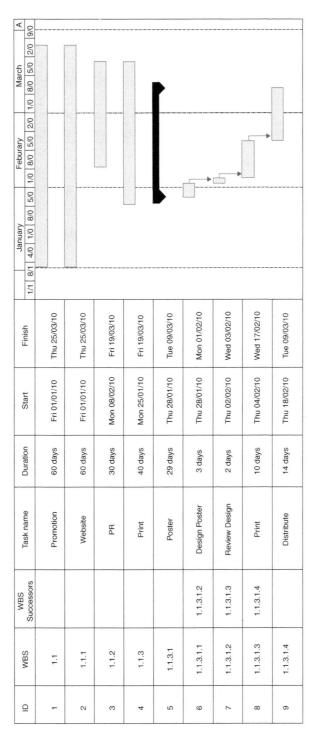

Figure 4.5   Gantt chart example

Holi Festival, 30 March 2008, Purulia, West Bengal				
TIME		ACTION /TASK	RESPONSIBLE	NOTES
Start time	Duration			
9.00 am	8 hrs	Greet guests at station and transport to site	Banglanatak.com offsite team	
5:00 pm	2 hrs	Register guests	Banglanatak.com onsite team	
7:00 pm	3 hrs	Inauguration	Chau, Jhumur and Baul artists	

Figure 4.6   *Run sheet for Holi Festival*

Box 4.2   Tips for Implementing Run Sheets

Goldblatt (2005) suggests circulating draft run sheets to stakeholders for approval. To ensure that the planner gets useful feedback, a memo should be included with specific instruction on how to review the run sheet along with specific tasks for each reviewer based on their expertise. In this way, the team not only gets feedback on the entire document but leverages the strengths of stakeholders.

Consider costing and budgeting

Once the resources and their source are finalized, it is now possible to determine overall event cost by tabulating costs in the WBS. For large events that require extensive preparation, an event cash flow determining financing requirements during preparation is also necessary. This can be generated using the compiling weekly or monthly work package costs using the event schedule. More detail on event costing is available in Chapter 7 by Kitchin, in this volume.

Put together risk management plan

Event managers also need to identify sources of risk, determine their possible effect and plan responses. Risks can be identified from the WBS and event flow chart which provide a detailed overview of event activities and processes. Once identified, an analysis is performed to determine their possible effect. If these effects are significant, a response should be planned. The activities required to mitigate risk should be used to update the WBS, flowchart, schedule and budget. More detail on risk management is discussed by Ritchie and Reid, in Chapter 8 in this volume. For large-scale events, the additional plans in Table 4.2 may also be employed.

Table 4.2 *Additional event plans*

Event Plan Element	Purpose
Change and Configuration Plan	Stakeholder demands are never static and they may request adjustments to the event plan over time. Successful event managers anticipate the need for change and design procedures in advance to incorporate the changing demands, in particular those that impact on function, feasibility or desirability.
Event Documentation Plan	Maintains central database of event documentation and controls who can access it.
Communication Plan	Determines the information needs for each event stakeholder: frequency, level of detail and format. For large events, this task should be included in the WBS.
Team Management	Evaluates the effectiveness of the event team, providing training or mentoring where necessary.
Procurement	Determines the need for external suppliers, sources a provider, manages delivery and evaluates performance.

Phase 3: Implementing Process Phase

In this phase, the event team ensures that the event scope is delivered in a manner that meets stakeholder needs within cost requirements. The event team, along with suppliers, executes the actions described in work packages to deliver outcomes described in the WBS. While event plans guide this process, the event environment is dynamic and the team needs to monitor and control activities to prevent unwanted outcomes. As work packages are executed, managers also need to determine the appropriate response to risks, generally using actions described in the risk plan.

Throughout implementation, the event team is required to evaluate performance against plans and communicate progress to stakeholders. If any variance occurs that can influence event outcomes, the team needs to decide on the necessary corrective action. The impact of these actions should be estimated and event plans updated, as necessary. Once work packages are complete, they may be formally evaluated to ensure that they meet performance requirements. In large events, this may take the form of testing by experts and the findings communicated to stakeholders. A pre-evaluation report may be completed at the end of implementation that can provide useful data for event staging such as expected attendance.

Phase 4: Event Execution

Based on the findings of the pre-evaluation report, stakeholders will decide whether or not to approve resources for event execution. If approval is granted, event activities are performed and monitored. Data from the pre–event evaluation report is also used to update the run sheet, ensuring that the document reflects the site and supplier realities. As shown in the case example, coordinators manage the process, from pre- to post-event, ensuring that activities are executed in the planned sequence and to the desired level of quality. At the end of the process, an event evaluation report is produced using the guidelines in Chapter 9 by Tull.

Phase 5: Event Closing

Like event initiation, the closing process is frequently overlooked by managers. However, it is a critical element in improving event planning and delivery. After resources are committed by stakeholders, the manager, in conjunction with the event team, organizes all documentation for archiving. During this process, the event team reviews event documents to determine any lessons learned. Once the review is complete, the team compiles a lessons learned report, which can be used to guide future planning. In the case example, attendance information was used to change performance times at the festival. The event team ensures that all event-related financial issues are resolved, including supplier contracts. Depending on the scale of the event, any assets created specifically for it are transferred to the relevant operating authority.

 Diary of an Event Manager – Tom Lunt, former Event Manager for Christian Aid

When asked about the most important lessons an event manager must learn about project management, Tom replied: 'prepare for the unexpected, both good and bad during event project management. While we can put everything in place, it's a good idea to have additional resources that can be drawn upon quickly.'

In 2008, his organization wanted to develop its fundraising event portfolio with underrepresented groups of donors, in particular younger males aged 25–45. While his team looked at a lot of ideas, the members wanted to embrace the idea of sustainability, so all concepts that included extensive travel were out. In the end the team decided on a sponsored bike ride through rural England.

The key to the event was finding potential riders who would make a commitment to fundraise and train for the event. This meant providing an efficient response to their initial enquiry and then encouraging them to sign up. Once signed up the key was to build a team ethos amongst a group of people who didn't know each other. This was done through social media and regular telephone calls. Tom remembers: 'The social media took on a life of its own and the participants used it to capture their training and riding experience. We were particularly lucky as a *Guardian* blogger mentioned the event, helping to build our presence at no cost to us. It was not something that we planned, but helped build camaraderie between the participants and, ultimately, this emergent action enhanced the event experience.'

However, not all the surprises were positive. There were 20 people of different riding ability trying to complete a long ride. They all completed the course at different rates, so there needed to be staff at the front, middle and back of the

(Continued)

(Continued)

group. During the second day of the event, one of the riders at the back had a minor accident.

Tom advises: 'While formal processes are important, managers need to keep the spontaneous nature of events in mind. It's a difficult balancing act, to be flexible enough to take advantage of opportunities but structured enough to ensure that goals are met.'

Case Study 4.2   Calabar Festival in Nigeria

Cross River is an eastern state in Nigeria with a population estimated at 2.89 million people. In the year 2000, the Governor introduced the Calabar festival, named after the capital, to attract visitors to the region. The first parade showcased the region's history, culture and products. The festival has since grown and now spans 32 days with dozens of events and attracts millions of visitors.

Planning for the event is conducted by the Events Management Unit and the Carnival Commission. Jointly, they form a programme organization called the Planning Committee that enables the delivery of events for the duration of the festival. The team then creates a programme infrastructure that incorporates management and technical elements to ensure a safe and successful festival. The management element incorporates all the personnel resources including volunteer recruitment and training. Technical elements include the systems, venues and procedures that facilitate festival delivery.

While planning for the festival is continuous, public activities begin in June when a theme is selected for the programme that reflects the culture of the region. In 2010, the theme was 'Our Strength and Resilience: The Bedrock of Our Future'. Bands also select their own themes – examples from 2010 include Seagulls, Bayside, Master Blasta, Passion Four and Freedom.

The festival formally begins at the end of November with the Xmas Tree Lighting Ceremony. Messages of goodwill are given and the Tree is visited by dignitaries at the Calabar Millennium Park. A 'Christmas Village' is set up at the Cultural Centre with shopping and food stands. The 32-day festival then begins and a number of events are staged that cater to different audiences. Over the period of the festival programme, visitors can attend fashion shows, food demonstrations, cultural exhibits, talent shows, music concerts, funfairs, carol services, parades and picnics. There is also an annual boat regatta which is a colourful display of flamboyantly decorated boats pitting local rivalling teams against each other. A summary of the programme is provided in Table 4.3.

(Continued)

(Continued)

Table 4.3   *The Calabar Festival programme*

	Week 1	Week 2	Week 3	Week 4	Week 5
Monday		Theatre Performance	Children's Carnival Dry Run	Sport Event: Golf Tournament	Calabar Carnival
Tuesday	(30 November) Tree Lighting Ceremony	Musical Performance: Canaan Rhythms	Theatre Performance	Water Carnival	Musical Performance: Carnival Rocks
Wednesday	City Walk	Musical Performance: Gyration Night	Final Carnival Dry Run	Youth Development Program Closes	Fashion Show
Thursday	Youth Development Program	Theatre Performance	Sport Event: Golf Clinic	Sport Event: Golf Tournament	Musical Performance: Naija's Most Wanted
Friday	Adult Carnival Dry Run	Sport Event: Power Women	Theatre Performance	Musical Performance: Carol Night	Musical Performance: Cross Over Night
Saturday	Musical Performance: Mixed Festival	Musical Performance: Roots Rock Reggae	Musical Performance: Jazz in Paradise	Family Funfair	Interdenominational Thanksgiving Service
Sunday	Choral Competition	Sport Event: Football Competition	Sport Event: Football Competition Final	Children's Carnival	

Over time, the festival has attracted international celebrities from the entertainment world who would perform at various events and act as ambassadors. The organizers have also upgraded the planning infrastructure, incorporating a website at www.calabarfestival.com. This site has been successful in promoting the festival worldwide, attracting tourists as well as sponsors. The vision of the committee is to become the biggest self-sustaining cultural event in Africa in 2012 and progress to date indicates that this goal is achievable.

Case Study Questions

1 Who were the key stakeholders in this case? How were their needs served by the event?
2 How would you evaluate this event?
3 In what way can project management processes contribute to the success of this event?

Chapter Summary

The forces of sustainability and austerity along with increasing customer expectations require event managers to adopt new methods in order to satisfy stakeholders. Successful event managers not only achieve their objectives but manage the realization process efficiently in order to provide accountability and capture learning. Adoption of project management tools and techniques enable the achievement of both goals by providing a structured approach to event delivery.

The event realization process can be divided into five stages: initiation, planning, implementing, delivery and closing. At the end of each stage, there is a formal review process that confirms stakeholder approval to proceed and resource commitment for the next stage. Once the event has been delivered, knowledge is captured in a database to aid in the design of future events.

Review Questions

1 For event success, why is it necessary to examine processes as well as outcomes?
2 Why is it important to engage stakeholders in the event delivery process?
3 How do event project management systems vary by event type?
4 For a given mega-event, such as the London 2012 Olympics, how does project management support event delivery?
5 Using the case studies, discuss the limitations of applying project management tools to events.

Additional Resources

Books, book chapters and journal articles

Goldblatt, J.J. (2008) *Special Events: The Roots and Wings of Celebration.* Hoboken: John Wiley & Sons Inc.
Includes a chapter which features 'Project Management Tools for Event Leaders'.

Kerzner, H. (2009) *Project Management: A Systems Approach to Planning, Scheduling and Controlling* (10th edn). Hoboken: John Wiley & Sons Inc.
This outstanding edition gives students and professionals a profound understanding of project management with insights from one of the best-known and respected authorities on the subject.

O'Toole, W. (2011) *Events Feasibility and Development: From Strategy to Operations.* Oxford: Butterworth Heinemann.
Presents tools, techniques and arguments for justifying expenditure on events and festivals.

O'Toole, W. and Mikolaitis, P. (2002) *Corporate Event Project Management.* New York: John Wiley & Sons Inc.
Applies project management tools to corporate event planning.

Robson, L.M. (2009) 'Event Management Body of Knowledge (EMBOK): The future of event industry research', *Event Management*, 12(1): 19–25.
Looks at the status of the EMBOK Model and how well it accomplishes what it says it can do.

Useful websites

http://www.epms.net/ft.htm
Presents the basis of competent event management and events portfolio management.

http://www.juliasilvers.com/embok.htm
Presents a knowledge domain structure as a captured and therefore explicit starting point for a multinational and multidisciplinary discussion on a global Event Management Body of Knowledge [EMBOK].

http://www.pmi.org/
The official website of the world's leading not-for-profit membership association for the project management profession.

References

Adema, K.L. and Roehl, W.S. (2009) 'Environmental scanning – the future of event design', *International Journal of Hospitality Management*, 29(2): 199–207.

Ali-Knight, J., Martin, R., Alan, F. and Adele, L. (2009) 'Part 4: Managing the event', in *International Perspectives of Festivals and Events*. Oxford: Elsevier. pp. 225–226.

Allen, J. (2000) *Event Planning: The Ultimate Guide to Successful Meetings, Corporate Events, Fundraising Galas, Conferences, Conventions, Incentives, and Other Special Events*. Toronto, Ontario: John Wiley & Sons Inc.

Allen, J., O'Toole, W., Harris, R. and McDonnell, I. (2002) *Festival and Special Event Management* (2nd edn). Brisbane: Wiley.

Baccarini, D. (1999) 'The logical framework method for defining project success', *Project Management Journal*, 30(4): 25.

Berridge, G. (2009) 'Event pitching: The role of design and creativity', *International Journal of Hospitality Management*, 29(2): 208–215.

Bitran, G.R. and Lojo, M. (1993) 'A framework for analyzing service operations', *European Management Journal*, 11(3): 271–282.

Bowdin, G.A.J., McDonnell, I., Allen, J. and O'Toole, W. (2001) *Events Management*. Oxford: Butterworth-Heinemann.

Bowdin, G., Allen, J., O'Toole, W., Harris, R., & McDonnell, I. (2006) *Events Management* (2nd edn). Oxford: Butterworth-Heinemann.

Crowther, P. (2010) 'Strategic application of events', *International Journal of Hospitality Management*, 29(2): 227–235.

Getz, D. (1997) *Event Management and Event Tourism* (2nd edn). New York: Cognizant Communication Corporation.

Getz, D., Andersson, T. and Larson, M. (2007) 'Festival stakeholder roles: Concepts and case studies', *Event Management,* 10: 103–122.

Goldblatt, J. (2005) *Special Events* (4th edn). New York: John Wiley & Sons Inc.

Heineke, J. and Davis, M.M. (2007) 'The emergence of service operations management as an academic discipline', *Journal of Operations Management,* 25(2): 364–374.

Jugdev, K. and Macœller, R. (2005) 'A retrospective look at our evolving understanding of project success', *Project Management Journal,* 36(4): 19–31.

Lawson, B. (2005) *How Designers Think The Design Process Demystified* (4th edn). Oxford: Architectural Press.

Lester, A. (2007) 'Work breakdown structures', in *Project Management, Planning and Control* (5th edn). Oxford: Butterworth-Heinemann.

Matthews, D. (2008) *Special Event Production.* Oxford: Butterworth-Heinemann.

Melton, D. and Iles-Smith, P. (2009) *Managing Project Delivery: Maintaining Control and Achieving Success.* Oxford: Butterworth-Heinemann.

PMI (2008) *A Guide to the Project Management Body of Knowledge (PMBOK ® Guide).* (Vol. 6). PA: Project Management Institute.

Robertson, M., Rogers, P. and Leask, A. (2009) 'Progressing socio-cultural impact evaluation for festivals', *Journal of Policy Research in Tourism, Leisure and Events,* 1(2): 156–169.

Robson, L.M. (2009) 'Event management body of knowledge (EMBOK): The future of event industry research', *Event Management,* 12: 19–25.

Salem, G., Jones, E. and Morgan, N.(2004) 'An overview of events management', in I. Yeoman, M. Robertson, J. Ali-Knight, S. Drummond and U. McMahon-Beatie (eds), *Festival and Events Management.* Oxford: Butterworth-Heinemann. pp. 14–31.

Shone, A. and Parry, B. (2004) *Successful Event Management* (2nd edn). London: Thompson Learning.

Silvers, J. R., and Nelson, K. B. (2009) 'An application illustration of the event management body of knowledge (EMBOK) as a framework for analysis using the design of the 2006 Winter Olympics opening ceremonies', *Event Management,* 13: 117–131.

Tum, J., Norton, P. and Nevan-Wright, J. (2006) *Management of Event Operations.* Oxford: Butterworth-Heinemann.

Van der Wagen, L. (2007) 'Event project planning', in L. Van der Wagen (ed.), *Human Resource Management for Events.* Oxford: Butterworth-Heinemann. pp. 37–55.

Wilson, J.M. (2003) 'Gantt charts: A centenary appreciation', *European Journal of Operational Research,* 149(2): 430–437.

5
Building an Events Team

Bruce Johnson

Learning Objectives

By reading this chapter students should be able to:

- Explain the importance of effective Human Resource Management (HRM) in creating effective events.
- Understand the fundamental principles of HRM in organizations and how they apply to building events teams.
- Identify and apply the basic processes of HRM to building events teams.
- Understand the particular characteristics of events that pose challenges for HRM.
- Recognize the need for formal management of volunteers.
- Assess the HR issues that may arise when managing international events.

Introduction

Effective Human Resource Management (HRM) leads to a positive impact on employee performance by enhancing the competence of staff, promoting motivation and commitment and designing work in such a way that staff are encouraged to make the fullest possible contribution (Guest, 2000). However, for the events industry HRM can be particularly important.

Boxall and Purcell (2011) give four reasons why good HRM is important in a service industry. First, labour can be a very large proportion of total costs and a relatively small percentage saving in these costs and therefore has a significant effect on bottom-line financial performance. Second, the intangible elements of services such as quality of service or friendliness of staff, rely heavily on 'the skills, personalities and moods of those who provide them'. This is particularly true in events teams, where there can be a lot of last-minute time pressure bringing the various elements of the event together. Third, the need for services to be produced and consumed simultaneously requires a highly flexible workforce to cater for variations in demand. Lastly, customer service plays an extremely important part in overall customer satisfaction (Boxall and Purcell, 2011: 147).

We might also add to this list the fact that many events, whether they are flagship sporting events and a matter of national pride or if they are vital to the promotion of companies and their products, depend heavily on effective teams of staff in order to achieve their basic marketing objectives.

All of these factors contribute to the need for a well-thought-through HRM strategy when building events teams. This strategy will involve making effective use of the principles and practices of HRM to be discussed in this chapter.

The Fundamental Principles of Human Resource Management in Events

For the events industry there is a particular need to energize one's staff so there is a positive atmosphere for both staff and customers (Van der Wagen, 2007). Essentially, no matter what size or type of event, success is determined through the staff knowing what is required of them and then having the ability and motivation to do what is required. To achieve the objectives of a committed, flexible, quality-orientated staff (Guest, 2000), organizations need to consider how they will plan their management, organizational and communication structures. Even when running a small event, staffed totally by volunteers, clear divisions of responsibility and authority will help all concerned contribute to its success.

HRM for events integrates with all aspects of event process management. Issues such as the need to have a clear design strategy and vision for one's event, as well as effective project management to control costs and enable effective planning, and the need to understand the event environment in terms of culture and politics all require effective event teams. Indeed, knowing how one wants staff to behave towards customers is a critical part of the event design and therefore integral to what one is trying to market. Equally, staff being clear on how they can contribute to the overall customer or audience experience can enhance their motivation and therefore their effectiveness.

Once the objectives of the event are agreed, HRM strategy is created through the creation of policies (Beer et al., 1984) that have been formulated taking into account stakeholder interests, as well as situational factors, such as the labour market, business strategy and conditions, technology, workforce characteristics and legal and societal values. Once implemented, these policies aim to achieve the commitment, competence and cost effectiveness of the workforce. In addition to policies, specific procedures are created to support the delivery of HR objectives (Fombrun et al., 1984) in several ways. Selection of appropriate staff enables job performance, which can then be appraised in order to inform reward and training decisions, both of which enhance performance, while also providing important feedback on the effectiveness of the selection process.

HRM Processes in Events, Planning and Organizational Structures

Once a well-defined design and a clear strategy are established, HRM planning can start to ask what staff will be required, in what quantity, from where and how they will be empowered or controlled.

Central to the planning of events staff is consideration of three different forms of flexibility: numerical, temporal and functional. Organizations would always like staff to be available in the perfect number to satisfy peaks and troughs of customer demand throughout the event, thus providing numerical flexibility, only when they are required, providing temporal flexibility, to do whatever is required, which is functional flexibility. In practice, of course, this completely just-in-time approach to staffing is rarely totally achievable. A well-trained, highly motivated and totally reliable workforce who can be asked to deploy generic skills in a wide variety of contexts would take time to build up and the costs of this are a luxury that many events organizations, operating in increasingly internationalized and competitive markets, simply can't afford. Equally, this highly trained workforce is unlikely to put up with the insecurity and anti-social nature of unpredictable hours and therefore income. There is therefore a balance to be struck between securing the perfect workforce and the costs of doing so. Often the core staff is relied upon heavily to train and lead teams of casual or voluntary staff during an event. Additionally, team-work may form an important part of the training, motivation and performance management of staff.

For a large event, subcontractors, or the venue, may provide many of the staff. Typically this might cover catering, cleaning, security, technicians, maintenance staff, car park attendants and even customer service staff. An organization may also be using volunteers, who will be discussed in more detail later in this chapter. It is also worth mentioning that even a small event, totally dependent on volunteers, is unlikely to turn away many willing people. Therefore structures and plans may need to adapt around the skills that emerge from the volunteers, rather than seeking specific staff to fit into a narrowly defined set of plans and job roles, imposed from the top of the organization. Despite this, events will still benefit from a well-defined strategy, as a tool to unite the efforts of all towards the satisfaction of goals.

Typically, events organizations rely on a very small number of core staff, who might or might not be employed on either a full- or a part-time basis. This core staff is then responsible for expanding the organization substantially, often including large numbers of volunteers, to help run the event itself. This characteristic of events organizations has been described as 'pulsating' (Toffler, 1970) and is discussed further later in this chapter.

A framework which can help organizations identify and differentiate between types of staff, identifying their different needs and therefore different approaches to management of the varying groups or segments is provided by the model of the flexible firm (Atkinson, 1984). This model suggests that staff can be divided into various groups. The core staff is most important to the organization, because of its unique knowledge and experience of the event's operations. The organization would like this core of staff to be as stable as possible and should therefore reward them appropriately and provide development and career opportunities, in order to help retain them to the event.

Outside this core there are two peripheral groups, who are also employed, and then beyond them there is agency and subcontractor staff. The first peripheral group has generic skills that are relatively easy to replace from the job market, such as electricians or stage managers, and may be employed on regular contracts but would not attract the same level of development or training as the core group because they are relatively easily replaced and do not necessarily have knowledge unique to the organization. The second peripheral group is in a similar bracket in terms of skill availability in the job market but would be on temporary or short fixed-term or casual contracts, still with the parent organization. Beyond the peripheral groups are subcontractors, agency staff or the staff of outsourced companies and, important in terms of events, there could be a large number of volunteers.

In reality a small minority of events staff are engaged on full-time permanent contracts, and might therefore receive a significant amount of career development or long-term training from their employers. This core staff may be crucial to the longer-term survival of the organization, by providing an organizational memory of lessons learnt from previous events, and present a particular challenge in terms of retention, to be discussed later in this chapter.

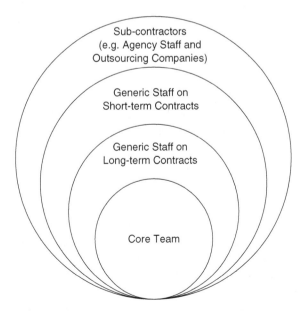

Figure 5.1 *Event staff types*

Job Analysis

In terms of planning what people do and when, a combination of the HRM planning described earlier in this chapter and the project management processes described in the previous chapter would be used to create a work breakdown structure. This will identify the functions staff have to perform both in the preparation for and during events and indicate the number of staff required. The next steps in the process are concerned with techniques for finding the right people to do these jobs. This starts with job analysis.

Job analysis is a process by which the main purpose of jobs, the principle duties or tasks and the reporting lines are established. However there are decisions to be made about which tasks that need to be done can be batched into jobs. The purpose of this is to design jobs that can be managed effectively by the organization and are manageable by the staff doing them. This connects with the need to create a flexible, committed and quality-driven event team as well as the previous section on HRM planning and organizational structure.

Kanter argues that in a service-oriented culture, clear standards achieved by standardized procedures facilitate effective employee performance (2008: 45). If one considers the complexity of running a large event and the fact that large numbers of staff, including volunteers, are coming together for a short time with an immovable deadline and that the need to learn from mistakes during the event must be minimized, the importance of well-established procedures, or at least well-defined objectives, becomes evident. In other words, all staff need to have a very good idea of what it is they are supposed to be doing and how they are supposed to be doing it, as soon as possible in the event. This could be through the use of procedure manuals, staff handbooks, job descriptions or simply through effective briefing. However it is the purpose of job analysis to identify the tasks and responsibilities of all roles in order to inform the content of these documents or the briefing.

Before finalizing any job description it is worth considering if one has created jobs that staff, whether they are employed, subcontractors or volunteers, will enjoy doing. It may be easier to manage an organization in which all staff have single functions, however if the single function in your job is always to spend an entire shift checking tickets at an entrance one might reasonably succumb to a degree of boredom. Considering the variety of tasks (job enlargement or job rotation) and level of responsibility (job enrichment) that a job entails, may pay dividends in terms of employee or volunteer satisfaction, which in turn could have big benefits for customer service and retention of staff. This could be expressed in terms of a mechanistic or motivational approach to job design (Bloisi, 2007).

A major consideration in the design of jobs is the need to have a flexible workforce, alluded to in the section on HRM planning and organizational structure. This can be incorporated into a job description by ensuring there are clauses about following any reasonable management request or about the changing nature of requirements. Alternatively one might use deliberately vague descriptions of duties such as 'taking responsibility for all aspects of customer care and responding to information requests in a variety of contexts' rather than 'staffing the enquiries desk'.

An alternative approach might be to define the job in terms of the competences required to carry it out successfully, rather than specify duties in a limiting or prescriptive way. Competences describe what a job holder should be able to do. For instance, our customer service staff on the enquiries desk might need to be competent in terms of communication, problem solving, customer focus and working under pressure. A competence-based approach can be particularly helpful when recruiting large numbers of staff against tight deadlines because the best way to establish the competence of staff is by questioning them about their previous experience. In an events environment in which there is very limited time to train staff, well-defined competences which can be inferred from applicants' previous relevant experience will facilitate quick recruitment decisions.

In simple terms, the design of jobs is the result of job analysis and the outputs of this process are a job description and person specification for the jobs that need to be filled. These two documents form the foundations of the recruitment and selection, then training and performance management of staff. They do this by specifying what tasks need to be done and what knowledge, skills and abilities are required to do them.

The person who will be responsible for management of the relevant staff once they are in post normally carries out the job analysis. This person may gather information by interviewing staff who have done the job in the past or are currently doing it, from colleagues, from a human resources specialist if there is such a person in the organization, from group discussion amongst the design team and senior managers or through analysis of critical incidents at previous events. A job description includes the following information:

- Job title
- Position (voluntary or paid) and grade
- Summary of job's main purpose
- Reporting lines; subordinates and managers
- List of main tasks
- Reference to any other relevant documents such as training manuals or procedures

The job description then feeds into the person specification. This document identifies what skills, experience, knowledge, qualifications and personal attributes are required in order to carry out the duties in the job description, generally identifying elements which are essential or only desirable.

Person specifications have various purposes. However it is worth noting that the objectivity and accuracy of the specification is essential for recruiters to identify the best people for jobs and therefore for organizations to defend themselves against any allegations of unfair recruitment and selection practices. The need to provide equality of opportunity in employment is enshrined in the employment laws of many countries. The accuracy of the job description is crucial in creating the person specification and therefore the job analysis process needs to be as accurate as possible. The objective and job-specific criteria for selection in the person specification then allow selectors to compare candidates as objectively as possible.

Recruitment and Selection

Having created the job description and person specification, we now have the information with which to carry out the recruitment and selection processes. Recruitment is the process of attracting sufficient candidates for a job and selection is the process by which the best of these candidates are selected. In order for these processes to be fair, they need to be based on the objective and relevant criteria that have been established in the job analysis and are now part of the job description and person specification. The first process in recruitment is to advertise the job. Adverts have to be drafted that will give a clear idea of what the job entails and what the selection criteria are. There is a balance to be struck here, between making a job sound attractive so that there are sufficient applicants and ensuring that there is enough information for inappropriate candidates to deselect themselves on the basis of the advert.

There is no single prescription on what should be in a recruitment advert, although legislation on equal opportunities may well dictate what should not be included. Taylor (2008) suggests issues to be considered should include how many candidates need to be attracted, how honest to be in terms of the challenges of a job and whether to focus on the organization or the job. De Witte (1989) found that clear information on job titles, workplace location and salary levels helped attract more candidates and there is evidence that a clear statement of skills will likewise attract more suitable candidates.

Internet advertising is now used by 75 per cent of employers in the UK for at least some of their jobs (CIPD, 2007) and increasingly sophisticated systems are being developed by which the recruitment and selection process is administered online and candidates can be taken through a series of exercises by which they either progress or are politely rejected as part of this process. Whatever media are used to advertise jobs, it is a good idea to monitor their effectiveness. This should help identify where suitable candidates are coming from, which media are attracting candidates from different ethnicities and backgrounds and which attract the highest number of suitable candidates. A quotation, often attributed to Lord Leverhulme, the creator of what is now Unilever, sums up one of the major issues in advertising: 'I know that half of my advertising budget is wasted, but I'm not sure which half.' Effective monitoring of how candidates hear about jobs and where the most suitable candidates are coming from is essential to identify the most cost-effective systems of advertising.

Once a suitable pool of candidates has been attracted then selection of the best candidate for the job can commence. Traditionally, this would use what Cook (2004) describes as the classic trio: an application form, interview and the taking up of references. In small organizations the use of application forms may be replaced by CVs, however an advantage to having information on an application form is that it is easier to compare candidates when their data is always presented in the same format, as it would be on a form.

When it comes to interviewing, the requirement that candidates be objectively compared suggests using a structured interview, in which all candidates are asked the same or similar questions. This helps selectors, of whom there should be at least two, to make these comparisons. The questions should be structured around the essential criteria for the job listed in the person specification and be specific to the job or opportunity being offered by the organization. A written record of candidates' answers will help selectors compare candidates after the interview.

Induction and Training

Having defined the strategy, planning, structure and job designs for an event, then recruited the best person for the job, the over-riding purpose of induction and training is to ensure all staff understand how their efforts will enable the organization to get the event right on the day. Given the need to provide the best possible experience for customers, there may be little opportunity for learning on the job, therefore if only a little learning is needed to do a job it can be taught on the day with very little cost attached to that training. Staff members who have learnt from experience of previous events will clearly need less training, so particularly if volunteers are involved the retention of previous staff will be helpful.

In terms of the need for an energized workforce, even where national pride was an important motivator for volunteers, as at the Olympic Games in Beijing, an enormous amount of training was also used (Ketter and Wang, 2008). In practice, for large events, contractors to whom functions such as security, cleaning or catering have been contracted will have done much of the training. Despite this, the parent organization should still be clear what standards of service they require their contractors to provide and this will have formed part of the contract for that service. For mega-events such as the Olympic Games or a football World Cup, there would be some common orientation training for all staff that would have to include important health and safety issues such as major incident and evacuation procedures. This training provides a certificated pool of staff that has also cleared any necessary security checks in order to work at the event.

One way to potentially reduce the costs of induction is through the use of operational, staff or procedure manuals (Hanlon and Stewart, 2006). Available in hard copy or online, these documents can allow staff to understand as much of their job as possible before induction and training, which then becomes more a matter of testing what has already been learnt and filling any job-specific gaps in knowledge or understanding.

Performance Management

Performance management is an area in which the conventional practices of HRM need careful adaptation to the complex and varied staffing of events. If managing a cohort of volunteers, one might reasonably assume that motivation and the desire to get the job right are a given. Effective recruitment and selection should have supplied staff capable of doing the job, while appropriate induction and training should have made clear what would be expected in terms of job performance. These steps provide organizers and team leaders with the understanding needed to tell good performance from bad in order to ensure event success and to provide job satisfaction for staff.

This need to communicate what constitutes effective performance on the day is a particularly important tool in the management of volunteers, for whom recognition of their efforts plays an important part in their reward. Equally, performance of contract staff should be evaluated on the day to ensure that jobs are being carried out correctly.

Performance management also provides feedback to core staff so their post-event evaluation can become one of the important tools of retention (Hanlon and Jago, 2004). Staff development for both paid and volunteer staff, creating the manuals for the following year and providing staff with the satisfaction of knowing they did a good job all spin off from the performance management system. Overall event evaluation can therefore be significantly enhanced by feedback from staff performance management systems.

Reward and Retention

In HRM, the issues of reward and retention are closely linked. This is also the case in events organizations, even those that rely on a large proportion of their staff being volunteers. However, with both paid and voluntary staff it is important to appreciate that reward is not just about money.

The discussion of volunteers, later in this chapter, will consider the question of motivation for volunteers. However it is also important to note that for staff who are employed, rewards may come in a host of forms. These could include career development within the organization, career development beyond the organization in terms of creating a strong CV with the necessary experience and training to progress, or the intrinsic satisfaction of being involved in a particularly worthy enterprise and the satisfaction of being part of a highly effective and highly motivated team.

Retention can be particularly problematic for event organizations that are running one event during the year, or even one mega-event like the Olympics every four years. The problem relates to both volunteers and core staff and is caused by the highly energized, team orientation of the run-up to the event itself, followed by the relative vacuum immediately afterwards. For both employed and volunteer staff, a post-event evaluation provides important information about the success of the event that has just passed, in terms of capturing the knowledge acquired to improve future events and also in terms of recognition for staff of the often incredible efforts they have just made to make the event a success.

As well as recognition, this is an opportunity for the organization to look at the future prospects for staff. For all staff, having a sense of what can be looked forward to at the next event, new or bigger roles, more challenge, or indeed less, may be the thing that will retain them with that organization. Additionally, there are some who suggest that making a proportion of pay dependent on completion of the event can help to encourage retention (Hanlon and Jago, 2004.)

Cross-cultural Factors, HRM and Events

As stated throughout this text, events are increasingly international in nature, either through use of foreign inputs or serving foreign audiences. Events teams are therefore required to work across countries and this demand raises additional personnel challenges for the event practitioner. Countries may vary in several dimensions that influence HRM practices including legal regulations, the structure of employment markets (availability of workers) and national culture. While the first two factors are formal and data will be available from secondary sources, national culture is a concept that has great influence on HR management, but is difficult to understand. Recently, models that have emerged that attempt to explain the effect of national culture on organizational performance include Hofstede (1991) (see also Ferdinand and Wesner, this volume) and Globe (see Chhokar et al., 2007). Hofstede (1991) identified five factors listed below:

- *Power Distance Index (PDI)* – the extent to which unequal distribution. of power is accepted by subordinates.
- *Individualism (IDV)* – the extent to which individuals act alone or are integrated into groups.
- *Masculinity (MAS)* – the extent to which roles are shared between genders.
- *Uncertainty Avoidance Index (UAI)* – the extent to which members of a culture can deal with unstructured environments.
- *Long-Term Orientation (LTO)* – the extent to which members of a culture respect tradition and social obligations.

The effect of these factors has significant implications for HRM policy design as they need to incorporate the communication preferences and views of authority of varying cultures. For example, in western, individualist cultures with low power distance, staff may approach management directly with concerns or issues. Staff from other cultures may not and critical problems may be hidden, resulting in excessive cost or even event failure.

The GLOBE studies build on Hofstede's work evaluating both societal culture and leadership styles. The latter is of particular interest to events HRM as it is a team-driven activity. Five styles were identified (Chhokar et al., 2007):

- Performance-focused leaders articulate a vision and attempt to motivate members to achieve it within parameters set by values and standards.
- Team-focused leaders attempt to build a cohesive group that is focused on achieving a common goal through collaboration.
- Participation-focused leaders attempt to minimize inequality within teams and delegate responsibility.
- Humane leaders focus on the feelings of their team members and coach individuals to achieve performance.

- Autonomous leaders emphasize the performance of individual team members to achieve team goals.
- Protective leaders focus on the security of the team through procedures and risk-minimizing behaviours.

While incorporating these factors may be complex for events managers, they are critical for ensuring event success.

Table 5.1   *Hofstede's leadership styles*

Performance Oriented *Higher*	Team Oriented *Higher*	Participative *Higher*	Humane *Higher*	Autonomous *Higher*	Self or Group-Protective *Higher*
Anglo	SE Asian	Germanic	SE Asian	Germanic	Middle Eastern
Germanic	Confucian	Anglo	Anglo	E. European	Confucian
Nordic	L. American	Nordic	African	Confucian	SE Asian
SE Asian	E. European		Confucian	Nordic	L. American
L. European	African			SE Asian	E. European
L. American	L. European			Anglo	
Confucian	Nordic			African	
African	Anglo			Middle Eastern	
E. European	Middle Eastern			L. European	
Middle Eastern	Germanic	L. European	Germanic	L. American	African
		L. American	Middle Eastern		L. European
		African	L. American		
			E. European		
		E. European	L. European		Anglo
		SE Asian	Nordic		Germanic
		Confucian			Nordic
		Middle Eastern			
Lower Performance Oriented	*Lower Team Oriented*	*Lower Participative*	*Lower Humane*	*Lower Autonomous*	*Lower Self or Group-Protective*

Diary of an Event Manager – Sonja Werners, Event Organizer War Child, the Netherlands

Sonja is an event organizer at War Child. She does not organize an event every week, but she works with the organization regularly. In the week of 25 March to 1 April 2011, War Child made a tour across the Netherlands with Radio 538

(Continued)

(Continued)

for the first time. As it was a new experience for the organization, it was a very hectic period.

Sonja relates: 'During the whole week we travelled across the Netherlands with two trucks in which a radio studio was built to collect as much money as possible for the war children. The team consisted of staff of Radio 538 and War Child and involved people for the contents of the radio programmes, for the fund raising, for the communication, for the organization of the events, and from the back office.'

While War Child is an international charity, an event of this type required a deep understanding of Dutch people. As a local Sonja provided the knowledge the charity needed to design appeals for Dutch people. While the language was not a major issue, understanding the local culture was critical to ensure participation and audience interest.

Sonja explains: 'Dutch people are very conscious of sustainability issues. Needless to say that with events like these we always try to take environmental aspects into account. For instance, we print "timeless" promotion material, travel by carpool as much as possible and arrange things locally. Without this effort, I'm not sure if the event would have been well received.'

During the tour, Sonja and her team visited 27 locations and were live on air for 24 hours per day. The public could follow their activities on www.538forwarchild. nl. On all locations ordinary citizens and celebrities were challenged to do a stunt to attract attention and raise money. She recalls: 'For instance we drove with a stretched limo through a car wash with celebrities on the roof; Marco Borsato, one of the most famous Dutch singers and also representative of War Child, presented the weather forecast at TV-station RTL4; it was possible to *abseil* from the town hall in Apeldoorn, and much more. We also visited Leeuwarden. For each €300 they raised, the employees of City Marketing Leeuwarden ran on pumps and wooden shoes to the highest floor of a high office tower which was 115 meters or 24 storeys.'

During the tour, War Child received many positive and enthusiastic reactions. In total it raised €650,000! With this money it can help more than 54,000 war children. Because of its success the organization also decided to make the tour an annual event.

Sonja says: 'What I've learned from my experience is that international teams can bring the best of both worlds – international best practices and local knowledge.'

HRM Issues Particular to Events

Building highly effective teams at work is a challenge for most organizations. However, when your organization can vary dramatically in size, when it relies on large numbers of volunteers or casual staff coming together for a short time on an occasional basis, when it serves very large numbers of customers at high-profile events, the challenges increase. Add to this the likelihood that events could be happening in a number of different countries and in a variety of contexts and it becomes clear that building high-performing events teams brings with it a particular collection of challenges.

Pulsating organizations

A pulsating organization is one which expands and contracts during the life-cycle of its regular activities (Toffler, 1970). In events management this is a fundamental part of most organizations and can happen to an extreme level. Hanlon and Stewart (2006) give the example of the Australian Open Tennis Championships in which a staff of 20 expands to over 4000 personnel and then back to its original size in a matter of weeks.

One issue of pulsating organizations is about creating structures that can grow rapidly, on a just-in-time basis, so staff are not paid to hang around waiting for an event to happen but are available to be properly briefed and trained for their tasks. Often involving a large proportion of staff who are volunteers, as in the case study on the National Student Drama Festival (NSDF), it is important for events organizations to achieve high levels of flexibility, in responding to the staffing needs of their events, while ensuring that all involved know what is required of them and how to achieve it.

This suggests another issue relating to the pulsating nature of organizations. This is the need to find ways of effectively inducting large numbers of staff, particularly in relation to issues of public safety, as efficiently as possible. Hanlon and Cuskelly (2002: 232) identify a generic four-step management induction process common in most organizations. These steps involve providing a broad understanding of the organization and its goals, establishing the working relationships which might also include some sort of team building, providing resources such as policy and procedure manuals and finally evaluating the induction process itself. They go on to argue that this process needs adaptation to the event environment, to take into account the needs of different groups such as those who are outsourced or already have experience of the organization.

The earlier section on HRM planning and organizational structures discussed ways to plan for pulsating events organizations, including outsourcing and subcontracting, while the section on job analysis has discussed how jobs can be designed to help provide flexibility and motivation.

A common way of bringing large numbers of appropriately inducted staff together for events, is for functions such as security, catering and customer service to be outsourced. This would require a specialist supplier, who in turn will have a pool of suitably certified staff on whom they can call. It is worth noting that in the case of mega-events, all staff who are likely to be used during the event, whether employed, subcontracted or volunteering, may need a common training programme covering basic knowledge such as venue orientation and health and safety, as well as some form of security screening (Van der Wagen, 2007).

Case Study 5.1   National Student Drama Festival: A Pulsating Organization

The National Student Drama Festival (NSDF) attracts productions, participants and professionals from across the UK, to create a unique week of workshops, performances, discussions and training.

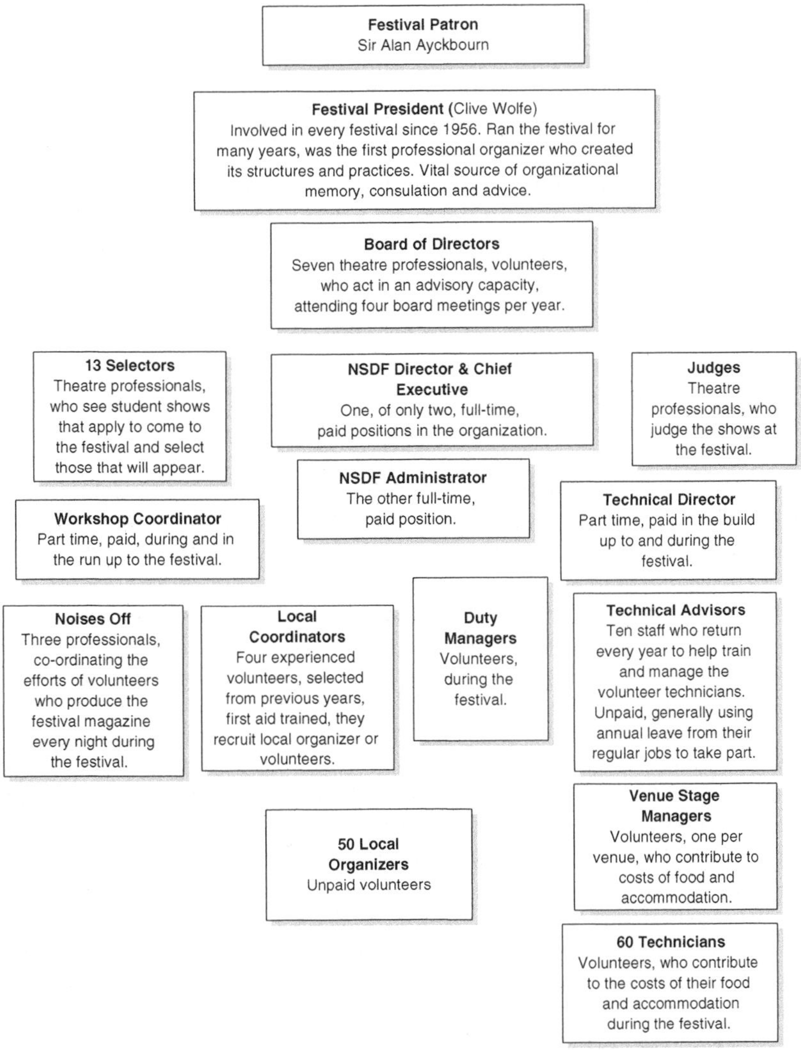

Festival Patron
Sir Alan Ayckbourn

Festival President (Clive Wolfe)
Involved in every festival since 1956. Ran the festival for many years, was the first professional organizer who created its structures and practices. Vital source of organizational memory, consulation and advice.

Board of Directors
Seven theatre professionals, volunteers, who act in an advisory capacity, attending four board meetings per year.

13 Selectors
Theatre professionals, who see student shows that apply to come to the festival and select those that will appear.

NSDF Director & Chief Executive
One, of only two, full-time, paid positions in the organization.

Judges
Theatre professionals, who judge the shows at the festival.

NSDF Administrator
The other full-time, paid position.

Workshop Coordinator
Part time, paid, during and in the run up to the festival.

Technical Director
Part time, paid in the build up to and during the festival.

Noises Off
Three professionals, co-ordinating the efforts of volunteers who produce the festival magazine every night during the festival.

Local Coordinators
Four experienced volunteers, selected from previous years, first aid trained, they recruit local organizer or volunteers.

Duty Managers
Volunteers, during the festival.

Technical Advisors
Ten staff who return every year to help train and manage the volunteer technicians. Unpaid, generally using annual leave from their regular jobs to take part.

Venue Stage Managers
Volunteers, one per venue, who contribute to costs of food and accommodation.

50 Local Organizers
Unpaid volunteers

60 Technicians
Volunteers, who contribute to the costs of their food and accommodation during the festival.

Figure 5.2

(Continued)

(Continued)

The NSDF can involve as many as 60 performances, 180 workshops, 6 discussions, 7 late night events and can attract up to 1000 students. Outside the festival itself, the NSDF organization runs a free two-day workshop weekend in Leeds, when they programme a range of technical and creative workshops led by professionals. They also run the NSDF and Methuen Drama Emerging Artists' Competition during the Edinburgh Fringe Festival, they programme the North Wall summer festival in Oxford, and run a national workshop programme and the NSDF ensemble.

Despite the size of the festival and the numerous other commitments throughout the year, there are only two full-time members of staff: the Festival Director, who is also the Chief Executive, and the NSDF Administrator. These two core personnel then call on a small team of professionals, who could be described as the first peripheral group referred to in the section of this chapter on organizational structures, as and when required for specific roles. The festival then relies heavily on a large number of volunteers, the second peripheral group.

The first peripheral group is made up of the Selectors and Judges, as well as two seasonally employed staff, who manage the technical aspects and workshops at the festival. The seasonally employed staff, the Technical Director and the Workshop Coordinator, assisted by four Local Coordinators and ten Technical Advisors, then manage the second peripheral group, of up to 130 volunteers, who make up the technical team and the local organizers.

This structure, a core staff of two full-time employees, growing to include the Technical Director and Workshop Coordinator in the run-up to the festival, allows the organization to expand rapidly in the immediate run-up to the week of the festival and then contract again afterwards. The core paid staff, local coordinators and technical advisors provide the organizational memory, allowing lessons to be learnt from year to year, and also play an important part in the recruitment, briefing and coordination of the duty managers, venue stage managers, local organizers and technical team. These latter roles require staff to have competences that are generally identified in those who have volunteered during previous festivals.

On the technical side, the technical team consists of around 70 volunteers from a variety of backgrounds who come for the unique opportunity to work and learn together. In ten days they build four theatres from empty rooms, run performance venues, support visiting companies, attend workshops and get involved with fringe events. It is important for a significant proportion of this team to have core competences in technical theatre and this will be established from their previous experience. Often this may have involved working in youth, school, college and university theatres as well as some professional experience. Technical volunteers may also be identified during the workshops and at other events that the organization runs during the year.

On the organizational side, during the six months leading up to the festival, the Local Coordinators appoint, train and manage a team of around 50 volunteers – the

(Continued)

(Continued)

Local Organization team. This team coordinates the front of house, box office, workshops and evening entertainments and much more. A large proportion of these local organizers may never have been involved in NSDF before and may be attracted to volunteer because they have an interest in theatre; being part of the organization provides them with free access to shows they would otherwise have to pay for. Equally, if they are studying theatre and want to work in the industry then their involvement would become part of their CV by providing vital work experience and may provide networking opportunities that could also enhance their future prospects.

It is worth noting the role of the Festival President. For many years the festival was completely dependent on Clive Wolfe, who dedicated much of his life to it. When Clive was ready to pass on responsibility for managing the festival he was still able to provide a vital link to the past, in terms of organizational memory and practical briefing for those who were taking on the responsibilities. This would have been invaluable to both the board and the incoming director.

Having identified the structure of the festival organization it is worth noting the way that activities are planned and scheduled. The beginning of the annual cycle is also the end of the previous year's cycle. This takes the form of a review meeting that is held every September. This meeting draws on formal feedback from previous participants, such as a technical feedback form, as well as the recollections and notes of those who are present.

During the year, the schedule for the local organizers involves a social meeting around Christmas time, giving those who worked together previously, and those thinking of joining, the opportunity to see the venues and network with each other. During the year it is the Local Coordinators who liaise between local volunteers and Festival Director.

On the technical side, the Festival Director, Technical Director, representatives of the Technical Advisers and the Venue Stage Managers meet with all of the companies selected to bring shows to the festival during a technical weekend, several weeks before the festival, in order to plan the equipment, staffing and logistics of the various shows.

The board meets four times per year in a voluntary and advisory capacity. Immediately before the festival the technical team arrives two days earlier to allow time to build the venues. This time is also used to disseminate the health and safety policy documents which everyone has to sign for, and to run workshops on safe working practices and emergency procedures. The local organizational team also arrives early to allow safety briefings, to get to know each other and to be trained on how to do their jobs. During the festival there are daily risk assessment meetings as well as regular liaison between the Duty Managers and security staff at the venues.

Overall, the NSDF is a good example of what Toffler (1970) describes as a pulsating organization, which also relies heavily on the support of a large proportion of volunteers.

(Continued)

(Continued)

Case Study Questions

1 How does the NSDF manage their 'pulsating' organization?
2 How do they attract and motivate volunteers?
3 If the NSDF management decides to invite teams from other countries, what HR processes do they need to put in place?

Chapter Summary

High-profile events undoubtedly attract support from many people interested in their content, and wanting to be connected to the event can become a major motivator in its own right. Effectively, all of the HRM processes and practices discussed in this chapter are important when creating an effective events team. A clear strategy, with structures, policies and procedures designed to create a committed, flexible, quality orientated staff; well thought-out jobs, aligning the efforts of staff with the strategy and goals of the organization; effective recruitment, reward and retention strategies ensuring appropriate staff have a clear understanding of how their own performance contributes to the event, along with well defined performance management and event evaluation – all of these elements support the delivery of successful events.

Review Questions

1 What are the primary functions of HR events management?
2 How can an HR manager ensure that volunteers perform effectively at an event?
3 Using an example of a conference, design an HR structure to manage a multicultural team.
4 What are the implications of 'pulsating organizations'?
5 Discuss this statement using HR theory: 'We've got a good plan. Once people follow it, the event will be fine.'

Additional Resources

Books and journal articles

Hanlon, C. and Cuskelly, G. (2002) 'Pulsating major sport event organisations: A framework for inducting managerial personnel', *Event Management,* 7(4): 231–243.
This article highlights the need to ensure staff is inducted as efficiently and effectively as possible, in pulsating organizations.

Hanlon, C. and Stewart, B. (2006) 'Managing personnel in major sport event organizations: What strategies are required?', *Event Management,* 10(1): 77–88.
This article focuses on strategies developed specifically for events management.

Huczynski, A. and Buchanan, D. (2008) *Organisational Behaviour: An Introductory Text* (6th edn). London: Prentice-Hall.
This book provides a comprehensive introduction to organizational behaviour. Using theory and examples, it examines the dynamics of human behaviour in a range of working environments.

Rayner, C. and Adam Smith, D. (2009) *Managing and Leading People* (2nd edn). London: Chartered Institute of Personnel and Development.
This text takes an evidence-based approach to evaluate the tools, techniques and processes of leadership in public, private and voluntary organizations. It provides a wealth of practical evidence in the form of case studies drawn from small, medium and large organizations.

Watson, G. and Gallagher, K. (2005) *Managing for Results* (2nd edn). London: Chartered Institute of Personnel and Development.
This book presents a strategic approach to management with critical perspectives on the human resource area. Using cases and examples along with discussion questions and exercises, it integrates HR and general management theory.

Useful websites

http://www.CIPD.co.uk
The office website of the Chartered Institute of Personnel and Development (CIPD) is Europe's largest HR and development professional body. It works to support and develop those responsible for the management and development of people within organizations.

http://www.HR.com
Contains templates, tips and ideas for HR management.

http://www.SHRM.org
The office website for the Society for Human Resources Management, a comprehensive resource for HR and personnel theory and practice.

References

Atkinson, J. (1984) 'Manpower strategies for flexible organisations', *Personnel Management*, 16: 28–31.
Beer, M., Spector, B., Lawrence, P.R., Quinn Mills, D. and Walton, R.E. (1984) *Managing Human Assets*. New York: The Free Press.
Bloisi, W. (2007) *Introduction to Human Resource Management*. London: McGraw-Hill.
Boxall, P. and Purcell J. (2011) *Strategy and Human Resource Management* (3rd edn). New York: Palgrave Macmillan.

Chhokar, J.S., Brodbeck, F.C. and House, R.J. (2007) *Culture and Leadership, Across the World: The GLOBE Book of In-Depth Studies of 25 Societies*. New York: Lawrence Erlbaum Associates.

CIPD (2007) *Annual Survey Report 2007: Recruitment, Retention and Turnover*. London: CIPD.

Cook, M. (2004) *Personnel Selection: Adding Value through People*. Chichester: John Wiley and Sons.

De Witte, K. (1989) Recruiting and advertising. In P. Herriot (ed.) *Assessment and Selection in Organisations*. Chichester: John Wiley and Sons.

Fombrun, C., Tichy, N.M. and Devanna, M.A. (1984) *Strategic Human Resource Management*. New York: John Wiley and Sons.

Hanlon, C. and Cuskelly, G. (2002) 'Pulsating major sport event organisations: A framework for inducting managerial personnel', *Event Management*, 7(4): 231–243.

Hanlon, C. and Jago, L. (2004) 'The challenge of retaining personnel in major sport event organisations', *Event Management*, 9(1–2): 39–49.

Hanlon, C. and Stewart, B. (2006) 'Managing personnel in major sport event organizations: What strategies are required?', *Event Management*, 10(1): 77–88.

Hofstede, G. (1991) *Cultures and Organizations: Software of the Mind*. New York: McGraw-Hill.

Guest, D.E. (2000) *Human Resource Management: Employee Well-being and Organisational Performance*. Warwick: CIPD.

Kanter, R.M. (2008) 'Transforming giants', *Harvard Business Review*, 86(1): 43–52.

Ketter, P. and Wang, W. (2008) Sprinting toward the finish line. CBS Interactive [online]. Available from: http://www.google.com/search?sourceid=ie7&q=sprinting+toward+the +finish+line&rls=com.microsoft:en-gb:IE-Address&ie=UTF-8&oe=UTF-8&rlz=1I7SMSN_enGB341.

Taylor, S. (2008) *People Resourcing*. London: Chartered Institute of Personnel and Development.

Toffler, A. (1970) *Future Shock*. New York: Bantam Books.

Van der Wagen, L. (2007) *Human Resource Management for Events: Managing the Event Workforce*. Oxford: Butterworth-Heinemann.

Acknowledgement

The Diary of an Event Manager in this chapter was kindly provided by Elena Cavagnaro, Albert Postma and Thomas Neese.

6
Event Marketing

Rumen Gechev

Learning Objectives

By reading this chapter students should be able to:

- Identify the peculiarities of event marketing.
- Develop appropriate event communication strategies aimed at event participants and attendees.
- Use the event marketing mix to develop an event marketing strategy.
- Appreciate the need to alter the marketing mix for event audiences in different countries.
- Understand the role of event marketing in the global economy.

Introduction

Over recent years, the organization and holding of events has become an almost ubiquitous phenomenon. Organizations, communities and countries throughout the world have embraced events and they are now an integral part of organizational growth and development strategies. This is because of the many benefits that are attributed to the hosting of events, which include:

- A high rate of investment return
- The positive thoughts and feelings events generate for attendees
- The potential for organizations that stage events to carve out distinct market positions
- The opportunities events provide for meaningful interactions amongst those that attend

On the one hand, events are subject to market forces much like any other product or service. Consequently, they obey basic market laws and principles, as well as the major requirements and mechanisms of marketing itself. On the other hand, they possess a number of peculiar characteristics, differentiating them from traditional goods and services. This implies the need for adapting existing marketing mechanisms specifically for events.

This chapter starts off by examining the differences between event marketing and the marketing of other products and services. It then outlines how successful event marketing strategies can be developed by utilizing the event marketing mix. It also highlights that event marketing mixes may need to be altered for event audiences in different countries. The chapter closes with an exploration into current trends in event marketing. Particular attention is paid to how the global financial crisis and technological developments are impacting the practice of event marketing.

Is Event Marketing Different from Marketing?

The dual meaning of event marketing

Today event marketing is an increasingly important part of modern business practice. It has opened up new opportunities for cost-effective and very beneficial communication to market segments. As Hall and Sharples (2008: 30) note, this type of marketing

> *... can keep in touch with the event's participants and consumers (including visitors), read their needs and motivations, develop products that meet these needs, and build a communication programme which expresses the event's purpose and associated product's purpose and objectives.*

However, this statement fails to encompass all the levels of interaction and dependencies of event marketing because it only focuses on the relations between the organizer of a given event and the respective participating companies on the one hand, and between the organizer and the visitors, on the other. The relationship between the participating companies and the visitors of an event is also of great importance, as this is a key outcome of event marketing. Companies frequently seek to participate in other organization's events in order to build relationships with the event attendees. They may seek to introduce themselves, build their brand awareness or encourage brand trial or switching.

Thus event marketing can involve the marketing of an organization's event to attendees and/or the marketing of the participating organization(s) brands/goods/services to event attendees. In one sense it follows the traditional understanding of marketing as in the marketing of a particular product – in this case an event – and in another sense it describes a particular type of marketing that organizations that participate in events undertake to promote their brands, products and/or services. It is a type of marketing which seeks to build relationships with event attendees even though the organization may not be responsible for hosting the event.

Marketing Events – A Unique Challenge

Marketing is defined as 'the management process responsible for identifying, anticipating and satisfying customer requirements profitably' (CIM, 2009: 2). Is this definition applicable to the marketing of events? The reply is affirmative, but with the stipulation that there are several peculiarities in the application of marketing principles, depending on the nature of the event itself. For example, events can be divided into 'for profit' and 'non-profit' events. An exhibition for manufactures would likely belong to the former group, whereas an event such as an anti-war rally would belong to the latter. Between the organizer of the latter and its participants there will be relationships and interactions, which will not be motivated by profit or typical market forces, such as raising awareness and recruiting supporters. Similarly many events hosted by governmental institutions or non-governmental organizations (NGOs) would fall into the non-profit category. For these events, very often the government or NGO will host these events to achieve some social objective and usually these organizations will not seek to recover the costs of these events from participants. As such the revenues from the tickets sold usually cover just a fraction of the costs involved in holding such types of events.

The preparation, actualization and marketing of an event is a great challenge indeed. Unlike classical marketing, which focuses on the market success of a given product or service, the marketing of an event has to secure a certain balance between the goals of all stakeholders, so that the objectives of the organizer, for instance, could coincide, or at least come close to aligning with the objectives of participating organizations and also those of the attendees. Additionally, like services, events are intangible and cannot be turned into stockpiles to be kept for more favourable times. In other words, there is not much room for any modification of marketing strategy in response to customer demands as the event is being produced as it is being consumed. Thus, any tickets that remain unsold after the event cannot be re-sold, so it is vital that the marketing strategy be effective as mistakes will be very costly to the event organizer. Other important similarities between services and events are listed in Box 6.1.

Box 6.1   Events' Similarities to Services

- Intangibility – Events cannot be experienced before they have taken place.
- Inseparability – Events cannot be separated from the people who produce them.
- Variability – People are involved heavily in delivery of events hence there are numerous opportunities for variation.
- Perishability – Tickets that remain unsold for an event cannot be re-sold at a later date.

To illustrate the range of stakeholders involved in the marketing of events, the marketing strategy involved in the staging of an international exhibition for manufactured goods will be considered. Such a strategy has to combine a range of goals, expectations and outcomes which arise from the organizers, participants and also exhibition attendees. The organizers of such an exhibition will be interested in:

- The occupancy rate of the exhibition areas
- The price at which exhibition space has been rented
- The revenues from the accompanying services at the exhibitions
- Revenues raised from visitor entrance fees
- The attainment of the highest possible return on investment
- The maintenance of competitiveness with respect to the organizers of similar events
- The positioning of the exhibition in the international market for such events

However, organizers will not necessarily be interested in which specific companies do take part in the exhibition or what their specific goals and interests are. For instance, if there was an increase in Japanese participants at the expense of American or European ones, this will be of no consequence to the organizer. However, such a situation would signal a change in the market positions and/or the need for modifications of the marketing strategies of the participants at the exhibition.

The marketing strategies of exhibition participants directed to attendees, and the possible communication among the participants themselves will also possess a high degree of autonomy and independence. Each participant will have their goals, expectations and desired outcomes for the exhibition. These may include displaying their products and services to potential new customers as well as finding out what competitors or companies in related industries are doing. In this case, the marketing strategies of the exhibition organizer will be less important to the participants as compared with the importance of their marketing strategies to the exhibition organizer. Moreover, the participants are the customers of the exhibition organizer, whereas the attendees are basically customers of the participants and are only indirectly clients of the organizer.

This situation demonstrates the complexity of satisfying the needs and requirements of two sets of customers at the exhibition – participants and attendees – whilst meeting the exhibition organizer's need for profitability. It signals the need for different marketing strategies to be developed to target the needs of each stakeholder, which raises the question of balance. Which set of needs and requirements should the exhibition organizer prioritize? Ultimately, the market success achieved by the participating companies contributes to the success of the entire event and vice versa. The more successful the event, the more attractive it becomes for future participants, because it offers adequate conditions for the realization of the various market targets and objectives. This creates conditions for a more successful branding of the event and/or the company responsible for its realization, which in turn will attract more attendees. A chain of success will be created when the needs of all stakeholders are satisfied (see Figure 6.1).

This chain can be equally applicable to music festivals which cater to the needs of artists, sponsors and audiences, as well as sporting events which need to appeal to athletes, sponsors and spectators. In both instances, as was the case for the exhibition, the satisfaction of participants (whether artists, athletes or sponsors) will directly impact the satisfaction of the event organizers, which will in turn impact the satisfaction

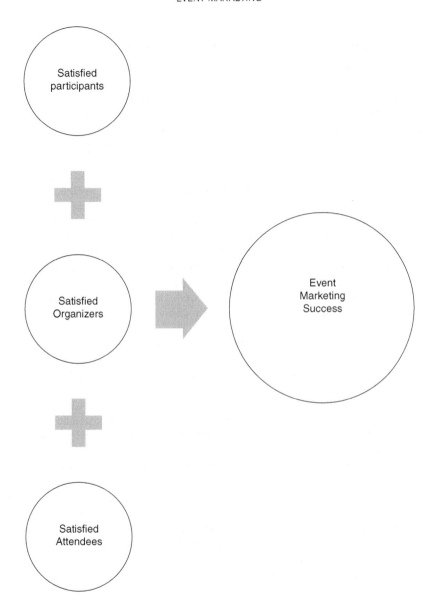

Figure 6.1   *Chain of event marketing success*

of participants and audiences/spectators. All three will then impact the event's over-all marketing success. One event that has been very successful in leveraging the interactions of organizers, participants and attendees is the Dayton International Hamvention. Case Study 6.1 details how the event has succeeded in satisfying the diverse needs of its stakeholders.

Case Study 6.1   The Dayton International Hamvention, Dayton, Ohio, USA

The Dayton International Hamvention is the most popular and the most prestigious amateur radio convention in the world. It combines trade show, retailing, flea markets, interest group meetings, licence examination sessions and other activities. It is held each May at the Hara Arena near Dayton, Ohio and not-for-profit Dayton Radio Amateur Association (DRAA) is the main sponsor of the event. The event attracts more than 20,000 radio amateurs (also called 'hams') from all over the world who see it as an opportunity to buy and/or sell new or used equipment, to meet with fellow hams or to take the licence examination sessions. Numerous companies, among them leaders in the field of radio such as ACOM, Ameritron, ICOM, Kenwood, Orion, Palstar and Yaesu, offer electronic components, receivers, transceivers, amplifiers, antenna systems, specialized software programs and books for sale. The event combines a number of commercial, institutional and social activities. The DRAA's expenses for the organization of the event (advertising, rent payments, printing materials and overheads) are covered by two main income sources: entry tickets and re-renting space to commercial companies and organizations.

The multidimensional character of the event creates excellent opportunities for mutually supportive marketing activities. These activities are organized by different event stakeholders (for example, radio manufacturers, radio amateur groups and societies, retailers and charity groups). The objectives of the marketing activities of the stakeholders are quite diverse and the hams as well have several distinct reasons for attending the event. For instance, hams who sell used equipment at the flea market often buy new equipment. Some will come to the event to simply upgrade their old equipment, prompted by the renewal of their licences. At the event both groups will find both buyers and sellers that satisfy these objectives. Other attendees will bring their families along for a fun day out. There are participating organizations at the event which provide opportunities for shopping in Dayton and visiting museums, exhibitions and theatres.

There are multiple levels of interaction amongst the organizers, radio manufacturers, amateur radio associations, retailers and attendees – creating a dynamic and enjoyable atmosphere.

Developing an Event Marketing Strategy

As in the case for products and services, the marketing strategy of an event can be developed with the classical marketing mix of the four Ps – product, price, place and promotion (Kotler et al., 1999). However, there need to be slight variations in how each one is interpreted.

Product

One of the key product attributes of many events is one of the other four Ps – promotion. Meetings, music festivals, trade shows, exhibitions, theatrical performances, cultural and charitable events can all be viewed as channels for promoting the product offered by the participants to the audience attending the event. This makes events unique when compared to other products and services which typically do not include promotion as part of their benefits. In support of this offering, the event product can also include sponsorship packages, television and broadcast rights and public relations opportunities.

Other key offerings of the event product are: the infrastructure constructed at the event venue, services to both participants and visitors (such as food and beverages, entertainment, financial and telecommunication services), the staff and the atmosphere. These offerings highlight both the intangible and tangible nature of the event product. Like many other products and services, events are a mixture of intangible and tangible qualities. By using Brassington and Pettitt's (2006) anatomy of a product, it is also possible to divide the event product into the following attributes (see Box 6.2).

Box 6.2   Anatomy of the Event Product

- Core attributes – Provide the main reason for the event, for example opportunities for event organizers, participants and attendees to interact and distribute and/or receive information, entertainment or key messages.
- Tangible attributes – Visible cues that the event organizer uses to communicate the core benefits of the event such as the venue infrastructure, food and beverages.
- Augmented attributes – Add-on or extras that the event organizer provides to the event's core attribute. These include sponsorship packages, broadcast rights and public relations opportunities, entertainment and atmosphere.
- Potential attributes – Cater to the evolving nature of events allowing them to be updated in response to changing trends and situations. For example, many events can be staged virtually in response to emerging concerns about the environment and the economy.

Adapted from: Brassington and Pettitt (2006)

Price

Event marketers, like their counterparts in other professions, base their prices on the fundamental law of demand and supply. However, event pricing will be based on a number of other factors such as the prestige of the event, the quality of services on offer, the expected effectiveness, the purchasing power and number of attendees, the price levels of similar events, the costs of the event and the organizers' profit expectations.

Skimming (charging higher than normal market rates) and promotional pricing strategies (offering discounted or incentive prices to encourage attendance) can be done for events as well. For instance, if the particular event is a one-off exhibition of not often seen works of art, a concert of a reclusive artist, a film festival with highly popular film stars, or a launch of a new software package (for example, an operational system of a new generation or a new generation of video games), then the application of a skimming strategy is appropriate. Apart from the higher income the strategy generates for the organizers, it is also effective for solving the problem of there being far more people interested in attending the event than there is capacity to accommodate them at the venue.

Likewise promotional pricing can encourage attendance at an experimental event or one that takes place in a remote location. Some events are free to encourage participation. Event organizers staging such events must factor in the opportunity and other costs that attendees will incur to attend the event even though there is no ticket price. It may cost some attendees more to attend a free event as opposed to a ticketed event depending on their individual circumstances.

Place

For events place refers to the venue at which the event is held and also to the geographic traits of the location, which include transport accessibility, level of prestige, natural environment and the security and safety of the area. Apart from these, this element of the marketing mix is connected with the way in which the tickets for the event are sold, whether via the internet, at cash desks located at the venue, at cash desks located elsewhere, by means of direct sales, or a combination of all these methods.

Promotion

Promotion is typically regarded as the most important element of the marketing mix – as it is through promotion that a product's or service's message or attributes are communicated to the consumer, which initiates his/her engagement with said product or service. Indeed an attendee must first know about an event before he/she can attend. It has already been stated that the event product itself is a channel for promotion, which though typically used by the producers of other products and services can also be used by event managers to promote their events. These may come in the form of taster or tester events which run prior to an event or in the form of publicity stunts or media events organized to publicize an event. For other promotional methods that can be used in event marketing, see Figure 6.2.

Steps to Event Marketing Strategy Success

Beunk and Älmeby (2008) propose the following six key steps to building a successful event marketing strategy, which can be adopted by event organizers to ensure the

Figure 6.2   *Promotional options for events*

Source: Harrell (2001)

success of their marketing efforts. It outlines a logical, methodical approach to developing, implementing and evaluating event marketing strategies.

Know your market and target audience inside out

This involves the study of the key parameters of the event market and includes both secondary or desk and primary market research. It is on the basis of this research that answers to the following questions can be found:

- What is the size of the specific market segment(s)?
- What are the key trends?
- Which are the target and reference groups?
- Which are appropriate mechanisms and instruments for communicating with participants and attendees?
- Which are the major direct and indirect competitors?

Other market research that can be undertaken include PEST/STEP/PESTEL analyses and research into the cultural, customs, language and communication styles of those likely to be involved in an event. Refer to Ferdinand and Wesner's 'The International Events Environment' in this volume (Chapter 2) for more information on carrying out this type of research.

Set clear objectives

The conclusions made on the basis of marketing research make it possible to define the objectives in more precise terms, including prioritizing which objectives are the most important. The number and type of attendees the event organizer hopes to attract are usually included among the most important objectives. See Box 6.3 for other types of event objectives that can be set by event organizers.

Box 6.3   Examples of Event Marketing Objectives

- Number of tickets to be sold.
- Number of exhibitors/performers/athletes/businesses to participate.
- Financial value of sponsorship to be raised.
- Percentage increase in market share to be achieved (if the event is competing directly with other similar events).
- Percentage of attendees from different market segments (e.g. local residents, ethnic minorities and disadvantaged groups).

Determine a communication strategy

This step specifies the content, the attractiveness and convincing power of the main message to be delivered to the potential event attendees. An effective communication strategy should demonstrate to attendees the value-added qualities of an event, how this event differs from other similar events, the distinctive features it has to offer and its unique selling point.

Determine the marketing mix

As has been stated previously, the classical four Ps of marketing can be harnessed effectively by event organizers to market their events provided their interpretation is adjusted to address the unique characteristics of events. However the event marketer may also choose to use alternative marketing mixes designed specifically for events. For example, Hoyle's (2002) 5Ps includes product, price and place but excludes promotion. The Ps which are put in its place are positioning and public relations. Recalling that many events are themselves a form of promotion, the omission of this P in favour of positioning and public relationships which play to the event's unique and attention-grabbing qualities is understandable. Getz (2007) in contrast has proposed adapting Morrison's (1995) 8Ps approach. He also groups the Ps into 'experiential' and 'facilitating' elements. The experiential elements refer to product, place, programming and people – which most directly affect attendees' experiences at an event. The facilitating elements are those that indirectly impact or facilitate attendees' experiences at an event and refer to promotions, partnerships, packaging and price. Regardless of the model that is utilized, the marketing mix must be in keeping with the market research findings, objectives set and the communications strategy specified.

Execute marketing activities

The time-frame and resources needed to accomplish marketing activities depend on the scope and nature of the event. For large-scale, annual, national and international events, the preparation can last for an entire year, commencing immediately after the completion of an event in the previous year, and the resources required can necessitate funding be acquired from many different sources including donations, sponsors, concession sales and public sources. Other marketing activities may be staged in a single day with minimal resources.

Prior to executing event marketing activities most event organizers will design an event marketing action plan which includes the key activities, personnel and resources required to deliver the marketing strategy. Execution addresses the who, where and when and how of marketing, whereas previous steps address the what and why (Kotler et al., 1999). Event organizers will very often make use of project management tools in developing and implementing their event marketing action plans. Williams in 'Event Project Management' (Chapter 4 in this volume) outlines how such an approach can be utilized.

Learn lessons

Important lessons can be learnt by conducting research of pre-, during and post-event evaluations. Methods for gathering information can include surveys undertaken pre-, during and post-event, on-site observation and participant focus groups. Findings from this research will be crucial for the marketing of the event when next it is run as it will tell event organizers about levels of participation, the promotional tools that were most effective and what participants thought of the event.

Local versus Global Event Marketing Strategies

Event marketers, like their counterparts in other industries, must be aware of the need to tailor the product, pricing, place and promotional elements of their event marketing strategy for attendees in different countries. Thus event marketers will be required to undertake market research to educate themselves about local conditions before developing market objectives, an overall communication strategy, marketing mix and implementation plan. For example, the poor attendance at the International Cricket Council's 2007 World Cup (see Ferdinand and Wesner, in this volume) could be seen as the failure of the event organizers to sufficiently adapt the event's marketing strategy. In particular, the pricing was out of sync with the purchasing power of the local population and the core product was not sufficiently augmented to encourage West Indian spectators to attend. Music and the ability to enter and leave matches freely proved to be key attributes that were needed to augment the core product of interacting with other spectators at the Cricket World Cup.

However, this is not the case for all events and all countries. In some instances it may be appropriate to pursue a 'global marketing strategy' when promoting events in different countries. When such a strategy is utilized an event's marketing is standardized in all countries where an event is held. In some cases event managers will be staging events in countries quite similar to their own or due to the requirements of an event franchiser they will be required to follow a standardized marketing strategy. It may also be the case that the event has universal appeal and thus the marketing strategy does not require adaptation. The following event management diary brings to light some of the other local and global considerations of marketing events in different countries.

 Diary of an Event Manager – Maria Schuett, Independent Event Marketing Consultant, Germany and the United Kingdom

Maria Schuett offers services to outdoor sporting companies in Germany wishing to enter the market in the United Kingdom (UK) and vice versa. She provides clients with press releases, press kits and marketing plans as well as arranging for them to attend major trade shows. She also stages media events to raise awareness of her clients' products and brands. A few years ago she realized that there was an opportunity in the market for a company that was able to provide insider knowledge and understanding of the German and UK markets for outdoor sports, which were becoming increasingly interlinked since the formation of the European Union.

She explains: 'I saw I was in an excellent position to take a hobby and make it into a business. I loved outdoor sports and was born in Germany and educated in the United Kingdom – where I made many contacts in the outdoor sporting community.'

Currently, 60 per cent of her clients are from the UK, where she spends most of her time, and 40 per cent of her clients are from Germany. In working with both sets of clients she has noticed that 'working with German clients is more complicated when compared to British clients. German companies are far more formal and hierarchal and their decision-making is a lot slower'.

As she looks towards the future of her business, she says: 'the main thing these days is social media and staying on top of technology, whatever country you are in. The recession and sustainability are also things I need to consider.'

She advises new event marketers to pay close attention to 'creative networking' as this is a valuable source of business opportunities, especially internationally. Maria also suggests that they constantly scan the environment for emerging trends and potential threats.

Global Trends in Event Marketing

In the first chapter of this text, event marketing is described as a method of communicating an organization's message, which echoes the secondary meaning which event marketing is given in this chapter – 'a particular type of marketing that organizations that participate in events undertake to promote their brands, products and/or services'. Very often organizations' participation in events is achieved through sponsorship, but they can also host their own events in order to achieve the benefits of this promotional tool.

The popularity of event marketing has proven to be an enduring trend over the last two decades and is proving resilient even after the 2008 financial crisis. Additionally, social media marketing and event marketing have emerged as complementary tools that can be used to enhance the effectiveness of one another. The following outline these and other trends and issues in event marketing.

The recession, events and event marketing

The financial and economic crisis of 2008 imposed substantial restrictions on the costs incurred by companies and institutions. This has affected the frequency, duration and organization of events. A study undertaken by the Event Marketing Institute (EMI) (2010) has shown that the attendance rate of events dropped by around 10 per cent in 2009. However, at the same time, certain types of events managed to attract more visitors, despite the effects of the crisis. They include conventions and tradeshows, where the visitor growth rate stands at 3 per cent. The EMI (2010) has predicted that the latter will continue due in large part to the growing interest in various events as a means of implementing business strategies and/or improving the market positions of companies. For many organizations, event marketing is a cost-effective alternative in hard economic times as it allows marketers to stage effective, efficient promotions as an alternative to pricier media messages (Tedesco, 2008).

Social media and event marketing – complementary marketing tools

Social media marketing tools can often enhance the effectiveness of event marketing and vice versa. Event attendees frequently continue their communication about an event via the internet site of the hosting organization – in blogs, discussion groups and chat rooms or via the organization's Facebook page. Research published by EMI and mktg.com (2010) found that three quarters of consumers would be more likely to communicate with a company using social media as a result of a good experience with that company's event. Additionally, some 45 per cent of respondents said that they had posted a photo/video/message from an event to their own social media page. Events combined with social media marketing is proving for some organizations a successful recipe for making their events/products/services go viral as customers, with the help of social media applications, are becoming effective company spokespersons. Box 6.4 provides some helpful guidelines on using Twitter to get event attendees talking about an event.

Box 6.4   Twitter and Events Marketing

Twitter is a micro-blogging and social networking media tool that can be harnessed by organizations managing events. Since 2006 the site has been accessible through any internet-capable devices but has gained significant traction with the emergence of portable devices such as smart phones and tablet computers. To post to twitter is termed 'to tweet' and tweets can lead to an effective communications stream for event marketers. Tweets are limited to 140 characters and can contain anything from general musings to links on breaking news, promotions and many other topics.

Steps for Tweeting Success

1 *Follow your followers* – once the event gains followers, the event should follow them in return. Dependent on the size of the event it is unlikely the event team can track each individual follower but by following a twitter user it can appear to facilitate a genuine two-way conversation between the event and followers. Tools such as Twittergrader allow managers to track prolific tweeters with large followings (power users) and ascertain their level of influence.
2 *Use hashtag-ing* – the use of a dedicated hashtag (#), such as #FIFAWC2010, can provide the event team not only with a way of managing their tweets into categories but also a way to track other users' tweets about the event. This can be an effective public relations tool, particularly when dealing with negative tweets about the event. Negative feedback is a part of all events, however the timeliness of twitter allows the marketing communications function to keep abreast of all manner of insights.
3 *Don't be shy about cross-promotion* – many sponsors provide substantial support for international events. Tweets can be managed to cross-promote official sponsors and other partners to create a fluent communication feed. If an individual who receives the tweet is interested then they will examine the tweet and possibly re-tweet it (giving your partners' exposure to their followers), if not then the feed will soon fill with other tweets.
4 *Spread the News* – any news relating to the event, its partners and its performers can be released through tweeting. This keeps all followers abreast of the information they may require and can generate and sustain interest in the event.

The growth of virtual event marketing

With the advance of technologies and the revolutionary development of the internet, which is now accessible to hundreds of millions of people, further growth of virtual event marketing is expected, not only because of the lower costs of reaching participants and attendees and communicating with them, but also because of other factors. Virtual marketing events eliminate the need for non-productive meeting time and can be promoted as sustainable alternatives to real-life events. Additionally, these types of events can extend a company's reach to new global markets and to individuals that are unable or cannot afford to attend traditional physical events.

The continuing importance of 'live'

Despite the growing popularity of virtual sales meetings and events, and online sales, customers have shown themselves persistently loyal to mediums in which they can get first-hand impressions of the products and services they purchase. The ability of virtual meetings to take the place of face-to-face meetings has largely been dismissed by meeting industry experts, who cite the continuing importance of the 'intimacy of social engagement' (Paxon, 2009: 138). Research published by EMI (2010) has also found that marketers think events are the best marketing tool for building customer relationships and over a third of them are of the opinion that event marketing is increasing in importance. Table 6.1 shows other highlights from the survey which suggest event marketing will prove a persistent trend for many years into the future.

Table 6.1   *Event marketing survey findings published by the Event Marketing Institute in 2010*

The top three rated marketing tools for building customer relationships are:

1   Event marketing
2   Social marketing
3   Web marketing

The marketing tools that give the best ROI are:

1   Web marketing (40 per cent of respondents agree)
2   Event marketing (22 per cent of respondents agree)

The percentage of marketers who rank the future importance of events as increasing has risen from 29 per cent to 36 per cent

34 per cent of respondents plan to move to an experience-driven portfolio within the next three to twelve months, while 31 per cent say they have already done so

Case Study 6.2   The 'Made in Bulgaria' National Trade Exhibition of Producers from Bulgaria

The 'Made in Bulgaria' National Trade Exhibition of Producers from Bulgaria is held by a non-profit association called the Made in Bulgaria Union set up by the National Palace of Culture, the Bulgarian Chamber of Trade and Industry (BCTI) and Business Center-Bulgaria Ltd. The major objective of the association, according to the Chairman, Hristo Droumev, is 'to encourage Bulgarian companies and grant them assistance for their further development'. Since 1995 to date, the trade show has been held on an annual basis. It has been attracting sizeable public interest ever since its inception and in the week it is held, it is visited by more than 250,000 people.

The marketing activity of the exhibition runs for the entire year, prior to its staging. Direct marketing is targeted to the members of the BCTI through personal letters, e-mail messages and telephone calls. Interactive marketing is also done through the trade show's website.

The BCTI has set up a special unit which is assigned the task of promotion, organization and actual hosting of the exhibition. The leader of the unit, Marin Manzelov, says 'the advertising campaign for the next trade show starts on the day the current event is closing'. Yordanka Chavdarova, manager of the business centre-Bulgaria Ltd, has found 'newspaper advertising has proved to be the most effective for attracting company participants, whereas TV clips mostly contribute to attract the attention of visitors'. She also thinks that newspapers provide the highest rate of return on marketing costs incurred for the exhibition.

The annual advertising budget of 'Made in Bulgaria' is US$100,000 (£60,910) which amounts to just around US$0.40 (£0.24) to attract each visitor. Thus the free publicity that results from hosting press conferences with the media before and after holding every successive trade show is very important. It is also traditional for the Prime Minister and several other ministers to participate at the opening ceremony of each annual event and that their opening speeches are delivered in the presence of members of parliament, ambassadors and representatives of international organizations. This provides another opportunity to attract free media attention. Event coverage is broadcast during prime-time slots of the country's leading television stations.

In November 2010 the 16th edition of the exhibition was hosted under the slogan 'Choose Bulgarian' (National Palace of Culture, 2010) in the emblematic National Palace of Culture, which is located in Bulgaria's capital Sofia. It is an impressive structure consisting of 11 floors – eight above ground and three below. The structure also has the unusual distinction of being built with more steel than the Eiffel Tower (National Palace of Culture, 2008). Entry to the exhibition is free and visitors can spend anywhere from half an hour to three hours looking around. In addition to providing the opportunity to learn about and purchase Bulgarian products, the exhibition also provides visitors with the opportunity to learn about Bulgarian culture. For the more than 300 exhibitors that participated in the exhibition,

(Continued)

(Continued)

'Made in Bulgaria' offered several benefits. For first-time exhibitors, it was an opportunity to introduce themselves to the Bulgarian public. For well established companies, it was an opportunity to enter new markets or to showcase their new product lines. A special poll conducted especially for the exhibition revealed that 27 per cent of the respondents bought goods made in Bulgaria to encourage local industry while 16 per cent preferred them because of their lower prices. The 2010 edition also featured for the first time a display of healthy food, beverages and other products under the banner 'Bio and Eco Expo' (Novinite Ltd, 2010).

Over the years the exhibition has continued to be extremely useful, especially for small and medium sized businesses in Bulgaria, as it serves as a springboard for entry into the national market. Very often visitors to the exhibition are surprised to find that Bulgarian products compare favourably to imported ones in terms of price and quality. Positive feedback like this gives Bulgarian manufacturers encouragement and confidence in the European Market.

Case Study Questions

1 Describe the range of stakeholder needs that must be satisfied by the 'Made in Bulgaria' exhibition.
2 How does the product offered to the visitors to the exhibition differ from the product offered to exhibitors at 'Made in Bulgaria'?
3 Other than free publicity, what benefits are derived from the public relations activities staged by the exhibition organizers?
4 What features could be included in the potential exhibition product to position 'Made in Bulgaria' for the future?

Chapter Summary

Event marketing can be defined in two ways. Firstly, it can be defined as CIM (2009) suggests, as a process of serving customers (whether these are event participants or attendees) profitably by manipulation of the marketing mix. Secondly, it can be defined as a particular type of marketing that organizations undertake, which involves the sponsorship or hosting of events.

When the CIM definition is applied to event marketing, although its practice is quite similar to the marketing of many other products and services, there are a few important distinctions. Firstly, there is the array of stakeholder needs that must be addressed by the event product, which includes participants, attendees and sponsors. Secondly, because events bear many of the same characteristics as services, they are highly perishable, making deficiencies in an event's marketing strategy especially costly as once an event has been held any unsold tickets cannot be offered for sale at a later date. Thirdly, due to events' unique characteristics, Kotler et al.'s (1999) 4Ps of event marketing must be adapted in designing appropriate marketing mixes for them. Event organizers can also adopt other marketing mixes which cater to the particular characteristics of events, such as Hoyle's (2002) five Ps and Getz's (2007) eight Ps of event marketing.

Marketing strategies for events, like those that are designed for other products or services, should be based on sound research from which clearly defined objectives, communication strategies, marketing mixes and implementation plans are developed. Event marketers, like their colleagues in other sectors, can benefit greatly from conducting pre-, during and post-event marketing research, especially if they are staging an event annually, as they can learn how to adjust their marketing efforts for the next time round. As with other products and services, it is often necessary to tailor an event's marketing strategy to cater to specific local conditions in different countries.

Event marketing as it relates to the practice of using events to promote organizations' brands, products or services is proving to be an enduring trend even in the aftermath of the 2008 financial crisis. Social media marketing, which facilitates continued audience interaction after an event has ended, has proven to be a strong ally of event marketing, enhancing its effectiveness. Event marketing has proven itself resilient to the increasing prevalence of virtual sales meetings and events and online sales, as many customers continue to value the experience of having first-hand experience of the products and services they buy.

Review Questions

1   What is the difference between event marketing and events management?
2   How can virtual events extend a company's reach to new global markets?
3   What are the advantages of event marketing over traditional advertising?
4   Why is return-on-investment (ROI) important to event marketers?
5   Explain the role of event marketing in the marketing mix of an event.

Additional Resources

Books, book chapters, journal articles

Allen, J. (2009) *Event Planning: The Ultimate Guide to Successful Meetings, Corporate Events, Fundraising Galas, Conferences, Conventions, Incentives and Other Special Events*. Ontario: John Wiley & Sons Canada, Ltd.
Provides concrete examples of how different types of events are marketed.

Close, A.G., Finney, R.Z., Lacey, R.Z. and Sneath, J.Z. (2006) 'Engaging the consumer through event marketing: Linking attendees with the sponsor, community, and brand', *Journal of Advertising Research*, 46(4): 420–433.
Examines the relationship among event attendees, sponsorship, community involvement, and the title sponsor's brand with respect to purchase intentions.

Kahle, L.R. and Close, A. (2010) *Consumer Behavior Knowledge for Effective Sport and Event Marketing*. New York: Taylor and Francis LLC.
Shows how consumer behaviour research can be applied to sport event marketing.

Raghunathan, R. (2008) 'Some issues concerning the concept of experiential marketing', in B. Schmitt and D.L. Rogers (eds), *Handbook on Brand and Experience Management*. Glos: Edward Elgar Publishing. pp. 132–143.
Provides a theoretical discussion on the usefulness of experiential marketing.

Stevens, R.P. (2005) *Tradeshow and Event Marketing: Plan, Promote, Profit*. Toronto: South-Western, Division of Thomson Learning.
Examines how tradeshow profits can be maximized.

Useful websites

http://www.eventmarketing.com
The Event Marketing Institute provides insights and business intelligence for strategic event management. It highlights the benefits of integrating social media into events.

http://socialmediatoday.com/
Social Media Today is an independent, online community for professionals in PR, marketing, advertising or any other discipline where a thorough understanding of social media is mission-critical.

http://www.worldeventmarketing.com
Highlights creative and innovative strategies to deliver key brand messaging points in the event marketing industry.

References

Beunk, S. and Älmeby, J. (2008) *Marketing Your Event: 6 Steps for a Successful Marketing Strategy*. Congrex [Online]. Available from http://www.congrexnetwork.com/cnt/files/whitepaper/WhitePaper_Marketing_your_event.pdf.
Brassington, F. and Pettitt, S. (2006) *Principles of Marketing* (4th edn). Harlow: Pearson Education Limited.
CIM (2009) *Marketing and the 7Ps: A Brief Explanation of Marketing and How it Works*. CIM [Online]. Available from http://www.cim.co.uk/marketing_resources.
Event Marketing Institute (EMI) (2010) *The Viral Impact of Events: A Study on the Power of Word-of-Mouth Strategies to Increase the Impact of Your Events*. Event Marketing Institute [Online]. Available from http://evalu8pro.com/_pdfs/ViralImpactReport.pdf.
Getz, D. (2007) *Event Studies: Theory, Research and Policy for Planned Events*. Oxford: Butterworth-Heinemann.
Hall, C.M. and Sharples, L. (2008) *Food and Wine Festivals around the World: Development, Management and Markets*. Oxford: Butterworth-Heinemann.

Harrell, G.D. (2001) *Marketing: Connecting with Customers* (2nd edn). Englewood Cliffs, NJ: Prentice Hall.

Hoyle, L. (2002) *Event Marketing: How to Successfully Promote Events, Festivals, Conventions, and Expositions*. New York: John Wiley & Sons, Inc.

Kotler, P., Armstrong, G., Saunders, J. and Wong, V. (1999) *Principles of Marketing*. London: Prentice Hall.

Morrison, A. (1995) *Hospitality and Travel Marketing* (2nd edn). New York: Thomson Delmar Learning.

National Palace of Culture (2008) *About NPC*. National Palace of Culture [Online]. Available from http://www.ndk.bg/staticpages.php?par=about.

National Palace of Culture (2010) *Events: The Made in Bulgaria National Trade Fair Under the Slogan of Choose Bulgarian!* National Palace of Culture [Online]. Available from http://www.ndk.bg/eventsdesc.php?eid=2834&langid=2.

Novinite Ltd (2010) *Made in Bulgaria Expo Opens in Sophia*. Novinite Ltd [Online]. Available from http://www.novinite.com/view_news.php?id=122078.

Paxon, M.C. (2009) 'Changing trends in the American meetings industry', in R. Raj and J. Musgrave (eds), *Event Management and Sustainability*. Oxford: Cab International. pp. 132–139.

Tedesco, R. (2008) 'Direct impact: Marketers find events affordable and efficient. Industry Trend Report 2008', *Promo Magazine*, October: 24.

7
Financing Events

Paul J. Kitchin

Learning Objectives

By reading this chapter students should be able to:

- Understand how organizational context provides the need for sound financial management.
- Explain the importance of the accurate determination of event pricing and budgets.
- Critique the relationship between aspects of financial reporting and highlight the relationships present for assessing the financial health of an event company.
- Gain insight into the role of the manager in reporting back to stakeholders who may be interested in the event's financial information.

Introduction

Box 7.1   The Importance of Finances for Events

Perhaps more than ever, effective allocation of a festival's limited resources is a critical managerial decision that must be addressed by all organizers (Smith et al., 2010: 242).

As the statement above indicates, the importance of financial management and resource allocation for international events cannot be understated. International events are an important part of cities', regions' and countries' cultural make-up and represent more than simply entertainment for interested consumers. Given this importance it is imperative that their ability to operate on a regular and ongoing basis is supported by a strong financial awareness of their management teams. How will we price the event to ensure that our objectives are met? How can we ensure that the management team and staff stay on time and on budget? How can we determine if we are generating enough revenue from our event to cover our costs, and how important is our cash-on-hand for our immediate survival? These are all finance-related questions that managers of international events should have a sound understanding of.

Depending on the size and scope of the event, managers have different financial processes. The organizational context (Stewart, 2007), or basic business model of the event business is crucial for determining these reporting needs. These models consist of a number of types; the basic types are that of sole traders or partnerships where the owners are the legal entities that make up the business. For international operations this is a risky form as if an event fails to be held the owner or the partners are legally responsible for all the debts that the event incurs. Therefore other legal forms are required. The formation of a company that is a legal entity in the eyes of the law is generally the preferred option for managing large-scale, international events. Andersson and Getz (2008) claim that many event organizations seek these legal, institutional forms in order to establish legitimacy and promote sustainability in the event industry. Stewart (2007) identifies two types in particular, the proprietary, or limited company and the company limited by guarantee. A limited company is a form of organization that is limited by shares. The company can either be private and owned by a number of shareholders, or it can have its shares publically traded on a stock exchange. In the UK, Ireland and Australia, a Company Limited by Guarantee is a private legal entity that consists of a company backed by a group of members who make a contribution if the business is wound up. Getz's (1997) event types consisted of a variety of these forms of organizations with varying company structures. However, even in the case of government organizations, the pricing, budgeting and reporting requirements have similarities. Therefore the finance issues discussed in this chapter should be of relevance to all event management organizations.

This text is aimed at students wishing to enter the events management industry. From our experience a number of students of event management show a keen interest in mastering the area of operations, or commercial and public relations aspects of events – however few talk about finance with the same passion. The saying 'do the math' is absolutely fundamental to successful event management, even if it is not many enthusiasts' first choice of career. While this chapter will not make the reader an accountant, it will provide a first step in thinking about finance from a managerial perspective. A dictionary-based knowledge of finance terms will not save the event from impending financial doom, but possibly an understanding of the relationships between pricing, budgeting and financial reporting could do so.

This chapter is structured into three main parts. The first part will examine pricing considerations for event management. There are many strategies in determining the price to charge participants, spectators and other organizations who may use festivals and events. The key factor in price determination is having a clear understanding of the reasons why we are staging the event. This second part is an introduction to budgeting and how this financial tool is important for internal stakeholder planning and controlling the finances of the event. The final section will address the three main types of financial reporting. Financial reporting is not simply constructing these statements but understanding the relationships between the economic entity of the business, its profitability and its solvency. This chapter also has an extended glossary – it is stressed that the reader familiarize themselves with this section as finance is full of its own jargon that requires defining as it can complicate the process for the novice manager.

Pricing

There are two key considerations that the event manager must address when seeking to establish price. For those managers who are stewards of existing events there is a wealth of historical data that they can use (including last year's price) to establish their pricing levels. Alternatively, for managers involved in establishing new events, the organization/event objectives and the costs involved in the event's staging are fundamental considerations. However financial management planning can be an extremely accurate consideration of what you aim to achieve and what it costs but the final key question is: can the customer afford it? Therefore, in addition, knowledge of the event's target market and each segment's willingness and ability to pay is vital. Good marketing research will provide managers with the results required to target, acquire and retain customers for the event while sound financial management should establish accurate budgets that will control costs and allow the correct price to be set. In academic terms determining price fits within the function of the marketing manager. This is suitable when addressing traditional organizations that have complex product portfolios. These pricing decisions have an important impact on the organization but small errors in the pricing of one product will not bring down an FMCG brand, however given the importance of pricing for event entry as an all-in product like an entertainment event it is crucial. Therefore pricing will probably not be left to the marketing manager but the senior members of the event management team, if not the director her- or himself.

Many large-scale events seek to achieve a wide range of objectives for their many stakeholders. Determining the full range of objectives is a difficult task but it can be simplified for finance terms by establishing whether the event company is a for-profit or not-for-profit enterprise (this is a gross simplification but for the purposes of this chapter it should suffice). A for-profit enterprise seeks to maximize its return on the funds invested in the business. This does not mean that every activity is carried out simply to maximize profit (that is, there can be social objectives achieved by for-profit event companies that incur costs), but that a return on investment is a sign of business success and sustainability – important for attracting further patrons, sponsors and other commercial partners.

There are many costs that event organizations must incur in order to manage the event. These costs are broken down into two main categories: variable and fixed. Variable costs are those costs that change with each additional ticket sale that might arise during the event. Fixed costs are those that remain constant over the duration of the event, such as insurance and electricity. Fixed costs can be further broken down into fixed and semi-fixed costs. Semi-fixed costs remain relatively stable but can increase with a step-change once certain capacity levels are reached (Stewart, 2007). For instance, when an indoor venue like a stadium is used for an event, it will require cleaning. Unless the event is a sell-out the stadium will have empty banks of seats. If these seats are kept clear then they will not require cleaning and therefore require less cost, not in a variable sense but by a step-change amount. Proper planning will ensure these costs are incorporated into an estimation of the break-even point.

Break-even analysis is a first step in determining the financial management of any project or event. All fixed and variable costs should be calculated to gain an understanding of the relationship between increased sales and increases in costs giving the manager the total cost. By then ascertaining the contribution sales make a total revenue figure is made clear. Once this is achieved the intersect between total cost and total revenue is the break-even point for the event. In a simple situation this would apply for the entire event, however in a situation where an event has much capacity the step-change of semi-fixed costs incurred would create a number of break-even points. Nevertheless, for new events regardless of their potential size, once the break-even point is achieved the process of pricing strategies and budgeting can begin.

Pricing strategies

There are a wide range of pricing strategies that management teams may adopt. It is not the purpose of this chapter to review every pricing strategy available to managers, however the following options are provided to introduce the reader to some basic approaches. The establishment of the break-even point is crucial for these strategies to provide maximum benefit to the event organizers.

Cost-plus pricing

Cost-plus pricing is one of the most common approaches to costing for managers (Verma, 2008). Cost-plus pricing means once all costs are considered and an estimate of total sales is made, a margin is applied to the figure that provides profit or surplus for the organization. As each unit is sold the margin allows the organization to generate profit. For capital intensive events such as the FIFA World Cup of Football, the fixed costs are high therefore sales revenue from tickets, broadcasting rights contributions, merchandise sales and commercial sponsorships are vital if a margin is to be achieved.

Prestige pricing

While events of international significance exist in a competitive field, certain events are positioned at the exclusive end of the quality spectrum. Events such as the European Champions League Final, Cannes Film Festival and Glastonbury Festival are synonymous with certain expectations and obtaining tickets to these events can be difficult for consumers. This exclusivity allows for the creation of ticket packages that cater for this demand. Prestige pricing is also used to reinforce this exclusivity, allowing the event hosts to leverage higher margins on top of the total unit costs of staging the event.

Discriminatory pricing

International events that are looking to achieve a number of accessibility objectives or those wishing to maximize their ticket sales may use discriminatory pricing in order to attract the widest array of visitors. The range of target groups that may be interested in an event vary considerably and so too does their ability to pay. By offering a discriminatory pricing strategy, the event can attract those groups that can afford high prices and those groups that can't; for instance, the Singapore Grand Prix contains 13 ticketing categories (Henderson et al., 2010). This can be arranged through providing seating areas of different proximity to the event itself or by offering a range of tickets to a multi-activity event. Box 7.2 highlights the ticketing policy of the Summer and Winter Olympic Games. As the event costs a great amount of money to stage, the policy was established to ensure host cities would make the Games accessible.

Box 7.2   Ticket Pricing Policy and the IOC

The Olympic Charter and the Technical Manual on Ticketing assist organizing committees that host a Summer or Winter Olympic/Paralympic Games to determine the systems governing the allocation of tickets during the event. Discriminatory pricing methods are used to ensure that all of the sporting and cultural events that take place within these two-week periods are well attended. Kitchin (2007) highlighted how this can be a minefield for the event managers. The profile of the ticketing systems, the availability and price of tickets to certain events (such as the Opening and Closing Ceremonies and the 100m Men's Final in athletics) lead to many public relations issues for organizers. However the discriminatory pricing policies allow the event managers to maximize ticket revenue. In the case of the Olympics this is vital as all ticket revenues flow to the host city, assisting in the recuperation of the immense costs of the Games. Considering the bill for the Athens 2004 Summer Olympic Games was estimated at US$11.6 billion, getting the policy right is important (Smith, 2004).

Budgeting

Planning and control of finance

For small-scale events budgets can be prepared quite quickly and can rely on a manager's experience and judgement. However, the more significant the event, the greater the need is for the budget to be prepared with precision. To ensure that events are managed effectively, a budget outlining the major financial activities involved in the project must be established from the outset. Budgeting is an important planning and control function for event management. Ongoing calendar events may have different planning mechanisms to one-off events but Schneider and Sollenberger (2005: 236) view planning 'as a framework within which managers anticipate future events, develop a plan of action, and estimate future revenues and costs'. Once a budget is created it should then be analysed by the senior management team, as each manager may have expertise in certain areas, allowing greater specificity on expected costs and revenues. The control function in financial management seeks to ensure that funds spent during the event project are in line with what is portrayed in the budget. The cost control process during an event ensures that the amount spent on staging the event is within the planning framework.

Why budget?

There are a number of reasons to budget. The most important of these is that most major events have a variety of stakeholders that are interested in how funds are spent and earned during the project period before, during and after the event. The downside to budgeting is of course the time it takes for the management team to create the master budget. The use of contingency funds can always be factored in to the budget in order to cater for cost overruns or unexpected items. However the physical act of getting management to agree on the budget can be tiresome itself. A budget can also create an environment that is not suitable to creativity, as staff will see it as a way of limiting their ideas. Regardless, the benefits of taking the time to budget are numerous:

- *To provide a plan of action* – the budget outlines the relevant cost and revenue centres within the event project. It will allow each section manager within the event to view their financial responsibilities and ensure that the event strategy is followed. If the plan is not working it can be monitored and alterations made if necessary.
- *To work as a communication and integration tool* – the budget acts as a way of communicating management priorities across the project and galvanizing the various elements of the event team towards one set of priorities.
- *To foster control over the event project* – the budget allows managers to keep track of all outgoings and incomings and identify areas of weakness or cost overrun. It allows the manager to implement financial changes that can benefit the event's operations.

Master budgeting for event operations

A feature of many events is their service orientation, relying on extensive human resources that would not be required by a manufacturing organization. Many events rely on the contributions of a volunteer staff force. However, research by Smith et al. (2010) and Getz (2007) highlights that in some cases the larger the event, the greater the need for professional human resources in lieu of these volunteers. Therefore one of the significant areas of event budgeting is allowing for the human resource – having an appropriate level of staff supporting an event is not only good for customer service but is also vital for health and safety requirements. Overstaffing is in many cases a must in case incidents occur, such as a medical emergency that keeps staff away from their initial activities. This is why many large-scale events manage their master budget on a project basis. Many projects like outdoor music festivals, international arts festivals, outdoor/recreation or participation events require flexible organizational event team structures and therefore budgets which can also operate in the same flexible manner. Master budgets are prepared up to one year in advance and are linked to the overall strategic plan. Project budgeting for special events may show that the budget system does not work around an annual calendar. Project budgets can form master budgets but be organized around the timeline leading up to, during and post-event. Once the event is over, the event management company moves on to other events or in some cases disbands. Therefore project budgets are more flexible in their scope but fulfil all the same advantages of a full master budget. Box 7.3 contains some tips from Arthur Somerset, an event consultant on budgeting in a recession. Even with increased cost control and a reduction in available funds, certain areas of events must be ring-fenced (or protected) from cuts.

Box 7.3   Budgeting in a Recession

Clarity is key.

Underestimating is not an option – don't leave anything out.

Treats and some extras need to be kept for events to have a 'wow' factor.

Staffing is critical, especially in tough times – don't skimp on human resources.

From where do you start the budget?

The master budget is a similar concept to the business strategic plan. From this one document, smaller departmental or unit area budgets are created. Within any large event there are cost centres and profit centres. The key difference is in the name – a cost centre is generally in charge of ensuring that this unit of the event is run to the budget levels. In an opposite sense, the profit centres are responsible for generating revenue, for instance in selling tickets, arranging commercial sponsorship or increasing the number of trade stalls present at the event. A profit centre still incurs costs but these are generally expenses consumed in the feat of acquiring revenue.

The event manager needs a good understanding of how the organization is structured to see where cost and profit centres lie. The presence of an organizational chart helps determine the responsible areas for cost and revenue. Schneider and Sollenberger (2005) stress the importance of designing the cost system to ensure that it is not too general, to the point where costs can be missed, but also not too intricate in that it could adversely affect the flow of cost-relevant information. They recommend the use of roll-up reporting to guide cost information through different event areas, such as administration, marketing and operations. Each level of activity reports to the manager in charge, and although this can be overly formal and bureaucratic it can also increase control.

Forecasting sales

The first step involved in budgeting is establishing a sales forecast. This is a prediction on the level of income that the event will generate from its range of income sources. There are many factors that can influence sales. External elements such as the economic conditions in a certain market, whether it is in recession or boom, is a primary consideration. Stallholders can form a solid stream of income for events, and difficult times for small businesses impact on their ability to stay in business, thus having a knock-on effect for events. This is particularly important when evaluating markets for entry as do some international events that can pick their next location. Internal factors such as pricing policy (as mentioned above), historical data on sales and market research can also be used.

The process can be assisted by using some mathematical formula that links a number of independent variables to a dependent variable. For instance, if the event is an outdoor arts and culture event that takes place in the summer months, the possibility of heavy rain or other bad weather could have a drastic impact on ticket sales. These are drastic, short-term effects – however, there are other examples of the impact of socio-cultural shifts in consumer tastes and preferences that can also impact on sales forecasts.

Box 7.4   Budgeting Planning Tips

Prepare yourself by talking to suppliers to get an idea of how much event inputs cost.

List all elements in a template to create a working budget that can be easily adjusted.

Allocate budget for crew and associated costs for travel, accommodation and subsistence carefully – these can really add up.

Never count on perfect conditions – always have a contingency and plan for the worst.

Revenues and expenses

The major sources of revenue for events are ticket sales and sponsorship. Sponsors are a function of event size as even smaller local or community events can attract sponsors but naturally they are smaller in size than those required for international events. There are a number of other sources of revenue such as concession sales, merchandise sales, donations, grants and broadcast rights from which events can also raise money. These items, along with ticket sales, comprise the revenue or income that would be shown on a budget. Damien Eames, Marketing Chair Volunteer for the Sydney Mardi Gras, highlights the importance of ticket sales and sponsorship for an international event such as the Sydney Mardi Gras.

 Diary of an Event Manager – Damien Eames, Marketing Chair Volunteer, Sydney Mardi Gras

Working with our business partners, we are starting to leverage the captive audience of several hundred thousand who attend the parade. By far and away the largest revenue source remains ticket sales to the Mardi Gras Party held at the Royal Hall of Industries and Hordern Pavilions at Moore Park, and our annual Sleaze Ball – held at the same venue in the spring of each year. We also derive a significant amount of income from annual membership fees ... Sponsorship is another key revenue source. Last year we signed a three-year $1.5 million agreement with gaydar.com.au, which is now the presenting partner of the Sydney Gay and Lesbian Mardi Gras. There are a number of other significant sponsors such as GAL Home Loans, Coca-Cola Amatil, The City of Sydney and Carlton United Breweries who also support the festival ... The Sydney Gay and Lesbian Mardi Gras has a good track record of attracting mainstream supporters and we continue to do so. A gay and lesbian focus is not a big hindrance with the big brands anymore. The future is about leveraging the broader appeal. Mardi Gras stands for tolerance, diversity, colour and fun, with a dash of edginess. It stands for these things in the eyes of not just a gay audience, but also with the young and well-educated generally. New Mardi Gras will focus on partnerships with brands with similar brand values.

Source: cited in Goodwin (2006)

Expenses are all the costs that are incurred by running an event. For many events the major expenses are derived from the event venue and supporting elements involved in venue preparation such as equipment hire, catering, décor and staging. Other large expense items include entertainment, wages and insurance (depending on the type of event).

Financial Reporting

Financial reporting is going one step further from the budget and feeding back to those who may be interested in the event company's financial performance. If events are to attract a range of financial and commercial partners, due diligence reports should ensure that the business behind the event is sustainable. Financial reporting systems are a feature of a pro-active risk management system and a requirement of many nations' company law legislation.

Financial reporting is required to allow managers and other stakeholders to make decisions regarding the use of resources. It allows interested parties to review the profitability, liquidity and solvency (sustainability) of the business as a going concern.

Main report types

Balance sheet

The balance sheet is a formal document outlining an event company's accounting equation. The accounting equation represents the relationship between a company's assets, liabilities and equity (see glossary). As assets are in some manner acquired from a funding source (either the company's own funds or from a borrowed funding source), the accounting equation that governs the investment made in a business should always equal the following formula:

$$\text{Assets} = \text{Liabilities plus Equity}$$

$$(A = L + E)$$

Profit and loss

These activities are represented in the profit and loss statement (P&L). The P&L statement allows us to estimate the profitability of the business. The P&L statement can be calculated through another equation:

$$\text{Revenues} - \text{Expenses} = \text{Profit (Loss)}$$

$$R - Ex = P (L)$$

Cash flow statements

The final statements indicate the ability of an event company to generate the cash required to fulfil business obligations (for instance, the repayment of bank loans if and when they fall due). In the balance sheet, cash can be seen changing from year to year, and the profit and loss statement can highlight profitability. Regardless, managers should always be querying how any profits are actually being made. Lee and Wines (2000) indicate that cash flow information is important because it identifies where the money in the business is coming from. You could, for example, (in the short term) feasibly sustain the business on borrowed funds, which could demonstrate profitability in the profit and loss statement. But if these backers are lending you the funds based on a rate of return, the business will not survive unless it can generate cash to service those debts. Also, having cash allows an organization to trade efficiently with others and given the just-in-time nature of most event management projects this is vital.

The cash flow statement examines the solvency (see glossary) of an event company. International Accounting Standard (IAS) 7 indicates that cash flow information is useful in determining the ability of a company to borrow funds and to indicate how cash flows will be distributed.

Cash reconciliation statements

Determining what cash flows go into which categories is one of the reasons accounting relies on a series of internationally recognized accounting standards. The need for the reconciliation of cash is to provide greater accuracy for determining working capital within the organization – it gives the manager a closer idea of the financial position by knowing how much cash is present. The reconciliation of cash takes another look at the cash flows arising from operating activities as covered in the cash flow statement above. The aim is to ensure that the reader can see that cash generated from operating activities is clearly identified.

The importance of financial reports

Understanding how to construct a balance sheet and a profit and loss statement, and knowing which items go where, is an important part of an event manager's repertoire of knowledge and is linked back to the budget process. However, even more important is understanding the relationship between the two statements. As a business increases its profitability, it can either re-invest the funds back into the business as assets or pay out dividends to its investors (if it is a for-profit company). This reinvestment then increases the equity contributions made, subsequently balancing the sheet. A business that fails to make a profit must keep drawing funds from either its own cash reserves or from outside the business through loans. Each of these eventualities impacts on the equity within the business.

Analysing financial reports: Financial ratio analysis

There are other levels to which potential and current investors and other stakeholders can go to determine the profitability, solvency and liquidity of the business – one of these is ratio analysis. These ratios allow the reviewer to determine the financial health of the business by examining relationships between current assets and current liabilities, debt to equity and profit margins. As these are tools for improving the awareness of the existing statements, they are not covered in this chapter. However, a good source for further information can be found in the supplementary materials that support this chapter.

Case Study 7.1   The Financial Performance of Sydney Mardi Gras

Background

A symbol and statement of pride in the gay and lesbian community, the Sydney Mardi Gras has been in existence since 1978. From very humble beginnings, the Mardi Gras is now one of the top series of events for the gay, lesbian, bi-sexual, transgender (GLBT) community in Australia and around the world. Members of the GLBT community and tourists from inter-state Australia and around the world make their way each year to Sydney for the festivities; the parade itself is preceded by a range of cultural activities. However, soon after the Millennium, the management of the Sydney Gay and Lesbian Mardi Gras went into insolvency. There were a number of reasons given for this insolvency, some ranging from increases in public liability insurance to poor financial management. This brief case will focus on the recent financial reports of the New Mardi Gras Limited (NMG). This new organization was established to create a not-for-profit sustainable organization and financial platform on which each year's events are built (Goodwin, 2006).

The event has a significant impact on the city and the local economy of Sydney. The organizers theme the activities under the banner of Nations United, which aims to promote human rights for all members of the GLBT community across the globe. Altman (1997: 420) addressed a wide range of Gay Pride events around the globe and considered the event 'uniquely Australian' due to its flamboyance and irreverence (cited in Markwell and Waitt, 2009). In 2009 there were over 300,000 Mardi Gras party-goers, and 134 floats took part in the main parade.

Although the case highlights the use of financial reports it makes NO evaluation of the financial management of NMG Ltd. – it is for illustrative purposes only. An organization such as New Mardi Gras Ltd. is a limited company that has to adhere to policies and standards required under Corporations Law in Australia, where the organization is based. While this is an Australian example most companies registered as a legal entity will be required to publish financial reports.

Under this Corporations Law all of these reports must be independently audited. Chapter 15 of NMG Ltd's constitution outlines that the company must prepare and disseminate financial information in the form of a balance sheet, a profit and loss account with a statement of cash flows, with a reconciliation of that cash flow. This case example will introduce these reports and highlight how NMG Ltd reported this information over the two accounting periods from 2007/08 and 2008/09.

Balance sheets NMG

For NMG Ltd the major sources of revenue are ticket sales and sponsorship which many major international events also attract. There are a number of other sources but they are not as significant as these two (interestingly the contra revenues involve business support offered in lieu of cash, and one of these deals was the

(Continued)

(Continued)

Table 7.1   *NMG Ltd's balance sheet as at 31 March 2009*

	31 March 2009 AU$	31 March 2008 AU$	31 March 2007 AU$
ASSETS			
Current Assets			
Cash and cash equivalents	1,469,307	1,538,460	774,687
Trade and other receivables	527,384	96,728	31,278
Other current assets	90,212	94,896	134,284
Total Current Assets	2,086,903	730,084	940,249
Non-Current Assets			
Property, plant and equipment	53,178	14,731	12,833
Intangible assets	9,465	25,431	29,096
Total Non-Current Assets	62,643	40,162	41,929
TOTAL ASSETS	**2,149,546**	**1,770,246**	**982,178**
LIABILITIES			
Current Liabilities			
Trade and other payables	441,499	410,416	178,544
Other current liabilities	97,038	138,722	39,481
Financial liabilities	0	0	26,695
Total Current Liabilities	538,537	549,138	244,720
TOTAL LIABILITIES	**538,537**	**549,138**	**244,720**
NET ASSETS	**1,611,009**	**1,221,108**	**737,458**
EQUITY			
Retained Earnings	1,611,009	1,221,108	737,458
TOTAL EQUITY	**1,611,009**	**1,221,108**	**737,458**

broadcast of the event. This broadcast is a significant factor in the increase in sponsorship fees a major event can attract – which highlights relationships between various income sources).

Some examples of significant expenses in this case are equipment hire and entertainment (one area where Arthur Somerset stated above not to shirk on), and venue hire for staging the festival. Other activities such as depreciation charges on non-current assets, equipment and venue hire charges and insurance payments which occur throughout the reporting period are also accounted for in the P&L statement.

It is clear from the table that companies stating that revenues are increasing year on year are not actually reporting the entire picture. Expenses understanda-bly must be taken into account. It should be noted however that 2008 was the 30th anniversary of the Sydney Gay and Lesbian Mardi Gras and this could have been a cause of the decrease in profitability between 2008 and 2009. Nevertheless, as stated throughout this example, it is best to use a variety of financial indicators assessed over a series of reporting periods to accurately iden-tify probable causes.

(Continued)

(Continued)

Table 7.2   *NMG Ltd's Profit and Loss for the year ended 31 March 2009*

	2009 AU$	2008 AU$	2007 AU$
REVENUE			
Ticket sales	2,842,799	3,269,426	2,429,696
Sponsorship	1,050,853	581,855	575,812
Bad debts received	0	0	9,091
Membership income	116,907	74,277	60,887
Stallholder fees for Fair Day	104,770	91,949	90,133
Sale of goods	106,772	208,929	278,953
Grants	0	0	2,000
Licence fees	48,381	79,856	51,451
Interest income	82,184	35,331	16,969
Other	0	0	10,755
Insurance recoveries	56,838	0	0
Festival entry	63,316	30,842	28,776
Contra revenue	434,689	422,062	170,625
Parade entrance fees and viewing room	38,992	48,545	23,748
Donations	27,782	39,098	15,599
TOTAL REVENUE	**4,974,283**	**4,882,169**	**3,764,495**
EXPENSES			
Occupancy costs	−10,103	-38,591	−28,497
Employee benefits expense	−465,850	−310,241	−274,051
Amounts paid to contractors	−223,984	−293,137	−185,274
Insurance	−125,284	−136,623	−174,237
Venue hire	−445,074	−557,316	−422,188
Amortisation of intangible software	−15,965	−13,085	−3,754
Depreciation of property, plant and equipment	−4,307	−9,319	−12,325
Operating lease rental expenses	−57,394	−55,261	−53,206
Marketing & communications	−142,068	−116,999	−192,510
Security	−286,865	−290,048	−231,862
Entertainment	−464,803	−295,587	−271,383
Cost of goods sold	−11,852	−112,598	−181,161
Cost of ticketing	−198,173	−199,029	−153,898
Party staging	−188,301	−189,226	−151,018
Equipment hire	−888,653	−757,892	−664,286
License expenses	−141,365	−189,421	−55,280
Professional fees	−30,368	−35,983	−64,021
Contra expenses	−434,689	−422,062	−170,625
Donations	−43,322	−142,823	−14,602
Other expenses	−405,963	−231,648	−217,418
TOTAL EXPENSES	**−4,584,383**	**−4,396,888**	**−3,521,596**
PROFIT BEFORE INCOME TAX EXPENSE (INCOME TAX BENEFIT)	**389,900**	**485,280**	**242,899**
FINANCE COSTS	**0**	**−1,630**	**−2,475**
PROFIT FROM CONTINUING OPERATIONS	**389,900**	**483,651**	**240,424**

(Continued)

(Continued)

The original company that staged the Sydney Gay and Lesbian Mardi Gras went out of business due to insolvency (Goodwin, 2006). Table 7.3 below shows that there has been a dramatic drop in net cash from operating activities and an increase in funds spent on investing activities (the purchase of property, plant and equipment). As no borrowings have had to be repaid in the last financial year (see balance sheet) there are no outgoings in this area. NMG Ltd has negative cash flows from this period's activities which should raise some questions. However the significant increase in cash holdings at the start and end of the year could put this result in another perspective. A view over several years should always be undertaken. No single result should indicate overall performance.

Table 7.3   *NMG Ltd's Cash Flow statement 31 March 2009*

	31 Mar 2009 AU$	31 Mar 2008 AU$	31 Mar 2007 AU$
CASH FLOWS FROM OPERATING ACTIVITIES			
Receipts from customers	5,361,681	4,092,080	3,136,312
Receipts of government grants			2,200
Payments to suppliers and contractors	−5,470,264	−3,314,375	−2,957,789
Interest received	82,164	35,331	16,969
Interest paid	0	−1,631	−2,475
NET CASH PROVIDED BY OPERATING ACTIVITIES	**−26,399**	**811,405**	**195,217**
CASH FLOWS FROM INVESTING ACTIVITIES			
Purchase of property, plant & equipment	−42,754	−11,218	−2,655
Purchase of other non-current assets	0	−9,419	−32,850
NET CASH USED IN INVESTING ACTIVITIES	**−42,754**	**−20,637**	**−35,505**
CASH FLOWS FROM FINANCING ACTIVITIES			
Repayment of borrowings	0	−26,995	−1,885
NET CASH USED IN FINANCING ACTIVITIES	**0**	**−26,995**	**−1,885**
NET INCREASE IN CASH HELD	**−69,153**	**763,773**	**157,827**
CASH AT BEGINNING OF FINANCIAL YEAR	1,538,460	774,687	616,860
CASH AT END OF FINANCIAL YEAR	1,469,307	1,538,460	774,687

(Continued)

(Continued)

Table 7.4   *NMG Ltd's Reconciliation of Cash from operations with profit from ordinary activities after income tax*

	2009 AU$	2008 AU$	2007 AU$
Cash at bank	1,469,307	1,583,460	774,687
Profit from ordinary activities after income tax	389,900	483,651	240,424
Non cash flows in profit from ordinary activities			
Amortisation	15,965	13,085	3,754
Depreciation	4,307	9,319	12,325
Bad debts written off	0	0	−80,000
Changes in assets and liabilities			
Increase in receivables	−430,655	−65,450	146,919
Decrease in other assets	4,684	39,387	45,776
Increase in payables	31,084	232,172	−148,059
Increase/(decrease) in other current liabilities	−41,684	99,241	−21,667
Increase/(decrease) in provisions	0	0	-4,255
Cash flows from operations	−26,399	811,405	195,217

From a look at Table 7.4 year on year it is clear that the cash situation in NMG Ltd is changing quite dramatically. One negative indicator is not enough to warrant drastic action in the management of the event. It is best to examine what other event companies are recording for their cash flow levels before appropriate analysis can take place. The key point when using financial reporting is that the various sources of information all work together to paint an accurate picture of the event company's financial health.

Case Study Questions

1 What key changes do you observe between the 2007/8 and 2008/9 NMG balance sheets?
2 What could the changes between the 2007/8 and 2008/9 profit and loss statements reveal about the financial strategy of the NMG?
3 What conclusions would be drawn about the financial viability of the NMG if the cash flow statement for 31 March 2009 was viewed in isolation?

Chapter Summary

Finance should not be an area that is left to the responsibility of others in event management. All event managers should have some understanding of the basics of financial management to the point where they could converse with specialists and interpret resultant recommendations for managing the future direction of the event.

The principles covered in this chapter are a level above a general introduction to the area. This is deliberate as we could fill four chapters with introductory information whereas this work demonstrates the key principles in action for international events.

This overview of financial management sought to introduce the reader to these event-finance management issues by examining organizational context, the importance of the accurate determination of event pricing and budgets, and the relationship between aspects of financial planning and reporting for assessing the financial health of the event company. This chapter was structured into three main parts. The first part examined pricing and the strategies used for determining price. A key factor in price determination is having a clear understanding of event companies' objectives and purpose.

The importance of budgeting for service operations such as events was then discussed. The preparation of a master budget is important for controlling the flow of funds throughout the organization. The final section introduced the reader to the importance of financial reporting by examining the balance sheet, P&L statement and cash flow statement (including reconciliation of cash). The financial reports of New Mardi Gras Ltd were used to examine the relationships between the economic entity of the business and its ongoing sustainability.

Glossary

Asset: A resource controlled by the entity as a result of past events and from which future economic benefits are expected to flow to the entity. [F 4.4(a)] ★

Balance sheet: A statement that represents the financial position of the company at the end of the accounting period.

Break-even point: The sales volume figure where total revenues and total costs intersect.

Cash flow statement: A statement that highlights how changes in the balance sheet and profit and loss statement impact on the cash and cash equivalents of the company.

Current assets: Cash; cash equivalent; assets held for collection, sale or consumption within the entity's normal operating cycle; or assets held for trading within the next 12 months. All other assets are noncurrent. [IAS 1.66] ★

Current liabilities: Those to be settled within the entity's normal operating cycle or due within 12 months, or those held for trading, or those for which the entity does not have an unconditional right to defer payment beyond 12 months. Other liabilities are noncurrent. [IAS 1.69] ★

Equity: The residual interest in the assets of the entity after deducting all its liabilities. [F 4.4(c)] ★

Equity Contributions: Involves the owners of the company contributing additional assets to the firm.

Equity Distributions: Involves the distribution of assets to the owner of the company.

Expenses: Decreases in economic benefits during the accounting period in the form of outflows or depletions of assets or an incurrence of liabilities that result in decreases in equity, other than those relating to distributions to equity participants. [F 4.25(b)] ★

FMCG: Fast Moving Consumer Goods (companies), goods that are sold quickly at low cost where branding plays an important role, for example washing detergent.

Financing Activities: Activities that alter the equity capital and borrowing structure of the entity. [IAS 7.6] ★

Fixed costs: The costs incurred to be in the business, for example plant, machinery. These costs remain constant throughout increasing sales.

For-profit: A business that exists to generate a return on income.

Going concern: The underlying assumption for accounting that the financial statements presume that an entity will continue in operation indefinitely or, if that presumption is not valid, disclosure and a different basis of reporting are required. [F 4.1] ★

IAS 7: The objective of IAS 7 is to require the presentation of information about the historical changes in cash and cash equivalents of an enterprise by means of a cash flow statement which classifies cash flows during the period according to operating, investing and financing activities. ★

Investing activities: The acquisition and investing activities disposal of long-term assets and other investments that are not considered to be cash equivalents. [IAS 7.6] ★

Liability: A present obligation of the entity arising from past events, the settlement of which is expected to result in an outflow from the entity of resources embodying economic benefits. [F 4.4(b)] ★

Liquidity: The ability of the company to settle its short-term obligations from its current assets.

Not-for-profit: A business that uses funds generated to reinvest in its business activities.

Operating activities: The main revenue operating activities of the enterprise that are not investing or financing activities, so operating cash flows include cash received from customers and cash paid to suppliers and employees. [IAS 7.14] ★

Organizational context: The legal form an organization may adopt (sole-trader, partnership, company limited by guarantee, limited company). These legal forms have implications for the complexity and formality of financial reporting (Smith, 2007).

Profitability: The ability of the company to generate a profit from its business activities.

Profit and loss (income) statement: A document that represents the revenues (income) and expenses for a financial period resulting in a statement of business profitability.

Reconciliation of cash: A statement to provide greater accuracy for determining working capital within the organization and to ensure that cash and cash equivalents generated from operating activities are clearly identified.

Revenue (income): Increases in economic benefits during the accounting period in the form of inflows or enhancements of assets or decreases of liabilities that result in increases in equity, other than those relating to contributions from equity participants. [F 4.25(a)] ★

Roll-up reporting: A method of departmental budget reporting where budgeted costs are measured against actual costs from the lowest entity through to the highest.

Solvency: The ability of the company to settle all of its obligations from its assets.

Stakeholders: Parties internal and external to the organization that have a stake, or interest in the operations and future directions of a company.

Total cost: A line on a break-even graph representing the cumulative costs incurred by all variable, semi-fixed and fixed costs.

Total revenue (turnover): The total value of sales and revenues generated by a company.

Variable costs: The costs incurred by generating business, for example labour. These costs increase in a relationship with total sales.

(★ *Source:* Deloitte, 2010)

Review Questions

1 In determining the break-even point for your event, what is the relationship between variable and fixed costs?
2 How should an event manager respond if a business with a history of profitability reports a loss on the P&L statement?
3 What pricing strategy would you use if you were managing a multi-activity event with a high level of fixed costs? Why would you choose this?
4 What internal considerations would you consider when establishing a sales forecast for an international modern arts festival?

Additional Resources

Books and book chapters

Atrill, P. and McLaney, E. (2008) *Accounting and Finance for Non-Specialists* (6th edn). Essex: Pearson Education Limited.
An introductory text for students learning about the subjects of accounting and finance.

Ciconte, B.L. and Jacob, J.G. (2009) *Fundraising Basics: A Complete Guide.* Sudbury: Jones and Bartlett Publishers.
A useful guide to raising funds, especially for non-profit event managers.

Kitchin, P.J. (2007) 'Financing the games', in J. Gold and M. Gold (eds), *Olympic Cities: Urban Planning, City Agendas and the World's Games, 1896 to the Present.* London: Routledge. pp. 103–119.
A general introduction to the major income and expenditure items of the Summer and Winter Olympic Games.

Stewart, B. (2007) *Sport Funding and Finance.* Oxford: Elsevier.
A good introduction to financing issues in sport.

Supovitz, F. and Goldblatt, J.J. (1999) *Dollars and Events: How to Succeed in the Events Business.* New York: John Wiley & Sons Inc.
An overview of the issues involved in running an events business.

Useful websites

http://www.duncanwil.co.uk/
An excellent resource that delivers accounting information to the masses.

http://www.eventscotland.org/funding-and-resources/event-management-a-practical-guide/
A practical guide to budgeting and financial planning for events.

http://www.iasplus.com/standard/framewk.htm
An official overview of the International Accounting Framework.

References

Altman, D. (1997) 'Global gaze, global gays', *GLQ: A Journal of Lesbian and Gay Studies*, 3(4): 417–436.

Andersson, T.D. and Getz, D. (2008) 'Stakeholder management strategies of festivals', *Journal of Convention and Event Tourism*, 9(3): 199–220.

Deloitte (2010) *Summaries of Interpretations.* Deloitte [Online]. Available from http://www.iasplus.com/standard/framewk.htm.

Getz, D. (1997) *Event Management and Event Tourism.* Putnam Valley, NY: Cognizant Communication Corporation.

Getz, D. (2007) *Event Studies Theory, Research and Policy for Planned Events.* Oxford: Elsevier.

Goodwin, E. (2006) 'Queer as folk', *Marketing Magazine Australia*, April: 16–19.

Henderson, J.C., Foo, K., Lim, H. and Yip, S. (2010) 'Sports events and tourism: The Singapore Formula One Grand Prix', *International Journal of Event and Festival Management,* 1(1): 60–73.

Kitchin, P.J. (2007) 'Financing the games', in J. Gold and M. Gold (eds), *Olympic Cities: Urban Planning, City Agendas and the World's Games, 1896 to the Present.* London: Routledge. pp. 103–119.

Lee, T. and Wines, G. (2000) 'Cash flow reporting and analysis', in G. Carnegie, F. Clark, G. Dean, M. Evans, C. Ikin, C. Ng and G. Wines, *Financial Reporting and Analysis.* Geelong: Deakin University. pp 3.1–3.31.

Markwell, K. and Waitt, G. (2009) 'Festivals, space and sexuality: Gay pride in Australia', *Tourism Geographies*, 11(2): 143–168.

Schneider, A. and Sollenberger, H.M. (2005) *Managerial Accounting: Manufacturing and Service Applications* (4th edn). Cincinnati, OH: Custom Publishing Company.

Smith, D. (2004) 'Bill for Athens to top $11b', *Sport Business International*, 15 November.

Smith, J.A. (2007) *Handbook of Management Accounting.* Burlington: CIMA Publishing.

Smith, W.W., Litvin, S.W. and Canberg, A. (2010) 'Setting parameters: Operational budget size and allocation of resources', *International Journal of Event and Festival Management,* 1(3): 238–243.

Stewart, B. (2007) *Sport Funding and Finance.* Oxford: Elsevier.

Verma, H. A. (2008) *Services Marketing: Text and Cases.* Noida, India: Dorling Kindersley/Pearson Education.

8

Risk Management

Brent W. Ritchie and Sacha Reid

Learning Objectives

By reading this chapter students should be able to:

- Understand the importance of undertaking a systematic approach to risk management.
- Understand the influence of event context in identifying and treating relevant risks.
- Develop relevant strategies and tools to identify, analyse and treat event-related risks.
- Understand the importance of risk communication and monitoring for both internal and external stakeholders.

Introduction

Events have the potential to generate internal and external risks and crises, due to their size, scope, use of equipment and attraction of large numbers of people to a particular site(s) during a defined period. Potential risks can cover all areas of operation, including health and safety of guests and workers, crowding, environmental risks, and compliance with local laws and regulations. Further, risks can be internal and external to the organization and could be created by audience members, suppliers or even event organizers themselves through inaction. Getz (2002) reveals that festival crises and failures are common. Getz (2002) identified the primary reason for event failure as the lack of advanced or strategic planning. This could be attributed to the limited capacity and knowledge of event organizers to plan for and deal with risks in a systematic way. Allen et al. (2008) also note that most event incidents occur as a result of management incompetency, thus making it necessary for all event managers to be familiar with the concept of risk and risk management.

Risk management assists event organizers in devising and conducting events in the safest possible manner, whilst mitigating losses (Berlonghi, 1994). Therefore, it is essential that event organizations formally plan for and develop strategies to deal with the possible consequences of unplanned events. This chapter provides an overview of risk management for event managers and identifies a range of tools to assist managers in planning and managing risk in the context of hosting an event. The chapter begins by defining risk and risk management from an events perspective, before providing a systematic framework for understanding and managing event risks. The remainder of the chapter addresses the components of the framework, providing examples throughout the text. Finally, a case study is provided at the end of the chapter integrating the chapter content.

Understanding Event Risks

Risk is generally defined as any threat that will negatively impact an organization's ability to achieve its objectives and execute its strategies successfully. The Australian and New Zealand Standard (AS/NZS ISO 31000: 2009) defines risk as the 'effect of uncertainty on objectives'. Glaesser (2006: 38) defines risk as 'the product of magnitude of damage and the probability of occurrence', while Berlonghi (1994: 19) views risk as 'an actual possibility of loss or exposure to loss'. As can be deduced from these definitions, risk involves some form of uncertainty and the potential for this uncertainty to create damage or loss to an organization. Such damage may include physical damage such as injuries, deaths, property damage, negative public image, lawsuits or financial losses.

Risk, in the event context, is defined as 'the likelihood and consequence of the special event or festival not fulfilling its objectives' (Allen et al., 2008: 588). This could be due to anything that might affect the outcome of an event or event activities, or anything that might expose an event or an event organization to loss. Risk can arise from the dangers which may be linked to environmental characteristics at the site where the activity is conducted or to the type and manner in which any equipment is used.

According to Leopkey and Parent (2009a), risk affects not only the organizing committee of an event, but all event stakeholders (including participants, spectators, sponsors, etc). Risks can be divided into those caused by internal forces and those caused by external influences. Therefore, event managers must understand and manage risks that are not just related to the host organization, but potential external risks from the broader political, economic, environmental, social and technological environment in which the event operates.

Getz (2007: 291) defines risk management as 'the process of anticipating, preventing or minimizing potential costs, losses or problems for the event, organization, partners and guests'. Leopkey and Parent (2009b: 164) consider risk management as 'a process that involves assessing all possible risks to the event and its stakeholders and then strategically avoiding, preventing, reducing, diffusing, reallocating, legalizing or using relationship management to mitigate the identified risks'. Effective risk management helps to ensure that the event is conducted in the safest possible manner and that any losses will be mitigated and assets protected (Berlonghi, 1995).

Risk management should be recognized as an integral part of good management practice, consisting of well-defined steps which support better decision-making and contribute greater insights into risks and their impacts. The prime objective of risk management is to minimize the potential for physical, social, emotional or financial loss arising from participation in an activity in an unfamiliar environment with unknown outcomes (Ewart and Boone, 1987). Wideman (1992) considers risk management as a process that lasts throughout the life cycle of the event and should begin during the event preparation stage to allow for alternative action plans and strategies to be developed. The process requires 'thorough and thoughtful procedures that proactively examines and analyses each possibility, then takes the necessary steps and allocates the proper resources to control the risks' (Silvers, 2008: 24). In this way potential risks may be able to be turned into opportunities, perhaps through improving practices and possibly even reducing insurance costs.

Risk Management: A Systematic Framework

Effective risk management requires a systematic approach to control the range and impact of potential losses. Figure 8.1 presents the international standard for risk management (AS/NZS ISO 31000, 2009) which provides a systematic process for managing risks through establishing the context, identifying, analysing, evaluating, treating, monitoring and communicating risks associated with any activity or function.

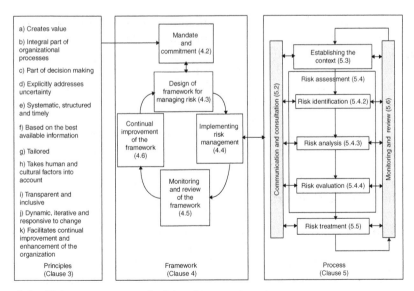

Figure 8.1   *Risk management principles, framework and process*

Source: AS/NZS ISO 31000, 2009. This is a copy of the relevant standard. Permission to reproduce this illustration has been approved by SAI Global Ltd. The complete standard can be purchased from http://www.saiglobal.com

Importantly, it also highlights five parts of a *framework* that assist the risk management process and should occur before risk management begins. The international standard also highlights seven *principles* that should underpin the initial framework and risk management process. Standards help provide a consistent approach to understanding and managing risk across industry sectors and organizations, including the events sector, as they provide principles and generic guidelines on risk management. The remainder of this chapter will discuss the application of the risk management *process* in an events management context providing examples, starting with communication and consultation (see step 5.2 in Figure 8.1).

Communication and Consultation

Communication and consultation with stakeholders is vital to help with the identification, assessment and treatment of event risks and is an ongoing function of effective event risk management. Internal stakeholders such as paid staff and volunteers have a wealth of experience which can help identify relevant risks and effective risk management actions. External stakeholders can include government authorities such as police, health and meteorological agencies as well as suppliers, sponsors, participants and spectators. These external stakeholders may provide important information which can help assess the likelihood and severity of a risk occurring and its implications. Information may come from secondary data such as that provided by weather or health agencies or from primary research with sponsors and spectators undertaken on behalf of event organizers.

Effective internal and external communication is important to ensure that stakeholders understand the issues relating to the risk and the process to manage it. As noted by Goldblatt (1997), effective communication will ensure that all stakeholders are aware that event risk management is everyone's responsibility. It is only when all the stakeholders become proactively and cooperatively involved in developing a coordinated event that the frequency of risk occurrence can be reduced. Communicating and consulting with internal stakeholders (such as volunteers and staff) are not only vital in implementing risk treatment strategies, but also in the monitoring and feedback stage to help improve future event risk management plans.

Establishing the Context

The risk management process often begins with understanding the environment or context in which the event or event host organization operates. The context includes the financial, operational, competitive, political, social, client, cultural and legal aspects of the organization's functions (described as the International Events Environment by Ferdinand and Wesner, this volume) as well as the goals and objectives of the organization hosting the event. From an event management perspective, it includes understanding the type of event, the management structure and resources, organizational culture, stakeholder analysis and a SWOT analysis of the organization in the context of its internal and external operating environment (Allen et al., 2008). The event context is dynamic with changes to the political, economic, environmental, social and technological environment.

Event managers need to understand these changes and their likely impact on their event. For instance, recent terrorist attacks and threats on sporting teams in Pakistan and India have heightened concerns surrounding potential risks to travelling sporting teams and the need for risk management procedures to be tightened. Further, the 2008 financial crisis has had an impact on the number of business events and exhibitions being held (Allen et al., 2011).

Understanding the type and nature of an event will give an indication of possible risks that the event will be exposed to; while the event purpose, goals and objectives will indicate what risks can be tolerated by the organization. For instance, if the host organization is a private enterprise where individuals live off anticipated profits, then financial risks may be more important than perhaps a community-based event whose purpose is to provide entertainment for the local community.

Risk Assessment

A comprehensive identification of risks using a well-structured systematic process is critical. Berlonghi (1994) purports that identification of risk factors should take place before an event. A number of tools outlined below can help managers to think through the possible causes of the risks, the parties who would be affected and the possible consequences (Berlonghi, 1994). The approaches used to identify risks include using a work breakdown structure, fault diagram, brainstorming, incident report, scenario analysis or environmental scanning (Allen et al., 2008).

Project management techniques, such as the work breakdown structure (described in detail in Williams, this volume) and fault diagrams, are useful for identifying risks based on operations and help identify possible risk problems and issues. Risk events or actions can be worked backwards to determine the possible causes of the potential risk effects (Allen et al., 2011). Poor ticket sales may be a potential risk for an outdoor festival that does not have many sponsors and is therefore heavily reliant on ticket sales for revenue. Poor weather may reduce ticket sales during the event, so the event managers may decide to sell tickets in advance to reduce possible consequences of poor weather on ticket sales, revenue and ultimately profit.

The convening of a risk assessment meeting to pool together the experience or expertise of event staff and volunteers can be useful to identify risks. Brainstorming and testing a range of scenarios of potential risks and their likely impacts can also be useful (Allen et al., 2008). This allows event managers and stakeholders to consider possible risks, possible actions and their consequences in advance. Managerial experience and the event context are crucial in identifying and assessing relevant risks. Previous experience needs to be captured and used to develop even better risk management plans, and highlights the importance of risk monitoring and review both during and after an event. Test events are also useful to determine possible risks, and are often used for large international events such as the Olympic Games.

This chapter highlights a range of risks for various event types and locations to provide the reader with an overview of the main event risk categories.

Health and safety risks

The event organizer is responsible for providing a safe and healthy environment for those attending or involved in running the event. As noted by Sönmez and Graefe (1998) and Hall et al. (2003), the heightened awareness of terrorism following the September 11 2001 terrorist attacks has caused many travellers to make their destination choices using security as a criterion. This is confirmed by a study conducted by Kim and Chalip (2004) on the 2002 FIFA World Cup, where it was found that attendance at the World Cup was affected by respondents' concerns over safety risks. Sporting events are often potential targets of terrorist threats due to their scale and the amount of media attention (Cieslak, 2009; Taylor and Toohey, 2006) they receive. The results also demonstrate the importance of sustaining the event with effective safety and security practices.

Box 8.1   SARS and Business Events

Conferences and trade shows postponed due to the SARS outbreak include the 2003 International Machine Components Exhibition in Shanghai which was supposed to attract almost 400 manufacturers and around 65,000 visitors (Metal-Powder.net, 2003), as well as the 6th Asia Pacific Hotel Investment Conference in Singapore which was to have been held in April and then was postponed until June 2003. The Asia-Pacific Economic Cooperation (APEC) Tourism Forum that was to be held in Pattaya, Thailand on 8–10 April was cancelled completely (Deloitte and Touche, 2003). A number of companies, including the Bangkok-based Wright Company, replaced travel by using video-conferencing facilities, in order to overcome the risk of SARS, thus contributing to the decrease in business travel (Newman, 2003).

Health hazards are also a primary concern for event organizers (see, for example, Box 8.1). Communicable diseases can be easily spread in places with large crowds. In the city of Mecca, for example, the population surges during the Hajj season. Annually, millions of pilgrims congregate within a confined space at this high profile religious event. This has resulted in outbreaks of a series of infectious diseases, such as meningococcal disease, the influenza virus and tuberculosis (Memish and Ahmed, 2002). Many pilgrims have to struggle against these public health hazards throughout the pilgrimage. The outbreak also has the potential to quickly turn into a global pandemic as overseas pilgrims carry the diseases or viruses back to their home countries. In addition to the above viruses, male pilgrims are also at risk of being infected with blood-borne infections such as hepatitis B and hepatitis C, through sharing or using communal razors during the head-shaving procedure after the pilgrimage.

Both security and health risks can be magnified as the size of the crowd increases. It is therefore important for safety and health management procedures to be established to protect the participants and attendants from health and safety threats (Getz, 2007). In addition to the concerns over the health and safety of the event audience, event managers also have the legal responsibility to provide a safe working environment for their workers, ensuring that they are protected from injury, damage or disease (Silvers, 2008). Hence, workplace health and safety measures must also be set in place to protect employees and volunteers. These measures may differ depending on the country where the event takes place and their respective regulations.

Crowding

Crowding can be defined as a negative assessment of a certain density level in a given area, and may negatively influence the quality of festival participants' experience and their activities (Lee and Graefe, 2003). Overcrowding has also become an inevitable problem at major events. For example, on New Year's Eve in Innsbruck, Austria, between 35,000 and 40,000 visitors gather at 'Bergsilvester' to observe the fireworks spectacle every year (Peters and Pikkemaat, 2005). The huge crowd poses major transportation and security problems for the event organizer.

Stampede as a result of overcrowding has also occurred at other events such as rock concerts and religious events such as the Hajj. Overcrowding is expected in an event of such a huge scale, as the population of Mecca swells to well over two million during the Hajj season (Gatrad and Sheikh, 2005). As shown in Table 8.1, the most severe stampede at the event took place in 2006 and resulted in 380 deaths and 289 wounded (Ahmed et al., 2006).

Table 8.1   *Tragedies at the Hajj*

Year	Number of pilgrims
1990	1426 killed by stampede/asphyxiation
1994	270 died in a stampede
1997	343 pilgrims died and 1500 injured in a fire
1998	119 pilgrims died in a stampede
2001	35 pilgrims died in a stampede
2003	14 pilgrims died in a stampede
2004	251 pilgrims died in a stampede
2006	Stampede wounded 289 and killed 380

Source: Ahmed et al., 2006

Environmental risks

Weather has become a universal issue for event organizers. This is because weather and climate can strongly influence the quality of visitor experiences and the success of outdoor events (Jones et al., 2006). Jones et al. (2006: 64) further state that climate marks out the timing and duration of outdoor events as it is the 'principal determinant of the natural resources that define the event's theme and attractions'. For example, climate influences the timing of tulip development, thus affecting the dates of Tulip Festivals (Jones et al., 2006). Natural disasters such as earthquakes and poor weather conditions can also create a crisis situation for any event as they may lead to cancellations, financial losses or legal liability claims against the host organizer.

In a survey to examine the reasons leading to the failure of special events, Getz (2002) found that weather is the foremost factor that could lead to an event's failure as it can drastically affect turnout and sales. This is further confirmed by Jones et al. (2006) who examined the impact of weather on climate-sensitive special events in Ontario, Canada. Their research demonstrated that the overall success of the events and quality of visitor experience are largely affected by weather and climate. Similarly, Scott et al. (2004) projected that winter tourism will be highly vulnerable to future changes in climate. Due to global warming, the average winter season is now shortened and natural snow is becoming an increasingly scarce resource. This phenomenon will seriously impact the winter recreation sector – which includes activities such as skiing, the use of snowmobiles and other related snow events.

The Hajj provides an excellent example of heat-related risks experienced at an event. The journey to Mecca for Hajj during the summer season is no ordinary undertaking as the temperature can rise to as high as 50 degrees Celsius. According to Gatrad and Sheikh (2005), heat exhaustion and heatstroke during the Hajj are common and can be fatal. The excessive heat in the summer can also cause pilgrims to suffer from deep burns and skin infection to the soles of the feet sustained from standing and walking barefooted along the religious route.

Alcohol and drug risks

Events featuring alcohol consumption, dependent on the type of event and their audience, may face various problems such as unruly crowd behaviour. Getz (2005: 287) lists the following risks associated with alcohol sales at events:

- Personal injuries and criminal acts due to drunkenness
- Additional insurance costs against the possibility of law suits
- Additional security and clean-up costs
- Major financial losses arising from law suits
- Vandalism
- Image problems and resultant lost patronage
- Attracting the wrong target segments

It is therefore important that event organizers carefully consider the distribution, sale and consumption of alcohol at an event (Abbott and Geddie, 2001) and put security measures in place to prevent drug consumption. Getz (2005) suggests that events with the intention to serve alcohol should have an alcohol risk management system in place, including practising responsible service of alcohol. Local law enforcement and city/council organizations should be involved in this planning process, to mitigate unwanted risks to staff, volunteers, attendees, participants and the local community.

Legal risks

As mentioned by Silvers (2008), operating an event legally and responsibly is the cornerstone of effective risk management. Hazards faced by persons attending an event can translate into legal risks for event organizers; especially if it is proven that the organizers have been negligent in identifying and preventing those hazards (Getz, 2005). Thus, it is essential that event organizers ensure compliance with the law and exercise duty of care to safeguard all those involved in the event. This in turn will reduce their risks and potential consequences such as their legal liability.

In practice this means complying with local regulations and ensuring appropriate licences and permits have been secured by event organizations for activities within an event. Furthermore, regulations, such as those concerned with noise, may differ between jurisdictions. Allen et al. (2011) provide a list of 12 regulations to be aware of, including:

- Liquor licensing laws
- Health regulations
- Building regulations
- Fire regulations
- Licenses governing security personnel
- Police acts
- Local government acts
- Banking acts
- General contract law
- Environmental Protection Authority for noise levels

Other event risks

The types of event risk factors discussed above are certainly non-exhaustive. Silvers (2008) listed several other risks associated with events, including internal risks such as the lack of event planning, finances and organizational structure as well as external risk factors. Different events are exposed to different risk factors and the severity of risks will vary in different contexts. Therefore, it is vital for event organizers to develop a culture of risk awareness and preparedness, so that they are in a better position to anticipate and manage risks, thereby rebounding quickly from any incidents or likely crisis situations.

Risk Analysis and Evaluation

The identification of threats and potential hazards should be followed by an assessment of the probability of occurrence and the severity of the consequences on the event goals and strategies. Management will need to rely on foresight and control to reduce either or both of the variables to an acceptable level in order to manage the risk. Priorities and actions will be determined following the risk assessment, with special attention awarded to those with negative and severe consequences.

Allen et al. (2008: 597) recommends that a risk's likelihood of occurrence be rated on a five-point scale from 'rare' to 'almost certain'. The consequence or severity of

Table 8.2 *Risk consequences and likelihood rating scales and descriptors*

Consequences

Level	Descriptor	Financial	Safety	Business Activities	Social Impacts	Reputation/ Public Image
1	Insignificant	Less than $10,000	No injuries	No disruption to event activities	No social impacts	No significant adverse impact on the organizational reputation
2	Minor	$10,001– $100,000	First aid treatment	Minimal disruption to event activities	Minimal social impacts	Adverse impacts on the organizational reputation
3	Moderate	$100,001– $1M	Medical treatment	Significant disruption to event activities	Significant social impacts	Direct adverse impact on the organizational reputation
4	Major	$1M–$10M	Extensive injuries	Major disruption to event activities	Major social impacts	Direct adverse impact on the CEO/ Accountable Officer
5	Catastrophic	Greater than $10M	Death	Severe disruption to event activities	Severe ongoing impacts	Extensive damage to organizational reputation

Likelihood

Level	Descriptor	Description
1	Rare	May occur in exceptional circumstances
2	Unlikely	Could occur at some time
3	Possible	Might occur at some time
4	Likely	Will probably occur in most circumstances

risks, on the other hand, will be given a rating of insignificant, minor, moderate, major or catastrophic. It is helpful that descriptors are provided and consideration is given to tolerance levels and potential impacts were the risk allowed to be untreated. Table 8.2 provides an example of an event manager's descriptors based on the management of a major cycling event in Australia.

Following the risk analysis, the next step is to evaluate the risks by determining which ones are acceptable and what needs to be treated. These assessments are then combined to evaluate the likely impact and possible risk treatment options (see Figure 8.2). For instance, a risk that was identified to have a likelihood of 5 (almost certain) and a consequence of 5 (catastrophic) would be rated 25 in the matrix and rated as a very high risk. The event host organizations should consider avoiding the risk completely, by cancelling/postponing the event or changing the part of the event that creates such a high level of risk. Consequently, an event risk that has a likelihood of 1 (rare) and an impact of 1 (insignificant) would be rated as having a very low level of risk. Event managers may decide to retain the risk and develop contingency plans to deal with it if it does indeed eventuate.

Risk is a subjective concept, and so rating scales are used by managers to try and create a more objective assessment of risk likelihood and consequence. Key questions to help determine the likelihood and consequences are:

- What happens if the risk is not treated?
- Who will it affect?
- Whose responsibility is it to deal with the risk?
- What information do we need to treat it?
- What risks will important event stakeholders accept?

Likelihood	Consequences				
	1	2	3	4	5
5	Medium-11	High-16	High-20	Very High-23	Very High-25
4	Medium-7	Medium-12	High-17	High-21	Very High-24
3	Low-4	Medium-8	High-14	High-18	High-22
2	Low-2	Low-5	Medium-9	Medium-13	High-19
1	Low-1	Low-3	Medium-6	Medium-10	High-15

Figure 8.2 *Risk assessment matrix*

Source: Assessment matrix taken from HB 436: 2004 Risk Management Guidelines Companion to AS/NZS 4360

ςs can be applied on certain risks if they are less tolerated by event organ-
increasing their consequences and overall rating respectively.

atment

Risk treatment strategies are considered important to reduce the vulnerability of
the event and control any problem that might arise. Risk treatment measures may
actually stop a risk incident from occurring (prevention), or they may reduce the
severity of the impact of a risk incident on the event (reduction). Other risk treatment options might include risk avoidance or transfer, through the use of third
parties such as suppliers or insurance companies. This step in the risk management
process involves identifying the range of risk treatment options, assessing the
options, preparing risk treatment plans and implementing them by allocating and
controlling event resources (financial or human).

Leopkey and Parent (2009a) believe that the use of proper strategies can directly
influence the organization's overall performance and the success of the event.
Strategies used for controlling risks may require additional documents, such as an
emergency evacuation plan, crowd management plan or crisis communication plan.
Studies on diffusion, reallocation and avoidance of risks do not seem to be as
prevalent compared to material related to prevention, reduction and legal risks. These
risk treatment strategies will therefore be the focus of this section of the chapter.

Prevention and avoidance

Prevention and mitigation are the first line of defence for event organizers. Planning
is the phase where the specifications for the event are determined, describing the
activities that will occur and how the resources will be organized (Silvers, 2008). It
is also at the planning stage where potential risks are identified so that preventative
measures can be devised and their effects considered.

Prior to conceptualizing event goals and strategies, a chain of command should be
established to facilitate the orderly operation of the event (Abbott and Geddie, 2001).
To improve event operations, the event manager should assemble a team that can
assist in identifying the risks and develop the risk management and evacuation plans
(Goldblatt, 1997). Operational plans should be developed that clearly specify the
responsibilities of the team members and that ensure potential risks and hazards are
communicated to all staff and volunteers. This is particularly important if regulations
and laws need to be followed.

Planning is a critical component in preparing for the annual Hajj event. The
authorities in Saudi Arabia have developed a comprehensive plan to ensure that
all aspects of the religious rituals are conducted safely (Shafi et al., 2008). Ahmed
and Memish (2008) state that preparations for the public health, safety and security of the event are extraordinarily challenging due to the scale of the event, the
fact that pilgrims travel from all over the world and that it occurs annually. Thus,
the planning of the event requires close and effective inter-Ministry collaboration.

Damage reduction

According to Getz (2005), if an event issue is perceived to be too risky or severe, it should be avoided or tried to be prevented. However, not all risks can be easily avoided and hence damage reduction strategies will help to reduce the severity of any potential losses. Leopkey and Parent (2009a) noted that reduction strategies are the most prevalent amongst event managers simply because many risks have to be retained and potential damage reduced. Therefore this risk treatment option involves actions taken to lessen or diminish the potential impact of risks on an event. Risk reduction can be accomplished through better management, training and emergency response procedures to improve response times to incidents, accidents and crises. Resolving a crisis situation also requires the team to carefully analyse the situation, examine the possibilities, selecting the least damaging option, and properly document every incident (Watt, 1998). Choosing the most appropriate option would also involve a cost–benefit analysis, whereby the cost of implementing each option is measured against the benefits obtained. The event context and tolerance levels are important considerations in conducting a cost–benefit analysis.

Risk transfer

Risk transfer (or diffusion) is a process to spread out potential risks. This could include storing equipment at different locations (Berlonghi, 1994) or selecting alternative training venues so as to diffuse the use or prevent destruction of the actual competition ground (Leopkey and Parent, 2009a).

Reallocation of risk involves transferring the risk to another company contracted to perform certain tasks and responsibilities. This may involve requesting vendors, suppliers and participants to obtain their own insurance (Getz, 2005). In Australia, for example, most performing groups are required to have public liability insurance before they can take part in an event (Allen et al., 2008). Another example is the hiring of private security companies to remove cash from ticket booths or to undertake security on behalf of the event organizers. The following interview with an event producer for a cultural festival in Australia demonstrates how event risk is transferred.

 Diary of an Event Manager – Anonymous, Event Producer for a Cultural Festival, Australia

An event producer for a cultural festival in Australia explains in an interview how he deals with risk. In 2009, the overall festival consisted of events in five restaurant venues and 20 events in various public spaces. These were managed by

(Continued)

(Continued)

each individual event manager but a marketing umbrella was placed over the top of the individual events to create the overall festival produced and marketed by the cultural festival producer. This meant that risks were transferred to individual event managers and individual venues. As described by the event producer:

> There is a principle in place that says everybody along the way needs to make sure they are covered. Whatever the regulations and rules are, for any venue that we might be in, or any event that we might be in, that partici-pants respect all their drills, electricians to certify their cabling. All this stuff they need to do it, before we participate. We will literally walk out of an event if they didn't, because it is just not worth it.

Further, the overall event producer has contracts with the different organizations or individuals to reduce the risk. It is therefore important that collaborators are chosen with a good reputation. This enables the event producer to minimize the risk. As the producer said:

> It's about minimizing the risks for us. They (the individual event organizer) deal with it – everything that they need. If it's the City Council, they got a pretty good chance that it's going to be great. They cover all the public lia-bilities, health and safety of the people that are involved.

Although transferring the risk to other parties may reduce the liability of the event organizer, should the other parties fail to manage the risks effectively, the event organizer may still need to find solutions to treat it.

Monitoring and Review

In light of changing circumstances, risks and the effectiveness of control, measures should be constantly monitored. Reviewing strategies is also an integral part of the risk management process to assess the effectiveness and feasibility of the risk manage-ment treatment plan. For effective evaluation and feedback, long-term learning from current experience needs to be captured and understood in order to ensure that (a) the same mistakes/problems do not re-occur and that (b) new strategies are increas-ingly better informed.

Preskill and Torres (1999) argue that evaluative enquiry is needed for organiza-tions to critically reflect on their strategies and their success. This requires that organization members 'critically consider what they think, say and do in the con-text of the work environment' (Preskill and Torres, 1999: 92). They use the term because evaluation is used to seek answers and information about an object or outcome, which should include not only the action or object itself, but also the values, standards and assumptions that relate to it. By critically evaluating all the aspects of risk strategy formulation, implementation and outcomes, it should be possible to gain important knowledge for the future and change the currently held collective mental models of organizational members.

Mechanisms often used to ensure ongoing review include setting up post-review meetings to de-brief and assist the event manager to evaluate strategies and avoid future repetition of mistakes. Incident reports that document the causes of incidents and actions taken during the event itself should be assessed at the meeting to help identify areas that need improvement or adjustment (Berlonghi, 1994). A range of stakeholders, both internal and external to the event, should be consulted, and, where appropriate, may include sponsors, participants, media, police and emergency services. Workshops and seminars with event managers can also be useful at communicating potential risks through previous experiences. Event associations may be best placed to organize and communicate such seminars or workshops to event organizers.

Case Study 8.1   Event Managers' Risk Planning Attitudes, Beliefs and Perceived Constraints

There has been a lack of research analysing event risk management planning attitudes, beliefs and factors inhibiting or facilitating adoption levels. The majority of research in the area has focused on mega-events, such as the Olympic Games, a significant yet small subsector of the events industry. Organizational behaviour can be explored at a systems, group or individual level. Although organizations ultimately implement risk planning activities, it is the role of individuals and their psychological factors which may influence the adoption of risk planning activities. A complex range of factors may influence risk planning including experience, values and beliefs, messages, personal attributes and socio-cultural norms.

A research project was undertaken in Australia to identify event managers' attitude and beliefs concerning risk management as well as to explore social influences and perceived constraints to implementing risk management planning. The research adopted a qualitative methodology to address the research aim and used Ajzen's (1991, 2005) Theory of Planned Behaviour (TPB) as a framework for exploring event managers' risk, attitudes, beliefs and perceived constraints. To obtain a comprehensive sample, a matrix of events in the region, that were diverse across the area, by theme, size, organization structure and length of operation, was developed and events chosen. The sample was further refined to ensure representation based on the following criteria: size of event (large, medium and small), theme of event (music, sport, cultural, community) and organizational structure (professional, voluntary organizing committee). Semi-structured interviews with 11 event managers were undertaken, drawn from South East Queensland, Australia.

(Continued)

(Continued)

Respondents' understanding of risk and risk management varied from limited and generalized to a comprehensive in-depth knowledge. Respondents articulated that risk management entailed '... identifying before the event and trying to put measures in place to make sure that you minimize any potential risk or fall out' [I4]. Safety and physical risks were discussed by most respondents as the key risk factors to consider, however a respondent went on to note: '... also the financial risk and a multitude of other risk factors need to be taken into risk management' [I10]. There appeared to be a direct connection between the level of professionalism of the event organizational structure (i.e. voluntary or professional) and a respondent's depth of understanding. Nearly all respondents had positive attitudes towards risk management planning. One respondent enthused: 'I'm one of these ones that's all for it; let's bring it on; let's be doing it ...' [I10].

Respondents were influenced by beliefs related to safety, compliance, decision-making and professionalism. The most common risk identified by respondents related to safety of employees, volunteers, participants and attendees, particularly as a consequence of activities and planned programming. Compliance considerations, such as legislation and insurance requirements, were also found to influence event managers' attitudes and behaviours.

Internally, respondents identified organizational management, such as directors, section heads or event organizing committees, as well as staff and volunteers as key influencers in undertaking risk planning. One respondent commented: 'The senior management team's actually very supportive of the risk management, they're actually the ones that are pushing it ... he sees it as a priority for the business as a whole. So the senior management team takes it very seriously and they very much are seen as a priority' [I5]. Externally, event managers were also influenced by the attitudes and beliefs of clients, sponsors, venues, participants and attendees. Significant compliance facilitators such as government organizations, police, security officials and event insurers were also important in influencing the risk management practices of respondents.

However, seven perceived constraints were also identified as important in influencing risk planning in an event context: time, financial costs, human resourcing, knowledge/self-efficacy, adapting to change, restrictions and regulation. As one respondent commented on the time constraint: '... see, I still run a business so I can't give it 100 per cent' [I2]. Consequently, a number of respondents identified hiring external consultants to assist in this process. Time and consultant costs result in financial costs being incurred by event organizations. However, as one respondent stated: 'I've got private health insurance. I find it the same kind of thing. Like, what's more important? The fact that it costs a lot of money but it's your life. My business is my bread and butter. One incident could put me out of business for the rest of my life too and I wouldn't be employable again' [I9].

(Continued)

(Continued)

Interestingly, the research identified that event managers were largely concerned about physical and safety risks, followed by financial, weather and organizational risks. These findings are in contrast to the holistic risk planning approach advocated by the Australian and New Zealand International Standards (AS/NZS ISO 31000, 2009). There was some differentiation between respondents based on past experience: 'I think first of all, we are all very much aware of the concept of a risk management planning. We are conscious of it, we are developing policies and practices ... that will mean it's a lot easier for us and therefore more enjoyable' [I4]. The findings indicate that individuals who are active event professionals within larger organizations appear to be driving risk management planning within the sector.

However, event managers were found to have a wider range of reference groups that they considered influential. The social pressure to perform risk planning practices was exerted internally and externally of the event organization. The findings suggest that event managers may face increased complexity in planning and implementing effective risk management practices in their organizations compared to other sectors. More widely, the industry needs education to enhance the knowledge of practitioners as currently expertise is sought externally for many organizations. The use of external consultants and the time involved in establishing risk management plans, policies and strategies is a limiting factor for widespread implementation of risk management practices beyond simply the need for legal compliance and internal risks.

Professional associations, government organizations and tertiary institutions have a significant role to play in educating and assisting the development of event manager competence to understand and plan for a wide range of risks. The use of knowledge management tools to aid in the development of industry manuals, risk assessments and policy guidelines would assist practitioners limited by knowledge, time and available staff, factors uncovered in this research. Creating opportunities to share experiences and knowledge gained would also be beneficial for event managers. Professional event associations could assist through the provision of online portals or discussion groups.

For more detail on this case study, see Reid and Ritchie (2011).

Case Study Questions

1 Why do you think the risk managers in this study are mostly concerned with physical and safety risks?
2 Why does senior management in an event organization play such an important role in risk management?
3 Suggest ways in which your university can educate current and future event managers about the importance of risk management.
4 How do the events managers' views of risk management in this case study differ from those held by events managers in your own country?

Chapter Summary

As outlined in the introduction of this chapter, the nature of events creates potential for internal and external risks and crises. Potential risks cover all areas in an event's operation including health and safety of guests and workers, crowding, environmental risks and compliance with local laws and regulations. Risk management assists event organizers in devising and conducting events in the safest possible manner, whilst mitigating losses and it is essential that event organizations formally plan for and develop strategies to deal with the possible consequences of unplanned events.

This chapter provided an overview of risk management for event managers and identified a range of tools to assist managers in planning and managing risk in the context of hosting an event. The chapter provided a systematic framework for understanding and managing event risks and used examples throughout the text. It also provided a concluding case study to highlight the importance of identifying, assessing. It also provided treating risks. It is hoped that this chapter has made the reader aware of the importance of risk management and the process that can be followed to systematically manage risks in an events context.

Review Questions

1   Select an outdoor and indoor event. Identify and contrast the likely risks and possible treatment actions for both of these events.
2   Legal liability is becoming a major risk for event managers. What is legal liability and how can event organizations protect themselves from its consequences?
3   What does it mean to transfer risk?
4   How important is communication and consultation in event risk management? Explain and justify your answer with examples.
5   How should event managers ensure that their risk management plans are kept up to date?

Additional Resources

Books, book chapters and journal articles

Allen, J., O'Toole, W., Harris, R. and McDonnell, I. (2011) *Festival and Special Event Management* (5th edn). Brisbane: John Wiley & Sons Australia Ltd.
Chapter 18 provides a good overview of event risk management.

Frosdick, S. and Walley, D. (1999) *Sports and Safety Management*. Oxford: Elsevier Butterworth-Heinemann.
A practical guide for event managers and all those involved in staging sporting events.

Kemp, C. and Hill, I. (2004) *Health and Safety Aspects in the Live Music Industry*. Cambridge: Entertainment Technology Press.
An outline of the health and safety requirements of concerts, festivals and other musical events.

Reid, S. and Ritchie, B.W. (2011) 'Risk management: Event managers' attitudes, beliefs and perceived constraints', *Event Management*, 15(4): 329–341.
A good research article on risk management from an event manager's perspective.

Silvers, J.R. (2008) *Risk Management for Meetings and Events*. Oxford: Elsevier Butterworth-Heinemann.
A comprehensive and detailed analysis of risk management for meetings and events.

Useful websites

http://www.hse.gov.uk/
A useful website which provides general guidance about health and safety at work, as well as free downloadable guides to health and safety at different types of events.

http://www.oshweb.com/
OshWeb provides links to, reviews of and comments on websites in the Occupational Safety and Health sector all around the world.

http://www.safeworkaustralia.gov.au/
A guide to safe working practices in Australia.

References

Abbott, J.L. and Geddie, M.W. (2001) 'Event and venue management: Minimizing liability through effective crowd management techniques', *Event Management*, 6(4): 259–270.

Ahmed, Q.A. and Memish, Z.A. (2008) 'Hajj medicine for the Guests of God: A public health frontier revisited', *Journal of Infection and Public Health*, 1(2): 57–61.

Ahmed, Q.A., Arabi, Y.M. and Memish, Z.A. (2006) Health risks at the Hajj. *The Lancet*, 367 (9515): 1008–1015.

Ajzen, I. (1991) 'The theory of planned behavior', *Organizational Behavior and Human Decision Processes*, 50: 179–211.

Ajzen, I. (2005) *Attitudes, Personality and Behavior*. Maidenhead: Open University Press.

Allen, J., O'Toole, W., Harris, R. and McDonnell, I. (2008) *Festival and Special Event Management* (4th edn). Brisbane: John Wiley & Sons Australia Ltd.

Allen, J., O'Toole, W., Harris, R. and McDonnell, I. (2011) *Festival and Special Event Management* (5th edn). Brisbane: John Wiley & Sons Australia Ltd.

AS/NZS ISO 31000 (2009) *Risk Management: Principles and Guidelines*. Sydney: SAI Global.

Berlonghi, A. (1994) *The Special Event Risk Management Manual*. Dana Point, CA: Alexander Berlonghi.

Berlonghi, A.E. (1995) 'Understanding and planning for different spectator crowds', *Safety Science*, 18(4): 239–247.

Cieslak, T. J. (2009) 'Match day security at Australian sport stadia: A case study of eight venues', *Event Management*, 13(1): 43–52.

Deloitte and Touche (2003) *SARS Impacts Asian Hotel Performance in March*. 17 April, Deloitte and Touche [Online]. Available from: http://www.hotelresource.com/article5874.html.

Ewart, A. and Boone, T. (1987) 'Risk management: Defusing the dragon', *Journal of Experiential Education*, 10(3): 28–34.

Gatrad, A.R. and Sheikh, A. (2005) 'Hajj: Journey of a lifetime', *BMJ*, 330(7483): 133–137.

Getz, D. (2002) 'Why festivals fail', *Event Management*, 7(4): 209–219.

Getz, D. (2005) *Event Management and Event Tourism* (2nd edn). New York: Cognizant Communication Corporation.

Getz, D. (2007) *Event Studies: Theory, Research and Policy for Planned Events*. Burlington: Elsevier Ltd.

Goldblatt, J.J. (1997) *Special Events: Best Practices in Modern Event Management* (2nd edn). Hoboken, NJ: John Wiley & Sons, Inc.

Glaesser, D. (2006) *Crisis Management in the Tourism Industry*. Oxford: Butterworth-Heinemann.

Hall, C.M., Timothy, D.J. and Duval, D.T. (2003) *Safety and Security in Tourism: Relationships, Management and Marketing*. New York: Haworth Press.

HB 436: 2004 (Guidelines to AS/NZS 4360: 2004) Risk Management Guidelines Companion to AS/NZS 4360: 2004 published by SAI Global.

Jones, B., Scott, D. and Khaled, H.A. (2006) 'Implications of climate change for outdoor event planning: A case study of three special events in Canada's National Capital Region', *Event Management*, 10(1): 63–76.

Kim, N.S. and Chalip, L. (2004) 'Why travel to the FIFA World Cup? Effects of motives, background, interest and constraints', *Tourism Management*, 25(6): 695–707.

Lee, H. and Graefe, A.R. (2003) 'Crowding at an arts festival: Extending crowding models to the front country', *Tourism Management*, 24(1): 1–11.

Leopkey, B. and Parent, M.M. (2009a) 'Risk management in large-scale sporting events: A stakeholder perspective', *European Sport Management Quarterly*, 9(2): 187–208.

Leopkey, B. and Parent, M.M. (2009b) 'Risk management strategies by stakeholders in Canadian major sporting events', *Event Management*, 13(3): 153–170.

Memish, Z.A. and Ahmed, Q.A. (2002) 'Mecca bound: The challenges ahead', *Journal of Travel Medicine*, 9(4): 202–210.

Metal-Powder.net (2003) *SARS Routs China Trade Show As Visitors Shun Travel*. Metal-Powder [Online]. Available from: http://www.metal-powder.net/june03news.html.

Newman, S. (2003) 'Executive on a leash', *Far Eastern Economic Review*, 166: 35–36.

Peters, M. and Pikkemaat, B. (2005) 'The management of city events: The case of "Bergsilvester" in Innsbruck, Austria', *Event Management*, 9(3): 147–153.

Preskill, H.A. and Torres, R.T. (1999) 'The role of evaluative enquiry in creating learning organizations', in M. Easterby-Smith, J. Burgoyne and L. Araujo (eds), *Organizational Learning and the Learning Organization*. London: Sage. pp. 92–114.

Reid, S. and Ritchie, B.W. (2011) 'Risk management: Event managers' attitudes, beliefs and perceived constraints', *Event Management*, 15(4): 329–341.

Scott, D., McBoyle, G. and Schwartzentruber, M. (2004) 'Climate change and the distribution of climatic resources for tourism in North America', *Climate Research*, 27(2): 105–117.

Shafi, S., Booy, R., Haworth, E., Rashid, H. and Memish, Z.A. (2008) 'Hajj: Health lessons for mass gatherings', *Journal of Infection and Public Health*, 1(1): 27–32.

Silvers, J.R. (2008) *Risk Management for Meetings and Events*. Oxford: Butterworth-Heinemann.

Sönmez, S.F. and Graefe, A.R. (1998) 'Influence of terrorism risk on foreign tourism decisions', *Annals of Tourism Research*, 25(1): 112–144.

Taylor, T. and Toohey, K. (2006) 'Impacts of terrorism-related safety and security measures at a major sport event', *Event Management*, 9(4): 199–209.

Watt, C.D. (1998) *Event Management in Leisure and Tourism*. Harlow: Addison Wesley Longman.

Wideman, M.R. (1992) *Project and Program Risk Management: A Guide to Managing Project Risks and Opportunities*. Newton Square: Project Management Institute.

9
Event Evaluation

Jo-anne Tull

Learning Objectives

By reading this chapter students should be able to:

- Articulate the nature and importance of evaluation to the events management function.
- Describe what event evaluation should focus on.
- Explain the purpose of event evaluation, including the needs and expectations of stakeholders.
- Describe the cyclical, holistic nature of event evaluation using the three critical Ss of events.
- Assess the different forms of evaluation models and methods.
- Formulate and prepare an event evaluation report.

Introduction

This chapter focuses on the role and function of event evaluation. It offers some insight into the main practices, models and methods that are employed in conducting event evaluation. Event evaluation is now widely accepted as a critical component of the events management function, given the complexities involved in planning and executing events usually in very dynamic contexts. Event managers cannot simply rely on a single metric such as patron head count or net profits as the main indicator of determining whether the event has fulfilled its objectives.

Experiences of events that operate beyond these early traditions of evaluation demonstrate that events management must give strong consideration to determining, understanding and analysing the nature, relevance, performance and impacts of events to gauge a range of key markers of success. In essence, effective use of event evaluation rests on its integration throughout the entire life of the event, from planning through to execution through to event shutdown. The London 2012 Olympic and Paralympic Games website, for example, offers a detailed account of how evaluation with a focus on sustainability has been incorporated from the planning stages of the Games, and includes targets for evaluation and progress reports (LOCOG, n/d).

Event evaluation can, therefore, take a holistic approach that would aid event managers in making prudent decisions at each stage of event development and execution. When executed well, event evaluation offers a solid guide for improvement and allows event managers to give an accurate account of all aspects of the event to its stakeholders.

Conceptualizing Event Evaluation

Evaluation is concerned with assessment, which usually involves measuring a set of key variables, as well as monitoring those variables to determine positive and negative outcomes. It is a subjective determination that can utilize objective quantitative measures (Getz, 1997). It denotes a continuous process of checking and re-checking, measuring and re-measuring, assessing and re-assessing towards achieving results.

With respect to events, evaluation is focused on measuring, assessing and monitoring whether events have been able to achieve their stated intent in a systematic manner. Measuring, assessing and monitoring may be based on numerical data or descriptive data, or a combination of both as is further explained later in this chapter. Event evaluation can be considered a critical component of event planning and the overall project management of any event. It offers a means by which decisions made at each stage of the project management cycle can be checked for efficiency and effectiveness. In this regard, Forrester's definition of event evaluation is instructive. He suggests that event evaluation for sports, recreation and tourism events, is 'the systematic collection and analysis of data in order to make judgments regarding the value or worth of a particular aspect of an event ... which can then be used to make decisions during the renewal phase of the event planning model regardless of the improvement of the event' (2008: 112–113).

At the practical level, event evaluation is often guided by what is perceived as the main purpose of the event. For example, evaluation of corporate events addresses two distinct areas – 'the content' viz. the speakers, activities and entertainment; and 'the destination' viz. venue, facilities and services. By extension, event evaluation for events ought to focus on determining how well the content matched the purpose of the event and whether the destination fitted the content and purpose of the event (O'Toole and Mikolaitis, 2002).

The use of specialized definitions of events can, however, 'pigeon-hole' the event evaluation process and limit the choice and range of variables examined in collecting data on the festival. For example, where a festival is deemed primarily a tourism product, focus rests on evaluating the components that relate to tourist activity,

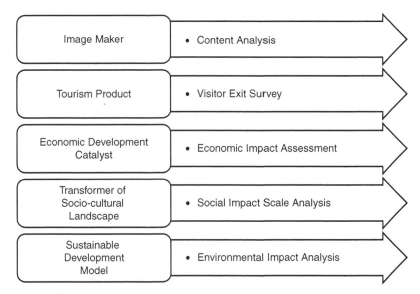

Figure 9.1   *Event types and evaluation tools*

usually through a visitor exit survey. Often times, less effort is allocated to evaluating local patron activity or impact on the community which can also have relevance to evaluation of these event types.

Consequently, as much as possible, the event evaluation exercise should be multi-faceted to satisfy a range of purposes, while minimizing complexity in its implementation. This requires having a clear understanding of the various purposes of the event, apart from its primary mandate. From this, the event manager can identify the broad approach to be taken and the corresponding model and methods to be used for measuring, assessing and monitoring. Complexity can be minimized by utilizing a particular evaluation model and a complementary set of methods that would allow for the collection of a diverse range of data on the event, thereby making the event evaluation process more cost-effective and time-efficient.

Whatever choices are made, the general steps for conducting event evaluation are as depicted in Figure 9.2.

Why Evaluate?

Event evaluation can satisfy a range of purposes as depicted in Figure 9.3. Fundamentally, event evaluation is a useful means of determining success or failure. It is a contributor to the lessons learned component of project management as it captures information that can articulate how more informed decisions can be made towards greater efficiency and more positive results. Between these two ends are a

Step 1
• Determine the purpose of the event evaluation exercise, including whether the evaluation is necessary.

Step 2
• Identify what should be the focus of evaluation.

Step 3
• Select the most suitable approach for conducting the evaluation exercise.

Step 4
• Select model(s) for evaluation as a framework for data collection based on suitability, praticality and relevance.

Step 5
• Develop appropriate instruments and data collection strategies based on the methods selected.

Step 6
• Collect and analyse data and findings.

Step 7
• Prepare and disseminate event evaluation report.

Step 8
• Formulate and implement decisions for improvement based on findings of event evaluation report.

Figure 9.2   *Steps for conducting an evaluation exercise*

number of other purposes that are driven by the internal needs of the event organization and the external context within which the event operates. For example, many event managers conduct event evaluation not only for the purpose of determining whether functions such as event programming, logistics and revenue generation are meeting their targets – an internally driven concern – but also to satisfy the expectations of stakeholders and provide accountability to investors, funders and sponsors, which are externally driven factors.

Event managers are accountable to multiple stakeholders. This has made event evaluation particularly critical to building the reputation of the event and its events management team. Stakeholders' needs and expectations can vary according to their level of interest and power with respect to the event. Event managers should therefore be cognizant of the needs and expectations of each stakeholder group and have these adequately addressed through evaluation reporting and documentation. A Stakeholder Concerns Checklist can be developed beforehand and reviewed upon completion of the evaluation exercise to ensure that the key areas of concern for each stakeholder group have been addressed.

The event manager must be very clear as to the reasons for conducting event evaluation, given that significant amounts of resources are needed to carry it out. In this regard, it is useful for the event manager to be aware of the following, particularly when the event is not new:

- Does the event organization/event host have, or have access to, the requisite resources to conduct an evaluation exercise?
- Have event evaluations been conducted on the event in the past? If so, how often, and what kinds of evaluation?
- What use was made of the evaluation report?
- What is the nature of the environment in which the event operates?
- Can it facilitate the execution of an event evaluation?
- Does the event have access to a wide range of information it can use to conduct the evaluation exercise?

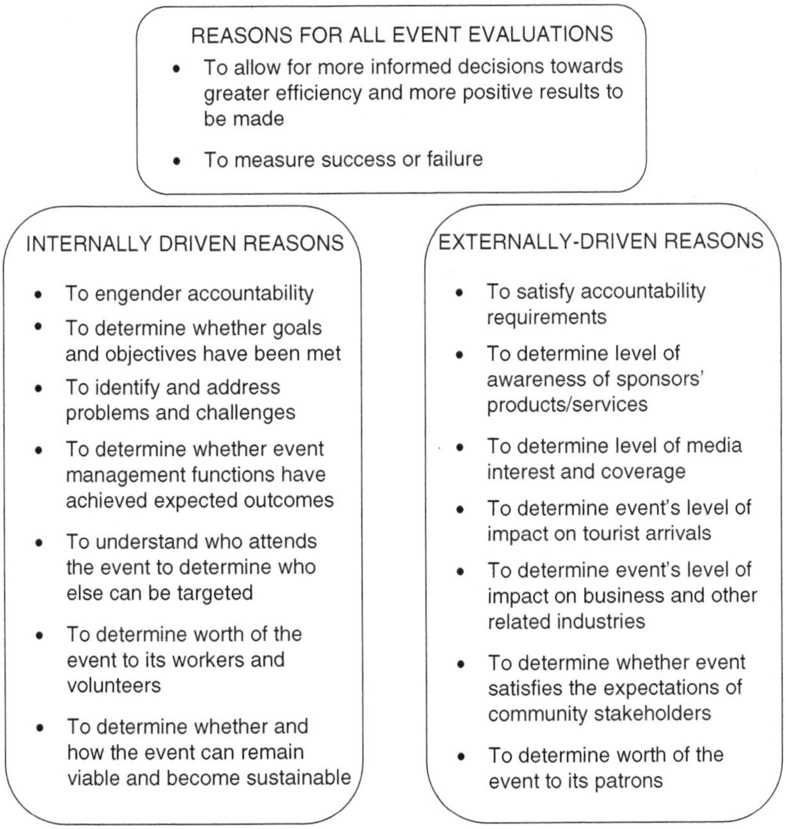

REASONS FOR ALL EVENT EVALUATIONS
- To allow for more informed decisions towards greater efficiency and more positive results to be made
- To measure success or failure

INTERNALLY DRIVEN REASONS

- To engender accountability
- To determine whether goals and objectives have been met
- To identify and address problems and challenges
- To determine whether event management functions have achieved expected outcomes
- To understand who attends the event to determine who else can be targeted
- To determine worth of the event to its workers and volunteers
- To determine whether and how the event can remain viable and become sustainable

EXTERNALLY-DRIVEN REASONS

- To satisfy accountability requirements
- To determine level of awareness of sponsors' products/services
- To determine level of media interest and coverage
- To determine event's level of impact on tourist arrivals
- To determine event's level of impact on business and other related industries
- To determine whether event satisfies the expectations of community stakeholders
- To determine worth of the event to its patrons

Figure 9.3   *Reasons for conducting event evaluation*

What to Evaluate?

To begin, the event manager should think of the main components of the event, the key event management functions and the context in which the event operates to decide what should be evaluated. This determination should therefore be made before the evaluation methodology is chosen so as to assure its suitability and practicality. The elements for evaluation range from basic information such as number of patrons to more complex queries such as social impacts and ROI. Some researchers have suggested particular typologies of elements that can guide event managers in making the appropriate choice of elements for evaluation (see Henderson and Bialeschki, 2002; Getz, 2005 and McDavid and Hawthorne, 2006). Examples of elements for event evaluation are:

- *Event Elements*: number of patrons; size of group; demographics of patrons; origin of event patron; attendees' address; source of information on the event; number of times attending event; patron satisfaction; quality and impact of event programming; quality of merchandise, food and beverage; the extent to which the event uses 'green' practices; quality of service.
- *Event Organization Elements*: nature and quantum of resources; number of staff; number and percentage share of volunteers; volunteers' perceptions working on the event; income and expenditure; cash flow; level of investment; number of sponsors; sponsorship dollars; nature and quantum of resources; extent to which event organization follows green practices; quality of service.
- *Event Context Elements*: nature and amount of local suppliers used; impacts on event; impacts of event; community perceptions; level of media coverage; media value; internet presence.

How to Approach Event Evaluation

What, then, is an effective way of approaching event evaluation? Some regard event evaluation as focused on measuring and monitoring the implementation of an event (Bowdin et al., 2006; Allen et al., 2008). Notwithstanding, it is argued that in actuality, event evaluation is mostly conducted after the event (Tum et al., 2006). This involves success being measured against objectives (Van der Wagen, 2005). Others still maintain that every aspect of the event must be evaluated (Tum et al., 2006), including factors such as human resource management and volunteerism, facilities and access, and hospitality (Wendroff, 2004). This approach requires that evaluation is conducted in a timely manner – relatively soon after the event has occurred in order the capture the experiences of all those involved lest they forget (Shone and Parry, 2001; Wendroff, 2004).

However, use of post-event evaluation as the sole mechanism for evaluating performance can have its challenges. The event manager can miss opportunities to correct any problems detected from the evaluation exercise as the event would have ended. There tends to be minimal or no focus on evaluating the planning phase of the event, which is vital to understanding many of the decisions implemented during the executing phase of the event. Evaluation conducted after an event may also result in key elements of the evaluation exercise not being effectively deployed, such as a patron satisfaction survey or crowding assessment. Post-event evaluation as a singular approach may therefore be too narrow in scope, thereby precluding the event manager from obtaining a comprehensive understanding of the event. The box below highlights the impact of short time frames on the decision of how an event is evaluated.

Diary of an Event Manager – Roberta Quarless, Event Manager, The Old Yard, Carnival Masquerade Heritage Fair, Trinidad and Tobago

The Department of Creative and Festival Arts (DCFA), University of the West Indies (UWI) is involved in numerous events every year, and one such event is The Old Yard. Roberta explains: 'The Old Yard was an inherited event for the DCFA, and one that I "adopted". The decision to pass the baton of this event onto our Department was made a mere five weeks prior to the date carded for the event, and so we had a small window of time to implement the planning and designing phases.'

It was apparent to Roberta from the start that evaluation had to be included, for very little had been documented about the event. She remembers: 'Because of the short time frame for planning and execution, I focused evaluation on event execution.'

The tools used to evaluate the event were a survey, informal interviewing and observation. Throughout the event, at varying intervals, the event team walked around, mingling with patrons questioning them about the event. The team also chatted with the performers and enquired about their experiences at the event as compared to its previous instalment and also looked out for problems arising such as long queues and crowding at the entrance, and immediately reported them to Roberta.

Interview sheets were distributed to a cross-section of the patrons: tourists, nationals, teachers, children, performers, academics and practitioners in the arts. From the collective responses, the team was able to make recommendations for next year's event. Roberta recalls: 'We discussed how we could improve logistics on the day of the event; as well as how to further improve marketing of the event. We discussed attracting sponsors that would not compromise the theme of the event and how we might expand on opportunities for greater revenue generation.'

The evaluation then served as a starting point for planning the event the following year.

The nature of the evaluation approach is also a key determinant in deciding on the evaluation methodology for a particular event. Evaluation approaches are generally characterized as numerically based or descriptive-oriented and are classified accordingly as:

- Quantitative and qualitative approaches
- Financial and non-financial approaches
- Economic and non-economic approaches

Quantitative approaches are primarily concerned with counting complex data sets such as attendance levels, information sources and event activities to make certain general conclusions and causal explanations about the event. There is the prevailing view that anything worth measuring ought to be counted, and that counting is the way of knowing. As a result, quantitative approaches are predominantly used in event evaluation, although exclusive use of such can have its drawbacks. One possible challenge is the limitations of particular data collection methods such as surveys, which may have low response rates among particular populations and settings. Additionally, inconsistencies may arise where terminology used in the survey may be interpreted differently by respondents based on cultural nuance. This may lead to over-calculation or over-estimation, thus affecting the reliability and accuracy of the evaluation exercise.

On the other hand, qualitative approaches focus on capturing opinion and attitudes on matters such as reasons for attending the event; benefits sought; level of satisfaction; stakeholder attitudes; quality of event and service offered at the event. Qualitative approaches tend to utilize open-ended questions to allow for in-depth responses. While qualitative approaches may be considered more cumbersome to administer and challenging to compile, they can complement quantitative approaches because useful details emerging out of conversation when conducting surveys cannot be represented numerically and therefore may be lost in the evaluation exercise (see Table 9.1).

Like quantitative approaches, financial approaches and economic approaches to event evaluation focus on the collection of numerical data in their respective areas. Financial approaches are concerned with collecting, assessing and monitoring numerical data on the fiscal elements of the event such as cash flow, gate receipts and other sources of revenue, patron expenditure, profit, loss and debt. Economic approaches predominantly examine numerical data related to employment, tax, visitor expenditure and economic activity triggered by the event in other businesses and related industries, mainly to gauge event impact and context.

As with general quantitative approaches, financial and economic approaches can encounter similar challenges, which may be addressed through the use of non-financial and non-economic approaches. Non-financial and non-economic approaches essentially utilize qualitative approaches to monitor and assess fiscal and economic matters that cannot be easily quantified but which are relevant. These include assessment of intangible costs and benefits; assessment of net value; assessment of stakeholder perceptions; and assessment of economic and market factors that can influence the event.

Indeed, as mentioned earlier, depending on the focus of the event and the purpose of evaluation, event evaluations can be based solely on numerically based approaches, or solely on descriptive-oriented approaches. Consequently, the event manager must be aware of the uses of the event evaluation in designing and executing the evaluation models. Overall, event evaluation is considered more effective when approached as a cyclical process that is holistically concerned with the event's 'well-being' – from conceptualization and planning through to post-event, utilizing a mixed methodology.

Table 9.1 *Categories of data using qualitative and quantitative methods*

Categories of Data	Qualitative Methods Used	Quantitative Methods Used
Festival management and organization	• Interviews • Discussion forums • Staff and partner feedback • Management reports	• Clustering • Surveys • Budgets vs. actual agenda
Festival attendance	• Observation • Focus groups	• Ticket sales • Head counts • Surveys • Police statistics • Box office data
Patron profile		• Visitor surveys • Questionnaire to sponsors/VIP • Questionnaire (demographic questions)
Role of festivals in communities/locales	• Focus groups • Interviews	• Clustering • Survey
Economic impacts on the locale	• Feedback from vendors, hoteliers and other service providers on profitability and business gained from the festival	• Visitor surveys • Survey • Spending at festival
Socio-cultural impacts	• Focus groups • Interviews	• Clustering • Surveys
Market assessments	• Secondary competitor analysis	• Audits • Demographic questionnaire • Cumulative economic impacts
Media impacts	• Content analysis	• Visitor surveys • Advertising equivalents
Festival sustainability	• Interviews • Observation	• Surveys • Repeat attendance data
Environmental impacts	• Interviews • Observation	• Surveys
Tourist-related impacts	• Interviews • Discussion boards	• Clustering • Visitor surveys • Surveys • Immigration records
Destination branding	• Interviews	• Surveys
Contribution to development of host communities	• Interviews • Focus groups • Discussion forum	• Surveys

The event manager can gain an in-depth understanding of the positive and negative outcomes of the event and have a stronger basis from which to make decisions of improvement at each stage of the event. The event manager can also derive more diverse, substantive analysis on the event that can satisfy a range of reporting needs.

To achieve this, event evaluation ought to engage in assessment and monitoring of key expected outputs, referred to as the '*three Critical Ss of event evaluation*'. These are: event significance, event success and event sustainability, which can be paired with the stages of the event's life cycle, and can also be linked to the three key periods of evaluation identified by Getz (1997).

The three critical Ss of event evaluation fundamentally reflect the three major output factors that any event manager would reference in deeming whether an event has realized its outcomes. The three critical Ss would also involve other events management functions, thereby acting as a check and balance for these other functions. For example, evaluation of event significance is concerned with measuring, assessing and monitoring the nature, purpose and intent of the event and whether the event is able to meet these. This involves the planning function of the event. Evaluation of event success focuses on determining whether execution of the event and the elements contributing to event execution have achieved their outcomes. This involves the events management functions associated with implementation such as programming, marketing, logistics, staging and so on. Evaluation of event sustainability is two-fold: it is concerned with measuring, assessing and monitoring the event in relation to its natural environment and the community in which the event operates; and secondly, with determining and understanding the potential of the event to continue and remain viable in the long run. Sustainability evaluation would involve most, if not all, of the event's management functions.

Event Evaluation Methodology: Models and Methods

On a practical level, holistic event evaluation is conducted through a mix of models and methods. These make up the event evaluation methodology. The methodology is guided by an evaluation model, which is the overarching evaluation framework that utilizes particular methods and techniques to carry out the evaluation exercise. An evaluation method is essentially a particular process or practice used to assess and monitor events that encompasses an analytical tool or instrument used to gather and cull data on the event in keeping with the method. Evaluation models work naturally with certain methods as shown in Table 9.2. Both have their distinctive strengths and can also present some challenges in use. It is therefore important to understand how the main models and methods of evaluation work in order to achieve the most from event evaluation. This is now explained in greater detail.

Models Used in Event Evaluation

There are four models that are generally used when conducting event evaluation: impact assessments; cost-benefit analysis; triple bottom-line evaluation; and ethnographic profile. Of the four models, ethnographic profile can be easily used for any type and size of event, although not generally used exclusively, while the other three tend to be used for evaluations of festivals, expos and rallies and other such events regardless of size. Impact assessments, cost-benefit analysis and triple bottom-line evaluations are also commonly used to evaluate tourism-driven events.

Table 9.2 *Evaluation methods and models*

		EVALUATION MODELS					
		Cost-Benefit Analysis	Economic Impact Analysis	Social Impact Assessment	Socio-cultural Impact Assessment	Triple Bottom Line Approach (TBL)	Ethnography
EVALUATION METHODS	Questionnaires			√	√		
	Surveys	√	√	√	√	√	√
	Interviews			√	√		√
	Secondary Data Analysis	√	√	√	√		
	Observation			√	√	√	√
	Content Analysis		√	√	√	√	
	Situational Analysis		√	√	√	√	

Impact assessments

Impact assessment models generally focus on measuring economic, social and cultural impacts of events such as festivals for which there is often the need to justify relevance. Impact assessments can vary slightly depending on the focus of the evaluation. There is economic impact analysis; environmental impact analysis; social impact analysis; and tourism impact analysis. All impact analyses tend to utilize a broad range of indicators (see Table 9.3). This is perhaps the major strength of impact assessments in that this allows for a more in-depth assessment that can provide a high quality of analysis and have great validity. Impact assessments are fairly comprehensive and resource-intensive and thus require careful planning to yield data of a high and substantive quality. When effectively conducted, impact assessments can identify the costs as well as the benefits. Additionally, impact assessments can track changes as well as monitor trends over time.

A major drawback of impact assessments however is their perceived bias towards the event, since impact assessments are usually commissioned by event hosts and funders seeking to legitimize the event's relevance. This criticism is particularly levelled at economic impact assessments on festivals. There is the view that these studies tend to assess the benefits more so than the costs and thus engage in methods to serve this end. Although the focus of social impact assessments is considered critical to attaining a wider understanding of the changes in the communities and in social relationships resulting from their hosting events, the social dimensions of culture can

Table 9.3 *Sample of key variables typically utilized in impact studies*

Variables	Impact Assessment Studies			
	EIA	ENIA	SIA	TIA
Number of festivals in a group	√	√	√	√
Theme/type of festival	√	√	√	√
Purpose of festival	√	√	√	√
Duration	√	√	√	√
Structure of festival organizing body	√			
Patron size	√	√	√	
Patron spend	√			
Number of visitors	√		√	√
Demographics of patrons	√		√	√
Demographics of visitors	√			
Purpose of visit	√			√
Visitor spend	√			√
Spending apart from festival-related items	√			√
Motivation for attending festival			√	√
Source of information on the festival				√
Medium of transport to festival	√	√	√	√
Employment generated by festival	√		√	
Tax revenue derived from festival	√			
Increased job opportunities	√		√	
Source of funding	√			
Festival income	√			√
Festival expenditure	√			√
Significance of environmental initiatives to festival patrons		√		
Noise pollution		√		
Use of green energy		√		
Festival organizers' awareness of green initiatives and policy				
Practice of recycling measures		√		
Construction of new facilities, new infrastructure	√	√	√	√
Media value	√		√	√
Level of participation by host community/residents			√	
Identification with theme			√	
Community attachment			√	
Level of traffic congestion			√	
Level of crowding			√	
Level of crime		√	√	√

EIA = ECONOMIC IMPACT; ENIA = ENVIRONMENTAL IMPACT;
SIA = SOCIO-CULTURAL IMPACT; TIA = TOURISM IMPACT

be difficult to assess. In recent times, a few commonly accepted statistical standards that support the measuring of the social dimensions of culture in events are now being used in event evaluation. These include household and time use surveys to assess and monitor active and passive cultural participation; and the social impact perception (SIP) scale to assess event attendees' perceptions.

Some researchers argue that impact assessments should be conducted some years after the event, as this could more accurately reflect both the positive and negative impacts. In this regard, the longitudinal approach has been found to be useful, particularly in evaluating Expos (Edwards et al., 2004; Lim and Lee, 2006). Overall, while economic impact assessments do raise some concerns, they are useful for clarifying industry and sectoral interaction in the local economies (Hackbert, 2009).

Cost-benefit analysis

Cost-benefit analysis identifies and measures the costs and benefits of an event. Although first developed to evaluate alternate uses of public funds from a macro-economic stand-point, cost-benefit analysis has been proven useful in evaluations of special events and corporate events. Cost-benefit analysis can take either a quantitative or qualitative slant, where the quantitative refer to those costs and benefits that can be expressed in economic terms by the assignment of a monetary value and the qualitative to those that cannot be so valued. This approach also takes into account costs and benefits accruing to the host community – also known as externalities or spill-over costs and benefits (Burgan and Mules, 2000). The contingent valuation method is typically employed in this approach, and it relies on interviews with sample patrons to assess willingness to pay and thus evaluate how patrons perceive the value or worth of the festival.

The major benefit of this model of assessment is that it allows for non-monetary considerations of value and costs to be considered in relative terms. Additionally, it differs from economic impact assessment in that it allows for the inclusion of 'intangible' impacts that are traditionally omitted from economic impact analysis. The main weakness is the heavy reliance on the interviewees' honesty on questions pertaining to festival expenditure, which, if not reported accurately, can skew the balance between cost and benefit. Another drawback is that the projected benefits are often intangible while costs are tangible, which makes it difficult to engage in comparative analysis.

Triple bottom-line approach (TBL)

This model emerged out of calls for business and tourism events to produce valuations of their activity that went beyond economics to include the impact of their events on the environment. As a framework for measuring and reporting the event's performance against economic, social and environmental parameters, the TBL approach evaluates the event's performance in relation to these variables to determine whether they are positively or negatively impacting on their host communities (Fredline et al., 2005).

The TBL approach is noted particularly for its systematic approach for evaluating environmental or 'green' issues and concerns relating to the event. In this way, the TBL approach is able to draw attention to the 'green' responsibility and the overall environmental footprint of the event. The TBL approach measures the social and natural environmental impact of an activity and correlates this to its financial and economic performance, thereby lending depth to traditional ways of measuring success. Measures can include, for example, water and energy use, waste generation and recycling capacity within the event, along with the other usually evaluated elements related to economic impacts and social impacts. Perhaps the main drawback to this approach would be its heavy reliance on qualitative methods which could pose problems of validity. Notwithstanding, the TBL approach offers a systematic model for widening the evaluation net beyond the economic and financial concerns.

Ethnographic profile

An ethnographic profile is considered a useful means of triangulating data derived from the previously mentioned evaluation models. It is developed through the use of ethnography, which utilizes participant observation, interviewing and the use of documentary sources to yield valuable and valid data, particularly within the wider frame of experience-related studies. Ethnography has been used in the analysis of tourism since the 1960s and is often used in the evaluation of cultural festivals and cultural special events.

The drawback to this approach is that the fieldwork would be demanding in terms of time, financial and human resources. The benefit is that the evaluator as the event attendee/event volunteer/local resident (any of the roles that would offer an insider perspective) would capture rich details and nuances of the event (intangibles that have real value) that might otherwise not be accounted for in traditional methods such as visitor surveys, satisfaction surveys and event surveys. This approach would also allow for the understandings of the socio-cultural and environmental impacts of the event from a visitor perspective.

Methods Used in Event Evaluation

Methods are critical to the process of gathering festival data, since it is at this stage that misuse or incorrect use of associated instruments can render the results invalid. Table 9.4 outlines the main characteristics of each method, examples of their use in event evaluation, along with their strengths and shortcomings as evaluation techniques for events.

Evaluation output: Documenting and reporting

Event evaluation would not be complete without proper recording of the analysis derived from the evaluation exercise. This is the final stage of the event evaluation process before further decision-making. It is generally referred to as documentation and reporting. Documentation and reporting is critical to triggering the feedback loop that characterizes evaluation as a continuous process. After the evaluation report is disseminated and reviewed, decisions must be made about improvements to the event arising out of the report, which are in turn fed back into the event planning and preparation stage, thus re-starting the project management cycle and life cycle of the event.

Since the evaluation exercise is conducted in a systematic manner, documentation and reporting should similarly follow a structured systematic layout, which could also

Table 9.4 *Evaluation methods, and strengths and limitations*

Evaluation Methods	Examples of Use	Strengths	Limitations
Content Analysis	• Nature of the event documented • Information, especially historical, that would indicate event type, event content, event duration, event organizers and event sponsors, etc. • Impact of event's documented information • Compatible with documentation, situational analysis • Used in media audit, and triple bottom-line assessments	√ Inexpensive, comprehensive research tool, user-friendly √ Does not require contact with people – unobtrusive √ Very useful when combined with other methods such as interviews, observation	× Purely descriptive – gives the what but may not give the why and how × Analysis limited by availability of information × Observed trends in media may be inaccurate
Documentation	• Traces the history of the event in terms of programming, past evaluation reports and correspondence with stakeholders • Compatible with stakeholder analysis • Used in cost-benefit analysis, triple bottom-line and all impact assessments	See above	See above
Environmental Audit	• Level of green practice being followed by the event • Nature and level of impact of the event on the physical environment: pollution, impacts on wildlife, waste generated, traffic and crowding • Used for environmental impact analysis, triple bottom-line and cost-benefit analysis	√ Gives a comprehensive picture of event in relation to physical environment	× May be limited in scope – focus only on impacts and not on internal approaches to green issues and practice or vice versa
Focus Group	• Determines perceptions, opinions, beliefs and attitudes towards the event (for e.g. benefits sought, satisfaction) through an interactive group setting • Analysis of quality management • Used for ethnography, triple bottom-line, cost-benefit evaluation • Compatible with stakeholder analysis	√ Allows group members to freely participate in discussion especially √ Allows for detailed analysis – can attain specifics on the event √ Useful where participants may not like filling out surveys and questionnaires	× Does not occur in a naturalistic setting × May not be encouraging to participants × Members may be reluctant to share personal information/feel that they must conform to populist views × Difficult to collate results in a quantifiable manner × Time consuming
Financial Audit	• Cash flow, assets and liabilities, profit and loss, debt and financial worth of event • Used for cost-benefit analysis, economic impact analysis and business impact analysis • Compatible with resource audit and return on event audit	√ Useful in determining financial performance and status of the event	× Does not explain context behind numerical analysis presented

(Continued)

Table 9.4 (Continued)

Evaluation Methods	Examples of Use	Strengths	Limitations
Interviews Structured Unstructured	• Perceptions, opinions, beliefs and attitudes towards the event through a one-on-one face-to-face interaction • Compatible with volunteer value analysis, stakeholder analysis, content analysis and situational analysis • Can be used with all the evaluation models	√ Attain insights and specifics on aspects of the event √ Useful where participants may not like filling out surveys and questionnaires √ Allows for honest discussion √ Complementary with other methods	✕ Time consuming ✕ Requires use of other methods such as content analysis ✕ Difficult to collate results in a quantifiable manner ✕ Lack of flexibility in structured interviews makes it difficult to probe further
Media Audit	• Nature of media coverage • Extent of media exposure (quantity and quality) • Worth of media coverage • Worth of event for sponsors and funders • Compatible with interviews, questionnaires and surveys • Can be used in all evaluation models	√ Can be executed in-house by marketing/pr team members √ Gives comprehensive picture of event through the lens of the media	✕ Can be expensive ✕ May require outside expert assistance ✕ Can be time consuming
New Media Audit	• Nature of internet coverage • Extent of website exposure (quantity and quality) • Worth of internet coverage	See above	See above
Observation	• Quality of management • Level of guest satisfaction • Profile of visitors attending the event • Profile of patrons • Trip type • Impact on physical environment and community • Compatible with all methods • Used in all evaluation models	√ Best method for studying natural behaviour √ Allows for specifics to be incorporated in the evaluation	✕ May not be the most reliable method ✕ Can sometimes be too subjective ✕ Time consuming to collate information gleaned
Participant Observation	• Quality of management • Level of guest satisfaction • Profile of visitors attending the event • Profile of patrons • Quality of event programming • Compatible with all methods • Used principally in ethnographic sketch • Can also be used in triple bottom-line and impact assessments	√ Considered to yield rich description because evaluator is directly involved in the event while observing	✕ May be biased given the closeness of the evaluator to the event

(Continued)

Table 9.4 (Continued)

Evaluation Methods	Examples of Use	Strengths	Limitations
Questionnaire Closed-ended Open-ended	• Analysis of market and marketing issues • Visitor profile: activities and spending, attendance, reason for attendance, reasons for trip • Patron profile: patron origin, patron demographics and information sources on the event • Return on investment for sponsors and funders • Compatible with all methods with the exception of ethnographic sketch	√ Can reach numbers larger than focus group, although not generally used for the volume as would a survey (see survey) √ Easy to fill out √ Results easily quantifiable (for closed-ended questions) √ Easy to administer – can be done face-to-face or via email/post √ Not expensive to administer √ Allows for anonymity	✗ Does not give context behind results ✗ Response rate tends to be low ✗ Difficult to extract adequate sample sometimes
Resource Audit	• Nature and level of capacity of event organization • Internal workings of the event organization • Volunteer value • Compatible with stakeholder analysis, content analysis, documentation, situational analysis, questionnaire, survey and interviews • Can be used for most evaluation models	√ Contributes to SWOT analysis	
Situational Analysis	• Context in which event operates • Internalities of event organization • Compatible with stakeholder analysis, content analysis, documentation, resource audit, questionnaire, survey and interviews • Can be used for most evaluation models	√ Contributes to SWOT analysis √ Feeds into impact analyses	✗ Can be limited by availability of information
Stakeholder Analysis	• Level of power and interest of stakeholders in event • Impact of event on stakeholders • Stakeholder interests and expectations fulfilled • Compatible with most methods • Used in triple bottom-line, impact assessments and cost-benefit analysis		✗ May be sympathetic to stakeholders' views of the event in deference to the event
Survey Accommodation Business Exit Market Visitor	Same as for questionnaire (See questionnaire for more)	√ More appropriate for larger numbers of respondents, particularly in the case of polling visitors	Same as for questionnaire

be used when making presentations to major stakeholders. Evaluation reporting should essentially address what the evaluation exercise entailed; why the particular choices of methodology were employed; how the evaluation was executed; findings and analysis and finally recommendations. The findings and analysis derived from the evaluation models and methods selected and the ensuing recommendations should essentially answer the following questions:

- What went right?
- What went wrong?
- How can the positive outcomes be further capitalized upon?
- How can the negative outcomes be improved upon?

An example of an outline of an event evaluation report is shown in Table 9.5.

Table 9.5　*Framework for an Event Evaluation Report*

• Executive Summary	• Assessment of Event Planning
• Introduction	○ Methods used
• Rationale	○ Findings & analysis
• Aims	○ Event sustainability & event significance
• Evaluation Methodology	• Assessment of Event Execution
○ Justifications & limitations	○ Methods used
• Outline of the Evaluation Report	○ Findings & analysis
• Profile of the Event	○ Event sustainability & event significance
○ Nature, purpose, location, history, main products/services, profiles & facts and figures	• Post-event Evaluation
	○ Methods used
	○ Findings & analysis
• Profile of the Event Organizer	○ Event sustainability & event significance
○ Background, number and type of employees & events management team & their areas of responsibility	• Evaluation of Stakeholder Needs
	○ Methods used
	○ Findings & analysis
• Brief background on Event Partners	○ Event sustainability & event significance
○ Major funders &/or sponsors	• Financial Reporting and Analysis
• Strategic Analysis of the Event	• Recommendations and Conclusion
○ Situational analysis (SWOT)	

Case Study 9.1　In Search of a Host Country for CARIFESTA

Introduction

Following the recommendations of the most recent strategic plan for the Caribbean Festival of Arts (CARIFESTA), the search began again for another country host for this regional mega-festival. CARIFESTA now had a renewed vision and

(Continued)

(Continued)

needed a country host capable of re-defining and re-organizing this Caribbean celebration to make it a vibrant and sustainable cultural enterprise (Nurse, 2004).

Given that the core strength of CARIFESTA lies in its mobility, Caribbean appeal and multi-disciplinary approach to the arts, steps needed to be taken to ensure that these were maintained, and where possible expanded. The strategic plan has called for a systemic in-depth evaluation; and so any Caribbean country seeking to win the bid to host the next instalment of CARIFESTA needed to demonstrate a commitment to this new requirement.

Background

Over its 30-year existence, CARIFESTA has made a significant impact on Caribbean development, in terms of the arts, artists and arts infrastructure in its various host countries. CARIFESTA has also aided in deepening Caribbean integration by making Caribbean arts accessible and fostering a vision of Caribbean unity and a pan-Caribbean outlook. It is, however, acknowledged that these positive impacts are derivatives more-so of earlier CARIFESTAs, and have seldom been spin-offs of CARIFESTAs in the post-1990 era.

There are a number of external forces that have challenged the success of CARIFESTA in the 1990s. In particular, CARIFESTA has been staged within an increasingly competitive environment where consumer tastes and trends constantly shift at a rapid rate – particularly within the Caribbean, its primary market. It is therefore clear that part of the success of the next CARIFESTA would rest on the ability of the host to understand and respond to this dynamic environment.

Broad strategy

It has been recommended that the next host country should be open to staging CARIFESTA whilst another mega-event is being held in the Caribbean, such as a sporting championship event. This is considered a strategic choice given that there are many synergies to be gained from combining sport and cultural events. Additionally, many successful mega-events have followed the approach of hosting cultural fringe events that celebrate the multiculturalism of the destination, alongside the main event. The 2002 Manchester Commonwealth Games is one such notable example, where apart from hosting a superb sporting event, the host country was also able to promote cultural excellence 'to secure a lasting legacy' for the destination region (Bowdin et al., 2006: 23). It was felt that the Caribbean could similarly benefit from hosting CARIFESTA around the same time as the ICC Cricket World Cup (see Ferdinand and Wesner, in this volume), as a sporting event of this nature would give the Caribbean the opportunity to present a cultural/entertainment extravaganza to the world and give nearby destinations an opportunity to share in promoting the Caribbean's cultural and artistic excellence. To achieve these goals, particular attention was to be paid to attaining operational excellence and market leadership, and building and maintaining stakeholder partnerships.

(Continued)

(Continued)

Festival format, programming and marketing

CARIFESTA comprises ten days of arts and cultural celebrations spanning two weekends. The Festival usually encompasses a number of events that serve both the commercial/trade and artistic interests of artists and entrepreneurs. These include:

- The Grand Market
- Cultural Industries Trade Fair
- Book Fair
- Film Festival
- Visual Arts Festival and Exhibition
- Symposia
- Community Festivals
- Super Concerts

The Festival also strives to incorporate a number of innovative elements that will aid in transforming CARIFESTA to a 'hallmark' event. Consequently, the marketing strategy must be primarily aimed at re-branding CARIFESTA. The intention is to create a hallmark mega-event that draws people from the Caribbean and the Caribbean Diaspora. The goal is also to create a festival that further enhances the image of the host country and that of the Caribbean. Thus, the marketing strategy was to be based on building partnerships, packaging and programming, alongside the standard marketing principles of place, product, price and promotion (see Gechev, in this volume). Not to be forgotten is the role that public relations can play in rejuvenating the interest and enthusiasm of the festival's primary market of Caribbean citizens.

Finances

It was decided that CARIFESTA would continue to receive support form Caribbean governments but must seek ways to attract other sources of income. Bearing in mind that expenditure includes artist fees, venue rental and website development and maintenance, there must be a clear financial strategy developed and implemented to assure that the return on investment by all key stakeholders is realized.

Evaluating CARIFESTA

The host country must be fully committed to engaging in event evaluation and be able to clearly articulate the nature of that evaluation process, the approach to be taken and the methodology to be used. The host country must also be able to justify choices made in conducting the evaluation.

(Continued)

(Continued)

Case Study Questions

1 Based on the case study, list the possible elements of focus for evaluation of CARIFESTA.
2 Why would the successful country host need to conduct evaluation of CARIFESTA?
3 What would be the long-term benefits of a festival such as CARIFESTA?
4 Write a brief outlining how CARIFESTA might be evaluated, incorporating, where possible, details from the case study.

Chapter Summary

Event evaluation is an important function that spans the entire life cycle of an event – from planning and design, to execution and event shutdown and post-event. It is important that event managers determine and understand the reasons for conducting event evaluation given the quantum of resources that go into such an exercise. Knowing what to evaluate can be guided by the event manager taking into consideration: the main components of the event; the key functions of the event organization; and the contexts in which the event operates. Although event evaluations can exclusively employ quantitatively based approaches or qualitatively based approaches, a holistic approach to event evaluation, which includes a mixture of the two approaches, can offer a more in-depth and comprehensive analysis. Event evaluation is executed using an evaluation methodology, which comprises evaluation models and evaluation methods. Evaluation models and methods can have their strengths and limitations and should therefore be carefully reviewed for suitability and practicality in relation to the event to be evaluated. Reporting and documentation is the final stage of the event evaluation process. It is critical in triggering the feedback loop that characterizes evaluation as a continuous process and is essential for communicating with key stakeholders on the performance of the event.

Review Questions

1 Explain the event evaluation function. What are the main benefits of conducting event evaluation?
2 What is holistic event evaluation? How might such an evaluation be conducted?
3 Design a Stakeholders' Concerns Checklist for a community-based special event.
4 Describe the main models and methods used in event evaluation, and discuss their respective strengths and limitations in use, with reference to an event with which you are familiar.
5 Obtain three examples of event evaluation reports, and compare and contrast the methodologies used.

Additional Resources

Books, book chapters and journal articles

Andersson, T.D., Persson, C., Sahlberg, B. and Strom, L. (eds) (1999) *The Impact of Mega Events*. Ostersund: European Tourism Research Institute.
Provides a useful resource for those examining the impact of mega-events.

Hede, A. (2008) 'Managing special events in the new era of the Triple Bottom Line', *Event Management,* 11(1–2): 13–22.
Proposes a framework for applying the TBL to the planning stage of special event management.

Phillips, J.J., Breining, M.T. and Phillips, P.P. (2008) *Return on Investment in Meetings and Events: Tools and Techniques to Measure the Success of All Types of Meetings and Events*. Oxford: Butterworth-Heinemann.
Introduces and demonstrates Jack J. Phillips's well-established ROI measurement methodology to address the growing demands from stakeholders to prove the value of meetings through data analysis.

Preuss, H. (2006) *The Economics of Staging the Olympics: A Comparison of the Games 1972–2008*. Cheltenham: Edward Elgar.
Is especially useful to those interested in economic impacts of mega-events. Also covers tourism, urban regeneration and social impacts to some extent.

Sinclair-Maragh, G. (2011) 'A critical socio-economic assessment of the ICC World Cup Cricket on the hosting Caribbean', in L. Jordan, B. Tyson, C. Hayle and D. Truly (eds), *Sports Event Management: The Caribbean Experience*. Aldershot: Ashgate.
Assesses the socio-economic impacts of the ICC Cricket World Cup.

Useful websites

http://www.juliasilvers.com/embok.htm
Hosts the EMBOK project and includes information on all areas of the event management process including evaluation.

http://www.london2012.com/
The official website of the London 2012 Olympic and Paralympic Games features articles and reports on the how the London 2012 Games will be evaluated.

http://www.wrap.org.uk/
Provides a host of free evaluation tools for businesses, individuals and communities wishing to evaluate their efficiency in consuming and recycling resources.

References

Allen, J., O'Toole, W., McDonnell, I. and Harris, R. (2008) *Festival and Special Event Management*. Brisbane: Wiley.

Bowdin, G.A.J., McDonnell, I., Allen, J. and O'Toole, W. (2006) *Events Management* (2nd edn). Oxford: Butterworth-Heinemann.

Burgan, B. and Mules, T. (2000) 'Reconciling cost-benefit and economic impact assessment', in J. Allen, R. Harris, L.K. Jago and A.J. Veal (eds), *Events Beyond 2000: Setting the Agenda, Proceedings of Conference on Event Evaluation, Research and Education, Sydney (July 2000)*. Lindfield: Australian Centre for Event Management. pp. 46–51.

Edwards, J., Moital, M. and Vaughan, R. (2004) 'The impacts of mega-events: The case of EXPO 98 – Lisbon', in P. Long and M. Robinson (eds), *Festival Tourism: Marketing, Management and Evaluation*. Sunderland: Business Education Publishers. pp. 196–215.

Forrester, S. (2008) 'The event planning model: The evaluation and renewal phase, Part I', in C. Mallen and L.J. Adams (eds), *Sport Recreation and Tourism Event Management*. Oxford: Butterworth-Heinemann. pp. 111–130.

Fredline, L., Raybould, M., Jago, L. and Deery, M. (2005) 'Triple bottom line event evaluation: A proposed framework for holistic event evaluation', Third International Event Conference – The Impacts of Events: Triple Bottom Line Evaluation and Event Legacies, Sydney, July.

Getz, D. (1997) *Event Management and Event Tourism*. New York: Cognizant Communications Corporation.

Getz, D. (2005) *Event Management and Event Tourism* (2nd edn). New York: Cognizant Communications Corporation.

Hackbert, P.H. (2009) Economic impacts of Appalachian festivals. Proceedings of ASBBS 16th Annual Conference, Las Vegas, 19-22 February [Online]. Available from: http://asbbs.org/files/2009/PDF/H/HackbertP.pdf.

Henderson, K.A. and Bialeschki, M.D. (2002) *Evaluating Leisure Services: Making Enlightened Decisions*. State College, PA: Venture Publishing.

Lim, S.T. and Lee, J.S. (2006) 'Host population perceptions of the impact of mega-events', *Asia Pacific Journal of Tourism Research*, 11(4): 407–421.

LOCOG (n/d) *Sustainability*. LOCOG [Online]. Available from: http://www.london2012.com/making-it-happen/sustainability/index.php.

McDavid, J.C. and Hawthorne, L. (2006) *Program Evaluation and Performance Measurement: An Introduction to Practice*. Thousand Oaks, CA: McGraw Hill.

Nurse, K. (2004) *Reinventing CARIFESTA: A Strategic Plan Prepared for CARICOM Taskforce on CARIFESTA*. CARICOM [Online]. Available from http://www.caricom.org/jsp/community_organs/carifesta-strategicplan.pdf.

O'Toole, W. and Mikolaitis, P. (2002) *Corporate Event Project Management*. New York: John Wiley and Sons Inc.

Shone, A. and Parry, B. (2001) *Successful Event Management*. London: Continuum.

Tum, J., Norton, P. and Wright, J.N. (2006) *Management of Event Operations*. Oxford: Butterworth-Heinemann.

Van der Wagen, L. (2005) *Event Management for Tourism, Cultural, Business and Sporting Events*. Frenchs Forest: Pearson Education Australia.

Wendroff, A. (2004) *Special Events: Proven Strategies for Non-Profit Fundraising*. Hoboken, NJ: John Wiley & Sons.

PART 3

CONTEMPORARY ISSUES IN INTERNATIONAL EVENTS MANAGEMENT

The first two parts of this text have provided an introduction to the need for an international perspective and the founding principles of effective event management at an international level. The convergence of socio-cultural, economic, political and technological forces on current event management practice requires staff to be immersed in a process of continual learning and re-learning. Events are not simply a vocation for event managers – to many stakeholders they are the reason to travel abroad, the reason to save their hard-earned cash, the reason to discipline their bodies through training and the rationale for the allocation of public monies at the expense of other community initiatives. The personal, social and cultural importance should be at the forefront of management thought.

To this end, this third part of *Events Management: An International Approach* builds upon these initial, functional contributions and examines applied and emerging issues in events management practice. Each of the chapters in the following section applies event management principles to particular areas of concern. Contemporary event managers must be aware that these principles encapsulate the issues discussed above. This part gets to grips with ethical and social issues such as sustainability and ambush marketing (or guerilla marketing – depending on your perspective). It also examines the role of events in hospitality, the event-led internationalization of sport and the role of people, planet and profit in corporate events.

The nexus of Corporate Social Responsibility (CSR) and sustainability is the focus of Chapter 10 by Cavagnaro, Postma and Neese. These authors provide a timely analysis of the increasing need for sustainable guidelines to assist in the management of events. Through a series of case studies and an examination of international standards, the principles of sustainability are introduced and applied. The authors however question the importance of sustainability in event management with particular attention as to whether the green credentials of an event is an ante-cedent for attendance, that is – do consumers really care?

In keeping with this discussion of social/ethical behaviour, Marc Mazodier examines the practice of ambush marketing in Chapter 11. The unwarranted use of, or an association with, an event without the event owner's permission is a contentious marketing issue for international events. A comprehensive review of the high-profile cases where this has occurred is provided within. Despite notions that event management guidelines and regulations are reducing the number of overall ambushing cases, Mazodier examines the FIFA World Cup held in South Africa in 2010 and the persistence of some marketers' attempts to capture the benefits that arise from these types of international events.

Remaining with the focus on international sport, the following chapter considers the international growth of the once domestic sport event and leagues of Europe and North America. These leagues and their event products are branching out in order to seek new markets, to capture new fans and sponsors while competing against each other for these new territories. Chapter 12 by Kitchin examines these developments and seeks to provide a model for which such developments can be managed by event personnel. This process is highlighted by a case study focusing on how terrorism resulted in the Indian Premier League's staging of their annual cricket competition not in India but over 7000 kilometres away in South Africa.

Chapter 13 by Pantelidis examines the contribution of events to the hospitality industry. The importance of hospitality to many international events is paramount and well understood – however the numerous functions of these events and the role of the wider hospitality industry requires greater attention. This chapter both serves this purpose and addresses the future trends in hospitality events provision. This section closes with a final chapter by Reic, examining how experiential qualities are driving developments in the corporate events sector. Reic explores the types of corporate events and highlights the myriad categories that comprise this area. Through this analysis, Reic emphasizes the centrality of internal and external stakeholder concerns before highlighting a series of current issues in the field. The closing case study on AIESEC examines the framework that guides events for developing young professional talent within the wider industry.

10

Sustainability and the Events Industry

Elena Cavagnaro, Albert Postma and Thomas Neese

Learning Objectives

By reading this chapter students should be able to:

- Define the concepts Corporate Social Responsibility (CSR) and Sustainable Development.
- Understand and explain the relevance of CSR and Sustainable Development for the event industry.
- Identify the main approaches towards sustainable events.
- List the key indicators for sustainable events.
- Identify, analyse and evaluate existing events on the basis of sustainable events indicators.

Introduction

Celebrations, contests and gatherings have been part of all cultures ever since the beginnings of human history and in today's world, even though updated in appearance, they still have a vital role in our daily life. In the last decades, the event sector experienced an unprecedented boom in popularity. Events not only have an impact on the economy of the hosting country, city or community but they also have a positive or negative impact on the hosting community itself, its culture and its natural environment. Similarly to what has already happened in other industries, the growth in the number and size of events have made their impacts more visible and raised the question of responsibility for both positive and negative consequences on communities and the natural environment. In short: the quest for a more sustainable event industry has begun.

This chapter explores the challenges posed and opportunities offered by sustainability to events in four sections. In the first section the concepts of sustainability and Corporate Social Responsibility (CSR) are defined and the relationship between the two is highlighted, leading to a definition of CSR as a contributor to sustainable development and a better quality of life now and in the future. The second section refutes the idea that events by their very nature are incompatible with sustainability and shows how events and sustainability relate. Guidelines for sustainability events are briefly addressed in the third section while the fourth and last summarizes the results of research conducted by the authors on the awareness of customers of the social and environmental impacts of the events they visit and on how they perceive sustainable events.

On Corporate Social Responsibility and Sustainable Development

After a difficult start in the 1980s, sustainable development and Corporate Social Responsibility (CSR) have earned a stable position on the political and business agenda (Jamali, 2006). Even though both concepts are perceived as vague and imprecise by some scholars (Sutton, 2007), there is a growing consensus that CSR is rooted in the acknowledgment that businesses have obligations towards society that go beyond their economic responsibility (Carroll, 1991; Elkington, 1997; and more recently Idowu and Towler, 2004; Jones et al., 2005). John Elkington's proposal of a Triple Bottom Line, by which business measures and reports upon its economic, environmental and social impact (or people, planet and profit), have been embraced both by for-profit and not-for-profit organizations. In 2008 more than 1000 organizations have published their 'Triple P' reports on the Global Reporting Initiative (GRI) website, an increase of 46 per cent compared to 2007.

Sustainable development was set at the centre of academic and political debate by the UN World Commission on Environment and Development, also known as the Brundtland commission, so-called because of the name of its chair, former Norwegian Prime Minister Gro Harlem Brundtland (1987). The Brundtland commission recognized that the current path of development not only has a negative impact on the natural environment but also fails to successfully address social inequalities both among nations and between nations. Therefore it cannot and should not be sustained indefinitely.

It was decided that change was needed towards a sustainable form of development that 'seeks to meet the needs and aspirations of the present without compromising the ability to meet those of the future' (1987: 40). To have an end in mind of sustainable development is thus a better quality of life for present and future generations. The main point made by the Brundtland commission is that a better quality of life cannot be achieved by relying on economic growth alone. A healthy natural environment and equitable social development are also essential dimensions of a sustainable pattern of development.

Sustainable development was quickly embraced by multilateral organizations such as the UN, and several NGOs. Currently, it informs not only UN programmes, but also local, national and regional policy. To give only one example, the Maastricht Treaty, signed on 7 February 1992, states that the goal of the European Union is to achieve sustainable development (EU, 1992, article B). Additionally, thanks to efforts of the World Business Council for Sustainable Development, more and more companies answered the call to become agents of change towards sustainability by re-designing their operations to achieve a positive impact on people, planet and profit: the triple bottom line proposed by John Elkington (Schmidheiny, 1992; WBCSD, 2000).

Based on the above the following definition of CSR will be used in this research: CSR is the voluntary dedication of business towards sustainable development, resulting in benefits for society (people), environment (planet) and the economy (profit). At the level of consumers, sustainability requires the consideration not just of the price of a particular good or service, but also of its impact on people and the natural environment (UN, 1992; Jackson, 2005).

Sustainability and Events

It may be clear from the above that sustainability is not a new issue on academic, political and business agendas. Yet, the event industry is only recently and quite reluctantly responding to sustainability issues. The reluctance to consider sustainable development and CSR as relevant and applicable to the event industry may be explained by the tendency to understand both as referring to something that should go on indefinitely, and then contrasting this definition with the unique and ephemeral nature of events. It is true that one of the meanings of the verb 'to sustain' is to endure and be long lasting. Yet, though sustainability aims at a form of development that can be sustained indefinitely, the message of sustainable development and CSR is that activities are unsustainable if they do not benefit the people involved, the community in which they take place and the natural environment. The stress is on the impacts of a specific activity, not on how long that activity lasts.

It is undeniable that events have an impact on the people involved, the hosting community and the natural environment – take, for example, the Sziget Festival in Budapest (Hungary). This festival was born as a student music festival with 43,000 visitors in 1993. In 2006 it reached 385,000 visitors and generated 2200 cubic metres of waste: an amount similar to the waste accumulated by residents of a ten-storey building in about nine to ten years (Dávid, 2009). As Getz has argued: 'sustainable events are not just those that can endure indefinitely, they are also events that fulfil important social, cultural, economic and environmental roles that people value' (2007: 70). Similarly Smith-Christensen argues that responsible events are 'sensitive to the economic, socio-cultural and environmental needs within the local host community, and organized in such a way to maximize the net holistic (positive) output' (2009: 25). Moreover, following a long tradition connecting CSR with stakeholders' thinking (Carroll, 1991; Elkington, 1997), Getz argues that to achieve sustainability 'accountability has to extend beyond internal shareholders to encompass all stakeholders interested in, and affected by planned events, including visitors and especially the affected communities' (2007: 71).

On this basis sustainable events can be defined as: events that impact positively on people, planet and profit and thus contribute to fulfil the economic, socio-cultural and environmental needs of the involved stakeholders, including the hosting community. Impact is chosen above output or outcome following the recent debate on the relative strengths of these concepts in the context of sustainability (Maas, 2009). In brief, while output and outcome highlight the results of a business activity, for example a well attended event, impact focuses on the positive or negative change and legacy that it leaves behind, for example disruption in a community that had to be relocated to make space to host a mega-event such as the Olympic and Paralympic Games. As Elkington (1997) observed, organizations have learnt to address environmental issues rather quickly, but the socio-cultural aspects of sustainability and CSR are still difficult to deal with properly. The efforts at greening the Olympic Games offers an excellent illustration of this point (see Figure 10.3).

To achieve positive impacts on the triple bottom line (people, planet, profit) and thus contribute to sustainable development, an organization should set sustainability principles at the centre of its vision and mission (Edwards, 2005). A quite early attempt involving the event industry consisted of the Hannover Principles, a set of nine maxims proposed as guidelines in designing competitions and projects for the World Exposition in 2000 in Hannover, Germany (McDonough and Partners, 1992; Musgrave and Raj, 2009). Sustainable design decisions were set in relation to the elements *earth* (for example, life-cycle analysis of all materials and recycling), *air* (for example, minimized air and noise pollution and artificial indoor climate control), *fire* (for example, on-site energy production and heating), *water* (for example, minimal water use and use of impermeable ground cover) and *spirit* (for example, embracing people's feeling of belonging to the earth).

The Hannover Principles clearly demonstrate that, although a mission based on sustainability principles is essential, sustainable impacts are primarily the result of sustainable processes and operations. The degree of sustainability of an activity depends primarily on its impacts on people, planet and profit, even when sustainability is the theme of that activity, as is the case, for example, with an event held yearly in the Netherlands: the Frisian Solar Challenge (see Case Study 10.1).

Case Study 10.1   The Frisian Solar Challenge, the World Cup in Solar Boat Racing

Fryslân, a Northern Province of the Netherlands, is renowned for its many lakes, rivers and canals, and can be regarded as a unique water sport region. The Frisian provincial government has set sustainable development as a goal of its policy since 2007. In this context, the Frisian economic policy is geared towards supporting innovative entrepreneurs and the development of sustainable technology. In the Frisian Solar Challenge these two elements are combined successfully.

The Frisian Solar Challenge is an international racing event for boats driven by solar energy. The participating boats race in six days on a route touching all 11 cities of the province of Fryslân, starting and finishing in the capital of Leeuwarden.

(Continued)

(Continued)

Almost 50 international teams participate every year. They compete in three classes: one sailor, a two-sailor team and an elite class. The event offers a stage on which innovative technology can present itself to a large public in a safe, pleasant and naturally beautiful environment. In this way the Frisian Solar Challenge hopes to support the development of solar energy and to stimulate its use. A second aim of this event is to promote the province of Fryslân not only as a tourism destination for water sport lovers, but also as an innovative and entrepreneurial region.

 Box 10. 1   Critical Thinking Exercise

How does the Frisian Solar Challenge exemplify the principles of sustainable development?

Sustainability Guidelines for Events

Already from the examples briefly described above, it is clear that the word 'event' covers very different activities. Indeed, events differ greatly. Common classifications distinguish events by size and content. In size, events vary from a wedding involving only the families of bride and groom – to local events involving a community, such as Easter processions in many Catholic communities – to hallmark events that become synonymous with the city hosting them, such as the Salone del Gusto in Turin – to mega-events such as the Olympics – which affect whole economies and command global media coverage. Content wise, events can be distinguished as either cultural, business or sporting events (Bowdin et al., 2006).

This diversity is reflected in the impacts that specific events have on people, planet and profit. It therefore follows that different events will require specific sustainability indicators and guidelines. However, there are some general issues that apply to the majority of events and should therefore be of concern to every event organizer. These include transport, energy and water use, water and sewage, food consumption, accommodation and communication with the attendees. Before going into more detail, it is important to remember that the challenge is to integrate the well-known economic measures with indicators on environmental quality and social development. In this respect the event industry is in the same predicament as other businesses that embraced sustainability before it and can learn from their efforts. Accordingly Getz (2007), for example, proposed an examination of the efforts of the tourism industry, one of the first movers in sustainability.

Several checklists have been published, such as the 'Greening your event checklist' developed by the New Zealand Government that, despite the name, does not only focus on the natural environment but also considers the need to involve and educate the public (Sustainability.gov.nz, 2011).

Secondly, guidelines for specific events have been developed. The Hannover Principles have been briefly addressed above. A similar initiative is the Sustainable Exhibition Industry Project [SEXI] promoted by Midlands Environmental Business Company in 2002. The project primarily addresses the waste issue, a most pressing problem for an industry that due to 'time pressures, contractual relationships, extremely tight margins and need for the "WOW" factor results in some difficult, possibly unique, waste management problem issues'(Laybourn, 2002: 2). Estimated waste from UK exhibitions is 60,000 tonnes per annum (Laybourn, 2002: 12), making reducing waste indeed a good stepping stone to confront the event industry with sustainability issues. Moreover waste-reduction measures, like r educing consumption of energy and water, also makes perfect business sense (Schmidheiny, 1992).

Eco-efficiency is thus a smart thing to do, in all events and not only for exhibitions. Yet, as it was repeatedly observed, environmental quality is only one of the aims of sustainability – social and economic impacts should be considered, too. Efforts at setting guidelines to manage sustainability in events in its entirety have also been attempted. In November 2007, the British Standard Group (BSI) published BS8901, a general standard for sustainable events management that addresses all dimensions of sustainability. London's 2012 Olympic and Paralympic Games was a major driver in the development of BS8901. Following the Denim cycle common to similar environmental standards, such as ISO 14000 on environmental management, BS8901 insists on the need to start from the planning phase, so that sustainability principles are embedded in the policy and relevant impacts are established from the beginning. BS8901 was revised and re-issued in September 2009 (BSI, 2010) and became the starting point for the draft of international standards for Sustainability in Event Management (ISO 20121).

The G3 guidelines ('G3' indicates the version Guideline No. 3) by the Global Reporting Initiative (GRI) also include standards for sustainability reporting on an international level. The guide encompasses 79 key performance indicators addressing the economic, environmental and social performance of the organization with 50 considered as core to most stakeholders (GRI, 2006, 2007, 2010; Sherman, 2009). For event organizers, a separate supplement is under development which addresses the demands of event stakeholders such as industry associations, journalists, local authorities, investors and visitors on the sustainability credentials of the events they attend (GRI, 2010). The new event guidelines, independent of the GRI Working Group, has been adopted by the Austrian and the Swiss government (who hosted the European Soccer Championships 2008), Live Earth, WWF, the Organizing Committee of the Vancouver 2010 Olympics and the Organizing Committee of the London 2012 Olympics. Indubitably the latter plays an important role within the UK in regards to implementing sustainability in the event industry.

In concluding this discussion, it is important to stress that event impacts are both negative and positive in nature. It is also essential to consider that these impacts will accrue directly and/or indirectly, willingly and/or unwillingly to all stakeholders, including the host community and natural environment (Maas, 2009). In this respect, a good summary of the main issues to be considered by event organizers is offered by Musgrave and Raj (see Figure 10.1 below). These issues are also discussed in Case Study 10.2.

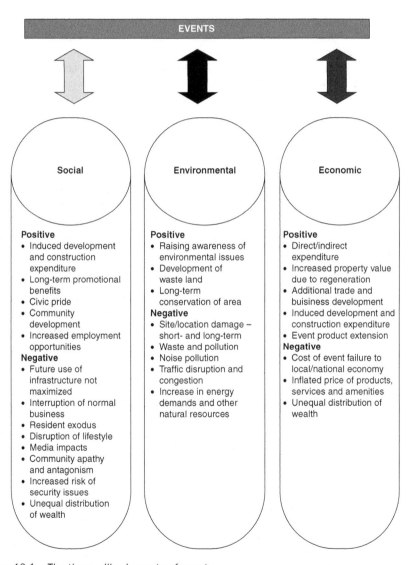

Figure 10.1   *The three pillar impacts of events*

Source: Musgrave and Raj (2009: 5)

Case Study 10.2   Oerol Festival

Each year in June, the West Frisian island of Terschelling (in the Netherlands) is the setting for the summer festival Oerol. The festival lasts for ten days and is focused on live public location theatre, music, visual arts and installations. As its name suggests (Oerol means 'everywhere'), the festival uses the entire island as its stage and source of inspiration, including for instance the beaches, the woods, the dunes and fields. A close relationship between Oerol and Staadsbosbeheer – a governmental organization in charge of natural parks and reserves in the Netherlands – assures a respectful use of the natural environment. Yet, it is not only the landscape that acts as a performance space. Man-made artefacts like farm sheds, boathouses and army bunkers are used for the acts and shows as well. Culture, nature and experiment go hand in hand.

Since launching in 1982 the festival has grown into a leading and internationally renowned multidisciplinary festival. Each year the festival is visited by more than 55,000 culture lovers. They are brought to the island by ferry and proceed further by bike or bus: no visitor vehicles are allowed on the island.

The festival is famous for its unique and innovative programming every year, which is focused around a specific theme inspired by the natural conditions and the special atmosphere on an island. For the residents and entrepreneurs the festival means hard work, day and night. However, a large part of the summer turnover on the island is earned in these ten days! The festival is important for the island economically, it involves large parts of the community and operates in harmony with nature. Thus it can be regarded as a good illustration of an event that is sustainable. However, a balance between the economic, social and environmental values needs to be maintained. In the past few years there have been criticisms about the increasing crowding on the island during the festival.

 Box 10.2   Critical Thinking Exercise

How can the organizers of Oerol festival maintain a good balance between economic, social and environmental values?

Is there a Market out there for Sustainable Events?

In December 2010 *The Guardian,* citing the annual Co-operative Bank's Ethical Consumerism Report, reported an 18 per cent increase in spending on green goods by UK consumers in 2009 compared to 2007. The report, which has been compiled since 1999, comprises expenditure figures on goods and services in the areas of ethical food and drinks, green homes, eco-travel and transport, ethical personal products, community and finances. While some areas show a more positive development than others, the sales figures however show a continuing positive trend when it comes to ethical or sustainable consumption – even in difficult economic times.

So far, consumer behaviour analyses have not included event-related consumerism. The omission therefore may give rise to the question as to whether people consider 'greener' or more environment–friendly options when it comes to attending an event. In other words: is there a market out there for sustainable events?

In research conducted in 2010, the authors explored answers to this question focusing on the UK market. The first step in the research was to measure the general environmental attitudes of events customers and their awareness of the environmental and social impacts of events. This has been done by adapting one of the most commonly used scales to evaluate environmental orientation, attitudes and behaviour – the revised New Environmental Paradigm or NEP (Dunlap, 2008; Dunlap and van Liere, 1978; Dunlap et al., 2000). Results show that while the vast majority of respondents (88.1 per cent) scored relatively moderate on general pro-environmental orientation, about the same number of respondents (87.9 per cent) scored relatively high in terms of awareness of event-related sustainability issues. These figures show that, even without being environmentalists themselves, people are aware that events do have environmental and social impacts. More specifically, they are quite sensitive to issues regarding waste, water and energy consumption, transportation and food consumption.

The big surprise? People want to know what is going on behind the scenes. On the question of whether they were willing to be informed about the environmental impact of the events they were visiting, the majority of respondents answered positively. Interestingly, respondents prefer information on what has been done to reduce the impact (for example, how much energy has been saved) above information on what the impacts are (for example, how much energy is consumed). The positive attitude by the majority of respondents about receiving information is significant because information is a first step in a chain, leading to the involvement of visitors and clients in enhancing the sustainability of events.

Additionally, about 70 per cent of respondents confirmed their willingness to actively contribute to reduce the impacts caused by the events they are visiting. Only 13 per cent did not want to get personally involved, while 16 per cent were unsure. Moreover sharing information on achieved impact reductions strongly enhanced the willingness of event attendees to contribute to sustainability efforts, whilst only giving information on how great (or minimal) the impact of the event is does not seem to have any influence on the willingness of the event visitor to join the effort towards sustainability. In this sense, visitors seem to be led by the example set by the organizer.

Several options for reducing impacts were offered to the respondents to choose from. Among the most popular selections were paperless promotion, correspondence and ticketing; changing from individual to shared and public transportation; and travelling by train instead of plane whenever possible. Of course, the choice to use public transport instead of their own car might also be influenced by other motives other than contributing to a more sustainable event. It may, for example, be the cheapest option. However, it is important to note that the attendees' willingness to participate in sustainability initiatives is essential to achieving sustainable events, alongside the efforts and contributions made by the organizer. In this sense, it is encouraging that a large majority of respondents – when properly solicited – were willingly to cooperate.

A further encouraging fact for everyone involved in planning, organizing and hosting sustainable events is that results show that efforts made towards a more sustainable approach will pay off in a higher level of satisfaction amongst visitors. In the research described here, satisfaction was measured by describing two scenarios for a congress event, where five aspects were examined in terms of sustainability. These five aspects were chosen from the event visitor's perspective and therefore included only areas that are visible and easily understandable for an event visitor. These areas were: promotions; invitation and ticketing procedure; offered transportation choices; food and beverages offered during the event; and the way additional information was distributed. Even though using scenarios as a research method has its limitations, the responses were so clearly skewed in favour of more sustainable events that the conclusion seems unavoidable. Attendees' satisfaction is indeed positively affected by sustainable choices (53 per cent vs. 81 per cent satisfied customers). In particular, respondents were satisfied with good connections to public transport and the offer of organic, fair-trade and locally produced food. The online distribution of event-related information packs rather than handed-out brochures also contributes to a higher average level of satisfaction.

To summarize, the research conducted showed that a vast majority of event visitors do have a high level of awareness about event (environmental) impacts. It also shows that a majority of them are willing to be informed about these impacts and that two out of three visitors do not exclude themselves from the responsibility of reducing impacts when they know that action has already been taken by the organizers. Moreover, respondents' satisfaction is significantly higher when they are asked to imagine themselves visiting an event that has clear sustainability policies as compared to one that does not. Thus it is clear that event sustainability is not just the obligation of the event organizer and his/her sub-contractors throughout the supply chain – it also involves the consumer. Additionally, rather than trying to shield attendees from their responsibility in making events sustainable, event organizers should ask for their cooperation as such action enhances the satisfaction of the attendee with an event. In short, there is definitely a market out there for sustainable events.

Case Study 10.3   Greening the Olympic Games

Though sustainability requires that positive impacts are achieved both on the people (social) and the planet (environmental) dimension, the main focus of many sustainability initiatives is on lessening the impact on the natural environment.

(Continued)

(Continued)

The event industry makes no exception. Lesjo (2000) analysed the first 'green' winter games in Lillehammer 1994. Even though the concept of 'Green Games' was not included in the original bidding requirements, disputes with environmental groups emerged in the planning process about the future of the Lillehammer region. Plans were changed and new policies introduced to develop an environment-friendly agenda based on four pillars of action: minimizing the use of natural material; conserving energy in heating and cooling systems; developing a recycling scheme for the winter games region; and avoiding 'visual pollution' by appropriately imbedding all facilities in the surrounding landscape.

Since Lillehammer major steps have been taken to maintain a 'green' image for both the summer and winter Olympic Games. Beijing 2008 and Vancouver 2010 have strengthened the focus on the environment, while the upcoming 2012 London Olympic Games are designed to be the most sustainable games to date. Non-Governmental Organizations (NGOs) were involved from the beginning, as *Towards a One Planet 2012*, the sustainability master plan for London 2012, testifies: it is based on the initiative *One Planet Living* by the World Wildlife Fund (WWF) and BioRegional (LOCOG, 2009a). The plan addresses five key themes: minimizing negative impacts such as greenhouse gas emissions; reducing waste throughout the project; reducing negative impact on wildlife and their habitats; enhancing positive impacts, such as promotion of diversity, creation of new employment and business opportunities; inspiring residents of the United Kingdom to take up physical activity and maintain a healthy lifestyle. This attempt at integration of the three dimensions of CSR (people, planet and profit) is also visible in other guidelines that have been published to support the organizer's aims. *The Sustainability Sourcing Code*, for example, explains strategies in procurement and unites 'internationally acceptable environmental, social and ethical guidelines and standards' for the event organizers' (LOCOG) internal buyers as well as for their suppliers and licensees (LOCOG, 2009b). As monitoring, evaluating and reporting are paramount in the process of sustainable events management, the Commission for a Sustainable London 2012 has been set up as an independent body to fulfil this role.

Case Study Questions

1 Would you consider the 2012 London Olympic and Paralympic Games 'sustainable'? Justify your answer.
2 Which environmental, social and economic issues should be considered in planning the 2016 Olympic and Paralympic Games in Rio?
3 Look at the lists of issues from question 2 above. How would you suggest measuring the impact of the Olympic and Paralympic Games on these issues?
4 Look again at your list of issues from question 2 above. How could positive impacts be maximized and negative impacts minimized?

Chapter Summary

Though the event industry has joined the sustainability challenge only in the last few years, progress has been swift and is still accelerating. In light of this, the coming years are going to be crucial. The sensibility of the market, already present in economically difficult times, will in all probability only be enhanced by these developments. Sustainability offers therefore not only a challenge to the event industry but also an opportunity to be seized with both hands.

Review Questions

1 What is the relevance of CSR and sustainable development for the event industry?
2 Which are the main indicators for sustainable events?
3 Which arguments could you put forward to convince the government officials in your city, or the manager of the event company you are working for, to organize sustainable events?
4 Imagine you are involved in a heated debate with someone who is very sceptical about sustainability and sustainable events. Identify at least three arguments you could use to convince this person to alter his/her position.
5 Using an event that has been recently organized in your home country as an example, critically evaluate whether you feel it was a sustainable event or not.

Additional Resources

Books, book chapters and journal articles

Dredge, D. and Whitford, M. (2010) 'Policy for sustainable and responsible festivals and events: Institutionalisation of a new paradigm – a response', *Journal of Policy Research in Tourism, Leisure and Events*, 2(1): 1–13.
This article takes a broad agenda on events policy research that embraces a wider range of epistemologies, ontologies and methodologies.

Freeman, R.E. (2008) 'Managing for stakeholders', in T.L. Beauchamp, N. Bowie and D. Arnold (eds), *Ethical Theory and Business* (8th edn). Englewood Cliffs, NJ: Prentice Hall. pp. 56–68.
A useful guide to involving stakeholders in ethical business operations.

Getz, D. (2009) 'Policy for sustainable and responsible festivals and events: Institutionalization of a new paradigm', *Journal of Policy Research in Tourism, Leisure and Events*, 1(1): 61–78.
Provides specific advice on what is needed to embed the new sustainable and responsible events paradigm in public policy.

Laing, J. and Frost, W. (2010) 'How green was my festival: Exploring challenges and opportunities associated with staging green events', *International Journal of Hospitality Management*, 29(2): 261–267.

Considers some of the challenges involved in incorporating green messages into an event theme.

McDonough, W. and Braungart, M. (2002) *Cradle to Cradle: Remaking the Way We Make Things.* New York: North Point Press.

A manifesto for a radically different philosophy and practice of manufacture and environmentalism.

Useful websites

http://www.defra.gov.uk/sustainable/government/
The Department for Environment, Food and Rural Affairs of the UK Government is deeply involved with sustainability issues, also concerning events.

http://www.eventsustainability.co.uk/pages/index.php
The objective of this website is to share resources, tools and ideas with the aim of increasing the positive impact events have on our economy, society and environment.

http://www.sustainable.org/
A website originally developed in the 1990s in the United States by the Sustainable Communities Network which hosts information on sustainability, including advice and further resources on how to plan a sustainable event.

References

Bowdin, G.A.J., Allen, J., O'Toole, W., Harris, R. and McDonnell, I. (2006) *Events Management* (2nd edn). Oxford: Butterworth-Heinemann/Elsevier.

British Standards Institution (BSI) (2010) *BSI 9801 – Sustainable Event Management Systems for Events.* British Standards Institution [Online]. Available from: http://www.bsigroup. com/en/BSI-UK/Assessment-and-Certification-services/Management-systems/Standards-and-Schemes/BS-8901/?sb=1.

Carroll, A.B. (1991) 'The pyramid of corporate social responsibility: Toward the moral management of organizational stakeholders', *Business Horizons*, 34(4): 39–48.

Dávid, L. (2009) 'Environmental impacts of events', in R. Raj and J. Musgrave (eds), *Event Management and Sustainability.* Oxfordshire: CAB International. pp. 67–75.

Dunlap, R.E. (2008) 'The new environmental paradigm scale: From marginality to worldwide use', *Journal of Environmental Education*, 40(1): 3–18.

Dunlap, R.E. and van Liere, K. (1978) 'The new environmental paradigm – a proposed measuring instrument and preliminary results', *Journal of Environmental Education*, 9(1): 10–19.

Dunlap, R.E., van Liere, K., Mertig, A.G. and Jones, R.E. (2000) 'Measuring endorsement of the new ecological paradigm: A revised NEP Scale', *Journal of Social Issues*, 56(3): 425–442.

Edwards, A.R. (2005) *The Sustainability Revolution: Portrait of a Paradigm Shift.* Gabriola Island, Canada: New Society Publishers.

Elkington, J. (1997) *Cannibals with Forks: The Triple Bottom Line of 21st Century Business.* Oxford: Capstone.

EU (1992) *Treaty on European Union. Official Journal C 191.* EU [Online]. Available from: http://eur-lex.europa.eu/en/treaties/dat/11992M/htm/11992M.html.

Getz, D. (2007) *Event Studies: Theory, Research and Policy for Planned Events.* Oxford: Butterworth-Heinemann/Elsevier.

Global Reporting Initiative (GRI) (2006) *Sustainability Reporting G3 Guidelines.* GRI [Online]. Available from: http://www.globalreporting.org/NR/rdonlyres/ED9E9B36-AB54-4DE1-BFF2-5F735235CA44/0/G3_GuidelinesENU.pdf.

Global Reporting Initiative (GRI) (2007) *Making the Switch.* GRI [Online]. Available from: http://www.globalreporting.org/NR/rdonlyres/D8AD5DDE-546A-4D5D-9617-20C75B242AAC/450/MakingtheSwitch.pdf.

Global Reporting Initiative (GRI) (2010) *Sector Supplement for Event Organizers.* GRI [Online]. Available from: http://www.globalreporting.org/ReportingFramework/SectorSupplements/Events/.

Idowu, S.O. and Towler, B.A. (2004) 'A comparative study of the contents of corporate social responsibility reports of UK companies', *Management of Environmental Quality,* 15(4): 420–437.

Jackson, T. (2005) *Motivating Sustainable Consumption: A Review of Evidence on Consumer Behaviour and Behavioural Change.* London: Policy Studies Institute.

Jamali, D. (2006) 'Insights into triple bottom line integration from a learning organization perspective.', *Business Process Management Journal,* 12(6): 809–821.

Jones, P., Comfort, D. and Hillier, D. (2005) 'Corporate social responsibility and the UK top ten retailers', *International Journal of Retail and Distribution Management,* 33(12): 882–892.

Laybourn, P. (2002) *Sustainable Exhibition Industry Project: A Waste Focused First Step Towards Sustainable Development by the UK's Exhibition Industry.* Birmingham: Midlands Environmental Business Club Ltd [Online]. Available from: http://www.mebconline.com/Portals/0/PDF/Sexi.pdf.

Lesjo, J. (2000) 'Lillehammer 1994: Planning, figuration and the green Winter Games', *International Review for the Sociology of Sport,* 35(3): 282–293.

London Organising Committee of the Olympic Games and Paralympic Games (LOCOG) (2009a) *Towards a One Planet 2010: London 2012 Sustainability Plan* (2nd edn). London: LOCOG [Online]. Available from: http://www.london2012.com/documents/locog-publications/london-2012-sustainability-plan.pdf.

London Organising Committee of the Olympic Games and Paralympic Games (LOCOG) (2009b) *LOCOG Sustainable Sourcing Code* (2nd edn). London: LOCOG [Online]. Available from: http://www.london2012.com/documents/locog-publications/sustainable-sourcing-code.pdf.

Maas, K. (2009) *Corporate Social Performance: From Output Measurement to Impact Measurement* (Doctoral Thesis). Rotterdam: Erasmus University Rotterdam [Online]. Available from: http://repub.eur.nl/res/pub/17627/EPS2009182STR9058922250Maas.pdf.

McDonough, W. and Partners (1992) *The Hannover Principles: Design for Sustainability*. Charlottesville: William McDonough Architect [Online]. Available from: http://www. mcdonough.com/principles.pdf.

Musgrave, J. and Raj, R. (2009) 'Introduction to a conceptual framework for sustainable events', in R. Raj and J. Musgrave (eds), *Event Management and Sustainability*. Oxford: CAB International. pp. 1–12.

Schmidheiny, S. (1992) *Changing Course*. Cambridge: MIT Press.

Sherman, W.R. (2009) *Making Triple Bottom Line Reporting Comparable: Adoption of the GRI G3 Framework*. Conference paper for 2009 Oxford Business and Economics Conference (OBEC) [Online]. Available from: http://www.gcbe.us/2009_OBEC/data/W.Richard Sherman.doc.

Smith-Christensen, C. (2009) 'Sustainability as a concept within events', in R. Raj and J. Musgrave (eds), *Event Management and Sustainability*. Oxford: CAB International. pp. 22–31.

Sutton, P.W. (2007) *The Environment: A Sociological Introduction*. Cambridge: Polity Press.

UN (1992) *Agenda 21* [Online]. Available from: http://www.un.org /esa/sustdev/documents/ agenda21/english/agenda21toc.htm.

World Business Council for Sustainable Development (WBCSD) (2000) *Eco-Efficiency: More Value with Less Impact*. Geneva: WBCSD.

World Commission on Environment and Development (1987) *Our Common Future (Brundtland Report)*. Oxford: Oxford University Press.

11

Ambush Marketing: Innovative or Immoral?

Marc Mazodier

Learning Objectives

By reading this chapter students should be able to:

- Distinguish between sponsorship, ambush marketing, incidental ambush and other communication tools.
- Understand the benefits of ambush marketing.
- List various ambush marketing strategies.
- Develop strategies to prevent ambush marketing opportunities and enhance event–sponsor partnership.

Introduction

The managers of major brands are competing to secure highly prized and very expensive rights to sponsor events, motivated by the belief that association with the event will favourably impact on the audience's recall, preference and behaviour. However, other brand managers – and those that missed out – may be tempted to stand in the wings and try and achieve similar beneficial effects without the requisite investments. Labelled 'ambush marketers' and hounded both by event organizers and their army of legal counsels, these mavericks aspire to associate their brands with an event through the use of related imagery, heavy advertising around the site or intense presence around the broadcast of the event, and other media-related tactics.

Ambush marketers are often competitors trying to negate any competitive advantage gained by sponsors from their association with an event, activity, sport or athlete. Several studies have observed public confusion as to which firms are official sponsors and which firms are ambushers (Quester, 1997; Sandler and Shani, 1989). Ambush marketing represents one of the biggest threats to the future of major sport events because they strike at the heart of the deals that finance them. If official sponsors cannot enjoy the exclusive rights they have paid for, there is no reason for them to continue supporting an event. Thus, sponsors of the 2006 FIFA World Cup in Germany demanded that sponsorship fees be reduced after several ambush marketing operations. This is also why IOC Marketing Commission Chief Gerhard Heiberd told Reuters (18 January 2008): 'We have taken this issue very seriously. These tactics cut to the heart of the commercial viability of the Games, and represent one of the biggest threats. Without guaranteeing exclusivity, it is harder to play competitive sponsors off against each other.' Therefore, sponsors and event organizers must fight against these competitors in order to defend and maintain these advantages. Several strategies to prevent ambush marketing are detailed in this chapter.

The Development of Ambush Marketing

Associating a brand with an event through sponsorship is a major brand leveraging tool (Keller, 2003) since it improves brand awareness, brand image and brand loyalty (see Cornwell, 2008 for an extended literature review). Leveraging a brand through associations allows the transference of desirable meanings to consumers in order to develop brand knowledge (Keller, 2003). Pairing a brand with positive affective stimuli such as an event may also improve brand attitude through indirect and direct affective response (Sweldens et al., 2010). Competition is fierce for sponsorship rights for high-profile events like the Olympic Games or the FIFA World Cup. Consequently, high fees and limited access have encouraged certain firms to use an alternative strategy: ambush marketing.

Ambush marketing refers to any form of communication around an event that uses its characteristic signs and symbols to mislead spectators by implying the brand is an official sponsor, in order to improve the ambusher's brand image. For example, during the Sydney 2000 Olympic and Paralympic Games, Qantas Airways featured two Australian athletes who were competing in the games and words such as 'Sydney 2000' or 'Olympic' in advertisements, even though the brand was not an official sponsor. Several factors have contributed to the growth of ambush marketing:

- *The rising place of sport events in our society.* Around the world, developed countries are increasing their spending on international spectator sports. People also have growing emotional connections to sport events that elicit passion and commitment. Therefore, sport events are more and more attractive for brands.
- *The effectiveness of sponsorship.* Many studies have shown the positive impact of sponsorship on brand awareness, brand image, brand loyalty and purchase intent. Sponsorship has become a convincing communication tool to leverage a brand.
- *The limited sponsorship opportunities for major events.* Most brands seek to be associated with global events with distinctive and relevant values. However, events of this kind are not numerous and the organizations in charge of these events tend to limit the number of partners to enhance the visibility of the sponsors. As a result, it is very hard to sponsor one of the major events.
- *High sponsorship fees.* The increasing number of companies willing to sponsor the major events has increased the cost of sponsoring one of these events. Thus, most companies cannot afford to pay the fee to sponsor a major event like the Olympic Games.

- *Multiple entities being involved in the staging of a single sporting event.* Sport events are convenient for ambush marketing because many stakeholders are involved in a sport event: sports federations or leagues, individual countries or teams, individual athletes, the media, the merchandise licensees with authorization to produce books, videos, recordings, tokens, etc. Each of these entities has the right to sell sponsorship. This makes it almost inevitable that there will be some confusion about the identities of the official sponsors.
- *An increase in the number of event broadcasters.* Several TV channels around the world broadcast major events. It is very complex to control every communication made around the event's broadcasting in every country. It has become almost impossible since a growing number of people watch the games on the internet. The number of authorized and unauthorized websites broadcasting sport events is almost infinite.

Ambush Marketing Definitions

A review of the literature suggests that ambush marketing is a field of activity that is difficult to define. Table 11.1 summarizes the different definitions found in the literature. The goal of the ambusher is to hijack the intrinsic values of an event and take advantage, for the least possible cost, of the interest it solicits in audiences and, finally, to improve its reputation and transfer the positive aspects of the event to its brand. As has been suggested (Sandler and Shani, 1989: 11), ambush marketing is 'a planned effort by an organization to associate themselves indirectly with an event in order to gain at least some of the recognition and benefits that are associated with being a sponsor'. Typically, the ambusher is not only seeking to create confusion, but also to make the consumer believe his/her organization is the real sponsor. However, being identified as a sponsor is not sufficient to qualify a firm as an ambusher. The ambusher must actively seek to mislead the public. As we can see in Table 11.1, the notion of deception is included in the definitions proposed by McKelvey (1994), Farrelly et al. (2005) and Walliser (2006).

However, while it is true that the ambusher does not pay sponsorship fees to the organizer, he must still invest heavily in implying his association with the event to reap the benefits of positive attitudes generated by sponsorship. It is exaggerated and incorrect to say that the ambusher takes advantage of the event 'for free' (French Olympic Committee, 2006).

The ambusher relies on several elements that characterize the event in his advertising campaigns in order to associate his brand implicitly with it. He can, for example, try to create an association with promoters or other parties involved in the event, use different symbols associated with a sponsored activity (playing field, ball, etc.) or the place where it is held (caricatures of the population, monuments, names of cities or countries, etc.) and even capitalize on other non-protected symbols associated with the event (similar generic names, colours, etc.).

Brands that buy advertising space around major events are not necessarily ambushers. They may simply want to take advantage of large audiences and potential media exposure. For example, the Nike Joga Bonito campaign, where the consumer saw soccer champions playing in everyday situations, insinuated that Nike was an official sponsor of the 2006 FIFA World Cup Germany but the Joga Bonito campaign is not a case of ambush marketing. On the other hand, Puma's campaign in France, with a

Table 11.1 *Definitions of ambush marketing*

Authors (year)	Proposed definition
Sandler and Shani (1989)	Ambush marketing is 'a planned effort by an organization to associate itself indirectly with an event in order to gain at least some of the recognition and benefits that are associated with being an official sponsor'.
Meenaghan (1994)	Ambush marketing is 'the practice whereby another company, often a competitor, intrudes upon public attention surrounding the event, thereby deflecting attention toward themselves and away from the sponsor'.
McKelvey (1994) cited in Meenaghan (1998)	Ambush marketing is 'a company's intentional effort to weaken or ambush its competitor's official sponsorship. It does this by engaging in promotions or advertising [...] to confuse the buying public as to which company really holds the official sponsorship rights'.
Fuchs (2003)	Ambush marketing is 'a technique where an advertiser – not accredited by the organizers of an event – tries to deflect public attention surrounding an event to his advantage, using marketing techniques, in order to gain some of the benefits associated with sponsorship'.
Farrelly et al. (2005)	Olympic ambushers are 'direct competitors striving to catch an illicit ride on the Olympic wave by deceiving or confusing consumers into believing they too are official sponsors'.
CNOSF (2006)	Ambush marketing is 'a set of behaviors by which an economic agent lurks in the wake of another in order to take advantage, free of charge, of his efforts and skills'.
Walliser (2006)	'Ambush marketing can be defined as a technique where an advertiser who does not hold official sponsorship rights, notably for an event, tries to make the public believe the contrary.'
VANOC (2009)	Ambush marketing 'capitalizes on the goodwill of the Olympic Movement by creating a false, unauthorized association with the Olympic movement, the Olympic Games or Olympic athletes'.

former soccer star (Pelé) and the German slogan 'Willkommen zum Fussball' was clearly designed to associate the brand with the World Cup by using the host country's language in addition to soccer images.

In contrast, when firms devise a strategy to pose as a sponsor, by using event-related imagery, intense advertising around the site or within the broadcast of the event, they become intentional ambushers, or ambush marketers. Instances of ambush marketing have been reported in the literature for decades, ever since Sandler and Shani (1989) first reported such behaviour in relation to the Los Angeles 1984 Olympic and Paralympic Games. Heavy media scheduling and outdoor saturation at the event location are common clues of ambush activities; their common aim is the formation of the mistaken belief that the ambusher's brand is also associated with the event in some official capacity. Hence, the intention of ambush marketers is clearly to mislead audiences, although the deception is not in relation to any product attribute claim but more specifically about the status of the brand in relation to the event.

There is evidence that ambush marketing can work. During the Atlanta 1996 Olympic and Paralympic Games, for example, Pepsi Cola invested heavily in a French sport magazine, showing one of the French track-and-field stars with the following caption: 'Marie Jose Perec, official representative of a non-official drink at

Atlanta.' During the games, Coca Cola's recognition actually decreased while Pepsi Cola benefited, despite their refusal to pay the sponsorship rights (Tribou, 2002).

During the Beijing 2008 Olympic and Paralympic Games, a brand of dairy product, Mengniu, was able, through the use of sport-related imagery, to generate recognition scores amongst Chinese consumers that compared with those of the official sponsor Coca Cola. Mengniu was actually identified by nearly 30 per cent of the Chinese public as an official sponsor, while Coca-Cola was recognized as such by 40 per cent (Madden, 2007). Because consumers almost never identify ambushers as such (Meenaghan, 1998), they will frequently form the same positive attitude toward official and ambush sponsors. According to the stimulus generalization theory applied to consumer behaviour by Miaoulis and D'Amato (1978), consumers react similarly to stimuli that closely resemble known stimuli. Consequently the practice of ambush marketing affords many benefits.

Box 11.1   Benefits of Ambush Marketing

- Increased brand awareness of any advertising message, depending on the exposure repetition and length.
- Improved brand affect through two potential persuasion processes. If the brand is perceived as a sponsor, it may benefit from favourable affective response according to evaluative conditioning theory (Sweldens et al., 2010). If the brand is not associated with the event, the brand may benefit from mere-exposure (Zajonc, 1968) like in classical advertising. In this case, people may develop preference to ambushers merely because they are familiar with them.
- Transfer of positive values related to the event to the ambusher. This goal may be achieved only if the ambusher is identified as a sponsor. Additionally, some brands seek to be perceived as more 'rebel', 'smart' and 'cool', thanks to ambush marketing compared to the official sponsors.
- Increased purchase intent as a result of the aims detailed above.
- Weakened link between the sponsors and the event by creating confusion about sponsors' identity. However, this benefit is very small when compared to the ambush marketing cost.

Ambush marketing seems like an attractive, relatively cheaper alternative to sponsorship but to date there is no evidence to suggest that ambush marketing improves brand image by leveraging a brand or by any other persuasion process. Ambush marketing creates confusion in consumers' mind about sponsors' identity and creates brand awareness. Nevertheless past studies overestimate the impact of ambush marketing on sponsor recall because they don't take into account the source identification process and message misunderstanding. When the link between the sponsor and event has not been perfectly encoded by the individual, he tends to infer the sponsor's name based on several criteria: the perceived congruence between the brand and the event, the brand's prominence (Johar and Pham, 1999) and his familiarity with the brand (Hoek and Gendall, 2002). These inferences can explain how brands involuntarily find themselves in ambush situations called 'incidental ambush' (Quester, 1997), that is, they are identified as official sponsors without seeking to associate the brand with an event.

To summarize, ambush marketing can be distinguished from other marketing and communication strategies by the following characteristics:

- Unlike the case with sponsorship, there is no official agreement with the event, no possibilities to use protected imagery of the event and no opportunities to do public relations in the event's venue.
- In contrast to classic advertising, ambush marketing aims to mislead people by creating an implicit association with the event.

 Box 11.2   Critical Thinking Exercise

As an event attendee, how might you be able to spot ambush marketers? How would their communication strategies differ from the official sponsors at an event?

Ambush Marketing Taxonomies

Previous studies have identified a variety of approaches favoured by ambushers (Crompton, 2004; Fuchs, 2003; Meenaghan, 1996). First, the firm may wish to exploit an association with the event broadcaster in order to create in consumers the idea of a more formal sponsorship relationship. This may result, in some instances, in different brands 'proudly bringing' to audiences in different countries the same event, sponsored by yet another brand, that of the official sponsor! Second, the ambusher may aim to saturate the physical environment of the event, or any available advertising space around it. Although such space may be 'protected' from ambushers, there have been several famous instances where ambushers were able to display their brands next to the location of the event, as when Nike placed its famous logo on an adjacent building to the Atlanta Stadium. Third, the ambusher may seek a sponsorship association with a related property, in order to secure access to an event for which it is not entitled to claim sponsor status. For example, sponsoring athletes or teams may enable some firms to leverage this sponsorship in a way that suggests that they are also sponsoring the event (Fuchs, 2003). This was the approach adopted by Qantas at the Sydney 2000 Olympic and Paralympic Games when large posters appeared throughout the city, extolling the relationship between the airline and two of the star athletes of the Games, swimmer Ian Thorpe and track-and-field champion Cathy Freeman, who both went on to cover themselves (and their sponsor) with glory at the Games. Surprisingly, an ambusher may also associate its brand name with the venue where the event takes place. For instance, spectators from the Telstra Festival of the Arts, in Adelaide, Australia, attended the shows at the Optus Theatre. More subtle but equally harmful from the sponsor's point of view, a forth method entails the ambusher using symbols or themes, or even musical tunes in its advertising, typically used by the event. Such advertisements, by virtue of their resemblance to the sponsors' ads, have the potential to suggest sponsor status for the ambusher's brand. In a particular instance, Kendall and Curthoys (2001) reported that an ambusher in its advertising campaign used the hymn of the English Rugby team, 'Swing Low, Sweet Chariot', during the 1999 World Cup. Finally, the ambusher can aggressively create a competing and simultaneous event to coincide with and divert from the sponsored event. For example, a press conference with the Basket Ball 'Dream Team' was scheduled by Nike to coincide with the Barcelona 1992 Olympic and Paralympic Games, exploiting the media saturation at the event (Fuchs, 2003). Festivals or award ceremonies are other opportunities to organize counter attractions like femmescougar.com during the 2010 Cannes Festival.

It should be noted that these classifications are far from definitive because they identify some marketing practices as ambush marketing that companies may engage in whilst not necessarily wanting to be associated with a particular event and/or ambush that event's official sponsors. For example, a company buying advertising spaces around the venue or on television, may just intend to benefit from the massive audience the event attracts. Also, placing advertisements based on celebrity endorsement during the staging of a mega-event is fairly typical because the event is the best time to activate a long-term partnership with a star athlete endorser.

To qualify as ambush marketing, the marketing practices need to use event-related elements to mislead the public into thinking the organization or brand is associated with an event. The list of potential event-related elements is vast but the list below provides some of the more common ones.

Box 11.3   Event-related Elements Utilized by Ambush Marketers

- Event broadcasters.
- People related to the event (e.g. athletes, coach, team, retired athletes, dead athletes and commentators).
- Symbols of the activity (e.g. fields, balls, uniforms and tickets).
- Symbols of the place (e.g. arenas, cities, countries and monuments).
- Unprotected symbols of the event (e.g. colours, generic names, generic sentences, generic goods and congratulatory messages).

A brand manager interested in ambush marketing should know these potential opportunities and check for the event elements that are legally protected to avoid being prosecuted and eventually fined.

Strategies to Prevent Ambush Marketing

Ambush marketing activities and the public's confusion about sponsors' identities have led sponsors to question the value of their investment in sponsorship, and have also motivated them to seek protection against the actions of ambushers.

Major event organizers and leading sponsors have first concentrated on legal protection as a means of fending off ambushers, with mixed results. The organizers forbid any non-sponsor companies to use elements identifying their event, such as the name, catchphrases, slogan, logo, symbols, designs, images, colours, jingles, songs or a combination of these elements. For instance, the Vancouver Organizing Committee for the 2010 Winter Olympic Games (VANOC) protected the following event elements thanks to the 'Olympic and Paralympic Marks Act' – the slogan, 'Faster, higher, stronger' and the following words/word combinations:

- Canadian Olympic Committee
- International Olympic Committee
- Olympic
- Olympic Games
- 2010 Canada
- Vancouver Games
- Canada Games, 2010 Vancouver
- Vancouver Organizing Committee
- Canadian Organizing Committee

The Olympic and Paralympic Marks Act was enacted by the Government of Canada to ensure that Canada kept its commitment to the IOC concerning protection of the Olympic brand and that VANOC met its obligation to protect the exclusive rights it had granted to its marketing partners. This act even forbade associations being made with the words: medal, games, 2010, Vancouver, gold, silver, bronze. The events' organizers established a clean zone around the events' venue thanks to on-site policy ambush patrol, which prevented unauthorized communications by destroying any unlicensed messages found and covering up any logos found from non-sponsors. The events' organizers set up contractual prohibitions with the broadcasters, the athletes and the spectators to oblige them to promote sponsors' communications and limit other companies' communication. For instance, Olympic broadcasters had to give priority to sponsors for TV advertising around the Olympics' broadcast. Spectators could not wear clothes with large logos of sponsors' competitors or organize promotions inside the stadium for these competitors. The size of the logos on athletes' uniforms was also restricted. However, anti-ambushing legislation is clearly not enough to avoid ambushing attempts (McKelvey and Grady, 2008; Michaelis et al., 2008) as these attempts are becoming more and more subtle and rarely infringe on protected words, symbols or emblems. An event organization cannot protect every event-related element and it cannot control and avoid all possible ambush tactics. For instance, VANOC officials admitted that they did not have the resources to stop every instance of ambush marketing (Cooper, 2008). Moreover, event organizers and official sponsors are often reluctant to file a claim for fear of negative publicity (McKelvey and Grady, 2008) and also because courts of law rarely support such claims (Miller, 2008). Finally, legal redress is usually costly and time-consuming.

A longer-term strategy, as indicated by Farrelly et al. (2005), involves sponsors building leverage in such a way as to ensure appropriate and secure exclusive access to the potential of sponsorship. Hence, purchasing saturation broadcast coverage and investing heavily in advertising to activate sponsorship may create barriers ambushers simply cannot afford to circumvent. Sponsors should integrate sponsorship into the marketing mix, use the event's identifying elements on their packaging and organize related promotion campaigns and point-of-sale strategies. Sponsors should also build long-term relationships to increase their brand or organization's authenticity and legitimacy. In collaboration with the event, sponsors should organize related events for its target market (for example, consumers, prospects, retailers or employees). Event organizers should also make an effort to protect sponsors' exclusivity and visibility. Many of them already limit the number of sponsors at their events and have sought to improve trademark protection legislation. However, event organizers also need to enhance the distinctive meanings of their event by utilizing integrated marketing communications. Event organizers must maximize their brand positioning, that is, the event's offer and image, so that it occupies a distinct and valued place in the target market's minds and their brand identity, that is, the unique set of associations that the event aspires to create or maintain. These associations represent what the brand stands for and involve a promise to people from the brand. Brand positioning and identity should help to establish a relationship between the brand and the spectator by generating a value proposition involving functional, emotional or self-expressive benefits. This added value is what is sought by the sponsors.

However, given that audiences are clearly misled in their beliefs by ambushers, another strategy open to official sponsors or event organizers is to simply disclose the 'real' status of ambush marketers in order to regain official sponsors' goodwill, in what some scholars have described as 'name and shame' campaigns (Farrelly et al., 2005). In 1996, for instance, the Atlanta Committee for the Olympic Games published advertisements in *Fortune*, *Sports Illustrated* and *Time* magazines, as well as selected newspapers, 'labelling the ambusher as villain' (Meenaghan, 1996: 110). The IOC launched similar campaigns for the Beijing and Vancouver Olympics. According to Frédéric Quenet, Marketing Director for the French Olympic Committee, organizers of major events, such as the IOC or FIFA, have created 'ready-to-broadcast' press releases to publicly denounce ambushers. To date, however, the practice has not been systematic. Only the IOC decided to launch campaigns in daily newspapers during the Olympics. The following statement was published for the 2006 Torino Olympics with the core message: 'By using Olympic emblems or imagery without authorization, or by presenting themselves as having an official association with the Olympic Games, these companies undermine the future of the Olympic Games' (IOC statement, 2006).

More common disclosing ambush attempts are done through public relations activities such as press releases and press conferences with the goal that numerous news articles describing ambush practices and naming the ambushers will be published (Humphreys et al., 2010). As mentioned by Humphreys et al. (2010) this is the usual way consumers actually learn about ambushing attempts. This strategy leads us to the question of public reactions to ambush marketing. Few studies have examined the effects of ambush marketing disclosure and the only empirical research available, which relied on laboratory experiments, is that published by Humphreys et al.

OLYMPIC ATHLETES
PROVIDE THE EXCITEMENT.

OLYMPIC SPONSORS
PROVIDE THE SUPPORT.

TOGETHER, THEY PROVIDE
THE DREAM.

However, some companies will claim to be Olympic sponsors or create
the false impression that they are. Those that do are cheating the dream.
By using Olympic emblems or imagery without authorization, or by presenting themselves
as having an official association with the Olympic Games,
these companies undermine the future of the Olympic Games.

Only Official Olympic Sponsors have the right to use Olympic emblems
or imagery in their advertising. A right they have earned by providing the products,
services and financial support that help make the Olympic Games possible.

With the Torino 2006 Olympic Winter Games fast approaching, show your support
for companies that are Official Olympic Sponsors and Licensees. Thank you.

Worldwide Olympic Partners

Coca-Cola   Atos Origin   GE   Kodak   lenovo   Manulife   M   OMEGA   Panasonic   SAMSUNG   VISA

Partners in Sport van NOC*NSF en het Nederlands Olympisch Team

Unlimited. DSM   NS   Unilever   randstad   ERNST & YOUNG   Lotto.

Suppliers: ATP, ASICS, Coca Cola, Achmea, Volkswagen, Nashuatec, NOS, Perry Sport, P&O Nedlloyd, Pfizer, PIET ZOOMERS, Rabobank, Oxxio
www.olympic.org

Figure 11.1   *IOC statement of ambushing*

(2010). Interestingly, they found that counter-ambushing communications in the form of press releases, mentioning the name and practices of the ambusher, could have the unintended effect of creating or reinforcing a link between the ambusher and the event in memory. Their study, however, only concerns memory effects and they suggested further research needed to be done on attitudinal effects.

The IOC (1996) and Shani and Sandler (1998) report that Americans agreed mainly with sentences like 'the practice of associating with the Olympic Games without being an Official Sponsor is unethical'. According to Meenaghan (1998), ambush marketers are poorly perceived by audiences once they have been made aware of the distinction between sponsors and ambush marketers. Empirical data from a three-country study showed that more than 20 per cent of the respondents would be less likely to purchase products from companies that use an Olympic message without paying the rights fee (Séguin et al., 2005). Recently, Mazodier et al. (forthcoming) have shown that ambush disclosure negatively influences perceived integrity, affective response and purchase intentions for the ambusher. Ambushers must therefore bear in mind the risk of negative consumer attitudes if they are unmasked.

Box 11.4   Critical Thinking Exercise

Under what circumstances would the risks ambush marketers take be appropriate and justifiable?

The Olympic Committee was the first organization to develop an integrated strategy against ambush marketing. Frédéric Quénet, Marketing Head of the French Olympic Committee, shared the following with the author about its strategy (see Box 11.5).

Box 11.5   The Olympic Committee's Anti-Ambush Marketing Strategy

Protecting our sponsors from Ambush Marketing is one of our main concerns. The CNOSF and the IOC have dealt with this issue for many years. We first developed legal measures. Thus, we legally protect the Olympic flame, the Olympic rings and other Olympic symbols, and some phrases like 'faster, higher, stronger', or 'Olympic Games'. Even the association of the words 'medal' and 'games' is protected. We protect the Olympic venues and areas around the venues from any advertising made by companies other than the sponsors. By doing so, we intend to increase the visibility of the sponsors and to avoid confusion about the identity of the sponsors. Additionally, we have taken strategic decisions. We have limited the number of sponsors in order to enhance the partnership with the sponsors and to meet the sponsors' needs. We also inform companies and the public about Ambush Marketing. The IOC has published many statements throughout the world in several newspapers and magazines to disclose Ambush Marketing. We attempt to educate the public to allow them to distinguish sponsors and ambushers. We also organize press conferences to inform professionals and to dissuade them from Ambush Marketing. Moreover we remind the public as often as possible to support the sponsors to the Olympic Games and we promote their communications. For instance, they have priority in advertising on TV during the Olympics' broadcasting. Finally, we highlight the specific values of the Olympics in order to distinguish the Olympics from other events. We emphasize strong values like 'respect', 'fraternity' or 'performance'. Moreover, we think that the Olympics symbolizes the social values of sport. Sport can educate the youth and build relationships between people from different social classes. Sport is part of the movement towards sustainable development. Our sponsors have a growing interest in these social values. For this reason, in collaboration with the sponsors, we support several local associations, which promote sport activity or develop social integration through sport or other social projects.

Frédéric Quenet – Marketing Head, French Olympic Committee (CNSOF)

Case Study 11.1 Ambush Marketing: The 2010 FIFA World Cup South Africa

The FIFA World Cup is the biggest event in the world next to the Olympics. Soccer is an obsession for a lot of European, African and South American people. This tournament evokes strong emotions from the fans. The 19th FIFA World Cup was held in South Africa. According to FIFA officials, the 2010 World Cup symbolized values related to South Africa's recent history, such as unity, success and pride.

Soccer is truly a global sport because there are soccer fans on every continent. Thirty-two national teams competed for the title of the 2010 FIFA World Cup. Moreover, with the advent of global media outlets and especially the internet, it was easy to watch the World Cup anywhere in the world. The final between Spain and the Netherlands was expected to attract more than 700 million television viewers, according to the tournament's organizers. Additionally, FIFA officials expected to exceed a global cumulative audience of 26 billion people. For all of these reasons, many companies tried to associate their brand with the 2010 World Cup.

Several other firms built ambush marketing strategies despite two Acts in South Africa which have restrictions against ambush marketing: the Trade Practices Act, No. 76 of 1976 and the Merchandise Marks Act, No. 17 of 1941. These Acts made it unlawful for anyone to display any false or misleading communication which implies or suggests a connection with the 2010 FIFA World Cup South Africa. Moreover these restrictions also state that no person shall use a trademark in relation to the FIFA World Cup to derive special promotional benefit from the event, without the prior permission from FIFA. A contravention to these Acts constitutes a criminal offence which is punishable by a fine and/or imprisonment. Civil liability can also arise from a breach of these provisions.

Pepsi Cola, direct competitor of Coca-Cola, an official sponsor, is famous for ambush marketing. In the 2006 World Cup in Germany, Pepsi Cola released an African soccer-themed advertisement. The advertisement had been launched on Pepsi's YouTube channel. In the video summarized in Figure 11.2, several soccer players participating in the tournament (Drogba, Messi, Henry, Lampard ...) played against African locals. Hundreds of Africans formed a virtual playing field. Many elements depicted were closely associated with South Africa: the music, the people, the landscape. The video has been watched over 400,000 times. It is available at: http://corp.visiblemeasures.com/news-and-events/blog/bid/12069/Pepsi-s-World-Cup-Campaign-Infiltrates-Viral-Video-Chart.

Moreover Pepsi Cola has used this themed advertisement for outdoor and press advertising campaigns. Eleven per cent of French people thought at the end of the tournament that Pepsi was a sponsor of the 2010 FIFA World Cup South Africa (Kantar Media, 2010).

(Continued)

(Continued)

Figure 11.2   *Pepsi CO's Youtube ambush*

Ferrero, another known ambusher, has developed an integrated ambush marketing strategy. Ferrero formed a partnership with the German soccer federation

Figure 11.3   *Ferrero and football involvement*

(Continued)

(Continued)

in order to be able to use German national team players in its communications. Ferrero also formed a partnership with the German soccer magazine *Goal*. Additionally, the company invited customers to take part in football-themed activities to win prizes at airports in South Africa and Europe. Customers took penalty kicks for a chance to win discount vouchers valid for all Kinder's products. Most surprisingly, Ferrero was able to put 'WM 2010' on its packaging. 'WM' stands for World Cup in German.

During the Holland vs. Denmark World Cup game, 36 attractive, supposedly loyal Dutch beauties, decided to take off their clothes to reveal skimpy orange dresses looking suspiciously similar to the sales promotion items given away with purchases of Bavaria beer six-packs in Holland. These women were arrested in a soccer stadium and accused of being part of an ambush marketing campaign to promote a Dutch brewery – Bavaria (Anheuser Busch's Budweiser was the official beer for the tournament). Millions of people read about this news story in their favourite newspaper (for example, *The Guardian*, *The Telegraph* and *The New York Times*) or on a website (such as, wikipedia.org, soccernet.espn.go.com and reuters.com). Bavaria ran a great global communication campaign at the cost of a few flights and a couple of orange outfits. According to internet analysis company Experian, Bavaria's website in the UK (that previously enjoyed little traffic, if any) was catapulted overnight to the fifth most visited beer site in the country.

Puma developed a classic ambush marketing strategy with advertisements showing tournament players wearing the national team's jersey. In the

Figure 11.4   *Bavaria blondes at the 2010 World Cup*

(Continued)

(Continued)

background is a typical African landscape. More innovative, Puma created two viral videos capturing the World Cup from spectators' point of view, by bringing the famous 'Love = Football' Puma slogan to life. Both videos were anonymous and included no branding. However all the discussions online by journalists and commentators referred to Puma, therefore providing strong promotion for the brand. As a result, Puma was identified by 19.65 per cent of French people as a sponsor (Kantar Media, 2010).

Many other ambush marketing strategies took place during the tournament, such as an advertisement with the slogan 'Unofficial National Carrier of the You-know-what' from Kulala, a South-African low-cost flight company, an ad from M&Ms showing a stadium in Johannesburg and soccer balls, and a lollipop company Astor naming a product 2010 Pops with packaging showing the South African flag and a soccer ball. Kulala and Astor had to stop their marketing at FIFA's request.

Case Study Questions

1 Which of the ambush marketing strategies identified in the case study was the most effective?
2 Was FIFA's reaction to the 'Bavaria's babes' justified?
3 Which event elements used by the ambushers in this case could be legally protected for the next FIFA World Cup?

Chapter Summary

The literature on ambush marketing, while still scarce, has aimed to develop a definition for this practice. Common in all of the proposed definitions is the clear intent by ambushers to: (1) avoid the cost of sponsorship and (2) mislead consumers. Hence, in the context of this chapter, ambush marketing can be defined as 'the deliberate attempt, by a non-sponsor firm, to falsely suggest an association with an event, person or idea, for the purpose of deriving a commercial benefit from that association, without incurring the costs of the acquisition of sponsorship rights in relation to that event, person or idea'. An ambusher can use many event-related elements to be associated with an event by the public: broadcasters, people related to the event, symbols of the sport, symbols of the event's venue, and unprotected symbols of the event. If the ambusher is successful in deceiving the public, it may enjoy the positive attitudes and associations that are derived from sponsorship. The questionable ethics of the practice aside, ambush marketing can be an effective strategy to associate a brand with an event, especially for smaller companies unable to afford official sponsorship. Some consumers actually find ambush marketing 'smart' and 'interesting', when it is done by challengers (Mazodier, 2008). Some marketing managers are also convinced that ambush marketing is more profitable than sponsorship. For instance, Vincent Prolongeau, General Manager at PEPSICO France, stated: 'The era of official sponsors is over' (*La Tribune*, 26 March 2006). Nevertheless, to avoid overestimating ambush marketing's efficacy, a manager must be able to distinguish incidental ambush, that is, when a brand is identified as a sponsor by the public without communication related to the event.

Sponsors and event organizers have to work together to develop strategies to prevent ambush marketing practices, whether by legal means (for example, contractual restrictions, establishment of clean zones and enactment of trademark protection legislation) or by optimized sponsorship management. Sponsors and event organizers should reinforce the link between the sponsor and the event by increasing sponsors' visibility to improve the legitimacy of the association by building long-term and congruent partnership. Additionally, the practices of ambushers should be made known to the public.

Review Questions

1 Why has the practice of ambush marketing become so popular?
2 How would you distinguish intentional ambush marketing from incidental ambush marketing during an international event?
3 In order to develop an ambush marketing strategy for the next FIFA World Cup, outline a plan to identify the best opportunities.
4 When should a firm undertake ambush marketing instead of sponsorship?
5 How can ambush marketing be prevented?

Additional Resources

Books and journal articles

Humphreys, M.S., Cornwell, B.T., McAlister, A.R., Kelly, S.J., Quinn, E.A. and Murray, K.L. (2010) 'Sponsorship, ambushing, and counter-strategy: Effects upon memory for sponsor and event', *Journal of Applied Experiential Psychology*, 16(1): 96–108.
Explores the effectiveness of ambush marketing in attaining sponsorship objectives.

Kolah, A. (2002) *Essential Law for Marketers*. Oxford: Butterworth-Heinemann.
Offers clear and concise explanations of the laws that impact on the practice of marketing, advertising, sponsorship, design and public relations, providing expert guidance on crucial issues for the busy practitioner, including a chapter on ambush marketing.

Meenaghan, T. (1996) 'Ambush marketing: A threat to corporate sponsorship', *Sloan Management Review*, 38(1): 103–113.
Explores the ethics and legality of ambush marketing and also how this practice can be prevented.

Sandler, D.M. and Shani, D. (1989) 'Olympic sponsorship vs. ambush marketing: Who gets the gold?', *Journal of Advertising Research*, 29(4): 9–14.
Attempts to weigh up the relative benefits of sponsorship and ambush marketing.

Scaria, A.G. (2008) *Ambush Marketing: Game Within a Game*. Oxford: Oxford University Press.
Offers insights into possible solutions to the problem of ambush marketing and includes an extensive discussion on the significance of event-specific anti-ambush marketing legislation.

Useful websites

http://www.advertisingcompliancelaw.com/
Provides news and updates on the laws and regulations governing marketing – including the practice of ambush marketing.

http://www.sportbusiness.com/
Features articles, news and research on sport event marketing – in addition to stories on ambushers making the news.

http://www.sportsmanagement.co.uk/
Provides daily news and jobs in the sports industry.

References

Cooper, B. (2008) 'Balance of rights – Getting it right, part 1', *Journal of Sponsorship*, 2(1): 85–95.

Cornwell, T.B. (2008) 'State of the art and science in sponsorship-linked marketing', *Journal of Advertising*, 37: 41–55.

Crompton, J.L. (2004) 'Sponsorship ambushing in sport', *Managing Leisure*, 9: 1–12.

Farrelly, F.J., Quester, P.G. and Greyser, S.A. (2005) 'Defending the co-branding benefits of sponsorship B2B partnerships: The case of ambush marketing', *Journal of Advertising Research*, 45(3): 339–348.

French Olympic Committee (CNOSF) (2006) 'La protection des marques et du territoire Olympiques', *CNOSF Conference*, 24 January, Paris, France.

Fuchs, S. (2003) 'Le pseudo-parrainage: une autre façon de faire du parrainage?', *Décisions Marketing*, 30: 31–39.

Hoek, J. and Gendall, P. (2002) 'Ambush marketing: More than just a commercial irritant?', *Entertainment Law*, 1(2): 72–91.

Humphreys, M.S., Cornwell, B.T., McAlister, A.R., Kelly, S.J., Emerald, A.Q. and Murray, K.L. (2010) 'Sponsorship, ambushing, and counter-strategy: Effects upon memory for sponsor and event', *Journal of Experiential Psychology: Applied*, 16(1): 96–108.

International Olympic Committee (IOC) (1996) *Marketing Fact File 1996*. Lausanne: IOC.

Johar, G.V. and Pham, M.T. (1999) 'Relatedness, prominence and constructive sponsor iden-tification', *Journal of Marketing Research*, 36(3): 299–312.

Kantar Media (2010) 4 jours après la fin de la Coupe du Monde en Afrique du Sud, KantarSport dresse le bilan de la competition [Press release, 11 July]. Available from: http://www.slideshare.net/RPMaroc/communiqu-de-presse-bilan-de-la-coupe-du-monde-en-afrique-du-sud-sponsors-annonceurs.

Keller, K.L. (2003) 'Brand synthesis: The multidimensionality of brand knowledge', *Journal of Consumer Research*, 29(4): 595–600.

Kendall, C.N. and Curthoys, J. (2001) 'Ambush marketing and the Sydney 2000 Games (Indicia and Images) – Protection Act: A retrospective', *E Law*, 8(2).

Madden, N. (2007) 'Ambush marketing could hit new high at Beijing Olympics', *Advertising Age*, 23 July.

Mazodier, M. (2008) 'An exploratory study of public attitudes towards the ambush marketing disclosure', *Revue Européenne du Management du Sport*, 1–24.

Mazodier, M., Quester, P.G. and Chandon, J.–L. (forthcoming) 'Unmasking the ambushers: Empirical evidence and conceptual framework', *European Journal of Marketing*.

McKelvey, S. (1994) 'Sans legal restraint, no stopping brash, creative ambush marketers', *Brandweek*, 35(16): 20.

McKelvey, S. and Grady, J. (2008) 'Sponsorship program protection strategies for special sports events: Are event organizers outmanoeuvring ambush marketers?', *Journal of Sport Management*, 22: 550–586.

Meenaghan, T. (1994) 'Point of view: Ambush marketing: Immoral or imaginative practice', *Journal of Advertising Research*, 34: 77–88.

Meenaghan, T. (1996) 'Ambush marketing: A threat to corporate sponsorship', *Sloan Management Review*, 38(1): 103–113.

Meenaghan, T. (1998) 'Ambush marketing: Corporate strategy and consumer reaction', *Psychology and Marketing*, 15(4): 305–322.

Miaoulis, G. and D'Amato, N. (1978) 'Consumer confusion and trademark infringement', *Journal of Marketing*, 42(2): 48–55.

Michaelis, M., Woisetschläger, D.M. and Hartleb, V. (2008) 'An empirical comparison of ambushing and sponsorship effects: The case of 2006 FIFA World Cup Germany', *Advances in Consumer Research*, 35: 527–533.

Miller, R.V. (2008) *Miller's Annotated Trade Practices Act*. Sydney: Thompson.

Quester, P.G. (1997) 'Awareness as a measure of sponsorship effectiveness: The Adelaide Formula One Grand Prix and evidence of incidental ambush effects', *Journal of Marketing Communications*, 3(1): 1–20.

Sandler, D.M. and Shani, D. (1989) 'Olympic sponsorship vs. ambush marketing: Who gets the gold?', *Journal of Advertising Research*, 29(4): 9–14.

Séguin, B., Lyberger, M., O'Reilly, N. and McCarthy, L. (2005) 'Internationalising ambush marketing – a comparative study', *International Journal of Sports Marketing and Sponsorship*, 6(4): 216–230.

Shani, D. and Sandler, D.M. (1998) 'Ambush marketing: Is confusion to blame for the flicker-ing of the Flame?', *Psychology and Marketing*, 15(4): 367–383.

Sweldens, S., Van Osselaer, S.M.J. and Janiszewski, C. (2010) 'Evaluative conditioning procedures and the resilience of conditioned brand attitudes', *Journal of Consumer Research*, 37:
473–489.

Tribou, G. (2002) *Le sponsoring sportif*. Paris: Economica.

Vancouver Organizing Committee (VANOC) (2009) *The Importance of Protecting the Olympic Brand*.
VANOC [Online]. Available from: www.vancouver2010.com/en/LookVancouver2010/
ProtectingBrand.

Walliser, B. (2006) *Le parrainage – Sponsoring et Mécénat*. Paris: Dunod.

Zajonc, R.B. (1968) 'Attitudinal effects of mere exposure', *Journal of Personality and Social
Psychology*, 9: 1–27.

12

The Internationalization of Sport Events and Leagues

Paul J. Kitchin

Learning Objectives

By reading this chapter students should be able to:

- Understand the organizations involved in the management of international sports events and leagues.
- Explain trends in the development of international sports events and leagues.
- Understand the environmental factors driving the recent development of international sports events.
- Critique the possible market entry and expansion tactics for internationalizing sporting events.
- Gain insight into the manager's process of selecting suitable markets for event hosting.

Introduction

Pop-economist Steven Levitt and journalist Stephen Dubner, in their work *Freakonomics* (2005), explained that sports, along with music, movies and fashion is one of the glamour professions. With the opportunity for staff within the industry to partake in international travel, to work in a fast-paced, constantly changing work environment with pressurized deadlines, life working in the field of international sports events is definitely at the coal-face of events management. Nevertheless Emery (2010) highlights that behind the supposed glamour there is a complex side to sport event management that must be considered. This chapter reviews this area by examining the development of international sports events and leagues.

The initial global development of sport occurred throughout the nineteenth and early twentieth centuries as Christian Missionaries and European colonization spread sport across the globe (Thoma and Chalip, 1996). Some of these events can still be seen today, represented in practices such as the Summer and Winter Olympic and Paralympic Games, the FIFA World Cup and other significant sporting events. However, over the past two decades, there has been another phase of development in global sport. This has been fostered by political, economic, social and technological developments such as shrinking domestic markets in Western countries, an increasingly global workforce and the proliferation of satellite and internet telecommunications.

Box 12.1   Game 39 – Soccer and Globalization

In 2007 managers at the FA Premier League in England, probably the world's most successful commercial sporting league, proposed a series of matches to capitalize on their international appeal. The Game 39 proposal involved 10 matches featuring Premier League clubs (including global names such as Manchester United, Liverpool and Chelsea) at 10 locations across the globe. However, regardless of how appealing the idea may be to Premier League fans in Mexico City, Shanghai or Melbourne, the proposal was met with fierce criticism by fan-supporter groups in England, national and international football governing authorities and politicians. But why would the Premier League want to provide an international event option for their domestic product? Possibly the landscape for international sporting events is evolving and so too must the clubs and leagues with it.

This chapter will focus on the secondary development of international sporting events. Hence it is important that the reader understands that in this chapter events such as the Olympic Games and other 'World Championship' events are not the main focus. Instead the growth of professional sports leagues, mainly from North America and Europe, into international markets are what, in this chapter anyway, is understood as an international sporting event. In doing so, this chapter will enable the reader to address the following pertinent questions: What considerations require attention by event management professionals when looking to internationalize their sporting events? And what skills are required by those wishing to work in this field of event management practice? A step-by-step approach to planning international development will provide the framework for this chapter. The closing case will examine the impact of terrorism on event planning for the Indian Premier League of Cricket and the processes involved in market selection.

The Development of International Sports Events

Many sporting events are famous for their tradition and heritage and have enjoyed strong following from within local regions and communities. Some of these sporting events are well known internationally and their geographic location is part of the attraction to the event, for example the Tour de France or the English FA Cup Final at Wembley Stadium. While these are high-profile sporting events, another perspective is to consider the international growth of sporting events. Events such as the Olympic and Paralympic Games and the FIFA World Cup are well established mega-sport events that take place once every four years. Many other international sports event organizers also host their major events in such a format. Although these may be the first international sporting events that spring to mind, they do follow a traditional developmental model.

Another approach to viewing international sporting events is through the calendar model. This model involves sporting teams from around the world competing in a series of events that take place over the calendar year. Although recent editions of this event take place across most continents it has not always been the case. This model has been operating in sports such as Formula 1 motor racing, professional men's and women's tennis tours, and has also been recently adopted by other sports such as the International Cycling Union's Pro Tour.

But why is there this trend to internationalize sporting events? A possible reason is increasing international competitive pressures that have lead sports organizations to look internationally for growth. Many sporting events have for many years enjoyed widespread international appeal. This appeal may be due to either long-standing cultural links that have followed the spread of emigrating populations, such as Barcelona FC in Mexico (Chadwick and Arthur, 2008), or due to a process of globalization whereby a combination of media, marketing and development programmes have created a platform for the sport's consumption in international markets. Clearly, in the following decades, many sporting organizations will look to extend their sports to new markets by internationalizing their events, thus creating a new battleground for those with the right techniques to facilitate the process.

A number of scholars have considered an organizational field approach to conceptualizing actors within a given industry (DiMaggio and Powell, 1991; O'Brien and Slack, 2004; Washington and Ventresca, 2008). Increasingly event promoters and managers are some of many field actors who seek to internationalize events and leagues. Actors within this field believe that the development of sport in a competitive landscape must cross national borders to tap into latent demand outside their traditional markets.

Within this field there are three main categories of organizational actors: sports organizations who have a primary responsibility for the delivery of sport training, events, information or goods; sports customers who comprise of individuals or groups who have committed interests in sporting organizations, their activities, and the goods and services they provide; and non-sporting organizations – organizations with an interest in the development of sporting organizations for a range of direct and indirect organizational objectives.

Box 12.2   Critical Thinking Exercise

Are any of the conditions discussed above impacting the sporting industry in your country? What can be learnt about sport in your country when the activities of the key actors in the sector (sports organizations, sports customers and non-sporting organizations) are examined?

Sport organizations

The first organizational form many think of are sporting teams and clubs. These are organizations responsible for the delivery of a particular sporting product. For the purposes of this chapter they do this as part of a league. Some of the biggest names in sport fall into this category: the New York Yankees, Manchester United, Real Madrid, Boston Celtics and, depending on your location, the Kashima Antlers, Collingwood Football Club, the Canterbury Crusaders or the Chennai Super Kings.

One such club is Arsenal Football Club of England. The club was based in a residential area that for many years provided strong local support and gate receipts. Since the 1990s an increasing amount of money has flowed into English football. Much of this has been through broadcast fees which have in turn increased the amount of commercial supporters each club has. Nevertheless the ideal funding situation for professional sport teams is to maximize not only broadcast fees and commercial partnerships but also gate receipts. As the importance of gate receipts increases, the utility of the older stadiums decreases as they are constrained by capacity issues. With the increased capacity of the Emirates Stadium (see Figure 12.1), the club generated many millions of pounds each year, much of this coming from naming rights, corporate hospitality suites and a range of executive club memberships. This ability to compete financially at home provides a solid foundation for international development. Many sports looking to develop internationally should have this sound platform from which to launch as international development activities can be a drain on resources.

Most sporting leagues, such as the NBA, or clubs, such as Manchester United, have adopted an international strategy which aims to grow their supporter bases in strong markets such as China and India. This type of international strategy is characterized by numerous business activities taking place in a small number of foreign markets. According to Douglas and Craig (1995), global strategies exist when the company is operating in many markets sequentially. The truth is that very few sporting organizations have the resources to do this on such a scale as it would imply having branches across the globe to coordinate business activities, hence arguably sport is not in fact globalizing. Therefore, while many sporting organizations receive global exposure, a few first-mover organizations, such as the NBA and European football clubs, are leveraging this exposure to support their international events.

Figure 12.1   *Arsenal's Emirates Stadium*

Sport customers

Much time has gone into researching, segmenting and targeting defined sets of sport fans. Traditionally sport fans were ranked on their devotion to their team through evidence of support. One of these factors for support was attendance at matches. As fans are now global in reach, we can see that attending matches is no longer a suitable method of judging devotion to a sport or club. Hence, if we try to classify fans based on the ability to attend alone, then we can misrepresent these potential new markets. There are a number of multidimensional models to explain sport fan behaviour that go beyond traditional approaches to loyalty and reflect considerations like geographical distance from the league (Hunt et al., 1999), motivation to watch on aesthetic and quality rationales (Westerbeek and Smith, 2003), and even those 'fine-weather' fans who just support while the team is winning. However, there is no definitive model of sport fan behaviour, so sport event managers need to communicate with their fans constantly through market research.

Over the past 15 years wider technological and economic developments have meant that sport customers have benefited from reductions in the real cost of travel and increases in consumer leisure expenditure. The growth in sport tourism around significant sporting events such as the Olympic Games (Weed, 2011) ensures managers need to be aware that event customers come from many backgrounds and can have many and different understandings of service quality. They can be domestic citizens of the country hosting the event. They could be travelling through the country or travelling to the event in particular, or they could be immigrant residents of a country that is hosting an event involving their sport or team.

Non-sport organizations

The commercial and global development of sport since 1990 has also been noticed by non-sport organizations who have, in partnership with many sports, been instrumental in assisting the proliferation of international sports events and leagues. Many of these non-sport organizations have been operating in international markets and have provided sporting organizations with vital local knowledge.

These organizations can be categorized into a number of forms: manufacturers, suppliers, sponsors and commercial partners, governments, and non-governmental organizations (NGOs). Manufacturers such as Nike, Adidas, Wilson Sports and Spalding dominate the sportswear and equipment markets. These companies internationalized their operations in the search for lowering the cost of manufacturing sports products. Increasingly these non-sport organizations are creating their own major events to cater for the needs of the sports market. Red Bull, the company that manages the Red Bull Energy Drink, hosts a series of sports events across a range of sports, from motor racing to extreme sports, to the fun and frivolous. In some cases these non-sport organizations are becoming synonymous with certain types of sporting event.

Many governments and politicians at all levels of the political system see sport as a way of achieving a number of direct and indirect goals. For example, in post-industrial economies, there has been a trend toward using sport for a number of social and economic goals. Cities and regions competitively bid for the right to stage these events and in order to increase their chances of success, these bidders use these sporting events as a catalyst for sporting and non-sporting construction; enhancing opportunities for regeneration benefits to local communities, even if these are sometimes keenly contested outcomes.

Sponsors and commercial partners are organizations involved in mutually beneficial commercial arrangements with sporting organizations. There are many reasons why non-sport organizations enter into these arrangements – however by working in partnership with sports organizations, these objectives can be realized for both parties. Commercial partners can also include broadcasting organizations on radio, on television and online. In addition, the management of sport and entertainment facilities and their need for bookings also enhances the demand for growth in international sporting events. One example is event and facility management specialists AEG Worldwide who work in partnership with the NBA to bring NBA matches to London on a regular basis. The final category of non-sport organizations includes the non-governmental organizations (NGOs) involved with sporting organizations who are jointly providing sports programmes and events for a range of developmental objectives.

Why Should Event Managers be Concerned with Internationalizing their Key Events?

Australian Rules Football is the leading professional sport league in the Australian market. 'Aussie Rules', as it is known, is an indigenous and domestic sport of Australia. Despite its cultural significance and popularity however, the sport has been geographically restricted (at a professional level) to its domestic market. Other sports such as gridiron football played in the National Football League in North America, and the Gaelic sports of Ireland also face these challenges. Global reach is becoming a major concern to indigenous sporting codes. The level of international development available to these sports is clearly dependent on a combination of factors, such as the financial and human resources at their disposal, the potential within international markets and also the interests of their non-sporting partners.

So how can sporting organizations begin a methodical focus on the international marketing environment and avoid using assumptions? International marketing academics Douglas and Craig (1995) proposed a five-step process to undertaking this task. This process was conceptualized primarily for non-sports organizations but in this chapter we will adapt the model to suit the sports industry. Figure 12.2 outlines the process which consists of five steps or stages.

Step 1: Establishing Your Organization's Mission

Sport events looking to develop globally need to ensure that the organization's mission is congruent with this desire. The mission should reflect these global aspirations and provide direction for the organization as a whole, but importantly not dislocate the organization from its roots (traditional supporters). The inclusion of the Corporate Social Responsibility programmes allows organizations to develop international

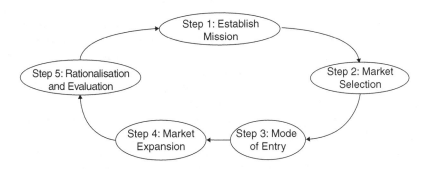

Figure 12.2 *Global marketing strategy*

Source: Adapted from Douglas and Craig (1995)

exposure and generate good will. Means and Nauright revealed the NBA's Basketball Without Borders programme mission:

> *Help young people from diverse national and economic backgrounds come together and learn through the sport of basketball. (2008: 374)*

This establishes direction for international development for the NBA without disenfranchising traditional supporters who follow the sport.

Step 2: Market Selection

The next stage is selecting the market, or markets, the sports organization wishes to enter. Much has been written about the potential of the BRIC (Brazil, Russia, India, China) markets and the extraordinary growth these have shown. Regardless of the trend of globalization that has proliferated since the early 1990s, many countries have environmental factors that confer a range of opportunities and limitations on sporting organizations who wish to develop their events in these regions.

Understanding the external marketing environment has traditionally focused on PEST analysis factors (see Ferdinand and Wesner; and Gechev, this volume; Kitchin, 2007). A PEST analysis should be the initial step a sport-event manager would take when evaluating the market options. Factors should include considerations of political, economic, socio-cultural and technological forces that could affect the market potential. In addition to this, a competitive analysis must be undertaken to assess the likelihood of incumbent events responding to your market entry. Each of these factors will now be addressed in turn.

Political

This force is influenced by a number of factors – for instance, the government support for, and recognition of, sport is a major factor in the awarding of major sporting events by international governing bodies. Governments may look to support or attract tours and related activities through partnerships. Urrutia et al. (2008) highlighted how the Catalan government supported FC Barcelona's tours of the United States and Athletico de Madrid's tour of South Korea. These tours provide tourist cross-promotions to the sponsoring region and can therefore be of particular economic benefit to tourism economies.

It is vital for sport-event managers to understand the possibility of regime change in the market they are studying. A stable political environment can be beneficial to leveraging benefits from events and tours, whereas an unstable environment places the key assets (that is, the coaches and players) in harm's way, resulting in dire consequences such as those seen in the 2010 African Cup of Nations. Problems in this area can also cast a negative light on local business activities and can prevent planned benefits from being realized. Regulations and laws within a given market are also extremely important. The EU-wide ban on tobacco sponsorship has dramatically impacted upon the marketing and financing of Formula 1 teams. This has a major impact on the financial sources that can arise through sponsorship to the point where these regulations have arguably pushed the Formula 1 motor racing competition into new international markets (Kitchin, 2007).

Economic

Closely linked to the political force are economic considerations. Sport-event managers can have little impact on macro and micro economic forces. The macro-economic environment consists of indicators of economic flow and growth. Since the mid-1990s many western economies have experienced good growth and low levels of inflation. Real disposable incomes have risen and this has benefited a number of sport entertainment offerings. However the credit crunch has affected a number of these markets. Outside these nations much has been made of the economic boom of the pan-Asian region and the Middle East. China's GDP growth was 10 per cent in 2007, followed by India at 7.9 per cent and even much smaller nations like Vietnam experienced strong growth of 8.1 per cent (*The Economist*, 2008). GDP growth is not the only indicator of a healthy economy but these markets present sporting organizations with more opportunities than their traditional markets. The boom has led to a growing sophisticated middle class, especially in India and China where the market size is attractive for many global companies. Further growth in the Middle East, Russia and certain countries within Africa will also see these markets becoming more appealing in the future.

The micro-economic environment is vital for non-sporting organizations looking to acquire inputs and resources for their international strategy. However the resources required for these endeavours are sometimes limited. For instance, the availability of playing talent and support staff is restricted, hence some international operations for a sporting organization are more akin to a travelling theatre group than a brick-and-mortar foreign investment. Additionally, the use of partners to assist with international operations can reduce the importance of micro-economic concerns as the sport can draw on their resources, or even local market knowledge. Global sponsors such as Coca-Cola, Visa and others have knowledge of many international markets that could benefit sports organizations.

An important consideration is the volatility of the market. Most sporting clubs and leagues operating internationally have little direct investment in the foreign markets. For those that do, stagnating growth in an economy can lead to fluctuations in the costs of doing business. Looking at the recent growth in the African market is promising but unsettled political conditions throughout the continent pose issues for long-term stability and foreign investment. Hence economic considerations should be carefully thought through.

Socio-cultural

Assessing the socio-cultural environment of a number of countries is difficult as cultural differences vary greatly in any given nation. China has 56 ethnic groups alone – although the majority are Han, one sport event cannot address all of these differences within the market. The growth of the Asian economy's consumer markets has demonstrated a strong demand for western sporting products. While these are consumed primarily over satellite television, tours of the region are well attended and provide new income streams. The success of these tours, led by European football clubs, and basketball clubs in the USA and Australia, represents a strong interest in high quality sporting products, sometimes to the detriment of their own domestic leagues and competitions.

The growing wealth of the Diaspora populations in many countries has provided opportunities for sport to market itself globally. While cultural differences can have an impact on consumption patterns within any given market, the rise of globalization has seen a paradoxical resurgence in national and regional identity. For example, the growing wealth of the Hispanic market in the USA has led to an increase in demand for European football with Barcelona and Athletico Madrid touring the region.

Nevertheless, sports fans consume their sport in slightly different ways which implies for sport-event managers that international activities need careful communication and promotion strategies if they are to appeal to a wider range of potential customers. For instance, the development of the so-called experience economy is a result of consumers expecting greater value and personalization in their consumption activities. Some consumers are attracted to events not solely for sport but also for the experience that comes with it. This desire to accumulate experiences instead of material possessions is one other aspect of changing consumer dynamics. Many spectators are motivated to attend international sports events and leagues for these experiential factors. Ferrand (2008) notes that for another global sporting event, the 2006 Turin Winter Olympics, six of the nine audience motives were experiential. Increasing the experiential qualities of sporting events in international markets can attempt to tap into these segments.

Technological

It is arguably the technological environment that has paved the way for sport in the international market. Factors such as the frequency and cost of travel, the efficient manufacturing of merchandise, and the availability of goods and services to many markets distributed over the internet (and its supporting mail network) has meant that Indian cricket fans in Santiago can order the latest kit and watch Sachin Tendulkar via satellite television. Sophisticated western markets and product-hungry emerging markets have made many international regions attractive for sports, and their partners, to leverage their technological competence and quality of competition to possibly overwhelm domestic competitions that cannot match these competences.

Competitive environment

It is the intensity of the competitive environment that is the catalyst for international marketing. Event managers need to understand the competitive characteristics of the regional markets they are selecting. An analysis of direct and indirect competitors is absolutely critical for successful market selection. For example, many markets have not only their own domestic competition, but also through satellite broadcasts, sports from other markets. A brief look at sport-entertainment competition in selected markets sees that in Europe association football is the dominant sport, in North America, the Big 4 and Nascar, while in the Middle East, East and South-east Asia it is also association football. Cricket is the major sport on the subcontinent and also across some areas of Australasia. Additionally in this market, rugby league, rugby union and Australian Rules football have significant market share. Sport-event managers seeking new markets should also be aware of alternate leisure-entertainment. Therefore an event manager's local market knowledge is vital when assessing the competitive environment as this environment can also be strongly influenced by the socio-cultural environment.

Step 3: Mode of Entry

The existence of international governing bodies has allowed many sports organizations to tap into a wealth of local knowledge and experience to advise on suitable market entry methods. Depending on the availability of organizational resources and the degree of resource exposure to these international markets, a number of options are available for market entry.

For a number of years, organizations such as Nike and Adidas have been structured around export manufacturing. The international networks these organizations have can provide suitable partners for sports organizations looking to export merchandise or even engage in international operations. The market entry options for sport in the international market include licensing, exporting, and joint ventures and alliances.

Licensing

Licensing has been used by organizations such as Arsenal in the community with their residential soccer schools in the Middle East. The licensing allows Arsenal Football Club a presence within the region and a contractually agreed control of the product while limiting their financial exposure in the market. Although the programme is running successfully, licensing as a choice of market entry generally suffers from issues in finding the correct local partner. Additionally, the products can be imitated if the legal environment (which is part of political considerations) is not robust on intellectual property.

Exporting

This method allows organizations to provide products in multiple markets without having to engage in outlaying significant resources. The effective use of the internet can instantly allow any sporting organization to export products, especially merchandise, to international markets. Some limitations of exporting include an over-reliance on intermediaries in the local market. Geographical and cultural displacement means managing across borders which can be difficult. The learning benefits from such arrangements are also limited, and with the importance of intellectual property to professional sporting organizations the wrong partner could be failing to adequately protect the assets.

Joint ventures and alliances

While it is unlikely Barcelona would use direct foreign investment to enter a version of the club in another nation's football league (as direct foreign investment would work for non-sporting organizations), joint ventures and alliances are a possibility in conjunction with international partners. This could include tours of international markets in alliance with the domestic sporting league or working with a sponsor in their 'home' market. European football clubs and the NBA have alliances with international markets to promote their sport and raise revenues. The advantages of this mode of entry are that the local partner can assist the sporting organization to achieve maximum benefits from its international tours, while sharing the resources to conduct the operations, hence reducing the financial risk. On the contrary, managing the relationship is an important consideration and generally the sport will have to pick and choose the most attractive markets to the detriment of fans and partners from markets that are less attractive.

Step 4: Market Expansion

Once the mode of entry is selected and the market has been entered and activities have taken place, an evaluation should be made on the outcome and benefits of these decisions. If the international development has been successful, the sport-event manager has three more considerations for further market development and expansion.

Positioning and segmentation

An assessment of the competitive market should allow the sport to be positioned and segmented effectively. For this, accurate consumer research needs to be undertaken on the market in order that the sport can satisfy the needs and interests of the market.

Localizing strategy

Taking consideration of local market perspectives can provide advantages for organizations. Santomier (2008) states that although ESPN–Star covers most of Asia, each major market has tailored programming to ensure that the fragmented market is served adequately. Conducting a tour involving local clubs or an all-star team of the national association may appeal more to local audiences than two or three foreign teams competing in their own tournament. This is important as spectators and participants in local markets can then feel some form of 'ownership' over the product. Without this local consideration, the international efforts may appear 'top-down' or not genuine.

Leveraging networks

As mentioned throughout this chapter, the use of partners is extremely important to enable sporting organizations to spread their financial resources further when marketing internationally. European football clubs are particularly proficient at this. Manchester United's use of Nike's competence in global merchandise distribution to ensure the replica kit can be found in multiple markets. Barcelona are building global brand equity through their partnership with UNICEF, the club's first shirt sponsor. Athletico de Madrid can call on the resources of Kia when considering tours of South Korea and other Asian nations (Urrutia et al., 2008). These networks have local knowledge which is valuable to the sporting organizations as it can help reduce financial risk and keep costs of international activities down.

Case Study 12.1   Cricket for Change International Sports Programme in Sri Lanka

Cricket for Change is a sporting charity based in London. Their international sport programmes work with local partners across the globe, including national governing bodies and non-governmental organizations such as UNICEF. As the charity is small and resource-constrained (despite being one of the leading cricket charities worldwide), their event planning systems are solid but they lack the financial resources to personally research event venues in the countries they are working in. Alex Basson, Coach and Sport-Event Manager, Cricket for Change, recalls:

> We had organized the final event without actually seeing the venue. Although this sounds odd we are only a small charity and could not afford any pre-event field trips to see for ourselves. We had to work with our local partners and take their word for it. Turning up at Colombo Cricket Ground I

(Continued)

(Continued)

looked out of the van and saw … well a field … I looked at the Development Manager as if to say, is this it? And he said 'just wait and see' …. We found a reception area and made our way through. As we walked through the walkway the saying 'never judge a book by its cover' came to me. As I walked along the path, there were these rivers of golden coy with palms and water-falls. It was amazing. At the end I walked through an arch onto the ground. As I walked onto the ground it was massive, the amount of seating and standing area was unbelievable. It was more than we needed for the event, however it provided an authentic setting. The peer leaders were already there as we arrived and were happy to see us. We brought the peer leaders in to explain what they were going to do and explained that this was part of what we had all worked for these past few days. In a way, if it was a sham-bles and didn't work it would be us in the 'dog house' not them, so we were more nervous than they were. As we turned up there were also the Sri Lankan Cricket Board and UNICEF. This was a big deal and everything had to look spot on. As it all kicked off, it was running really well, the music was blaring, the matches were flowing and the sun was shining. As I walked around the stadium taking it all in, it was then I thought this is exactly what it was all about. All the planning of the past few months and the local train-ing sessions with the peer leaders over the past four days provided the carnival atmosphere we were all expecting.

 Box 12.3   Critical Thinking Exercise

What lessons about hosting sporting events in foreign and unfamiliar countries can be taken away from the experience of Cricket for Change?

Step 5: Rationalization and Evaluation

The final stage serves as a check and balance on international operations. By ration-ing various international activities, the sport-event manager has to determine which efforts can provide the greatest benefit. This trade-off is important as touring clubs must choose some markets at the expense of others. The goals and timeline of the global strategy should make these choices less complicated. Urrutia et al. (2008) found that Athletico de Madrid had already faced these decisions by selecting China for their recent tour as the 400,000 Euro from this tour could not have been achieved with other international options.

An objective evaluation of each form of international exposure must be undertaken in order to ensure that these activities are not just a 'copy-cat' strategy. Evaluation against initial objectives is required to ensure that international activities are in the best interests of the organization.

Issues with Global Strategies

Upon critical reflection, international marketing and its related activities needs to be carefully considered. Not just for the business reasons listed above but also for the sociological underpinnings that do not always set the business of sport with the support of sport. One of the major issues with the exporting of western sporting events to international markets is the potential distaste for westernization in local markets. The westernization of sport is also important in many countries that do not easily equate with sporting principles based on confrontation and win/loss (Thoma and Chalip, 1996). Some sports fans have a strong dislike of being called customers and seeing their passion packaged as entertainment. Event managers should carefully consider all types of fans – those that are very loyal and even those that are fair-weather fans should be catered for. As the directors of Athletico de Madrid of Spain stated, the emphasis of their event was on developing real relationships with local communities which were 'nurtured not manufactured' (Urrutia et al., 2008: 208).

Implications for Event Managers

Event managers should be aware of the model outlined by Douglas and Craig (1995) that should assist them with sizing up the best markets for international events. This five-step model can assist in making these ventures successful by providing a framework for action.

The importance of the following key points cannot be overstated. First, the use of local partners, or partners with international experience, can provide timely and relevant information required to make better decisions. Sport-event managers should also perform a thorough analysis of the PEST and competitive factors for each market they wish to enter. This is a time-consuming task and in reality the final decision may be made for less than rational decisions by senior management.

Selecting the appropriate mode of entry is important when accessing new markets. The fewer the resources the organization has available, the more limited the range of options – however with clever localized strategies benefits can be obtained. Importantly sport-event managers need to be able to foresee any local market issues that may arise through international operations. Underpinning all of these points is the importance of market research. Rigorous preparation will allow for contingencies to be created in order to handle any given situation.

Box 12.4   Critical Thinking Exercise

What would be the most important considerations for international sporting organizations coming to your country?

Case Study 12.2   The Indian Premier League: Playing challenges with a 'straight bat'

The sport of cricket has been, for many years, a sport traditionally played by two teams over a five-day period. Shorter versions of the game have for many years been used to attract new audiences to the game that might not be interested in the original form. The version of the game called Twenty20 cricket was developed commercially by the England and Wales Cricket Board in 2003 (Kitchin, 2008a). By 2005 the format was sweeping the world and the biggest and most important cricket market of them all – India – launched their own official league in 2008 called the Indian Premier League (IPL) (Kitchin, 2008b; Pritchard and Hyde, 2009).

The IPL was an eight-team franchise model developed by Lalit Modi, the former Chair of the IPL and Vice-President of Marketing for the Board of Control for Cricket in India. Modi used aspects of other successful domestic leagues to design the competition. The level of commercial interest and broadcasting rights and the fact that the IPL attracted top-level players from around the world, and hence large attendances for the first season, meant the IPL was an instant success.

However, in the November before the second edition of the IPL, the city of Mumbai was attacked by terrorists and over 160 people were killed. Despite security issues being at the top of most sporting events' risk management programmes, the Indian police told the BCCI that they could not spare the police for the second edition as it coincided with the Indian national parliamentary elections. Instead of cancelling the IPL, Modi and his management team set about the task of finding an international location with venues that could hold the 61 matches of the second edition. The competition was scheduled to run between 18 April and 23 May 2009. There were a number of countries with the expertise to stage the event to a high standard. Australia, the West Indies, South Africa and England all had the capability to host the event. The following criteria could be used by an analyst to determine the first stage of selection. These criteria could have included the experience the hosts had at staging significant cricket events, the weather (Pritchard and Hyde, 2009) and chance of rainfall (cricket is played outdoors and hence climactic conditions such as rainfall can limit the quality and amount of play), and the logistics of moving eight cricket teams to another country. The country selection was also imperative in determining the starting time that a game could be played. The reason for this was that it was important to ensure that the event would be broadcast to India in prime-time viewing.

(Continued)

(Continued)

Table 12.1   *Stage 1: Market selection options for IPL2*

Qualitative Factors/Market	South Africa	Australia	West Indies	England/Wales
Event Experience	2007 T-20 World Cup	1992/93 World Cup	2007 World Cup Proposed Hosts for 2010 T-20 World Cup	1999 World Cup Proposed Hosts for 2009 T-20 World Cup
Suitable Climate During April and May	Good, dry autumn	Certain regions but not in major markets	End of dry season and start of wet	Moderate temperature and rainfall
Logistical Suitability	High	High	Moderate	High
Time Delay to Mumbai/ Convenience for Indian Broadcast Market	3–3.5 hours behind/ convenient play time	3.5–5.5 hours ahead/start play late	10 hours/start play very early	4.5 hours behind/convenient play time

In making their decision, the IPL management only ever considered the markets of South Africa and England. The final two contenders were very closely matched, however competitive factors may have been a deciding factor, as the English Domestic Season was set to begin in the scheduled time that the IPL required. There was a possibility that there might have also been some political factors in the decision as England and Wales' governing body was the second largest national cricketing board behind the BCCI (Kitchin, 2008b). For political reasons, not handing the event to their nearest competitor (despite them generating significantly less revenue each year) may have been a factor that in reality no research could plan for.

The deadline for the decision was made 25 March – only three weeks from when the IPL event team were notified about the unsuitability of playing in India due to lack of security coverage. Within three weeks of the decision being made to award the event to South Africa, the first ball was bowled in IPL2 in front of a big crowd in Cape Town. The match was broadcast live into millions of homes across the subcontinent. The quick thinking of the IPL management team set an excellent example for other sport-event managers on issues of overcoming adversity and the use of market selection processes.

Case Study Questions

1 Conduct a web search on the Indian Premier League. What factors about this sport and its supporters would make the process of international development easier?
2 In choosing South Africa as the host, the IPL managers have clearly based their decision on a number of factors. If for some reason South Africa was to withdraw from hosting, what country would you award the IPL to? Justify your answer.
3 Apart from hosting the event in another country, were there any alternative options the IPL could have chosen?

Chapter Summary

Internationalizing sport events should be a careful and calculated business decision based on accurate and timely research. The international development of sport strategies should be tailored and localized to cater for peculiarities in individual markets. While some global non-sporting organizations can apply a one-size-fits-all approach, the fragmented nature of sports fans will require event managers to use a different approach. Organizations should always work with partners to spread the risk, whether governments, sponsors, good manufacturers or any other organization that could assist in these operations. This network approach can lead to benefits for the entire group, not just for one organization. Rein et al. (2006) stated that the traditional competitive environments in many countries are limiting the opportunity for sport event growth, and hence a wider view is needed.

International sports events and leagues receive a very high profile on the sporting spectrum, hence the management complexities involved in their staging are significant. However it is clear that many domestic sports and competitions may soon start to examine how they can take the live experience to wider audiences. This chapter has intended to demonstrate the utility of a process model approach to internationalizing sports events. It has reinforced the notion that sport-event managers should consider the full range of issues that could impede on the effectiveness of their events. Therefore the use of this framework could be beneficial for organizations, or networks of organizations, looking to work together.

Review Questions

1 What domestic conditions are increasing the need for sporting organizations to internationalize their events?
2 Prepare a market selection analysis on the candidates for the 2020 Summer Olympic Games. Which market would you select from the PESTCOM factors?
3 What mode of entry would the Premier League's Game 39 involve? How could this be re-examined to ensure that the game's stakeholders may be more supportive of the initiative?
4 For a sporting league of your choice, suggest a range of market entry strategies that would take advantage of local networks.

Additional Resources

Books and journal articles

Jozsa, F.P. (2009) *Global Sports: Cultures, Markets and Organizations*. Danvers, MA: World Scientific Publishing Co.
Discusses the emergence and development of extremely popular team sports – baseball, basketball, football-soccer, ice hockey and cricket – since the 1800s in 15 different countries.

Rein, I., Kotler, P. and Shields, B. (2006) *The Elusive Fan*. New York: McGraw-Hill Inc.
Highlights the pressure sports clubs and leagues are faced with in domestic environments.

Richeliue, A., Lopez, S. and Desbordes, M. (2008) 'The internationalisation of a sports team brand: The case of European soccer teams', *International Journal of Sports Marketing and Sponsorship,* 10(1): 29–44.
Provides academic analysis of how the brand of a European football club is managed to increase international exposure.

Tomlinson, A. and Young, C. (2006) *National Identity and Global Sports Events*. Albany: State University of New York.
Examines the significance of international sporting events and why they generate enormous audiences worldwide.

Westerbeek, H. and Smith, A.C.T. (2003) *Sport Business in the Global Marketplace*. London: Palgrave.
Provides a very good title for an interesting, if now dated, analysis of the internationalization of sport.

Useful websites

http://www.aussierulesinternational.com/
Gives an example of a traditionally domestic sport managing international expansion.

http://www.redbull.com/
Provides details about the sporting events of international brand Red Bull and provides a contrasting perspective to the internationalization of sporting events focused on in this chapter.

http://www.sportbusiness.com
Focuses on events, clubs and leagues involved in international markets.

References

Chadwick, S. and Arthur, D. (2008) 'Mes que un club (More than a club): The commercial development of FC Barcelona', in S. Chadwick and D. Arthur (eds), *International Cases in the Business of Sport*. Oxford: Elsevier. pp. 1–12.

DiMaggio, P.J. and Powell, W.W. (1991) 'The Iron Cage revisited: Institutional isomorphism and collective rationality in organizational fields', in W.W. Powell and P.J. DiMaggio (eds), *The New Institutionalism in Organizational Analysis*. Chicago: University of Chicago. pp. 63–82.

Douglas, S.P. and Craig, C.S. (1995) *Global Marketing Strategy*. New York: McGraw Hill Inc.

Economist, The (2008) *The Year Ahead 2009*. London: The Economist.

Emery, P. (2010) 'The past, present, future major sport event management practice: The practitioner perspective', *Sport Management Review*, 13(2): 158–170.

Ferrand, A. (2008) 'Olympic marketing: The power of the five rings brand', in S. Chadwick and D. Arthur (eds), *International Cases in the Business of Sport*. Oxford: Elsevier. pp. 222–242.

Hunt, K.A., Bristol, T. and Bashaw, R.E. (1999) 'A conceptual approach to classifying sports fans', *Journal of Services Marketing*, 13(6): 439–452.

Kitchin, P.J. (2007) 'The sports marketing environment', in J. Beech and S. Chadwick (eds), *The Marketing of Sport*. London: FT-Pearson Education. pp. 61–82.

Kitchin, P.J. (2008a) 'Twenty20 and English domestic cricket', in S. Chadwick and D. Arthur (eds), *International Cases in the Business of Sport*. Oxford: Elsevier. pp. 101–113.

Kitchin, P.J. (2008b) 'The development of Limited Overs Cricket: London's loss of power', *London Journal of Tourism, Sport and the Creative Industries*, 1(2): 70–75.

Levitt, S.D. and Dubner, S.J. (2005) *Freakonomics*. London: Penguin Books.

Means, J. and Nauright, J. (2008) 'Sports development meets sports marketing in Africa: Basketball Without Borders and the NBA in Africa', in S. Chadwick and D. Arthur (eds), *International Cases in the Business of Sport*. Oxford: Elsevier. pp. 372–388.

O'Brien, D. and Slack, T. (2004) 'The emergence of a professional logic in English rugby union: The role of isomorphic and diffusion processes', *Journal of Sport Management*, 18: 13–39.

Pritchard, A. and Hyde, C. (2009) 'Twenty20 cricket: An examination of the critical success factors in the development of the competition', *International Journal of Sport Marketing and Sponsorship*, 10(2): 132–142.

Rein, I., Kotler, P. and Shields, B. (2006) *The Elusive Fan*. New York: McGraw-Hill, Inc.

Santomier, J. (2008) 'ESPN STAR Sports', in S. Chadwick and D. Arthur (eds), *International Cases in the Business of Sport*. Oxford: Elsevier. pp. 30–44.

Thoma, J.E. and Chalip, L. (1996) *Sport Governance in the Global Community*. Morgantown, WV: Fitness Information Technology.

Urrutia, I., Robles, G., Kase, K. and Marti, C. (2008) 'The internationalisation of Club Athletico De Madrid, S.A.D.: Creating value beyond borders, a differential strategy', in S. Chadwick and D. Arthur (eds), *International Cases in the Business of Sport*. Oxford: Elsevier. pp. 205–221.

Washington, M. and Ventresca, M.J. (2008) 'Institutional contradictions and struggles in the formation of US collegiate basketball, 1880–1938', *Journal of Sport Management*, 22: 30–49.

Weed, M. (2011) 'Olympic tourism', in J. Gold and M. Gold (eds), *Olympic Cities: Urban Planning, City Agendas and the World's Games, 1896 to the Present*. London: Routledge. pp. 194–212.

Westerbeek, H. and Smith, A.C.T. (2003) *Sport Business in the Global Marketplace*. London: Palgrave.

13
The Role of Events in the Hospitality Sector

Ioannis S. Pantelidis

Learning Objectives

By reading this chapter students should be able to:

- Understand the nature of events within the hospitality industry context.
- Recognize the key markets in hospitality and events management.
- Comprehend the range of different types of events within the hospitality sector.
- Appreciate the recent trends and changes in events in hospitality.

Introduction

Events play a key role in the strategic positioning and profitability of hospitality organizations and this chapter examines events from the hospitality management perspective. It provides an overview of the organizational logistics, market trends and key stakeholders of events within the hospitality industry. Current trends in events management mean that hospitality organizations have had to rethink their products. This often means introducing innovative ways of delivering a high quality product whilst maintaining minimal costs and thus competitive pricing. Different types of hospitality-related events are described focusing on meetings, conferences, weddings, christenings and special celebrations. The role of the conference and banqueting manager within hotels is examined as well as the nature of events in other sectors of hospitality such as restaurants and contract catering. The chapter closes with a case study that highlights the complexity of the organization needed for such events and the variety of management objectives such events satisfy.

The Relationship Between Hospitality and Events

Successful events, regardless of size or nature, will often feature the consumption of drink and food. In many cases, this is combined with the requirement for overnight accommodation. These characteristics of events management are identical to those of hospitality management. Changes in consumer behaviour and expectations have added demands to the traditional roles of conference and banqueting manager (a title commonly used in hotels) and that of catering manager (a title commonly used in the restaurant and contract catering sectors). These added demands, together with a more holistic understanding of the hospitality industry and the management qualities needed to perform the necessary tasks effectively, has led to the redesign of these job roles which now often appear in job advertising sites and magazines under the title of Events Management. For example, Marriott Hotels is one of the hotel chains (glassdoor.com) that has rebranded the traditional role into that of an Events Manager. Another example is Hilton hotels where when advertising for a Conventions Manager they give the job title as Events Manager. Upon closer inspection of the job summary, one can clearly see how what would be advertised as a Conference and Conventions role is now listed as an Events Manager role.

Box 13.1   Hilton Events Manager Job Summary

Executes all aspects of the convention resume and corresponding arrangements between the hotel and customer during the meeting or event. Serves on site group and catering customers in a proactive manner relative to logistics of group room block, food and beverage, public meeting space/exhibit hall, ancillary and vendor services, affiliates/exhibitors and related billing processes. Interviews, trains, supervises, schedules and evaluates staff.

Source: appclix.postmasterlx.com (2010)

At this point it is worth noting that the Meetings, Incentives, Conferences and Exhibitions market (known as MICE, see Chapter 16 in this text) was estimated to be worth US$650 (£400) billion, according to the corporate travel group CWT. North America accounts for US$260 (£160) billion or 40 per cent of the total, followed by Europe with US$227.5 (£140) billion (35 per cent) and Asia with US$162.5 (£99) billion or 25 per cent (Mintel, 2010a). A very large part of this market is served by hotels, restaurants and contract caterers.

It is essential to never forget that hospitality as a 'product' is largely intangible and because each customer perceives the product or service based on their own previous experiences and expectations, the product also becomes inseparable from the customer. Considering the three major key markets in hospitality events, it is worth remembering that events, like any other hospitality product, are also highly perishable. An unsold event ticket is a ticket lost; in a restaurant an unfilled cover is a lost opportunity for better profit margins. Unlike retail where the product can be sold at a later date, a hotel room night or a restaurant seat for lunch or dinner are defined by that time frame and time never turns back. Finally, the success of an event is determined by a number of unpredictable factors which can make the same event very different from the night before. For example, different service employees have varied levels of skills which may impact on the quality of the event.

For a hospitality organization, trying to ensure consistency of product becomes of paramount importance since creating a 'brand' largely depends on the experiences of previous customers. Increasingly word of mouth becomes a big part of that brand, especially with the increase in usage of review websites such as tripadvisor.com.

It should be noted however that events management is emerging as a separate area of research focus away from hospitality, tourism and leisure (see Allen et al., 2000; Shone and Parry, 2004). This shift has also been reflected in academic research with the emergence of journals such as *Events Management* and *Journal of Convention and Event Tourism*, as well as textbooks with authors such as Bowdin et al. (2006), who attempt to describe events as a subject in its own right. There has also been an increase in the number of qualifications offered in Events Management, especially within universities that have a long tradition in hospitality management.

 Box 13.2   Critical Thinking Exercise

Compare and contrast the events and hospitality industries. List the ways in which they are similar and in which they differ.

Defining Event Typologies for Hospitality

Considering the huge part that the hospitality industry has to play in all types of events, it would be important to define event typologies that are relevant to hospitality. Events are often categorized by their scale and size – Bowdin et al. (2006), for example, amongst many others offer the categories of local, major, hallmark and mega-events. A large number of local events may have a sporting, artistic, religious or even historical focus, often attempting to bring the community together and in some cases even evolving and becoming hallmark type events.

For example, the Cologne Carnival dates back to 1823 as a local festival that today is an event known worldwide, making Cologne a prime destination during the carnival season and the carnival one of the largest street festivals in Europe. Although the event itself and its organization are largely focused around the street events and parades, a visitor will discover that the event is supported by local hospitality businesses such as food stalls, restaurants and bars as once the festivities in the street come to a close, revellers will seek to continue the celebrations. As such, hospitality could be directly or indirectly a part of such an event's coordination. Another example of a local event that is directly linked to hospitality is the Maslenitsa religious festival in Russia, also known as pancake week or butter week. Blini (russian pancake) stands sell this type of pancake throughout the festival before the beginning of the Lent fasting period.

Many carnivals, such as the Cologne or the Notting Hill Carnivals, were once local affairs, yet today they define their respective destinations making them hallmark events. Classic sport events in the hallmark category would involve stadia and, considering the amount of food and beverage outlets each stadium has, it is evident that hospitality is an undeniable part of most local or major events, including the Olympics. For example, Wembley stadium features 60 bars and 41 food outlets (Wembley Stadium, 2011). For the London Olympics in 2012, it is estimated that 1.3 million meals will have been served to construction workers alone and a further 13 million meals to expected visitors (see Sustainweb.org, 2011). The *Sunday Times* reported that the 2012 organizers alone had pre-booked 1925 hotel rooms in some of the city's most exclusive hotels (*Sunday Times*, 2008).

From an operations point of view, it is important to distinguish the various events for a number of reasons. For example, from a strategic point of view a hotel chain may wish to delay discounting room rates during periods that an event will impact its reservations. From a tactical point of view as an example, a restaurant may wish to ensure it has enough members of staff to cope with the level of business expected during a period such as the Olympic and Paralympic Games.

A proposed classification of events for hospitality organizations would be to classify them by type of activity, such as internal versus external in terms of where the business is coming from. For example, a wedding organized at a hotel would be an internal event, whilst visitors for a hallmark-type event near the location of the hotel would be external. Furthermore each event could be characterized by:

- Length of time the event impacts the business.
- Revenue generation per day impact.

These two factors could help management determine the importance of the event in terms of revenue generation. For example, suppose we have two hotels – one at a prime location during a mega-event and another at a not so great location – both would have a high impact for a length of time but the first would also have a much greater revenue generation per day.

The event could then further be classified by:

- Business versus pleasure type events.
- Luxury versus budget.

Both these factors would dictate style and type of product to be delivered to customers. Of course, from an operations point of view no matter what factors or indicators are chosen to help classify an event they must be both measurable and meaningful to the business that is utilizing them. Such a classification can be a great help when attempting to forecast future business and that can have a great impact on all areas including pricing, staffing or stock control. The following sections of the chapter will focus on some of the major internal types of events in the hospitality sector and their key markets.

Business-to-Business (B2B)

Also known as corporate events these are events that are delivered to business clients. Typical business-to-business hospitality events include conferences, exhibitions or business shows and training events. These types of events are of great importance to a hospitality operator because they could lead to future sustained business. Unlike a dedicated events company that only focuses on organizational services, a hotel may be selling room nights, extra food and drinks and further entertainment over and above that pre-specified within the boundaries of the specific event.

City-based hospitality businesses largely rely on B2B types of contracts to make up the majority of their revenue. Winning over a business client for a hospitality organization is becoming increasingly challenging with the emergence of dedicated events management companies that may have developed a better portfolio of similar types of events to what the client may want. Having said that, for a hotel negotiating a contract, having the ability to reduce the margins of secondary services can be a great advantage – after all, for B2B contracts successful negotiation is the key.

Business-to-Customer (B2C)

Events targeted directly at the consumer from a hospitality operation can involve putting together an event and selling tickets, which can be a very time-consuming process but especially in slow periods it can be well worth the effort. Restaurants and hotels have been known to organize events that will attract customers that otherwise would not stay in that particular hotel or eat in that restaurant.

Theme nights are a good example of how hospitality operations are attempting to attract new customers by putting together events. Special days in the calendar are very popular for organizing these types of events and generating extra business. For example, Valentine's Day or St Patrick's Day themed nights are two occasions when restaurants will design specific menus and add extra entertainment, attempting to create that extra value that will allow them to pre-sell their restaurant seats. Of course, weddings and private functions also provide a great source of income for restaurants and hotels and they are promoted for such use, especially during slow periods.

Third Party – Organized Events

It is not uncommon for events management companies to partner with hospitality companies, such as hotels, to create events that they then sell directly to customers. Such a symbiosis has advantages for both the events management company and the hospitality organization. For example, the hotel does not need to focus on the selling of tickets or providing elements to the event, such as entertainment, and can focus on the quality of its core product, namely accommodation and food and beverage.

For the events management company, a successful partnership can mean delivering a successful event where the quality of the key parts of the event is guaranteed so that they can focus on the sales of the event.

Business-to-Government

These types of events are those that are organized by contract catering companies for government ministries or departments. Typically prequalified government contractors are given preference to supply services for these events. They may supply food and beverages only or organize and deliver the entire event.

Hotel Events

Some hotel companies would distinguish their event types by size or theme. For example, Hyatt categorize their events into four categories, namely small meetings, large meetings, weddings and social events (Hyatt, 2010), whilst Radisson Edwardian hotels split their categories into meetings and conferences, and private functions (Radisson Edwardian, 2010). Each hotel or hotel chain places emphasis on where their key business is focused but almost all will have good revenue streams from meetings and weddings.

It is important to note that the role of events management in hotels is changing so much that, as mentioned above, the traditional job titles of conference or banqueting manager are now replaced by titles such as events manager or events director. Hotels realize that they are in direct competition with highly sophisticated and experienced events management companies. Such companies could be run by people with hotel, restaurant or contract catering backgrounds and have insight knowledge as well as far more flexibility in their offering since they are not limited by physical space of only one hotel and can offer a range of properties to a potential client. As such, hotels have to respond with extremely competitive pricing with a higher quality of product and service than ever before. Hotel events are most commonly divided into the following categories:

- *Meetings* – These are generally categorized by their size with most hospitality companies simply listing them as small or large meetings. Seminars can also be categorized under this section as hotels are often used as venues for training purposes by companies and their size can vary greatly. The definition of a small meeting could vary between companies and could be anything up to 16 people for some, whilst others will suggest that anything more than 12 is a large size meeting. While these events have been traditionally profitable for the industry, the emergence of dedicated meeting and conference venues, which often may offer better technology or food and beverages, have made hotel operators rethink their pricing models. Often hotels will feature a 'day delegate rate' and some may charge room hire, especially for small meetings, whilst they may waive the room hire for larger scale ones. The day delegate rate will often include coffee breaks and lunch/dinner but may exclude the use of information technology which can come at an extra cost.

- *Banquets* – The idea of banquets (large meals or feasts) goes back to the Elizabethan era, although these types of events have found their use in the modern era. Business banquets are often used by companies as a way to say 'thanks' to current employees or to entertain prospective customers. This type of business is so important to many hotel operators that traditionally the events department of a hotel is known as the 'Conference and banqueting' department. Often hotel companies or contract caterers will be required to organize such events in locations that may or may not have food-production facilities and this can place an extra burden on the logistics of such an operation, which can be very complicated. Profit margins tend to be small and, as Davis et al. (2008) suggest, pricing is largely determined by the operation's fixed and variable cost structure.
- *Conferences* – These can be categorized by the type of conference but the main categories found in hotels are business, academic or sports conferences. News conferences also occur but these tend to be smaller scale, press release types of events. Conferences can vary in length from 1 to 5 days. They are a great source of revenue for a hotel as they utilize every single department of the hotel, generating both room revenue and food and beverage revenue. In the UK, for example, an estimated 5 per cent of all hotel stays are due to a conference or training related reason (Mintel, 2010b).
- *Weddings* – The wedding market is very large and highly contested. Some hotel chains have dedicated directors whose sole focus is the weddings trade. The market is so large that it can often be found in literature referred to as the 'wedding industry' (see Terrell, 2004) and although there is a large number of dedicated professional consultants and event managers, the hotel sector is still capitalizing on it, both on related room stays and the actual hosting of the post-wedding reception. In some cases, resorts in idyllic locations have created a segment whereby customers can have their whole wedding organized and catered by the hotel from the actual ceremony to the honeymoon.
- *Special Celebrations* – Other types of events, catered by hotels, are special celebrations such as parties, private functions and receptions. Many may have a religious theme (such as christenings or B'nai Mitzvahs), whilst others may simply be a private function celebrating a birthday or a momentous occasion. These events can vary greatly in size and their organization may require the hiring of extra specialized services, adding to the complexity of the organization. Most hotels however have developed contacts with suppliers over the years that allow them to cater for any needs the party organizer may have.

Restaurant Events

Restaurants tend to focus on event types that allow them to utilize their limited space and expertise. Without the luxury of large conference space, they tend to only focus on wedding receptions, parties and special celebrations. Some restaurants may feature small meeting room space but most will simply focus on their core business which is the selling of food and beverage. Often, and especially at quiet seasons, a restaurateur may take on an event that is not particularly profitable but which will have a beneficial public relations effect that may attract future business.

As restaurants have limited space, they have to consider the effect that the closing of their business for a day or two may have on their repeat business, especially on their most loyal customers. From a logistics point of view, knowing the exact numbers for the event can be problematic – for example, quite often a wedding organizer may not know the exact number of guests until very close to the reception date – therefore having policies in place that make the organizer aware of such issues at a very early stage is very prudent. At the same time, working with flexible suppliers who can deliver extra goods at the last minute, if needed, is equally important as the guest numbers may go rapidly up as well as down.

Contract Catering Events

These are traditionally contract caterers focused on B2B with five key types of contracts, as Davis et al. (2008) suggest. These are cost plus/management fee, fixed price/performance guarantee, profit and loss concession, total risk and purchasing.

However, as contract caterers branched out to run their own restaurants, they also branched out in running events for their existing clients as well as new clients, where the operation permitted. Typically they will cater for any type of event that a restaurant could, with the added benefit of economies of scale allowing them to provide better value for money to clients whilst ensuring the quality of the product is kept to standard. On top of events such as meetings and weddings, contract caterers can deal with large-scale events such as exhibitions or even mega-events. At the time of writing of this chapter three contract caterers – BaxterStorey, Do and Co, Sodexo and Amadeus – were believed to have become the first caterers to secure a series of multi-million-pound contracts at the London 2012 Olympic and Paralympic Games (Stamford, 2011).

 Box 13.3   Critical Thinking Exercise

What benefits are there for hospitality businesses that classify the events they do into different types?

Trends in the Hospitality Events Arena

The hospitality industry continually faces new challenges from the ever-increasing expectations of consumers, added taxation that minimizes margins, competition from new sectors, such as the specialized events sector that capitalize on what was once the domain of the hotel and restaurant sectors. However, these challenges are merely reminders to the hospitality industry that it needs to always reinvent its business models and ensure that as an industry it is a leader both in quality and innovation, and not just a follower. There are many trends that are worth exploring including food and beverage trends, sustainability issues and financial issues but due to limitations we briefly focus on only three trends that the author believes have great impact and will continue to have a great impact in the foreseeable future.

Technological innovation

The technological innovations of today can be both a challenge and an opportunity to the events manager in hospitality operations. New cooking technologies allow the caterer to provide speedier and better quality meals as well as keeping the meals far more consistent than ever before (Pantelidis, 2009). In addition to food production, advances in information technology enable operators to do far better than ever before. Beverage stock control technology and advanced electronic point of sales systems enable better cost control and minimization of losses. These technologies are now fully integrated with internet technology, enabling customers to purchase tickets for their event with so much more ease than in the past. The latter point highlights the fact that these technologies are available to both the customer and the hospitality manager. Event experiences can be captured using the now ubiquitous mobile phone and are easily uploaded to websites and social networks, making your operation much more open to scrutiny. The same technology however can offer opportunities for positive PR and effective branding, provided the operator is willing to communicate openly and honestly with her clients.

The changing competition

Consumers are far more demanding than ever before and they are able to choose from a wide range of options for events. Where once meetings and conferences were primarily the domain of hotels, there are now more and more dedicated conference and exhibition centres that provide excellent service and can cater for any size of group from the very small to the very big. For every hotel in the city of London that currently charges for wi-fi access, there will be at least one conference centre that will provide this service for free. Hoteliers will need to rethink their strategy and already there is a shift whereby hotels are now increasing their dedicated conference centre space. How does one stay ahead of competition, especially during times of financial crisis? Specialization could be the key, a focus on technology or green issues could be part of the answer but, for certain, assurance of flexibility, quality of product and value for money will be what attracts the consumer. Perhaps in certain instances, hotels, caterers and conference centres could work in synergy, rather than in competition, to ensure a more sustainable future for all concerned.

Sustainability and green issues

Green strategies, carbon footprints and water footprint (the concern over water wastage) have been taking an increasingly larger place in hospitality businesses' agendas. Although there has been research that shows that the consumer does care about the environment (Straughan and Roberts, 1999), there has been limited research that can quantify how much more consumers are prepared to pay for a 'green' product versus a 'non-green' labelled one.

In most cases market segments appear to be price-sensitive and more so in periods of economic downturn such as the current one. Therefore the question would be why should hospitality companies seek to design their events with sustainability and a green agenda in mind? The answer is twofold. The first point has to do with B2C. Although the average consumer may not actively be seeking green hospitality events, most companies are now engaging with green issues and in their strategies they often require their suppliers to mirror their green concerns. As such hospitality organizations cannot afford the potential loss of revenues when it comes down to corporate contracts.

The second point has to do with cost savings. There are numerous case studies that can show the cost-cutting effects of various green technologies (see Additional Resources). However that is not all as governments are now imposing 'Green Taxation' and green penalties and this approach is cascading to numerous countries, the pending approval of the carbon tax in Australia being one example. Butler (2008) argues the case for green hotels and Pantelidis et al. (2010) highlight the importance of good communication between managers and front-line employees when introducing green practices to maximize positive results. The fact remains that if currently taking a green approach is a choice, in the near future with green taxation and more demanding consumers, such an approach will be a necessity in most countries around the globe.

Measuring Success

Hospitality operations use a number of key performance indicators (KPIs) that enable them to monitor performance. Examples of such are RevPar, which is revenue per available room or Food Inventory Turnover (which is the cost of food divided by the average food inventory for the given period). Such measures of performance (MOPs) can be split into three categories:

- *Cross-sectional analysis*: MOPs from other companies, other departments or units in the same company, or industry norms.
- *Time-series analysis*: MOPs from departments and units within a company over a period of time (daily, weekly, monthly, etc.).
- *Variance analysis*: MOPs within the company's budget.

In order to effectively measure performance, the MOPs must reflect the goals of the organization and be meaningful and quantifiable. They must also be timely and accurate, actionable and economical. There is no point in investing too much effort in measuring performance indicators that could be better invested in taking care of customers. A good hospitality manager will ensure that the KPIs s/he uses reflect not only the financial viability of the operation but also the quality of the product delivered to the customer. After all, it is only by measuring the operations success that one can sustain an effective business and stay on top of competition.

Case Study 13.1   Hotelympia 2010

Hotelympia is the UK's largest food service and hospitality event. The exhibition originally began in 1998 and was hosted at Earls Court exhibition centre and by 2002 it was large enough to move to even bigger premises at ExCel London. The exhibition is held every other year and in 2010 the exhibition boasted an impressive exhibitor list of 600+, covering all areas of hospitality from Food and Drink (accounting for more than 50 per cent of exhibitors) to Catering Equipment, Tabletop, Décor and Design, Bathroom and Hotel Spa, Premises and Facilities, Technology as well as a dedicated Sustainability section.

On top of the exhibitors, Hotelympia features cook-offs by celebrity chefs, culinary arts competitions hosted at their 'Salon Culinaire', presenting over 800 awards to participating competitors. FreshRM is the company that organizes Hotelympia and Toby Wand, Group Exhibition Director at FreshRM, commented:

> Hotelympia 2010 has been a great success. Positive visitor feedback has been greater than ever before, particularly referencing our high profile Stage 75 Programme. We've brought innovation to visitors via our Innovation Award finalists, displayed at the Innovation Lounges, and we have received almost 2000 votes. Overall, Hotelympia has been a glimmer of light, after a tough 18 months for the industry, showing suppliers that business is starting to pick up and going from strength-to-strength. (cited in Rooke, 2010)

The difference in the 2010 exhibition was the focus on sustainability with seminars focusing on sustainability, dedicated awards and a dedicated area called 'Sustainability in Action', that was aimed at helping hospitality professionals better understand how to make their operation more green.

As with previous events, the Hotelympia 2010 featured a careers fair with dedicated seminars for hospitality students. The interesting aspect of the pricing for the exhibition is that if you pre-book you do not have to pay the £30 fee which suggests that the organizers are making their profit from the exhibitor fees as well as advertising.

Case Study Questions

1 What motivates the exhibition organizer to waive the fee for visitors that pre-register for this event?
2 Why do you believe there was a focus on sustainability in the 2010 exhibition and not in previous ones?
3 Why do you think organizers put an emphasis on the provision of dedicated space to be used for seminars for hospitality students?
4 What other events can you identify in your country that have a direct link to hospitality?

Chapter Summary

This chapter focuses on the key sectors of the hospitality industry and examines issues related to events management in hospitality. It illustrates parallels between existing events typology and proposes a typology that can be utilized in hospitality operations. The chapter examines the key markets in hospitality-related events and focuses on three sectors, namely the hotel, restaurant and contract catering ones. The chapter finally gives some insight into trends in technology and competition and provides examples on how performance is measured in hospitality organizations. The chapter concludes with a case study on a hospitality exhibition that has become a major event in London over the years.

Review Questions

1   Create a basic typology for events in hospitality. What makes hospitality events different from other events such as spectator sports?
2   Describe the key markets in hospitality-related events.
3   List the different types or categories of events that occur in the hospitality sector.
4   Name the three most important types of measures of performance that you would consider utilizing when operating an events management organization in hospitality. Why are these MOP so important to your organization?
5   Describe some of the key trends in hospitality-related events.

Additional Resources

Books and journals

Bowdin, G., McDonnell, I., Allen, J. and O'Toole, W. (2006) *Events Management* (2nd edn). Oxford: Butterworth-Heinemann.
A useful introductory text to understanding events management.

Cornell Hospitality Quarterly.
A hospitality academic journal written by both academics and industry specialists.

The International Journal of Contemporary Hospitality Management.
A multidisciplinary hospitality academic journal focusing on hospitality-related issues.

The International Journal of Hospitality Management.
Excellent academic journal that discusses major trends and developments in a variety of disciplines as they apply to the hospitality industry.

Useful websites

http://www.instituteofhospitality.org
A UK-based hospitality professional association with one of the most extensive hospitality-relevant online libraries.

www.greenpowerforum.org.uk/case_studies.php
A website with case studies on how to manage carbon emissions.

www.sustainablehotel.co.uk
A website with resources for sustainable practices in hospitality.

http://oxygen.mintel.com/index.html
Mintel Oxygen hosts a wide-range market of intelligence reports from across the globe with industry-specific reports both for hospitality and events.

www.caterersearch.com
An online magazine with useful hospitality-related articles including industry trends and statistics.

References

Allen, J., Harris, R. and Huyskens, M. (2000) *Event Management: An Australian Bibliography.* Sydney: University of Technology.

Appclix.postmasterlx.com (2010) *Event Manager.* First Advantage Recruiting [Online]. Available from: http://appclix.postmasterlx.com/index.html?pid=c216459d272d8d81012 72ed5126d03ee&source=indeed.

Bowdin, G., McDonnell, I., Allen J. and O'Toole, W. (2006) *Events Management* (2nd edn). Oxford: Butterworth-Heinemann.

Butler, J. (2008) 'The compelling "hard case" for "green" hotel development', *Cornell Hospitality Quarterly,* 49(3): 234–244.

Davis, B., Lockwood, A., Pantelidis, I.S. and Alcott, P. (2008) *Food and Beverage Management* (4th edn). Oxford: Butterworth-Heinemann.

Hyatt (2010) *Meetings and Events.* Hyatt [Online]. Available from: http://www.hyatt.com/ hyatt/meetings/index.jsp;jsessionid=BFFA153A610EE4F9D80C6772ECB5F784.atg02-prd-atg2.

Mintel (2010a) *Business Travel Worldwide – International – September 2010.* Mintel [Online]. Available from: www.mintel.com.

Mintel (2010b) *Hotels – UK – November 2010.* Mintel [Online]. Available from: www.mintel.com.

Pantelidis, I.S. (2009) *High Tech Foodservice: An Overview of Technological Advancements,* CHME 18th Annual Research Conference, May, Eastbourne. Londonmet [Online]. Available from: http://londonmet.academia.edu/IoannisSPantelidis/Papers/95209/High_tech_foodservice_an_overview_of_technological_advancements.

Pantelidis, I.S, Geerts, W. and Acheampong, S. (2010) 'Green generals jade warriors: The many shades of green in hotel management', *London Journal of Tourism, Sport and Creative Industries,* 3(4): 8–20.

Radisson Edwardian (2010) *Meetings and Events.* Radisson Edwardian [Online]. Available from: http://www.radissonedwardian.co.uk/meetings-events.html.

Rooke, S. (2010) *Crowded Halls at HOTELYMPIA Sees Inspiration and Innovation Delivered to Hospitality and Food Service Industry.* Hotelympia [Online]. Available from: http://www. hotelympia.com/page.cfm/T=m/Action=Press/PressID=246.

Shone, A. and Parry, B. (2004) *Successful Events Management* (2nd edn). London: Thomson Learning.

Stamford, J. (2011) *Baxterstorey and Sodexo in Line for Olympic Contract Wins*. Caterer Research [Online]. Available from: http://www.caterersearch.com/Articles/2011/01/27/336795/ BaxterStorey-and-Sodexo-in-line-for-Olympic-contract.htm.

Straughan, R.D. and Roberts, J.A. (1999) 'Environmental segmentation alternatives: A look at green consumer behaviour in the new millennium', *Journal of Consumer Marketing*, 16(6): 558–575.

Sunday Times (2008) *2012 Chiefs to Get 3000 Rooms*. The Sunday Times [Online]. Available from: http://www.timesonline.co.uk/tol/news/politics/article3822635.ece.

Sustainweb.org (2011) *Food and the London 2012 Olympics*. Sustainweb [Online]. Available from: http://www.sustainweb.org/olympicfood/.

Terrell, E. (2004) *Wedding Industry Research*. Library of Congress [Online]. Available from: http://www.loc.gov/rr/business/wedding/.

Wembley Stadium (2011) *Wembley NFL*. Wembley Stadium [Online]. Available from: http:// www.wembleystadium.com/brilliantfuture/learningResources/.

14

The Development of the Corporate Events Sector

Ivna Reic

Learning Objectives

By reading this chapter students should be able to:

- Appreciate the diversity within the sector of corporate events, both in terms of event objectives and in terms of event categories.
- Understand how corporate events fit within the overall business strategy of an organization.
- Understand the complexity of the relationships between various stakeholder groups related to corporate events and the importance of the effective management of these.
- Appreciate the importance of corporate event evaluation, as well as challenges related to it.
- Identify the current trends within the corporate events sector and discuss their implications for corporate events managers.

Introduction

The shift from the market-oriented economy to the experience-oriented economy (Pine and Gilmore, 1999) is creating a whole new playing field for product and service providers. Regardless of whether these companies operate in the public, private or not-for-profit sector, they need to be aware that customers no longer require just excellent quality of service – they are now also 'experience hungry'. This makes events (as an aspect of experiential marketing) the perfect tool for delivering the *brand experience* and inspiring customer loyalty.

Events represent a specific type of tourist activity (Getz, 2007) that was, until recently, completely unrecognized as a market segment. Today, however, events are increasingly being used as significant contributors to the overall global economy. Another important aspect of the developing events market is the synergies that are being created between various event types. Thus, for example, the UK government is using the London 2012 Olympic and Paralympic Games to boost the growth of the corporate events sector, trying to put London in the lead of the global conference and event destination market. It is estimated that the events sector will create an additional £2.1 billion in revenue in the period between 2007 and 2017 (DCMS, 2007).

Corporate events are significant revenue earners not just in the events sector, but also within the global economy as a whole. What started off as a spin-off from regular company needs for the training of their staff in specific business areas, has now grown into an industry of its own. Cosmopolitan cities such as London, New York, Paris, Singapore, Kuala Lumpur and Tokyo are competing for the lead in the sector and the situation has now reached a point where entire countries (most notably, the UK) are now relying on the corporate events sector as one of the strategic drivers of the economy in their local and national government plans for post-recession recovery.

This category of events is expansive as they are of many, varied types (Bowdin et al., 2011). Some authors refer to them as business events, framing them within the wider tourism industry (Bowdin et al., 2011; Tassiopoulos, 2010). Although corporate events are an important aspect of the tourism industry, this relationship will not be explored in this chapter. Alternatively, the chapter focuses on defining 'corporate events' as a category of events that support the delivery of an organization's corporate objectives, and explores the various core management concepts in relation to this particular event category. Corporate events can impact on the company's business by either directly or indirectly impacting on the achievement of business objectives. It is important to note that this definition is not rigid: what for one organization is an event that indirectly supports the achievement of its organizational objectives (for example, by sending an employee to a conference for professional development and networking, the company hopes to have future business benefit) can easily be an event that directly supports the achievement of another organization's objectives (for example, the mentioned conference is a direct source of income for the conference organizers). Recognizing that events tend to meet a multitude of business objectives for the varying stakeholder groups that are related to them (Rogers, 2008) is the first step towards understanding their complexity.

One of the main topics for debate in today's corporate events sector is the ambiguity of the term 'corporate events'. No clear definition exists, either professionally (within the industry itself) or within academia. As yet the sector has no clear or set structure (Shone and Parry, 2010), which makes it difficult to compile market data and define and assess the economic indicators related to the sector. Globally, in every country this sector will encompass different event categories. Hence it is understandable that there are big challenges with comparing the sector across countries internationally.

This chapter aims to clarify the concept of corporate events and highlight some of their key aspects. Issues of diversity of event objectives and event types related to these are explored. Core management concepts such as stakeholders and performance measurement are also applied within the context of corporate events and thus provide ample material for discussion. The closing case study highlights the role of corporate events in the non-profit sector.

Corporate Event Objectives

Corporate events, also known as business events, have multiple aims. Not only do they focus on creating added value to the businesses and individuals that are involved in their delivery (both participants and event providers), but also, on a macroeconomic level, they serve to support the growth and development of business tourism, thus boosting the local and national income, as well as the international profile of a particular destination. A global survey of 2300 *Harvard Business Review* subscribers conducted in 2009 showed that 95 per cent of them believed face-to-face meetings are a key factor in successfully building and maintaining long-term business relationships (Eventia, 2011). The idea is that forging strong relationships internally (between the company's employees) and externally (between the company and its various stakeholders) can ensure the company's financial sustainability in the long run.

As with any other business endeavour, the primary reason for organizing corporate events is to enable the achievement of intended business objectives (Getz, 2007; O'Toole, 2011). These objectives are directly related to the overall business performance. There is, however, another important distinction to be made: the term business performance denotes not only financial performance (in terms of revenues and profits), but also performance in terms of the product or service quality delivered to the customer, as well as the level of development and satisfaction of the employees and (in some cases) the impact of the business on its other stakeholders (for example, the local community). Therefore, the objectives of corporate events can be classified into two types, financial and non-financial, as seen in Table 14.1.

This classification creates some important questions. Does this classification mean that non-financial objectives should be considered secondary to, or less important than, the financial ones? Absolutely not. The achievement of non-financial objectives is still expected to have a positive impact on the company's financial performance. For example, a retail company investing in sales training for their newly hired sales staff will be expecting increased effectiveness of those staff in their selling efforts (by attracting more new business or successfully closing more sales), ultimately increasing the revenues of the company. Similarly, a boat producer, such as Sunseeker International, participating at the London Boat Show is looking to expand their customer base through establishing new contacts at the show and thus driving post-event sales.

Table 14.1 *Corporate event objectives*

Financial objectives	Non-financial objectives
Increasing sales	Improving staff skills
Increasing revenue from other sources (e.g. sponsorship)	Team building and improving staff morale
	Networking
Achieving a return on investment	Stakeholder appreciation
	Building brand awareness and loyalty

Box 14.1   Critical Thinking Exercise

Are there any circumstances in which a corporate event is not hosted to achieve a profit-making objective?

Corporate Event Categories

As an umbrella term, 'corporate events' include business events, but are by no means limited to them. Some authors and professionals will occasionally use the acronym MICE – Meetings, Incentives, Conferences and Exhibitions (Rogers, 2008; see also Chapter 16 by Edwards and Taylor in this text). However, the MICE sector does not do justice to the diversity of corporate events (Getz, 2007). It is rather restrictive in that it does not recognize other, equally relevant, categories of corporate events (for example, product launches and training and team-building events). However, this term shall not be widely used throughout this chapter. Even the term 'corporate events' itself can be somewhat misleading, implying that corporate events exist only in the corporate sector and only serve the purposes of corporate entities. It is, therefore, important to point out that corporate events can exist within the public and not-for-profit sectors as well. The term 'corporate' relates to the purpose of the event (that is, the event being the tool to achieve particular organizational objectives), rather than the particular sector of the economy it pertains to.

Depending on what objectives are to be achieved and which audiences are being targeted, corporate events can be classified into different categories. At the same time, holding a particular type of corporate event may achieve more than one objective for the host organization. Additionally, each stakeholder involved with that event will have their own reasons for participation, which are directly linked to their individual or organizational objectives (Rogers, 2008). Thus, corporate events serve a multitude of interests for varying stakeholders. From the host organization's point of view, corporate events can be classified as *internal* (or aimed at the employees of the organization) or *external* (aimed at other stakeholders outside of the organization itself). There are also events that can target *both internal and external* audiences, as can be seen in Table 14.2 below. So what does each particular category entail?

Internal corporate events are aimed at achieving internal organizational objectives. For example, incentive travel, and training and team-building (TTB) events target the employees of the company itself. External corporate events, such as product launches and exhibitions, are aimed at promoting the company and/or its

Table 14.2   *Corporate event categories*

Internal	External	Both internal and external
Incentive travel	Product launches	Corporate hospitality and entertainment
Training and team building events (TTBs)	Exhibitions	Meetings and conferences

products/services to external audiences. The primary focus of external corporate events is the strengthening of corporate reputation and relationships with different stakeholders, which is expected to boost business results, for example increasing sales and market share. Corporate hospitality and entertainment, as well as meetings and conferences, can be oriented both internally (aimed at the employees of the company) and externally (aimed at a company's business partners, suppliers and other external stakeholders). Sometimes one conference can perform as an externally oriented event (for example, meeting with representatives of the company's sponsors) and as an internally oriented event (motivation and professional development for the employees) at the same time.

Meetings and conferences

Meetings and conferences are categories of corporate events that are becoming more and more prominent. Even with all the digital advances enabling instant long-distance communication that supports virtual meetings, there is still a need for that personal, face-to-face communication to support the building of successful long-term business relationships. As seen in Table 14.2, meetings and conferences can be geared towards both internal and external audiences. This category of corporate events focuses on creating an environment for delegates to expand their network of contacts, whilst at the same time improving their knowledge of a particular business area. The format may vary, depending on the needs of the delegates, from half-day to two/three-day, or even week-long events with overnight stays. With longer events, often the official business-related content of the meeting is supplemented with more informal activities in the evenings, aimed to facilitate the networking between delegates and also provide a sense of enjoyment and fun to offset the formality of the day sessions.

The UK Events Market Survey conducted by Eventia (2011) estimates that there were approximately 1.32 million events held in the UK in 2009 creating a sector worth around £18.8 billion, which is impressive considering that the economy had been in recession for much of that time and the corporate budgets for these types of events had decreased considerably. Some recent numbers indicate that the industry has grown even faster since 2009, and has accounted for £36.1 billion in overall economic benefits in 2010 (Rogers, 2010). The stability in demand for these types of events has led to the creation of local, national, government and industry-wide strategic plans which focus on strengthening this aspect of the UK events industry in the hope of increasing revenues generated by business events tourism in the years to come.

Incentive travel

Incentive travel is all-expenses paid travel that is used to reward staff for their good performance and motivate them to continue with their good work (Rogers, 2008).

It aims to improve employee morale and job satisfaction. Whilst previously considered only a treat for the company's few high-fliers, today incentives are being employed to reward whole teams of employees in performance-driven fields, such as sales. It is not uncommon to incorporate participation in various other types of events into the incentive travel package.

Since the turn of the millennium, sustainability has been high on the agenda for many businesses, which resulted in the increased importance of Corporate Social Responsibility (CSR) programmes. Many incentives today attempt to incorporate an opportunity for the participants to participate in CSR-related activities and give something back to the communities they visit, with a stronger emphasis on short-haul, rather than long-haul destinations.

Exhibitions

Exhibitions are large corporate events focused on external audiences. They can be classed as B2C (business to consumer) or B2B (business to business) exhibitions. In the industry they are most commonly known as *consumer shows* or *trade shows* (Getz, 2007). The main purpose of participating in an exhibition is boosting product sales and raising awareness of the product and the company amongst the target audiences visiting the exhibition. Event organizers recognize the need for innovative environments and programmes that create a positive experience for the attendees, hence sales-focused formats are being complemented with a variety of educational (for example, seminars, workshops, master classes and key-note speeches), as well as entertainment elements (for example, designated relaxation areas, activity corners, themed bars and other areas linked to the theme of the event). These additional elements represent a new revenue stream for exhibition organizers, as they can be sponsored by some of the companies exhibiting at the show.

Often, the companies organizing exhibitions are based at the exhibition venue and focus on developing a strong portfolio of events held at that same venue. Examples of these include Messe Frankfurt, the world's leading exhibitions organizer that manages its own venue and organizes international exhibitions in five business areas: Technology and Production, Consumer Goods and Leisure, Textiles and Textile Technologies, Mobility and Infrastructure, and Media and Creation. Messe Frankfurt uses exhibitions as an integral part of its business strategy to create its competitive advantage and increase its market dominance. London's Earl's Court and Olympia, as well as the ExCel centre are also venues worth noting with a constantly growing portfolio of both B2B and B2C exhibitions.

Corporate hospitality and entertainment

Corporate hospitality and entertainment events serve to establish and maintain successful business relationships with a variety of company stakeholders (Bowdin et al., 2011). From participation-based outdoor activities (for example, hovercrafting and clay pigeon shooting) to sleek, themed corporate parties, awards and other celebratory events, the emphasis is always on creating a positive, engaging experience that will influence the perception of the attendees towards the host brand or organization. These events can be organized as standalone events, or they can piggyback on the existing landmark events in the social calendar. For example, corporate entertainment can often include booking a box at a football stadium which includes catering and corporate gifts. For the more creative, anything from casino nights to murder mystery events are an option.

Product launches

Globally, according to Lindstrom (2008), 52 per cent of all new brands and 75 per cent of individual products fail. Today's consumers are no longer happy with a product just satisfying a particular need; that same product needs to have something the customer will buy into, it needs to have an image or a story. For the customer, the story begins with the launch and continues through the first-hand experience the customer gets in using that particular product or service, supported by the brand marketing (Berridge, 2007) and media coverage the product gets over time. It is, therefore, imperative that the product gets off to the right start with a product launch that truly reflects the spirit and personality of the brand, thus effectively creating a 'live communication' between the brand and the consumer (Getz, 2007). Product launches provide the first step in the introduction of a new product or service to both the media and consumers. Depending on the product/service being launched and the profile and reach of the company, these events can range from small tasting sessions in the local shopping mall to big, high-end, flamboyant affairs with celebrities attending, such as the launch of a new designer perfume.

Training and team building events

Training and team-building events (TTBs) have been gaining popularity over the last decade and a half. These events are recognized as relevant and necessary by all companies that wish to see their business grow. The implication is that, in order to have great business results, the company needs to have content and motivated staff. This can be achieved in two ways. Firstly, focusing on boosting an individual staff member's confidence by helping them work on the particular knowledge and skills required in their role can help influence their level of motivation and job satisfaction. This can include role-specific or area-specific training (such as sales of a particular product) or development of transferrable skills, such as communication, negotiation and presentation skills (Bowdin et al., 2011). Secondly, the building of overall staff morale can be achieved by engaging staff in various team-building activities, thus allowing them to get to know each other on a more personal, rather than professional level. Improving interpersonal relationships in the working environment helps create a more positive job context that has an impact on overall employee satisfaction in the workplace, although no direct link to performance has yet been established (Reic, 2010).

Case Study 14.1 Authentic Corporate Events: Team Building on Eco-farms

One of the largest team-building events ever held in Croatia was delivered on a family-owned eco-farm in the small village of Zivika near the town of Slavonski Brod in Slavonija in the summer of 2011. The event was organized for the employees of Vaillant, the leading global producer of heating solutions and domestic appliances. Eight hundred of them, from all levels within the organization and from Germany, Austria and Belgium, spent a day relishing the authentic local cuisine, fishing and traditional local games, as well as riding the barouche and taking a spin on the local authentic river boat along the river Sava.

The aim of the event was to provide an engaging and authentic experience that would help the client's employees escape from everyday work pressures, but that would also encourage them to get to know each other and bond, in order to foster good communication and atmosphere among the staff. Enjoying the delicious authentic Slavonian cuisine, the guests tried their luck in a variety of traditional Slavonian village games, such as hammering nails into wood logs and sawing wood with traditional Slavonian saws. Those interested in fishing had the opportunity to participate in a fishing contest at the farm's fishing pond and the car lovers were encouraged to enter the barouche race and experience the driving style of the early twentieth century. The prizes for the winners reflected the authentic feel of the location and included a baked pig (a traditional Slavonian dish), kulen rolls (traditional Slavonian spicy sausage) and homemade wine. Throughout the day the guests were entertained by traditional Slavonian music bands – tamburasi – who fulfilled the guests' musical requests, enhanced by the authentic sound of the *tamburica* (a traditional Slavonian string instrument, related to the lute, mandolin and balalaika), thus adding a touch of rural feel to the audio background of the day. The perfect ending to the day was provided by a ride in the first ever Slavonian tourist river boat. The clients were extremely happy with the service and have reportedly already booked the venue for a future event.

The event was the largest of its kind ever organized in Croatia, costing over £25,000 and provided an excellent branding opportunity for the venue, the region and the country as a whole. Additionally, it provided work for the local villagers involved in the event preparation (building parts of the venue and equipping it prior to guests' arrival) and delivery of the event (local music bands were used as entertainment and local women helped with cooking and serving the meals for the clients throughout the day). As such, this is a good example of an event that focuses on creating win–win–win partnerships between the organizers, the clients and the local community. More importantly, it highlights the importance of authenticity in creating a unique event experience and provides a good blueprint for the development of authentic events that can be both original and sustainable – the kind of offering that would benefit any destination in the world.

Key Stakeholders in Corporate Events

In the corporate events area, stakeholders are one of the key components that need to be taken into consideration; from the event inception all the way through to the evaluation stage (Rogers, 2008). Stakeholders are important because their expectations of and attitudes towards the event will have a strong influence on the event experience (Getz, 2007).

Key stakeholders need to be identified and managed effectively in order to enable the event to be a success (O'Toole, 2011). Stakeholders can be classified as internal or external to the organization. Internal stakeholders would include customers, employees, suppliers, managing board members, a board of advisors and other internal bodies/groups of people. External stakeholders could include corporate partners of the organization, government bodies, media and special interest groups. Clarkson's (1995) concept of primary and secondary stakeholders can facilitate the process of prioritizing and effectively managing relationships with stakeholders. However, it is important to acknowledge that stakeholder management is a fluid process and although it is not appropriate to categorically claim one stakeholder group is more important than another, different situations will demand that particular stakeholders be put first. It is up to the event manager to have an overview of the situation and decide which stakeholders to prioritize over others in a bid to maximize the cooperation and goodwill amongst all stakeholders and ensure successful event delivery.

Relatively few companies have a dedicated in-house event manager, or events department, and it is mostly national and multinational companies that tend to organize a large number of events every year, which justifies the costs of employing an event manager or maintaining an entire events department. For smaller companies with a lesser volume of events to handle, it makes more business sense to outsource the event organization to an agency or a freelance event manager.

Demand-side stakeholders – the buyers

Within the corporate event management process, on the demand side, buyers can take many forms: corporations, associations, the general public and entrepreneurs (Rogers, 2008). Buyers are people in charge of organizing a particular corporate event at an organization. As mentioned previously, not many organizations have a dedicated events officer, much less a dedicated events department to take over the planning and operational aspects of corporate events. Thus, the responsibility for putting together an event may lie with someone in the marketing department, human resources department, public relations department, or even a personal assistant (PA), depending on the internal structure of the organization. In addition to this, the level of involvement of this staff member in the event itself can vary. With smaller and less challenging events, it is just a matter of getting a quote and liaising with the chosen venue, and the venue's manager will then manage the operational aspects. On the other hand, the situation is sometimes much more complex and time-consuming, so the corporate buyer is responsible for the conceptualization of the event, supplier selection, the overall operational management of the event and satisfying the event's stakeholders. This will, understandably, entail a high level of responsibility for the final success or failure of the event.

The financial and other considerations for buyers arise from the type of organization they are working for. Whereas corporate buyers will probably have greater flexibility in designing their corporate events supported by considerable budgets, association and public buyers will have to be very mindful of the costs related to the event, as their income streams (as well as their freedom of spending) are limited. The greatest financial risk is taken on by the entrepreneurial buyers, that try and predict the demand for a particular type of event and then organize it in the hope of attracting enough attendees to cover the costs and make money.

Supply-side stakeholders – the suppliers

The major players on the supply side of corporate events are venues and catering companies, without which the delivery of a corporate event would be nearly impossible. Venues can include purpose-built locations, such as exhibition halls, conference and convention centres or team-building grounds. However, it is also possible to use other, non-purpose-built venues for the delivery of corporate events. For example, annual awards and celebration events are often delivered in famous museums or galleries, whose grandeur is then used to emphasize an event's status. The catering function depends on the requirements of the buyer, but some venues can pose limitations on this, as they may have long-standing contracts with particular catering companies, which have a monopoly over food and drink provision in that particular venue. The decision of the venue will, therefore, include some consideration of the type of catering service that is required by the event. Other suppliers of corporate events can include a multitude of additional services, such as entertainment and activity provision, décor, audio-visual and information technology solutions, delegate registration, security services, transport services, speaker management agencies, etc.

Intermediaries

In the world of corporate events, intermediaries can take the form of full-service event production and event management agencies. More commonly, freelance event managers and producers work on a contract basis and can prove to be very cost-effective, particularly for smaller companies that do not have big budgets to pay the soaring event agency fees. For outsourced corporate events, 'client is king'. The organization commissioning the event from an event management agency or a freelance event manager has to be kept happy. It sets the budget and it demands must be accommodated as much as possible. Whether the event commissioned is small (for example, a senior management team meeting with only seven attendees) or large (for example, a global conference on sustainability with over a thousand attendees), the quality of the service offered is what will make or break the event. It is also important to keep in mind that the agency (or freelance event manager) organizing an event on someone else's behalf needs to pay close attention to making sure the client's standards are met throughout the event management process. This includes managing the client's stakeholders on their behalf with the utmost care and consideration. Any dissatisfaction on the part of the client's stakeholders will reflect negatively on the client's satisfaction with the event and can result in the client not using that particular intermediary for any future projects. In the events industry generally, and with corporate events in particular, the event organizer's reputation is what wins new and retains old business and that reputation is only as strong as the last event delivered by that organizer. Therefore, it is imperative for professional event providers to maintain their standards of service at all times.

Other important stakeholders

Other external stakeholders can include:

- *Trade media* – in countries where events are a recognized industry (particularly the United States and the UK) there are specialized media channels that support the growth and development of the industry. In the UK the leading trade publications are *Event Magazine* and *Access All Areas*. Many of the media channels focus largely on the digital content rather than printed versions. This enables them to provide much more than just articles and reviews. For example, there are designated areas for forums and blogs that incorporate the element of social networking and co-creation, areas related to job search in the sector and other useful tools.
- *Trade and professional associations* – as the events industry is very diverse and is still fairly young, there has been a lot of ambiguity and overlap between the trade and professional associations operating within it. In the UK, Eventia has been accepted as the official trade body of the industry, whereas the Association of Event Organizers (AEO) is a more informal body comprising event management companies, venues and other support services. On an international level, the International Special Events Society (ISES) and Meetings Professionals International (MPI) both provide educational and networking opportunities for event professionals globally.
- *National tourism organizations and destination marketing organizations (NTOs and DMOs)* – these organizations are important allies of the events industry. Events are intrinsically linked to tourism and are increasingly becoming one of its most important development tools – acting as tourist attractions and important elements in building a destination's image.
- *Educational organizations* – there is an increasing number of event management courses offered by various types of institutions today – from further education courses to university Bachelor and Master's degrees. Industry trade bodies also have their own certification programmes and certificates in, for example, event risk management or

sustainability processes auditing. For instance, the sustainability standard certification BS 8901 is becoming increasingly important in the UK events industry and has been adopted as a supplier requirement by the London Organizing Committee of the Olympic Games (LOCOG).

 Box 14.2   Critical Thinking Exercise

What type of corporate event is a university recruitment fair? Who are the most important stakeholders at such an event?

Measuring Corporate Event Success

In capitalist societies the goal of most businesses is financial sustainability. Sometimes the business may contribute to preserving the environment, give back to the local (or even global) community and create a legacy for the generations to come, but these are just side-effects. The ultimate goal of any business is to make a profit. The *experience economy* (Pine and Gilmore, 1999) relies on events which are face-to-face interactions between brands and their customers. It is becoming increasingly difficult to pinpoint the actual costs of producing and delivering events. It is also particularly challenging to ascertain the income and benefits created by the event, and more specifically how much new business is generated by it. Despite these challenges, *cost-benefit analysis* (O'Toole and Mikolaitis, 2002) is still one of the dominant models for measuring event success.

Return on Investment (ROI) has been a major theme in global business over the better part of the last half century, focusing mainly on calculating return on invested assets, capital, cash and/or other fiscal items. These are all fairly easily quantifiable and can provide a reasonably accurate calculation of how much money a particular resource is bringing in. With events, return on investment is very difficult to measure due to the fact that delivery of an event uses not only physical resources, but to a large extent depends on the creativity and skills of the people involved in its conceptualization and delivery. These are challenging to quantify in financial terms, which presents a difficulty in using them to calculate a particular return on investment. For example, can the creativity of the event production team be easily translated into monetary terms? Certainly, it is easy enough to calculate their cost for the organization – the amount of money that will be paid to the production team for the time they have put into conceptualizing the event and coming up with the ideas. The problem actually arises when we attempt to pinpoint exactly how the concept and design of the event have influenced the event's target audience. For one-off events the question usually is: has the event had such a significant impact on the attendees that it is certain to create new business for the organization? For long-standing events, it would be worthwhile to know whether the event experience, delivered through the event concept and design, is enough to create repeat visits by the same visitors. Another difficulty in calculating the return on investment is the distinction between various stakeholder groups that are associated with the event. As mentioned in the previous section, various stakeholder groups related to the event are all looking to gain something from their association with the event. This means all of them are looking for some sort of return on investment for whatever it is that they have invested in the event, whether it is financial or in-kind sponsorship (corporate sponsors), work hours (staff and volunteers), media coverage (media) or operational support (suppliers).

One of the most recognized methods for measuring ROI with events was developed by Phillips (2003) for calculating the return on investment in training programmes. The model builds on Kirkpatrick's (1998) four-stage model of evaluation and proposes five stages of evaluation of training and performance improvement programmes. It also highlights the aspects that can be evaluated at each level, ranging from attendee expectations and satisfaction at Level 1 all the way through to the actual ROI at Level 5. Since its first publication in the late 1990s, this model is slowly being introduced as a relevant evaluation tool for other types of events, although no consensus has yet been reached in terms of defining a standard model (or process) of ROI calculation for events in general, nor corporate events in particular.

Apart from return on investment, there are other indicators of business success that can be suitable for measuring the success of a particular event. Some authors and event professionals are now turning to measuring the Return on Objectives (ROO), as an indicator particularly suitable for events (Phillips et al., 2008; de Lisle, 2009). The idea is that achievement of the specific objectives related to the event can help identify the overall success of the event, particularly if those objectives have been well-defined and measurable. For example, if a conference producer identifies the target attendance for their event as 300 attendees, it is fairly easy to ascertain whether or not this objective has been achieved, thus establishing whether the investment in the event has been justified or not. Another example would be setting a target of £50,000 in sponsorship. If at the end of the event this amount has been reached or (even better) exceeded, the event could be deemed a success. Of course, events will usually have more than just one objective, so the overall success of the event will depend on how well all of the set objectives have been achieved and their relative importance to the organization.

It is important to note that each organization will usually define its own indicators of success, depending on the nature and profile of the business. It is the same with events. The event management team decides in the initial stages of event planning what the indicators of event success will be. Another challenge with events, however, is the fact that the success of the event itself depends largely on the satisfaction of other stakeholders involved (Getz, 2007). If the event organizing team has managed to achieve all of their event objectives, but other stakeholders have not managed to achieve their targets, this could impact negatively on the future sustainability of the event, as these stakeholders might withdraw their support or participation in the event in the future. It is, therefore, important to include the perspectives of these stakeholders when designing the success measurement framework for the event and setting the initial event objectives.

Sustainability in Corporate Events

As any other area of business, corporate event management has its own difficulties and challenges. One of the emerging areas of focus within the event industry in general, and with corporate events in particular, is sustainability. Sustainability has been on the global business agenda for the better part of the past two decades. More details on the evolution of the concept from the initial Brundtland Report (UNWCED, 1987) to the more recent introduction of quality standards are available in Chapter 10 by Cavagnaro et al. in this text. In the context of corporate events, two key developments are important to highlight. Firstly, the adoption of Elkington's (1997) concept of the Triple Bottom Line (TBL) within the events sector and its utilization by Hede (2008) to develop a stakeholder mapping tool which highlights the areas of impact a particular event can have on its primary stakeholders. The tool is useful not only in the planning stages of an event for mapping out stakeholders and event impacts, but also in the evaluation stage of the event for assessing the impacts (costs and benefits) in relation to various event stakeholders. The main benefit of the TBL model is that it helps to identify synergies between particular stakeholder groups which can then be used to effectively manage these and ensure stakeholder satisfaction with the event.

Secondly, sustainability initiatives are being incorporated into the day-to-day practice of corporate event management, although the majority of them focus only on the *greening* aspect of sustainability, that is, managing the environmental impact of events. In the UK, the trend of certifying processes related to event management is already well under way. With corporate events, sustainability is intrinsically linked to the choice of venue and suppliers, so the scope of implementation of the BS 8901 standard is widening. The overall aim is to incorporate sustainability in all levels of the event management process, in order to maximize the positive and minimize the negative impacts of corporate events. Companies are increasingly interested in obtaining the BS 8901 certification in relation to their corporate events, which is considered to improve the company's competitive edge and Jack Morton Worldwide, the leading brand experience agency, is one of the most recent proud owners of the BS 8901 standard. Business practices of many event providers currently support the implementation of sustainability initiatives in the environmental domain of the triple bottom line. Unfortunately, less focus has so far been put on economic and social sustainability, so the next steps would be to clearly define the indicators within the economic and social domains and move towards streamlining the processes in order to ensure sustainability in these areas as well.

 Box 14.3   Critical Thinking Exercise

What sustainability initiatives have you noticed being adopted by companies in your country?

Case Study 14.2   Corporate Events in the Non-Profit Sector

AIESEC is an international non-profit organization providing a platform for young people to discover and develop their potential. The organization was founded in 1948, following the Second World War, as an avenue for increasing intercultural awareness and establishing positive relationships between different countries, in order to promote peace and ethnic and cultural tolerance. Currently it operates in 107 countries and has over 45,000 members globally, focusing on providing challenging opportunities for students and recent graduates by enabling them to get involved in the day-to-day management of local, national and international offices, organizing a variety of projects and events, as well as spending some time on professional internships abroad. Although AIESEC is a student-run, non-profit organization, it enjoys a strong reputation globally and is held in high esteem by both students wishing to develop crucial professional skills and competencies and its corporate partners. Global giants such as Procter and Gamble, PricewaterhouseCoopers, Tata Consultancy Services, DHL and Alcatel-Lucent, who partner with the organization, regard it as a powerful source of talented young professionals with a global mindset and passion for being agents of change in society.

As an organization, AIESEC has a variety of both primary and secondary stakeholders. Firstly, AIESEC members are one of the key primary stakeholder groups, as they determine and manage the development of the organization. Secondly, the student population at universities across the world is an important stakeholder as well, as it can be targeted for recruitment purposes: to source members of local committees or local, national and international executive boards of the organization, as well as candidates for the organization's international professional internships programme. Managing boards of the universities where the local and national committee offices are hosted are an important stakeholder, as these boards have direct influence over the survival of the local and national chapters by providing in-kind sponsorship to the organization. There are also a number of corporate partners, from small SMEs to big multinational corporations (such as the ones mentioned above), that have long-standing partnerships with the organization with a view to sourcing talented young professionals with a particular mindset. Finally, there are also the organization's alumni, a large proportion of whom have built successful international careers and continue to support the organization in a variety of ways.

As just about any other large international organization, AIESEC has a specific organizational culture, which is underpinned by its structure and a variety of both internal and external corporate events. These events support the successful implementation of the AIESEC Experience Framework – a strategic tool for developing and managing young professional talent, which is the primary objective of the organization. These events also help strengthen the global brand of the organization.

(Continued)

(Continued)

Internally, the annual conference cycle is designed to support the members of the organization in developing the key skills and competencies required for managing the work within the organization. Conferences are themed according to the organization's requirements, usually last 2–5 days and are implemented on a national level. Members from all the local committees within a particular country come together to gain specific knowledge and skills, as well as to network with their peers to build their own network of contacts that will support them in their future work within the organization. With larger national conferences, aimed at bringing all the levels of the organization together, the agenda is split into multiple tracks which run in parallel and are tailored to the particular needs of the varying target audiences. For example, young members (affectionately known as 'newbies') attend sessions that focus on building their knowledge of internal organizational processes as well as building particular transferrable skills, such as communication or time management skills. The agenda for the members of executive boards maps out the meetings required to support the legislative process within the organization, deciding about the direction of the organization, as well as supporting functional meetings where the organization's officers can network and discuss any issues related to their particular functional area (for example, external relations, finance, human resources, etc.). Some of the conferences also offer tracks aimed at 'outgoing interns' (that is, students selected to go on internships abroad), focusing on developing their cultural awareness and preparing them for their journey ahead, as well as alumni, focusing on exploring possibilities for their involvement with the organization. With such a variety of objectives and target audiences, it is extremely important to get all of the operational elements completely right. Depending on the country, some of these conferences attract an attendance of 600–800 people and provide considerable logistical challenges so if things are not coordinated perfectly, disruptions to the agenda can severely affect the success of the conference.

Aside from the internal conference cycle, AIESEC also delivers a number of events aimed at external audiences. A prime example of these are career fairs that are designed to provide a platform for leading national and international companies to get access to up-and-coming young talent – students in their final years of study or recently graduated and about to start building their careers. These fairs are essentially employer exhibitions and tend to rate very highly with many of the leading national and international companies. These companies commit their staff to interacting with the students by manning the company stands and delivering company presentations to the attendees at the fairs. Past exhibitors have always emphasized how happy they are with the profile of the students they come into contact with, which is also confirmed by their continued involvement with these events and AIESEC as an organization. In their role of bringing together companies and young professional talent, apart from career fairs, some AIESEC chapters use various types of more focused business events to engage a number of their stakeholders.

(Continued)

(Continued)

These events serve several purposes. Firstly, the participating companies are able to gain fresh solutions to their current business problems. Secondly, participating students get the experience of working in teams to design business strategies and tactics in relation to real-life case studies, as well as contacts with companies that could potentially become their future employers. And finally, AIESEC members get relevant event management experience and strengthen their professional skills.

The type of external corporate events AIESEC organizes varies not only according to the needs of the organization itself, but also to the needs of its traditional corporate partners. However, the guiding principle for all events organized by AIESEC is to maximize their impact by creating synergies between various stakeholder groups. Thus, corporate partners are also invited to participate in the internal conference cycle, either via involvement in the official day agenda, or using the evening events as a form of corporate entertainment and expressing gratitude for the continuous support the partners offer the organization.

These are just a few examples of how an organization can use events to support its own purpose and deliver on its mission. It is crucial to recognize that events can be used to involve a number of different stakeholders and that it is these synergies that tend to give events momentum and ensure their success.

Case Study Questions

1 Who are the main stakeholders of AIESEC?
2 Which categories of corporate events does AIESEC use and for which purposes? How do they fit with its core business?
3 Suggest other examples of corporate events that might be useful for AIESEC to focus on. Justify your recommendations.

Chapter Summary

Corporate event managers can often feel like they are performing a balancing act: managing various stakeholders and deadlines while trying to achieve the final objectives set for the event within the budget approved. In designing and executing corporate events it is important to always keep in mind the following three questions: What need does the event fulfil? How does the event fit in with the overall business identity of the organization? Does the event share the specific business culture of the organization? Only when all these factors have been coordinated, will the event be considered an authentic representation of the business itself and have the chance to really engage its target audiences and deliver an engaging experience.

The chapter has highlighted the increasing relevance of corporate events in modern economies. It has demonstrated that, although the bottom line for any business venture (corporate events included) is financial sustainability, there are a number of non-financial objectives that corporate events aim to fulfil. Additionally, it is important to recognize the multitude of stakeholders related to corporate events, as each of these stakeholders will have certain expectations of the event and objectives of their own that the event is supposed to fulfil.

Review Questions

1   Are corporate events well developed in your country? If so, why are corporate events becoming increasingly important in the current economy?
2   What is the difference between return on investment (ROI) and return on objectives (ROO)?
    a   Which one would you recommend for a product launch and which one for a networking event, and why?
    b   Can you think of any other performance indicators that might be suitable for corporate events?
3   What type of objectives can corporate events help achieve for organizations? Provide examples.
4   What are the issues facing sustainability in corporate event management?

Glossary

BS 8901 – British Standard number 8901, the world's first quality standard on sustainable event management, published by the British Standards Institute (BSI).

Additional Resources

Books and journal articles

Allen, J. (2007) *The Executive Guide for Corporate Events and Business Entertaining: How to Choose and Use Corporate Fun*. Ontario: John Wiley and Sons.
A complete guide to using corporate incentives and hospitality in business.

Allen, J. (2009) *Event Planning: The Ultimate Guide to Successful Meetings, Corporate Events, Fundraising Galas, Conferences, Conventions, Incentives and Other Special Events* (2nd edn). Ontario: John Wiley & Sons.
A step-by-step text which provides guidance on hosting a range of corporate events.

Hede, A.M. (2008) 'Managing special events in the new era of the Triple Bottom Line', *Event Management*, 11(1–2): 13–22.
A theoretical investigation into the consideration of achieving 'people, profit and planet' objectives in event management.

O'Toole, W. and Mikolaitis, P. (2002) *Corporate Event Project Management*. New York: Wiley.
A good handbook on managing corporate events.

Phillips, J.J., Breining, M.T. and Pulliam Phillips, P. (2008) *Return on Investment in Meetings and Events*. Oxford: Butterworth-Heinemann.
A good clear guide to calculating return on investment.

Useful websites

http://www.aiesec.co.uk/
AIESEC was the focus of the main case study and the site contains a wealth of information including opportunities for event industry placements.

http://www.bsigroup.co.uk
BSI, the British Standards Institute, launched the first national standard in sustainable event management – the BS 8901 – and offers a good overview of the standard's requirements, as well as relevant industry-recognized training.

http://www.eventia.org.uk
Eventia is the official body of the events industry in the UK and offers a variety of event-related resources and opportunities for networking within the sector.

http://www.mpiweb.org
MPI, Meetings Professionals International, is the leading global association of event professionals focusing on meetings and corporate events.

References

Berridge, G. (2007) *Events Design and Experience*. Oxford: Butterworth-Heinemann.

Bowdin, G., Allen, J., O'Toole, W., Harris, R. and McDonnell, I. (2011) *Events Management* (3rd edn). Oxford: Butterworth-Heinemann.

Clarkson, M. (1995) 'A stakeholder framework for analysing and evaluating corporate social performance', *Academy of Management Review*, 20(1): 92–117.

De Lisle, L. (2009) *Creating Special Events*. Champaign, IL: Sagamore Publishing.

Department for Culture, Media and Sport (DCMS) (2007) *Winning: A Tourism Strategy for 2012 and Beyond*. London: DCMS [Online]. Available from: http://www.tourism2010.com/CMS/Resources/ResourceLibrary.aspx.

Elkington, J. (1997) *Cannibals With Forks: The Triple Bottom Line of 21st Century Business*. Oxford: Capstone.

Eventia (2011) *Green Shoots Forecast for Britain's Live Events Sector*. London: Eventia [Online]. Available from: http://www.eventia.org.uk/html/article/green-shoots-forecast-by-britains-live-events-sector.

Getz, D. (2007) *Event Studies: Theory, Research and Policy for Planned Events*. Oxford: Butterworth-Heinemann.

Hede, A.M. (2008) 'Managing special events in the new era of the Triple Bottom Line', *Event Management*, 11(1–2): 13–22.

Kirkpatrick, D.L. (1998) *Evaluating Training Programs: The Four Levels* (2nd edn). San Francisco: Berrett-Koehler Publishers Inc.

Lindstrom, M. (2008) *Buyology: How Everything We Believe about Why We Buy is Wrong*. London: Random House Business Books.

O'Toole, W. (2011) *Events Feasibility and Development: From Strategy to Operations*. Oxford: Butterworth-Heinemann.

O'Toole, W. and Mikolaitis, P. (2002) *Corporate Event Project Management*. New York: Wiley.

Phillips, J.J. (2003) *Return on Investment in Training and Performance Improvement Programs: A Step-by-Step Manual for Calculating Financial Return* (2nd edn). Burlington: Butterworth-Heinemann.

Phillips, J.J., Breining, M.T. and Pulliam Phillips, P. (2008) *Return on Investment in Meetings and Events*. Oxford: Butterworth-Heinemann.

Pine, B.J. and Gilmore, J.H. (1999) *The Experience Economy: Work is Theatre and Every Business a Stage*. Boston: Harvard Business School Press.

Reic, I. (2010) 'The role of teambuilding events in developing effective teams: A literature review', *London Journal of Tourism, Sport and Creative Industries*, 3(4): 21–27.

Rogers, T. (2008) *Conferences and Conventions: A Global Industry* (2nd edn). Oxford: Butterworth-Heinemann.

Rogers, T. (2010) *Britain for Events: A Report on the Size and Value of Britain's Events Industry, its Characteristics, Trends, Opportunities and Key Issues* [Online]. Available from: http://www.britainforevents.co.uk/pdf/Britain%20for%20Events%20Report%20final.pdf.

Shone, A. and Parry, B. (2010) *Successful Event Management: A Practical Handbook*. Andover: Cengage Learning.

Tassiopoulos, D. (2010) *Events Management: A Developmental and Managerial Approach*. Claremont, SA: Juta.

United Nations World Commission on Environment and Development (UNWCED) (1987) *Our Common Future* (Brundtland Report). Oxford: Oxford University Press.

PART 4

EXTENDED CASE STUDIES

The final section in *Events Management: An International Approach* considers a series of extended cases studies that seek to combine the numerous elements addressed in Parts 1–3 within a case structure. Case studies can assist students in understanding how the application of event management knowledge addresses the challenges that face event managers. There are four extended case studies which address a series of topics and elements from the first three sections; ranging from risk management in music events, to the importance of intellectual capital in MICE events and even a comprehensive overview of the many and varied operational activities of fundraising events.

The review questions asked in each of these cases are not intended to be addressed with quick and easy answers but considered using the theoretical and practical aspects covered in the first 14 chapters. Students are recommended to begin this section by reading through the semi-fictional case 'Sleeping Through the Static' by Stephen Henderson. This case deliberately differs from the other three as the review questions contain guided answers that demonstrate the complexity of case solutions. It is an attempt to break from a straightforward response to a given event situation – that may be the initial hunch of the student – and in some way addresses problems using a range of information from the myriad experiences of practising event managers.

Destination marketing in the twenty-first century requires cities and regions to have high-quality and well-managed facilities. The more successful a city or region in attracting MICE events, the more frequently these facilities are used. Knowledge generated from the operations of these events facilities are of great use to the many stakeholders that events engage. From an event organizer's perspective, competent and confident event and facility managers are paramount in making every event a success. Sarah Edwards and Liander Taylor's case, 'The Exportation of Event Expertise: Taking Best Practice to International Markets in the MICE Sector', examines how knowledge and competence in event-facility provision leads to competitive advantage for the facility to increase the number of MICE events held and also export this knowledge to assist in the establishment of facilities in new markets.

The development of the economies of the Gulf Region states since the turn of the new millennium has been phenomenal. Events and tourism have been central to this development, however the competition between these states (whether in Dubai, Abu Dhabi or Qatar) for visitors and investment has been intense. In the third case, 'The Marketing Strategy for the 13th IAAF Indoor World Athletics Championships 2010 in Doha: Creating a Value Constellation', Alain Ferrand is joined by Maher N. Safi and Tariq Saed Al-Abdulla from the Qatar Olympic Committee to present a comprehensive overview of how a local organizing committee approached the event marketing at the IAAF 2010 World Athletics Indoor Championships in Doha and used the process to create 'value-constellations' for the event's stakeholders.

The final case, 'Event Operations: The London City Airport's Fundraising Day' by Polly Larner, presents a detailed coverage of the complexities involved in managing a fundraising event. As the final case it is clear that many of the aspects covered in this title have relevance not only for the highest profile international events but even those events that emphasize local relevance. Larner provides students with an insight into the sheer scale of event operations; indeed the view 'from the coal-face' highlights the event-day duties of one of the event managers which reinforces our understanding of event work as, simply, eventful.

15

Sleeping Through the Static

Stephen Henderson

Please note that this case study uses a real-life example but a fictional narrative has been woven into the tale to enrich the case study as a means of learning.

Introduction

As global communications have become simpler but more sophisticated with new technologies, the market for entertainments such as music and sport has globalized. Add to this the reduced profits that artists receive from recorded music (due to the increase in downloads as opposed to CD purchase) and you have a situation where musicians are just itching to get out on the road. In contrast to this, environmentalists have complained about the scale of tours that seem to travel across the world carrying huge amounts of equipment. For example, U2 have been criticized for their '360°' tour with its large 'in the round' stage set moved from concert to concert around the world starting in 2009 and through to 2011 (see Figure 15.1).

Figure 15.1 *U2's '360°' tour*

A number of consulting organizations such as Julie's Bicycle (www.juliesbicycle.com) and Music Matters (a division of EFFECT) (www.effectpartners.com) have helped to provide information for artists to make better choices on their approach to touring. This case study looks at Jack Johnson's 'Sleep Through The Static' tour that crossed the world in 2008 and tried to address some of the criticisms of other tours.

Case Elements

The tour plan

The planning for the tour began in 2004 with a roundtable discussion between Jack Johnson, prompted and accompanied by his wife, Kim, and a leading consultant who had developed an environmentally friendly approach to artist contracts and riders. Going under the trademarked name of the 'EnviroRider' (see *Scientific American*, 2011), this approach meant that promoters on the tour had to support environmental aims by managing their use of power for lights and PA, adopting biodiesel fuels, offering recycling facilities at venues, etc. Additionally, there was an idea to create a small marketplace within each concert for 'not for profit' organizations, typically charities, that would help support the social aims of local communities.

With this innovative approach in place, promoters around the world were obliged to busy themselves putting together the infrastructure required at each concert and Jack Johnson's management began recruiting local organizations that would feature in the 'not for profit' village at each concert. Here, these local organizations were allowed to recruit members and promote their activities in an expectation that they would boost the support for their particular cause (see Figure 15.2). Before the concert itself, the local organizations were encouraged to organize events that would help to promote their activities as well as their involvement with the upcoming concert.

To complete the picture, it was suggested that an online network would usefully create a feeling of community with the fans and get across the environmentally friendly message. Taking its lead from Jack Johnson's 'All At Once' song, a website was developed to facilitate the online community (www.jackjohnsonmusic.com/allatonce). Fans were encouraged to sign up by the availability of free music downloads for those who became members and the intention was made quite clear by their marketing strapline 'An individual action, multiplied by millions, creates global change'. To support this, the site made available lots of information about the environmental activities and the 'not for profit' organizations involved in the work. Furthermore, the 'All At Once' front page carried Jack Johnson's fan forum and the whole site was integrated with his own music-related information.

During the tour itself, it was important that those involved at each concert behaved in a manner that respected environmental and social needs during the build, during the

Figure 15.2   *Surf Relief at Jack Johnson's Newquay concert*

event itself and at the breakdown at the end. So, Reverb (www.reverb.org/index.php) were engaged to act as monitors looking at how well the contractual needs of the 'EnviroRider' were being met and to record key quantifiable measures at each of the concerts in a way that would allow a retrospective audit reporting at the end of the tour.

Johnny and June

Johnny and June had been music fans for many years having met at college in their late teens. Now, in their late 20s, if Johnny wasn't writing songs, they were attending music events of one kind or another down near their home in the south-west of the UK. In this region, there was a healthy surfing community and they had been drawn into this by some surfer friends. They'd discovered that it wasn't all sea, sand and surf. Indeed, there was a strong community feel that led to wider socializing and activities such as campaigning for cleaner beaches.

Their taste in music was quite broad and they liked to kick the 'post-Christmas blues' by trying to figure out what they could do over the summer. As they were now both working, they had money to spend but were wary of going wild as they still had big student loans to pay off. In fact, they'd decided they could really only afford one decent sized event every summer alongside their other socializing. So, as they sat down with their last festive food, this was the list that was under consideration along with their personal notes:

Box 15.1   Johnny and June's Options

Kokua Festival – big on Jack Johnson (almost my own personal Jesus) but it's an expensive trip to Hawaii for his two-day festival despite the good weather.

Glastonbury – lots of different bands and varied entertainment across a few days but it's going to cost us and it may be time for another mud bath if it gets too wet.

Beach Break Live – good local festival over a few days but not many big name acts and full of students – cry, cry, cry – those were the days! Do you remember? No responsibilities – no mortgage!

Wakestock – love the idea of the surf but this one is as much about extreme sports as music and needs a weekend trip up to Wales. Isn't Wales just too rainy?

Jack Johnson – it's just one day down in Newquay and a few other decent acts. Last time I was down there, in the evening, there was a ring of fire on the beach where everyone was singing – could be the one!

The promoter and the purchase

While Johnny and June were busying figuring out where they should spend their hard-earned money, the promoter for Jack Johnson was working on getting the tour dates all sorted. For this major event organizer, in addition to selling the tickets, it required making sure the needs of the artists were met, including those of the 'EnviroRider'. With a mix of outdoor and indoor concerts in most of the major UK cities, there was a need to make sure that venues had suitable facilities both technically for the production and in terms of food and drink outlets for the attendees. There was more work to do with the outdoor concerts than the indoor venues because suppliers tended to be engaged on a one-off basis for each concert.

As well as sorting out these new sites, there were plenty of tickets to sell but there were plenty of fans too. The promoter's marketing team kicked into action with the usual mix of marketing communications aimed not only at the surfing-related fans but also at a wider audience that was generally thought to be aged between 15 and 35.

As a further part of the suggested approach, the promoter made arrangements with the online ticket distributor to allow ticket purchasers to have the option to carbon offset their travel to the concert. Initially, it was thought that this would be a simple change but it necessitated complex discussions with the ticketing outlet as to how this would work for different concerts. It also meant the promoter had to make a search for a carbon offset project that met sustainability standards. Hard work but it was worth it and much appreciated by the artist and his team.

The day of the concert

Johnny and June reviewed the different summer fun opportunities. Whatever it was that influenced them (cost, weather, artists, etc.), they bought tickets for the local Jack Johnson concert in Newquay. They didn't take up the carbon offset option but felt no guilt as they lived quite locally hence they were not travelling far. In the end, it was lucky that they chose to get tickets for the second concert in Newquay as the first date on the preceding day was cancelled due to bad weather. Howling winds turned the temporary stage into a hazardous place to be and one set of fans for the two sold-out concerts ended up being disappointed. Though this occurred with only 24 hours to go before the first concert, disappointed ticket holders were refunded their money and promised that he'd be back in the area on the next tour. So, when Johnny and June arrived in Newquay and parked, there was a long queue but they were happy to walk the line to get their tickets checked off.

On entering the arena, they found a large grassy area stretching out before the stage and noticed some stalls in the distance and a scattering of food and drink suppliers around the edge of the arena area. Despite bumping into their friend, Tammy, the 'typical' British summer weather was not inviting with wind and rain blasting across the cliff top where the site was positioned. Johnny thought how spectacular it would be if, even for a short time, the sun would just appear to set over the ocean. His mood was lifted by some friendly All at Once volunteers wearing branded T-shirts (see Figure 15.3) who offered them a 'passport' and suggested that they could visit the 'non-profit' stands in the village to collect stamps on their passport. Though it seemed a rather strange offer, there was time to kill and their passport could be added into a draw to win seats to watch the concert from the side of the stage. So, the three of them headed over to the stall in the distance.

When they arrived in the village, time flew by as they chatted with the stallholders who explained their activities. Though they were familiar with two local tourist spots – The Eden Project and Jamie Oliver's Fifteen restaurant (which helps some unemployed people to train as chefs) – they gained useful insights into the activities of other organizations. Indeed, though aware of the Surf Relief Festival, they did not realize that the proceeds of the event went to supporting disabled access to surfing by way of a range of special activities.

Having enjoyed some food from a vendor offering free-trade products in recyclable packaging, the time flew by, the sun came out and set behind the sea. Just as Johnny and June thought it could not get much better, an announcement from the stage declared them winners of the prize draw and they took their places on stage to watch the show. In the morning, as Johnny arose and remembered Jack Johnson's great show, he noticed the spare passport that he'd collected and it reminded him of the different aims of the 'not-for-profit' organizations. It also advised that the impact of the tour

Figure 15.3 *All at Once volunteers in their branded T-shirts greet the fans*

would be communicated by way of a report posted at a later date on Jack Johnson's website (see Figure 15.4). But that wasn't all. June suddenly announced that she was pregnant with their first child and she'd dreamt of a baby called Sue. There were hugs and celebrations. Later, as Johnny stared into the shaving mirror thinking of this premonition, he couldn't help but think that the baby would be a boy.

Case Analysis

This case study aims to provide the reader with a walk-through of how the case and the review questions can be answered by using the information contained within this book. Each of the following ten questions uses the case as a means of extrapolating and applying the textbook materials. The cases that follow each have a stand-alone case analysis section that is then developed further by the review questions.

Case Review Questions

1 What does this case tell you about the dynamics and range of internal stakeholders required to build an events team to work in a touring, global situation?
2 You are the promoter (event organizer) of these concerts. Detail who you would consider as the key external stakeholders and which communication methods you feel would be appropriate for them.

3 Consider how you might move a potential attendee through a sequence of steps that lead from total unawareness of Jack Johnson's interest in social issues to involvement with a not-for-profit organization at one of his concerts.

4 Compare the marketing of tickets for this event and encouraging people to behave in a sustainable manner before, during and after their attendance at the event.

5 Considering the issues around major events such as these concerts, how is sustainable development being addressed by the approach taken by Jack Johnson?

6 Evaluation is an essential factor to successfully manage major events like this. Consider how Figure 15.4 addresses the evaluation of Jack Johnson's 'Sleep Through the Static' concerts.

7 There were a range of options for Johnny and June to choose from. Define and evaluate perceptual maps that explain how they came to prefer the Jack Johnson concert above the other options.

8 Explain how the risks would be assessed prior to the cancellation of the first Jack Johnson concert.

9 Explain how the use of outdoor and indoor concerts on this tour would affect the event management.

10 The first concert in Newquay was cancelled due to bad weather. Consider the options that present themselves to communicate this news and present a suitable communication plan.

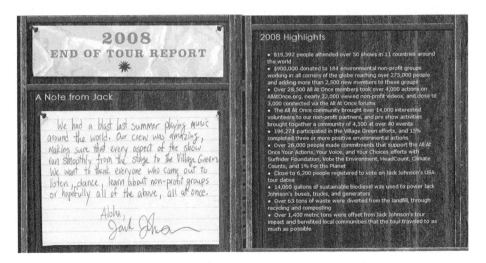

Figure 15.4 'Sleep Through The Static' tour report

Case Review Guided Answers

1 What does this case tell you about the dynamics and range of internal stakeholders required to build an events team to work in a touring, global situation?

The case shows the large number of internal stakeholders often found in an events team and, in particular, highlights the added complexity that a sustainable touring approach requires. These stakeholders include the following:

- The *artist* who has not only a music-based show to present to the audience but also a vision of sustainable touring.
- The *artist management* who are responsible for agreeing the events team, the commercial and practical relationships for the tour.
- The *consultant* who advises on the best way to meet the sustainable touring requirement.
- The *agent* who seeks promoters around the world who are able to meet the requirements of the sustainable production and marketing of the show.
- The *promoters* who can deliver the show requirements at a local level in terms of production facilities, marketing tickets and overseeing the sustainable elements.
- The *suppliers* to the event of food, drink, staging, PA, etc. as organized by the promoters.
- The *auditors* who observe the actual practices put in place by the promoter and suppliers at each show to check that they meet the sustainability requirements of the artist management.
- The *not-for-profit organizations* that become part of the advance promotion and on-site village after they have been approved by artist management.

Within the team, more stakeholders could be considered such as the volunteer teams working on the village and the 'All At Once' website developers. Nevertheless, the list above reveals a typical extensive, mixed events team who may only have temporary relationships for the duration of the tour planning and implementation. The reader should also recognize that the global nature of the tour means that stakeholders, such as promoters or suppliers, will be replicated at each stop on the global tour. Though some stakeholders may operate across a number of countries, some will certainly differ from country to country. As a result, there will be the usual range of cultural issues to manage such as the requirements of different languages and varying local customs. Similarly, there may be different levels of motivation to meet the sustainability objectives of the events team that will need to be addressed in order to get the most out of the group.

2   You are the promoter (event organizer) of these concerts. Detail who you would consider as the key external stakeholders and which communication methods you feel would be appropriate for them.

For marketing communications, it is important that the preferences of different stakeholders are identified. Hence, in addition to those internal stakeholders examined in question 1, the external stakeholders also have to be clearly identified at the starting point. In identifying all the stakeholders, we take those mentioned in the previous question and add in the ticket holders, media, local government and community, audience, local support artists, local fire and police service, amongst others, to complete the picture.

In communication with suppliers, it is clear that personal communication is likely to be more efficient and effective than posting information on a website as contract details will need discussing, whereas for the ticket holders this would be reversed. There is no clear answer to this question in terms of preference as a limitation of the case is that it does not reveal the scale of some stakeholders, for example maybe those suppliers are so large in number that less personal communication approaches, such as using standard emails and contracts, might be in place. In many of these cases, personal communication would meet the needs of both stakeholder parties, that is those sending and receiving communications. For example, members of the events team would make personal communications with the local police to work out how to manage the traffic movement to and from the event. However, it is important to recognize the different communication options that are available to the promoter. These might be broken down into the traditional media such as using posters, flyers, newspapers, magazines for mass-market communication and letters and phone calls for more directed communication, and the modern media of websites, email, viral marketing, social media, etc.

New technology lends itself to low-cost, mass communication and, in this example, it was identified that websites can be used for announcing matters such as the Jack Johnson tour dates. So, it can be seen that new technology is mainly used for communication with the audience who find this appropriate and convenient. However, the choice of communication method does not only depend on the target for the communication but also the communication objective. For example, announcing the tour dates on the website is suitable for an objective based on awareness (from AIDA) but, if evacuation of the event area was required, it would be illogical to announce this on the website. Instead, it can be anticipated that pre-planned announcements (from their emergency planning activity) would be communicated from the stage through the public address systems.

Also, this question allows the exploration of communication preferences. For example, as people receive more and more emails and SMS messages direct to their mobile devices, readers might want to consider the rising importance of these direct communication methods. However, wider issues such as the potential for individuals to receive information via other means such as printed matter arriving with their tickets, or the need for information to be communicated in different languages should be considered to optimize their effectiveness (in terms of reaching the target) and their efficiency (in terms of cost).

3   Consider how you might move a potential attendee through a sequence of steps that lead from total unawareness of Jack Johnson's interest in social issues to involvement with a not-for-profit organization at one of his concerts.

The process followed is the step-by-step hierarchy of a model such as AIDA (a model of consumer cognition that follows the sequence of becoming *Aware*, generating *Interest*, encouraging *Desire* and facilitating *Action*). Communications should be geared to follow this. So, using AIDA for example, the first task is to communicate with the stakeholder to make them aware (A) of the 'not-for-profit' activity. This is seen in the case by way of examples where the 'not-for-profit' organization arranges pre-concert events to publicize their own activities as well as the concert. Similarly, the 'All At Once' website helps to make people aware. Both of these approaches would, hopefully, raise interest (I) too. If not, the volunteers at the concert would raise both awareness and interest by their discussion with attendees and the explanation of the incentive of being added to a draw would create desire (D) in the attendees to look over the 'not-for-profit' village. Here, each stall member explains their 'not for profit' and tries to get an action (A) from the attendee, such as joining their mailing list or getting further involved with their activities, for example to help clean up a beach. It should be noted that this type of social marketing uses the step-by-step process to look for a permanent change in behaviour, whereas the single actions seen in the case may be forgotten after the concert. Interestingly, one might reflect on how much permanent change to behaviour has been achieved.

4   Compare the marketing of tickets for this event and encouraging people to behave in a sustainable manner before, during and after their attendance at the event.

Marketing tickets for an event has all the characteristics of services marketing, for example what is being sold is perishable and only available for the duration of the event. Similarly, what is on offer is intangible though memories of an event might be enhanced by tangible elements such as the merchandise available. The experience at the event is inseparable from the venue and its environment which means that bad weather would alter perceptions of the experience. These points alone make the overall experience of events variable, even before we consider variation introduced by the high level of human involvement from the person who greets you at the door to the artist on stage.

On the other hand, if we consider the earlier question, it can be seen that the promotion of sustainability within this event has more to do with social marketing than product or service marketing. In other words, the marketing is aimed at changing the behaviour of attendees and not selling them any kind of product or service. Generally speaking, the approach to marketing is the same in that a step model is followed, starting with raising the awareness of a product, service or need to change behaviour. Then, going on to encourage consumers to take action to buy that product, service or change their behaviour. However, once sold, a product or service is evaluated by the customer for repeat purchase but a change in behaviour may or may not be established forever and will not be purchased either way.

5   Considering the issues around major events such as these concerts, how is sustainable development being addressed by the approach taken by Jack Johnson?

It would be useful to begin by explaining the basic definition of sustainable development in terms of addressing 'people, planet and profit'. We might take for granted that a major artist such as Jack Johnson has structured the concerts such that 'profit' is not an issue for concern. Therefore, answering this question will mainly focus on the 'people' and 'planet' aspects of sustainable development.

In the case, it can be seen that the 'people' aspects of sustainable development are being addressed by the establishment of the 'not-for-profit' village at each concert. The choice of which organization to invite into the village defines the social aspects that are being addressed and may be assumed to have been directed by the artist and his management. Their approach seems to have involved a focus on organizations that are local to the concert and/or have a surfer lifestyle connection.

The 'planet' aspects of sustainable development in the case are being addressed by the 'EnviroRider' and the report indicates that the remaining carbon footprint of the tour is offset. So, the approach is aligned to sustainable thinking that proposes reducing the environmental effects, measuring the outcome and offsetting the remainder of the carbon offprint.

6   Evaluation is an essential factor to successfully manage major events like this. Consider how Figure 15.4 addresses the evaluation of Jack Johnson's 'Sleep Through the Static' concerts.

Figure 15.4 highlights three aspects of evaluation. Firstly, some of the points address the scale of the tour in order to set the other elements of evaluation into context. The opening statement in particular reveals the number of attendees, shows and countries involved on the tour. Secondly, the 'people' elements of sustainable development are addressed by noting the donations to the 'not-for-profit' organizations, the number of attendees engaging with them, and those registering to vote. Finally, the 'planet' aspects of sustainable development are noted through the amount of biodiesel used, the diversion from landfill by recycling, and the carbon offset that was made against the tour's activities.

7   There were a range of options for Johnny and June to choose from. Define and evaluate perceptual maps that explain how they came to prefer the Jack Johnson concert above the other options.

A perceptual map is a 2 by 2 matrix with two-dimensional representations of consumer perceptions that can be used to identify similar propositions (clusters of competitors) or strategic opportunities (gaps where no competitor is present). The dimensions of perception in this case can be aligned to the attributes of events though these need to be variable and operate along a dimension as opposed to offering a set of strict value, for example different sports. So, the attributes in this case may be drawn from the festival descriptions and summarized along the following dimensions:

- Duration of event – from short (single day) to long (multiple days)
- Cost of trip – from low cost to high cost
- Content – from music through a mix of sport/music to sport

- Distance away for consumer – from local to distant
- Weather – from cold/mild to hot/warm weather

It can be seen that Johnny and June have the choice of local events of short duration and long duration but only long duration distant events. As we might consider that the distance dimension is likely to be interchangeable with cost, this suggests that any other events that are distant would be at a higher cost. So, their higher cost might suggest that they offer less value to the consumer events, particularly if a short duration event, and this position in the perceptual map offers a gap but not one that meets the needs of these consumers (see Figure 15.5).

8 Explain how the risks would be assessed prior to the cancellation of the first Jack Johnson concert.

For all events it is wise to consider the preparation of a risk assessment. This requires the identification of any risks involved with the event and a calculation of the risk measured as a multiple of outcome severity times the chance of the hazard causing harm. If the calculated risk appears to be too high, controls must be introduced to reduce the risk of harm.

Grouping these hazards into those that might be addressed by a common approach is sensible. For example, if fire hazards were to cause harm, they would be tackled with a similar approach. In this case, the impact of weather might be seen as a way to group hazards as this would suggest that those managing this risk ought to make regular checks on weather forecasts to ensure a safe event.

In this case, high wind was the hazard to be addressed and suitable controls might be used to stabilize the movement of any temporary structures such as the stage or the catering outlets. However, the organizers must have viewed that these controls, potentially, would be inadequate in the high wind being experienced and decided upon the ultimate way to reduce harm – that is, limit the people involved to a minimum and cancel the event.

9 Explain how the use of outdoor and indoor concerts on this tour would affect the event management.

The key issues for event management tend to emerge from the fact that outdoor venues are often not intended for events like this, whereas indoor venues are often purpose-built for music. This means that not only are the former impacted on by the outdoor environment but also may lack an infrastructure to deal with large crowds. So, the former will provide weather hazards that cause people to be affected by hot, cold or wet weather as well as other natural problems like insect stings. In terms of infrastructure, the event team has to address site design in order to avoid potential hazards such as trees that might be climbed by the audience. Care has also to be taken in providing shelter from any problematic weather but also to consider the hazards that arise with temporary structures such as those experienced in the case. Also, it's important to consider access to the site from local roads and the availability of potential support services such as hospitals. In both cases, the event team will need to

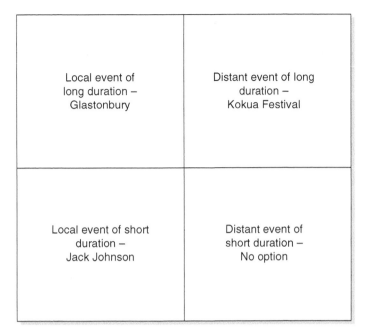

Figure 15.5   *A perceptual map of event choices*

consider how to manage medical and welfare problems on site but these will differ along the lines implied above. For example, slips and trips might be more common indoors and insect bites more likely to happen outdoors.

Whilst the above health and safety concerns will dominate event management thinking, it can be observed that there will be a freer hand to choose suppliers in outdoor situations as indoor venues are likely to have contracted suppliers for food and drink outlets. So, the event management team is more likely to find the outdoor venues offer flexibility to choose suppliers that meet sustainable development needs.

10   The first concert in Newquay was cancelled due to bad weather. Consider the options that present themselves to communicate this news and present a suitable communication plan.

Firstly, it should be recognized that the events team should have a contingency or emergency plan which explains the steps to be followed should cancellation be required.

Initially, it should be explained how the decision will be made to cancel the event, that is, how this is reviewed and who does the reviewing to decide on the outcome. Then, with decision made, it must be clear which individuals in the events team will communicate with which stakeholders and when this will occur. For example, in this case, the staff on site at the event would be aware of the high winds and might consult the local weather forecast to make the decision. This might be further considered with the local police to be clear as to the impact on the local vicinity. Once cancellation is agreed, a communications plan to advise both ticket holders and local public should be executed, whether as direct communication to the ticket holders and/or via use of the local media. In this case, Jack Johnson visited the local radio station as a guest on one of the programmes, played a few of his songs and spent some time making sure the radio broadcasted the key cancellation message. The latter message must also be planned carefully as, for example, ticket holders will want to know how to obtain refunds and those coming on the second day will need to be advised how to confirm that the concert will go ahead.

In this discussion, it should be recognized that the plan is interlinked with certain steps occurring in sequence and others occurring in parallel. So, the presentation of this plan in a flowchart, similar to those used to explain emergency procedures, would be a sensible means to explain these agreed actions.

Reference

Scientific American (2011) *Jack Johnson's Low Impact Summer. Scientific American* [Online]. Available from: http://www.scientificamerican.com/article.cfm?id=jack-johnsons-low-impact-summer-tour.

16

The Exportation of Event Expertise: Taking Best Practice to International Markets in the MICE Sector

Sarah Edwards and Liander Taylor

Introduction

This case study aims to provide students with an example of best practice in venue provision and operations in the MICE (Meetings, Incentives, Conference and Exhibitions) sector through an analysis of the International Convention Centre (ICC), Birmingham, UK.

In the context of the purpose-built conference centre, the case study will focus on two areas in particular. Firstly, it will identify key success factors for facilities in delivering events and includes the support that key stakeholders can provide when hosting major international events. Secondly, it focuses on the development of international consultancy projects as part of a strategic growth plan. Using the management of the Convention Centre Dublin (CCD) as a specific example, it subsequently identifies the necessary cultural considerations and the intellectual capital required to undertake such consultancy in international markets.

Aims and objectives

This case aims to make the reader aware of the key success factors in operating a convention centre in an international market. In particular, on completion of this case, students should be able to:

- Identify how a purpose-built convention centre contributes to a destination's economy.
- Explain some key success factors for venues in delivering successful events.
- Identify how internal competencies in event operations can be applied to international settings.
- Understand the importance of cultural awareness when operating in international markets.

Case Elements

The economic impact of a purpose-built venue

The momentum for the development of purpose-built venues presents an increas-ingly competitive global market. Huge investments are being made in the provision of purpose-built venues, with particular growth in Abu Dhabi, Dubai and Qatar – indeed the Qatar National Convention Centre is currently under construction at an estimated cost of US$1.2 billion (£730 million) (BMEIS, 2011). Britain's event sec-tor as a whole is worth over £36 billion per annum to the national economy, with business visitors spending an average of £131 per day – 72 per cent more than the amount spent by leisure visitors on a daily basis. In terms of segmentation, the con-ference and meeting market is purported to be £18.8 billion. These figures are presented in terms of net revenue to venues, but also in terms of the wider economic benefit to destinations through delegate spending on travel, entertainment, shopping and eating out, for example.

In terms of tourist spend, Rogers (2008) discusses the measurement of the eco-nomic impact of spending in terms of the 'multiplier analysis'. In these terms, a number of multipliers are used to calculate expenditure figures – for example, the number of delegates attending an event, the number of days the event is being held for, any addi-tional days (where guests might extend their stay) and the organizer's spending (which may, for example, include Corporate Hospitality and sightseeing trips).

The International Convention Centre, Birmingham, UK

The International Convention Centre (ICC) (see Figure 16.1) is part of the Birmingham-based NEC Group. Whilst originally conceived as a stand-alone venue, during planning stages it was decided to merge the ICC venue with the existing National Exhibition Centre (NEC) under the branding of the 'NEC Group' (Fenlon, personal communication, 5 May 2010). Today, the group comprises four main venues: the ICC, the NEC (National Exhibition Centre), the LG Arena and the National Indoor Arena (NIA). Across its venues, the NEC Group attracts over 4.1 million visitors to the region, with the business having an estimated economic impact of £2 billion for the West Midlands (Marketing Birmingham, 2011).

The ICC venue comprises 11 purpose-built conference halls, which sit alongside the Symphony Hall, an auditorium with unrivalled acoustics which seats over 2000 people. Today, the ICC venue hosts around 500 events per annum and maintains its position as one of the leading convention centres in the UK. Twice voted the UK's premier pur-pose-built conference venue by *C&IT* magazine, it is also one of only two venues in the UK to achieve international standards for quality (ISO 9001) and environmental (ISO 14001) management systems (Dwyer, personal communication, 1 July 2011).

The ICC was opened in April 1991, and was jointly funded by Birmingham City Council, the local Chamber of Commerce and the European Regional Development Fund. As a public/private partnership, it was seen as a project that could significantly

Figure 16.1   *The International Convention Centre, Birmingham, UK*

contribute toward the regeneration and redevelopment of the city. The continued success of the ICC today as one of the most popular UK venues has continued to generate significant income for the region. The Conservative Party Conference in October 2010, for example, was the sixth political conference that Birmingham has hosted in five years and generated £18.4 million in economic impact for the city (Marketing Birmingham, 2011).

ICC key success factors

Destination management – a team approach

In identifying the needs of the client, it is appreciated that in order to deliver a successful event for an international audience, it is not sufficient to purely consider the venue. In fact, in many instances, especially for international associations, it is the destination that is considered first:

> *Conference organizers attach greater importance to 'location' than to any other single criterion when selecting their sites. Location may be expressed in terms of 'town', 'city', 'region of the country'. The widely accepted term to describe each of these is 'destination' ... each conference destination must contain a range of venues, facilities, attractions, support services and appropriate infrastructure to help it to attract conference business. (Rogers, 2008: 59)*

Birmingham as a destination continues to be popular with event organizers. It has been selected as the top UK events destination outside of London, according to an in-depth study of the views of more than 600 British event organizers (The British Meetings and Events Industry Survey – BMEIS, 2010/11). However, the city as a destination needs to attract both national and international clients in order to remain competitive. To help ensure that the clients' needs are met and that the city has the best chance of winning event contracts, the city employs a unified approach. Key stakeholders are unified as 'Team Birmingham', and this includes Birmingham City

Council, the NEC Group, Marketing Birmingham and The Birmingham Convention Bureau. There are senior connections across all boards that ensure that communication channels remain open and information is disseminated effectively (Brown, personal communication, 24 November 2010).

This approach is perceived as being particularly effective in attracting and winning bids for major international events. Over the last 20 years, the ICC and Birmingham have hosted a range of international events to include The G8 Summit, the World Baptist Conference, International Lions Congress, the World Congress of Neuropathology and the World Small Animal Veterinary Conference (ICC, 2010).

For any conference organizer, particularly for a major international event, the demands can be far reaching. However, with a coordinated, unified approach, clients can be offered professional support across a range of services to include advising on the bidding process, preparing a bid presentation, sourcing Professional Conference Organizers (PCOs), booking hotel accommodation and advising on logistical and support services such as ground transportation, translators and florists. In addition, Marketing Birmingham will help 'dress' the city and ensure that international delegates are made to feel welcome from the time they arrive in the city, whilst helping to profile the event as appropriate. 'Dressing' the city may include welcome banners, electronic message boards and signage around the city.

As a result of this team approach and the tailored service that each client receives, the ICC is able to command a large percentage of repeat business. One particular client, The Association of Colleges (AoC), has recently signed a new three-year contract having considered three competing venues, and deciding on the ICC.

> While we have a long-standing relationship with the AoC, we understand that all associations need to ensure that they are providing their members with the best possible value. I am extremely happy to see that after sampling what our competitors have to offer, the AoC has not only returned to The ICC, but has shown such a tremendous degree of confidence in us.
>
> We worked very closely with our partners across the city including Marketing Birmingham and local hoteliers on devising this package, which once again proves the value of our Team Birmingham approach. I know that I speak for everyone here when I say how pleased we are and that we're all looking forward to hosting the AoC Annual Conference and Exhibition for the next three years. (Fenlon, personal communication, 5 May 2010)

This unified approach ensures that all aspects of an event are taken into consideration, and that clients feel comfortable in choosing Birmingham and the ICC for their event. Whilst 'Team Birmingham' helps attract clients to the city, there are a number of other key advantages that the ICC has over its competitors.

ICC's competitive advantage

Whilst being 20 years old, the ICC still remains one of Europe's premier conference and meeting venues and, even as competition increases, is able to attract and retain key clients. This may be attributed to a number of key competitive advantages that the ICC has over the competition, namely location, 'facilities design' and internal expertise.

Location

In terms of location, the ICC is ideally situated in the 'heart' of the UK and is therefore able to attract delegates on both a national and international scale. Birmingham is easily accessible by air, rail and road.

> *There are over 2000 flights a week to and from Birmingham International Airport with over 50 locations (including 16 European capital cities) benefiting from direct scheduled services ... there are trains every 10 minutes from the airport to Birmingham city centre, with the journey taking just 10 minutes to complete. Birmingham's central location at the heart of the country's road and rail system that is fast, frequent and reliable – makes it simple to travel around. (ICC, 2010)*

For international delegates, this means that access to the destination and venue is convenient and there is the opportunity to add on sight-seeing activities either pre- or post-conference.

'Facilities design'

The ICC was built for a specific purpose, which is the hosting of conferences – as opposed to being simply a multi-functional building. As such, each of the 12 halls was individually designed and constructed, and in effect were 'boxes' that could fit into the framework of the building (Fenlon, personal communication, 5 May 2010). Each hall is protected by a 'Faraday Cage' to prevent the spreading of electronic signals to enhance the acoustic quality. The individual design of each hall also means that occupants are well protected from any health and safety concerns.

This individual design and specifications allowed for unparalleled acoustics and a soundly engineered and designed building. Spaces are flexible allowing for tiered plenary sessions, exhibitions, dedicated registration areas, seminars, and product launches, alongside a range of catering services tailored for each client. Operationally, the building is designed for large numbers of conference delegates. Not only are delegates able to move around easily, but the operational aspects of providing for large numbers are considered. For example, the kitchen and serving space are aligned with service areas, there is both front-of- and back-of-house lift access, and sufficient cloakroom facilities to cater for the maximum number of delegates in the building.

The operational needs of exhibitors was also considered in the design phase. Access for large equipment that may be used in an exhibition or as part of a product launch, was also considered, with door widths, weight allowances, the provision of stand electrics and access all considered in the initial design. Such was the standard of the original fit that even today no major refurbishments are deemed necessary (Fenlon, personal communication, 5 May 2010).

Internal expertise

Whilst the NEC brand may have been in operation for over 30 years, and the ICC for 20, the team at the ICC are constantly looking for ways to improve their service and the client experience.

For event managers, this includes embracing company core values such as 'spirit and teamwork', whilst ensuring that they constantly question what they do and how they do it. In recruiting for event managers, company values are used as a benchmark when interviewing and hiring a team member with the view to these core values being used day-to-day in dealing with clients (Payne, personal communication, 7 January 2011). Key core competencies of an event manager in this environment are considered to be:

- Excellent communication skills
- Developing and building internal and external relationships
- Up-selling logistical and technical services
- Effectively working within financial budget/limitations
- Accurately recording and disseminating event information
- Being an independent and strong worker
- Problem solving (Payne, personal communication, 7 January 2011)

Employees are empowered to create a relationship climate where the customer is heard and valued. This not only equips employees with knowledge but they also feel trusted and valued. Whilst having the right team in place is considered essential, it is the relationship with clients that is key to the maintenance of a successful business. Clients are very much considered as partners, and only if a client's event is a success is the ICC seen as a success.

Therefore, client feedback is deemed extremely influential in the ICC's continued internal and external operational environments. Although important as in most industries, understanding and engaging with the client has been key to building and retaining business for the ICC.

The ICC has taken the concept of Customer Relationship Management (CRM) and focused on gaining valuable information and increasing their awareness about each of their clients whilst developing the event team's leadership behaviours, a radical move from the industry norm where the focus has historically been an inbound process of taking an enquiry, making a booking, and ultimately billing (Anton, 2005). CRM is defined by Buttle (2010: 15) as a 'core business strategy ... fundamental in building a stable economic platform for business'. This strategy facilitates the collection of customer information, allowing the ICC to build organizational, customer and supplier intelligence (Dyche, 2004). In turn, staff can proactively engage with clients and unlock information, strengthen communications and relationships whilst achieving a Return on Investment (ROI). Furthermore, this enhanced customer value and satisfaction has proven to positively impact employee behaviour which ultimately enhances customer satisfaction.

The ICC is a market-orientated company, whose goal is customer centricity, continuously striving to develop relationships which will provide opportunities, awareness, exploration, expansion and commitment within their business strategies, thus enabling them to adapt constantly to the changes in requirements and competition. This gradual but highly appropriate move towards Customer Experience Management (CEM) is an innovative move and has enabled the ICC to be 'outside in' focused, rather than purely CRM which is historically 'inside out'. This shift has enabled the ICC to look beyond just retaining clients, gaining recommendations and translating requirements into delivery; they now influence the industry, how it is formed and how it operates. The ICC's creation of this 'client experience strategy' has been developed through a top-down, strategic focus on improving the customer experience and has proven extremely important in the current economic climate. In this environment, client experiences hold even more substance and decisions are more contemplative with fewer margins for error. The ICC's adoption of CRM and CEM strategies communicates clearly to their clients that 'one size fits all' is not a viable business approach and strategies such as lifetime value where lifetime income streams are proposed and customer experience management is developed in line with their streams, are more beneficial to both client and the ICC.

Exporting the expertise – international consultancy projects

The development of a consultancy role was perhaps a natural extension of the NEC's core business. Expertise had been developed in many key areas such as design, construction, operations and feasibility studies (Fenlon, personal communication, 5 May 2010). The NEC 'brand' was well established and recognized, and consultancy projects both on a national and international level were a way of increasing revenue whilst transferring expertise in order to help other destinations/ venues. The reputation of the NEC means that approaches may be made through a number of ways, including referrals through the ICCA (International Congress and Convention Association) or simply through an existing client of the ICC. Consultancy may take many forms to include initial feasibility studies, advice on design and implementation, and operations and logistics, right through to a full consultancy role. Clients may visit the ICC to observe operations, or for international projects may conduct business remotely by conference call (Fenlon, personal communication, 5 May 2010).

Consultancy projects have included the Reykjavic Concert Hall and Conference Centre in Iceland where the NEC Group was able to advise on feasibility, design and also operational issues. For example, advice was given to include consideration of the potential markets (including local corporate or association clients), hotel availability for delegates and accessibility. In addition, design features such as rehearsal space, lifts and flexible meeting space were considered with a design consultancy brief. Consultancy has also undertaken for the Kontantinovsky Congress Centre in St Petersburg where specific operational advice was required. Again, the long-term project aims needed to be considered, as well as specific business outcomes. The building is complex in that it has a TV Studio, secure VIP apartments, an ice rink and a main auditorium incorporating an 80-metre-long projection screen. An operational manual was developed for this client, all the while considering the context of the brief. Approaches for consultancy have also been received from potential clients in Dubai, the People's Republic of China and Pakistan.

Cultural awareness and implications for consultancy projects

In developing and 'exporting' the cultural intelligence within the organization, consideration is needed on many fronts, including acknowledgment of the context of any bid, the needs of the client and the culture in which the client operates. The development of cultural intelligence is paramount here. Whilst the internal expertise may be considered the best in the sector, sufficient research and consideration of operating cultures is key to winning and conducting business.

The considerations necessary for the NEC Group in this context may be usefully adapted into the framework of a four-dimensional module of Cultural Intelligence (Livermore, 2010). Being rooted in many years of research on intelligence and cross-cultural interaction, the four dimensions consider Motivational CQ, Cognitive CQ, Metacognitive CQ and Behavioural CQ (Livermore, 2010).

Motivational CQ considers the interest, drive and motivations to adapt cross-culturally. In this respect, the Senior Management Team consider consultancy as a way of diversifying and applying best practice into other parts of the globe and in turn creating additional revenue streams. There are opportunities to apply expertise across a number of key areas of the business, including running arenas, exhibition spaces and conference centres. Expertise in operational areas such as logistics and catering can also be provided.

The consultancy role helps raise the profile of the ICC on a global scale. As a member of the Board of the AIPC (Association International de Palaise de Congress), the ICC has contacts worldwide and approaches for consultancy, particularly in the Baltic countries, have come through this channel.

In considering which consultancy projects to adopt, it is vital to understand the operating culture and how business is done (Cognitive CQ). For many clients this is likely to include the feasibility of a project, and specifically the business risk. In terms of CQ Strategy, or Metacognitive CQ (Livermore, 2010) it is thought necessary to continually observe cultures and continually check to see if expectations are accurate. This may be particularly relevant for a long-term project or for a complex scenario in a developing country.

When working in developing countries, Fenlon suggests that considerations should include the potential business risk. For example, the following questions could apply: Do you know your market? What are your sources of supply (for example, staff)? Cultural issues particularly should be considered. In developing a consultancy team for each project, it is therefore important to have someone who understands the culture, but is also able to gain trust from the client. This is also evident in working over the longer term in a consultancy role and developing operational teams.

Some particular challenges of operating in different cultures are in the day-to-day running of conferences and events, in effect CQ action (Livermore, 2010). The behavioural dimension of cultural intelligence can be considered in many operational guises. Health and safety, for example, has different interpretations in different countries and the idea of 'keeping people safe' might vary according to people's position in society (Fenlon, personal communication, 5 May 2010). Reactions to women may also vary – some more explicit than others. In the Far East, women may not get to the negotiating table, and in addition the practicalities of having women in operational roles need to be considered. Programming considerations are also subject to cultural awareness. In Chinese culture, for example, food and flowers take prominence, and sufficient time in a programme should be allowed for these elements.

Convention Centre Dublin, Republic of Ireland

Some of the considerations mentioned are evident in a recent project that the NEC Group has been appointed to consult on the Convention Centre Dublin (see Figure 16.2). The Convention Centre Dublin is Ireland's first purpose-built convention centre, established through a unique Public Private Partnership with the Irish Government. The parallels to the ICC are recognizable in that the project is seen as a catalyst for the economic regeneration of the city and will benefit the destination long term. From a consultancy perspective, the project has taken place over the last 10 years with the ICC team having had input into areas such as initial physical design, human resource and information technology systems.

Still in its infancy, the CCD has so far provided revenue to the economy in the region of £60 million. From a consultancy perspective, the project was first initiated in 1998, with the ICC account team selling the concept of the ICC and its expertise. The CCD, whilst looking at other competing bids, was impressed with the ICC's approach to business and how it provided excellent service and quality standards to the business market. It is this focus which CCD CEO, Nick Waight believes has been the foundation for what was and is being achieved at the ICC and has enabled the group to build a culture and ethos based on core quality and service standards which it has transferred to the CCD. By providing this excellence, value is added and reinvested to meet the needs of the client and delegate, thus building the confidence of the ICC and CCD to grow and develop their strategic objectives (Waight, personal communication, 22 July 2011).

With a build cost of around £380 million, the CCD is the most expensive convention centre since the ICC, and therefore required creativity and precision management. Waight notes that the ICC holds these skills in abundance. However exporting resources such as operating systems and knowledge can help in the formation of quality teams only up to a point. Cultural considerations, particularly in the way that business is conducted, have been a learning point for the team in Dublin. In the Republic of Ireland, a hand shake often forms a contract and networking is fast and influential. This is far removed from some professional and often protracted relations the ICC has formed with its stakeholders within the UK. However this relaxed, almost informal, relationship between the CCD and client has in essence made the DCC team analyse its core product and service offered to clients. Waight (personal communication, 22 July 2011) states that although it is operationally challenging,

Figure 16.2   *Convention Centre Dublin, Republic of Ireland*

having clients arrive who have either not stated what they want or make changes on the day, requires the CCD to not merely state that it is customer-centric but actually try to adapt to the client's needs and prove that it really does care about the customer. The promise of customer care, it is suggested, is rarely delivered within the MICE industry, but Waight argues that this approach is indeed the 'next generation of client centricity'; the group is striving to adapt its structure, systems and processes and move from an 'imposing to listening' relationship, which will be crucial in creating systems and processes which work for both parties.

The NEC's management is renowned for its knowledge of international markets, operational standards, quality managing processes and physical systems, and it has been the ICC's framework which has facilitated new growth. However, large-scale conference skills have been limited in the local Irish market and it has been imperative to bring in expertise to help train and develop an extremely bright, passionate and motivated team. This not only helps set standards, but instils the right attitude to work in a venue such as the CCD. Without these key individuals and their expertise, Waight suggests it would have been extremely hard to achieve quality from the outset. Whilst looking at external support services, the CCD has had to be exacting in its requirements. Companies such as AV specialists and production companies who were extremely small scale compared to their counterparts within the UK, had never worked with a venue that owned its own equipment or, for example, exceeded a capacity of 300. Therefore much emphasis has been given to building the trust of small companies and helping them realize the benefits of their relationship with the CCD, whilst growing expertise.

In the wake of successful management of the CCD, further international projects are planned, utilizing its expertise and reputation in areas such as facilities, operations, functionality, diary utilization and flexibility. With much internal re-branding taking place (for example, Amadeus Catering), the NEC Group is poised once again to increase the gap between itself and the competition. With a goal of five venue management contracts within a four-hour plane journey from Birmingham and projects in developing countries, the NEC is looking to increase its bottom-line profit and to continuously build its core skills and reputation.

Case Analysis

Purpose-built convention centres are globally a significant growth area. Destinations worldwide are looking to invest in such projects in order to increase business tourism and add to the local economy through the multiplier effect. The effective management of such centres, however, is crucial in delivering success. Key success factors include location, facilities design and internal expertise, as well as a team approach from the hosting destination.

Effective Customer Experience Management (CEM) and Customer Relationship Management (CRM) underpin a successful experience for the client. This approach needs to be flexible, and take into account cultural considerations and contexts. Developing expertise within the sector and nurturing an element of cultural intelligence within operational teams is thought to be key. This is keenly demonstrated through the development of international consultancy projects undertaken by the NEC Group.

Case Review Questions

1   What benefits might a purpose-built convention centre bring to a destination?
2   What particular skills and intellectual capital are required to run a successful venue?

3   When building an operations team, what cultural issues need to be considered when transferring skills in an international environment?
4   From a facility management perspective, what are the key considerations of managing successful customer relationships when operating in the events environment?

References

Anton, J. (2005) *CRM: Making Hard Decisions with Small Numbers.* Englewood Cliffs, NJ: Prentice-Hall.

British Meetings and Events Industry (2011) *The British Meetings and Events Industry Survey – 2010/11.* BMEIS [Online]. Available from: http://www.meetpie.com/staticpagedisplay. aspx?code=bmeismenu.

Buttle, F. (2010) *Customer Relationship Management: Concepts and Technologies.* Oxford: Elsevier.

Dyche, J. (2004) *The CRM Handbook: A Business Guide to Customer Relationship Management.* Boston, MA: Addison Wiley.

International Convention Centre (ICC) (2010) *ICC* [Online]. Available from: http://www. theicc.co.uk.

Livermore, D. (2010) *Leading with Cultural Intelligence: The New Secret to Success.* New York: American Management Association.

Marketing Birmingham (2011) *The Marketing Toolkit.* Marketing Birmingham [Online]. Available from: http://www.birminghamtoolkit.com.

Rogers, T. (2008) *Conferences and Conventions: A Global Industry* (2nd edn). Oxford: Butterworth-Heinemann.

17

The Marketing Strategy for the 13th IAAF Indoor World Athletics Championships 2010 in Doha: Creating a Value Constellation

Tariq Saed Al-Abdulla, Maher N. Safi and Alain Ferrand

Introduction

The International Amateur Athletics Federation (IAAF) World Indoor Championships (WIC) 2010 was held between 12 and 14 March at the Aspire Dome in Doha, Qatar. This international event involved a large number of stakeholders. The Doha Local Organizing Committee's (DLOC) mission was to move the event forward through adherence to the highest professional international standards to deliver quality to its stakeholders. In order to do so it worked closely with a range of stakeholders such as the IAAF, the event participants, the host city and its partners, and the media in providing what was an exceptional and innovative event that could be shared with the public.

This case study will present a framework for implementing international event marketing which demonstrates how value is created for the network of stakeholders. This framework is based on relationship marketing principles. It aims to create and develop valuable relationships in the stakeholder's markets. For the reader this case encapsulates issues presented in Chapters 6, 11 and 12. To highlight the application of these concepts this case study is developed in three sections. The first section will present the background to the event in order to provide relevant supporting information about the event's rights holder and Qatar's international sport-event hosting policies. The second section will present a series of case elements that will focus first on the WIC and its stakeholders; provide an overview of the event brief; and detail the event marketing strategy, its implementation and the key results. The final section, case analysis, will provide a critique of how a 'value constellation' was created and managed for the event's stakeholders.

Country brand

Qatar is one of the most dynamic economies in the Middle East. It has undergone remarkable economic and social development over the last 20 years. With an attractive business environment and a progressive national leadership, the country continues to be one of the fastest growing economies in the region. Having hosted numerous sporting events for over two decades, Qatar has become a major leader of sporting organizations and has helped accelerate the evolution of grassroots athlete development in Asia and the region. Since hosting the Asian Games in 2006, Doha has hosted many major sporting events and consistently invested in expanding its national athlete development programme, which is supported by the global sports training expertise of the Aspire Academy for Sports Excellence.

Major global sports events present an extraordinary opportunity to strengthen the Qatari national brand. When handled properly, a country such as Qatar with its unique values, natural assets and culture can be showcased on the world stage, creating a lasting positive legacy for trade, investment and tourism.

Sport in Qatar

Qatar is recognized as one of the region's top sports destinations and has built on the legacy of the Asian Games Doha 2006 by developing both its sporting and tourism facilities, in addition to reinforcing its strong external image as a country underpinned by strong economic, social and political stability. Sport is important to the people of Qatar and the government. The leader of the country, His Highness the Emir of Qatar Sheikh Hamad Bin Khalifa Al Thani, is a strong advocate for sport development in Qatari Society, and the Heir Apparent, Sheikh Tamim Bin Hamad Al Thani, is President of the Qatar Olympic Committee and an avid advocate of sport in the country.

Through the Qatar Olympic Committee (QOC), the state of Qatar has adopted a 360° approach to developing sport in the country, from grassroots development to the hosting of major international sporting events. The QOC is committed to providing support to its national sports federations so that the country may host world-class events that build Qatar's reputation as the sporting hub of the region. The QOC also seeks to host major international sporting events to ensure maximum utilization of Qatar's existing sporting facilities and sport tourism infrastructure. An indication of its status within the region, it will be the first member of the region to host the FIFA World Cup which will be staged in 2022. Qatar's sports leagues and competitions are growing every year and their international tournaments continue to attract leading athletes and a growing worldwide audience of live spectators and television viewers.

Previous success

Qatar has had remarkable success in welcoming the world's top athletes and sports professionals to its international events. These include the major popular sports as well as Olympic disciplines such as gymnastics and IAAF-sanctioned athletics summits. The Qatar Super Grand Prix has been one of the biggest draws in international athletics for many years and has built Qatar's reputation among the world's top athletes, helping to attract increasing interest in the IAAF World Indoor Championships in Athletics, Doha 2010. Recently, Qatar has built an outstanding reputation for hosting international sports events and, as a result, Qatar has won most of its event bids.

Sports tourism

Sports tourism in Qatar owes a great deal to the legacy of the Asian Games Doha 2006, which created a discernable change in the way Qatar is perceived in the sporting world. Today a large number of hotel rooms and hospitality services support a thriving sports tourism industry that features regular regional and international events hosted in Qatar at both indoor and outdoor venues, making Qatar one of the most popular sports tourism destinations in the Gulf region.

Bidding to host the IAAF World Indoor Championships, Doha 2010

In 2006, the Qatar Association of Athletics Federation (QAAF) approached QOC for support to bid for the 2010 IAAF World Indoor Championships (WIC). The bid demonstrated that athletics was a strong and well established sport in Qatar and subsequently it was the first sport to bring Qatar international sport recognition. It demonstrated that many stakeholders could be interested in playing a part in the event. The advantages of Qatar in terms of location, security and broadcasting-time-zone were central to the bid. Qatar submitted a strong bid to host the IAAF WIC 2010 in Doha. At an IAAF Council meeting in Monaco on 25 November 2006, Qatar was awarded the event.

Case Elements

The event

The International Association of Athletics Federation's WIC was inaugurated as the World Indoor Games in 1985 in Paris, France and was subsequently renamed in 1987. The Indoor Championships have been held every two years except for when they were held in consecutive years in 2003 and 2004 to facilitate the need for them to be held in alternate years to the main IAAF World Championship Outdoor Games.

Keys facts and data about the event

Table 17.1 presents the keys facts and data about the IAAF WIC 2010 in Doha, while the situation of the preliminary and final entries is summarized in Table 17.2.

Table 17.1　*IAAF WIC 2010 in Doha: Key facts*

Number of tickets sold	25,775
Number of flags produced and installed inside venue	150
Number of flags produced and installed around city	850
Number of outdoor mupies	560
Number of buses branded	10
Number of taxis branded	100
Number of faces in malls	21
Number of faces in airport	4
Number of lamp post banners	200
Number of outdoor signs	30
Number of way-finding signs	606
Number of items produced	49,500
Number of press release topics issued	42
Number of TV commercials	240
Number of radio promotions	700
Final number of entries by NF (include in bottom list of NFs)	145
Final number of athletes (male + female)	606
Final number of team officials (male + female)	482
Seating capacity of the venue (without extension)	2240
Seating capacity of the venue (with extension)	3620
Seating capacity of the venue (with temporary new seats)	5000
Number of VVIP seats	210
Number of VIP seats	464
Number of international media attending	100
Number of local media attending	52
Number of media accreditations issued	491
Number of international broadcasters	99
Number of rights holders attending	23
Host broadcaster	147
Number of hours of live TV broadcast	23

Stakeholder landscape

The IAAF WIC 2010 in Doha was a large-scale event which involved numerous stakeholders, namely:

- The Qatar Olympic Committee (QOC)
- The Qatar Association of Athletics Federation (QAAF)
- The International Association of Athletics Federation (IAAF)
- The National Athletics Federations
- The participants
- The IAAF worldwide sponsors
- The local event sponsors

Table 17.2   *Entries, participation and qualification*

	PEF	FEF	Participation	FEF/PEF	Real/FEF	Real/FEF
MF	163	150	142	−8%	−5%	−13%
Men	457	373	336	−18%	−10%	−26%
Women	331	282	249	−15%	−12%	−25%
Officials	481	481	444	0%	−8%	−8%
Total	1269	1136	1029	−10%	−9%	−19%

- The local, regional and international media
- The Aspire Dome
- The Qatar Tourism Authority
- The Ministry of the Interior
- Spectators and members of the public including:
  - Athletics fans (local, expatriates, tourists)
  - Sports fans in general (locally and internationally)
  - Students from schools, colleges and universities interested in sports and seeking alternative entertainment (locally)
  - Families (locally)
  - The public looking to experience a world-class sporting event

Stakeholder engagement

The Doha Local Organizing Committee (DLOC) utilized a strategy to encourage all stakeholders to collaborate and to experience the brand and its related values by turning these into a promise for target customers, and delivering the promise in a way which brought the brand alive (more details in the brand development section). It was important that a consistent DLOC approach was taken to ensure that each stakeholder felt their marketing objectives would be achieved. Below is an outline of the key considerations drawn up before the event:

- Delivering an event of unparalleled success and organizational creativity, adhering to the best standards in the world.
- Ensuring sufficient spectator capacity in the arena, whilst delivering an event that would draw global audiences to view the event via live and deferred coverage.
- Upholding and promoting the global brand image of the IAAF, QOC and QAAF.
- Promoting and delivering the marketing objectives of IAAF partners and local partners.
- Supporting the marketing efforts of the Qatar Tourism Authority and hospitality service providers in the country.
- Delivering an event and event environment capable of meeting the strict demands of the world's top media stakeholders.
- Partnering with the host broadcaster to ensure widespread viewership in local, regional and international media, whilst supporting the needs of media holding international broadcast rights in various territories.

- Exceeding the expectations of local and international spectators in terms of organizational excellence and access to the event.
- Supporting grassroots development of athletics at club and youth levels, both in Qatar and abroad.

Stakeholder prioritization

Considering the large number of stakeholders at the event, the DLOC decided to categorize and manage them according to their importance.

The QAAF and the QOC were deemed the most important because they were in charge of the event and they made decisions about resource allocation. However their strategy and actions were strongly influenced by IAAF and the QOC because they needed to ensure the highest level of services for all participants as was agreed in the IAAF contract.

The second most important were the two major partners: the Aspire multi-games complex and the media. These two were crucial in providing full support to the event as facilities and media/public relations were major players in the determination of the event's success, as the first was the venue for the competitions and the second was essential for generating quality exposure.

The third group of stakeholders, in terms of importance, were organizations with a minor partnership role in the organization of the event. Sports events and sport associations were mainly involved in providing human resources in all the fields required to run one of the major events for the IAAF. Sport management, marketing and hospitality, logistics and accommodation are some of the areas where cooperation was necessary to organize and produce the best services for this event.

The fourth important group of stakeholders included the Ministry of the Interior, which was responsible for the participants' entry into Qatar and other aspects such as venue safety and security. The Qatar Tourism Authority provided support in welcoming all VIPs, participants and other visitors who came to Qatar. The goal was to give all participants the best experience ever for a WIC event and judging from the IAAF final report on this event, they were successful.

The brief

The event's marketing strategy was conceived and implemented according to four principles which structured the brief for the DLOC. This section also presents the resources engaged by the DLOC and its stakeholders.

Delivering high standards

The event was the biggest IAAF event to be staged in the Middle East and Asia which bought with it a great deal of responsibility. The success of this event would outline the future legacy of athletics in the region and therefore was one of the most important joint projects undertaken by the IAAF and the QOC. The approach to marketing the event would be predicated on delivering value to all stakeholders, and positioning the World Indoor Championships in Athletics Doha 2010 as the premier athletics event ever held in the region.

Balancing commercial, social and environmental objectives

Arguably, the ultimate objective of every sporting event is to create value for the targeted stakeholders through sport, economic, social and environmental impacts in each host city or nation. In Qatar, during and after the event, the mandate included developing sporting programmes that would leave a lasting impact on youth and society, whilst striving to reduce the impact on the environment.

The majority of sport's mega-events are becoming increasingly focused on the development of their commercial objectives in order to achieve sustainability. This commercial focus can create a real dilemma for event managers, as it is difficult to optimize income from marketing activities while preserving and developing social priorities. The DLOC stressed the importance of the social marketing programmes related to the event. This involved applying marketing concepts and methods to create and implement programmes that influenced the behaviour of the organization's target groups and that aimed to improve the well-being of the groups to which these organizations belong. Furthermore, the environmental challenges posed by transportation and the use of sports facilities were included in the requirements.

Creating value for stakeholders

The marketing and communications programme developed for WIC 2010 had to consider the needs of each stakeholder group, identify key event opportunities and benefits, whilst also deliver on the contractual and ethical obligations to IAAF partners and local partners during the build-up of WIC 2010.

Enhancing Qatar's brand image

WIC Doha 2010 was a landmark moment in the history of sport in Qatar and provided a major opportunity to promote Qatar's role in sport, in the Middle East and the world at large. Prime among the objectives of hosting the event was the push to justify Qatar's positioning as the region's primary sporting hub and elevate the country's brand image to the next level.

Resources engaged

Like any strategy, marketing is based on resource mobilization and allocation. The Resource-Based View (RBV) approach has become a standard way of thinking about company strategy and has been developed over the past few years into the field of sport management (Gerrard, 2005). The marketing department's responsibility in the RBV approach included the following:

1 Marketing
2 Public relations
3 Branding
4 Publication
5 Merchandising
6 Signage: Way finding
7 Creating the Fan Zone

The marketing department also had the overall responsibility of the brand management and the look and feel of the IAAF WIC event. The importance of these marketing activities to the event's financial bottom line was vital as the activities generated approximately US$5.5 million (£3.4 million) in revenues from sponsorship, ticketing and the Fan Zone. This data on income and expenses is presented in Table 17.3.

Table 17.3   IAAF WIC 2010 income and expenses

World Indoor Championship, Doha 2010
Unaudited Income Statement

Income S.No.	Items	Actual Amounts (US$)
1	IAAF Contribution	
2	Administration/Authorities	14,819,901
3	National Partners	547,945
4	Entrance Tickets	45,411
5	Mechandising/Licensing Sales	
6	Adidas Uniforms (VIK)	250,00
7	Seiko Contribution	300,000
8	Other Income	76,386
	Total	16,039,644

Expenses S.No.	Items	Actual Amounts (US$)
1	Personnel	1,384,938
2	LOC Coordination	2,009,527
3	Marketing	1,151,060
4	Competition Site	2,261,934
5	Other Sites	612,345
6	Transportation	1,168,421
7	Accommodation	2,009,446
8	Team/Social Activities	54,219
9	Telecommunications	69,863
10	Medical Services	206,505
11	Press	78,728
12	Television	2,787,701
13	Protocol	2,244,957
	Total Budget (US$)	16,039,644

Outcomes

Marketing strategy

According to the principles highlighted previously, the WIC Doha 2010 marketing strategy focused on branding and building a relationship strategy which encompassed domestic and international audiences.

Branding

The branding strategy for WIC Doha 2010 was a comprehensive undertaking that saw for the very first time a new IAAF brand identity and event branding system used in a major IAAF event. It included the creation of a brand identity kit comprising full visual language and graphic devices, defined photography and illustration styles, specific fonts and rules for their usage, the development of an event mascot and specific mascot usage guidelines, as well as external and internal communications guides to ensure consistency in application of the brand across all communication. Among the myriad other factors considered were the tone of communication, stakeholder engagement principles, organizational behaviour and visual appearance, ensuring consistency in message delivery to support IAAF partners and local partners, and protecting intellectual property rights.

The brand mark

The process of brand development began with the creation of a unique logo, based on the IAAF event brand identity templates. The final design (Figures 17.1 and 17.2)

Figure 17.1   *IAAF WIC Doha 2010 logo landscape version*

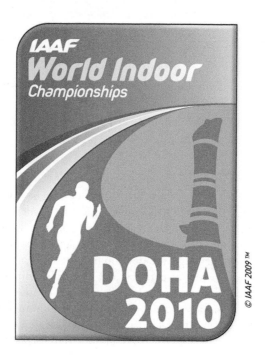

Challenging the limits

Figure 17.2   *IAAF WIC Doha 2010 logo portrait version*

featured the Aspire Tower, an icon of Qatar's emergence in Middle East sport, as its centrepiece, along with a running man completing a circuit of an indoor sports track. 'Energy, Passion and Determination' are the words that inspired the brand mark used in WIC Doha 2010. The Aspire Tower is one of the most recognizable sporting landmarks in the Middle East. It encompasses the energy and spirit of all athletes in one iconic image. The colours were chosen to capture the commitment and courage of 'pure athletics'.

The brand vision

> *'To be the benchmark in athletic events that brings people and athletes together in a world class competition environment; to be a reference of legacy as the hub of international Olympic sports in the region.'*

The brand mission

'To promote the city of Doha and the sport of athletics regionally and internationally by encouraging participation, cooperation and friendship between all stakeholders.'

The brand values

Table 17.4   *IAAF WIC 2010 brand values*

Integrity	Inspirational
Being unified in fair play regardless of race, religion or colour.	Providing motivation through athletics to encourage participation in sport and wellbeing.
Aspirational	**Leadership**
The ambition of performing at higher levels.	Being catalysts for positive action.
Camaraderie	**Collaboration**
	Bringing the world together through sport.

The mascot

The official mascot of WIC Doha 2010 was called 'Saham', a caracal, which is a mid-sized cat found across the Arabian Peninsula. It was, and is, especially important to Qatar because it is one of the few remnants of the desert heritage of its people.

The caracal in Arabian lore is a symbol of vitality and great skill. It has thrived in the region for many centuries, even in the face of adverse weather and the encroachment of urban areas into its natural space. Being a protected species, this mascot was also a channel for generating awareness within the local community of the presence of such majestic creatures that need the community's support to flourish in the future.

Box 17.1   Saham the Mascot

Saham, who was born Al Shahaniyah, on the outskirts of Doha, grew up with his family near Al Wabra Wildlife Preservation. The eldest of three children, Saham was groomed from an early age to carry on the family's great affection for sport. A natural athlete, he learnt from an early age, from his grandfather and father, that sport is about more than just performance.

(Continued)

(Continued)

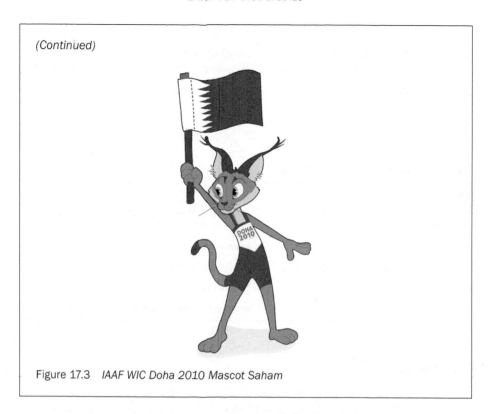

Figure 17.3   *IAAF WIC Doha 2010 Mascot Saham*

After completion of brand development by a specialist brand agency and approval by the IAAF, the brand identity and guidelines were managed by an integrated marketing communications agency and overseen by the marketing and public relations subcommittee of the WIC Doha 2010 OC.

Relationship strategy

Event marketing was based on the singular brand proposition of 'Challenging the Limits'. The DLOC developed this marketing campaign to show its commitment to 'Challenging the Limits'. This was a defining moment for the Arab world, and perhaps the entire world, as it was the first time that such a high-profile event had come to the region. One of the major ambitions for WIC Doha 2010 was that it would set the pace for a brand new age in athletics in the region.

Supported by the IAAF, the campaign 'Challenging the Limits' was implemented across geographic boundaries and celebrate past sporting achievement. The IAAF also encouraged Qatar and the DLOC to create an environment that 'Challenged the Limits' of human achievement, as well as redefined the role of athletics in the region. The brand proved an inspiration to people at every level and resonated throughout Qatar, as well as with the many visitors who attended the event. The event marketing strategy was structured and implemented in three phases:

- Phase 1 'Building interest' (September 2009 to November 2009)
- Phase 2 'Building demand' (December 2009 to January 2010)
- Phase 3 'Building desire' (February 2010 to March 2010)

Phase 1 'Building interest' (September 2009 to November 2009)

The WIC Doha 2010 marketing plan aimed first at raising event awareness by taking the following steps:

- Developing news coverage that outlined the positioning of WIC Doha 2010 and promoted international and domestic interest in the event.
- Finalizing sponsorship considerations and ensuring modification of branding elements to reflect the needs of IAAF partners and local partners.
- Developing interest in all grassroots athletics development programmes undertaken by the QOC and the QAAF.
- Engaging the media and the public at key sporting events in Qatar to generate interest in WIC Doha 2010.
- Building an advocates and volunteers programme for implementation during the final stages of the campaign.
- Utilizing media opportunities to publicize the new IAAF WIC Doha 2010 logo and brand identity.

Phase 2 'Building demand' (December 2009 to January 2010)

One of the goals of the WIC Doha 2010 was to increase the event's appeal for its success through the following process:

- Further developing news coverage that outlined the positioning of WIC Doha 2010 and promoted international and domestic interest in the event.
- Finalizing local partners and sponsors for WIC Doha 2010.
- Actively advertising in local and international specialist media to promote the event.
- Inviting international key media to attend the event in coordination with global National Olympic Committees and Athletics bodies.
- Finalizing promotional videos focused on 'Challenging the Limits' in partnership with the IAAF featuring IAAF president, Lamine Diack, IAAF Vice Presidents, Sergei Bubka and Lord Sebastian Coe, as well as top athletes such as Usain Bolt, Elena Isinbayeva, Daryon Robles, Blank Vlasic and David Oliver.
- Actively promoting the WIC at key youth engagement opportunities such as the Doha Gymnasiade and other key international sporting events in Qatar at the time.
- Finalizing city branding arrangements with event partners, both local and international.
- Supporting the IAAF media and technical staff, and completing the production of 13 official publications, including the WIC Doha 2010 Bulletin, Media Advisory Newsletters and guides for teams, volunteers and visitors.
- Commencing the roll-out of the volunteers programme to attract youth to participate in the event.

Phase 3 'Building desire' (February 2010 to March 2010)

Aside from building the interest and raising the demand, the organizers of the WIC Doha 2010 decided that it was time to shift the focus of their campaign to increase the local and international public desire to attend and actively participate in the event. To this end, the following were put into action:

- Development and production of all material that marketed the event in accordance with the guidelines.
- Active implementation of city look and feel supported by active branding of venue and city high visibility areas.
- Way finding and directional signage – to assist in the orientation of the event participants and spectators.
- Sponsorship contract management.
- Event ticket planning and sales – to increase ticket sales, ticket sales management, and stadium blocks management.
- International ticket sales management – to focus on among four countries: UAE, Jordan, Egypt and Bahrain.
- Merchandising sales and distribution.
- Fan Zone development and management.
- Fan Zone sales – a marketing strategy to increase involvement and promotion of the WIC.
- Website management – updating the data on a daily basis and live during the event.
- Taking the campaign to the streets and asking the public to 'Challenge the Limits' at fan zones and activity areas.
- Utilization of event Ambassador videos for promotion of event on Al Jazeera Sports and via social media.
- Launch of official event TV commercial built on 'Challenging the Limits' campaign.
- Final roll-out of a social media campaign on Facebook and Twitter to encourage followers.
- Scheduled media briefings and sponsorship announcements in local and international media.
- Targeted communication to drive ticket and merchandise sales and publicize sales outlets, as well as an online bookings portal.
- Participation in key events leading up to WIC Doha 2010.

Programme description

Communications programme outline

The DLOC marketing department developed a communication plan prior to the event to discuss specific topics before, during and after the event. This gave the DLOC more focus on how to communicate the event to the public and what topics were needed to be communicated or promoted as a result of successes and challenges. This communication was part of the public relations (PR) team's duties.

Once the topics below were selected, the PR team developed a timetable of when to release such press releases, interviews and/or articles to the media. This was used as a way to continuously generate information to the public and media on the event.

- Brand mark launch
- Ambassador's appointment (TBC by QOC)
- Announcement of star athlete participation (on availability in partnership with IAAF)
- Tickets on sale
- Economic impact (sport tourism and legacy)
- Sponsor announcements
- Announcement of host country participation
- One-month-to-go announcement
- Event final build-up
- Event participants' arrival in town
- Opening ceremony
- Daily event briefings and collateral
- Past champions
- The wrap-up (post-event reports, outcomes, success stories)

Other content development included:

- Accommodation information
- Competition timetable
- Event schedule and entry standards
- Event organization structure and details
- Frequently Asked Questions (FAQ)
- General event information
- Location information, venue, country profile
- Media information
- National partner supplier details
- News articles
- Ticket information
- Travel information
- Volunteer information
- Social media (Web 2.0): tools such as Facebook and Twitter have proven to be important in promoting events. They are successfully used by the PR team to promote and advertise sport events. The nature of these networks provides a worldwide social network exposure centre for sport events and the reach of these networks is beyond normal media borders and incredibly effective.

  o YouTube: Many event participants uploaded videos featuring their favourite segments of the event (see http://www.youtube.com/results?search_query=doha+2010+iwc).
  o Facebook: The WIC Doha event organizers created a profile page for the event on Facebook to encourage e-relationships (http://www.facebook.com/WIC2010).
  o Twitter: A regular stream of tweets was delivered through http://twitter.com/wic2010.

- Publications: Bulletin 1 (2000 copies); Team Manual (including technical manual) (1000 copies); Volunteer Manual (1000 copies); Bulletin 2 (2000 copies); Official Programme (2000 copies); Entry List (1000 copies); Start Lists (1000 copies); Final Results Booklet (1000 copies); Athletics and Doha (1000 copies); Media Guide (1000 copies); Post-Event Highlights Booklet (1000 copies).

Tier 1 Ambassadors Programme

The Ambassador Programme was developed to help generate interest in the sport of Athletics, and to speak about the athletes' own experiences. It was a chance for kids to participate in activities involving them and the community in general.

The Ambassador Programme was developed to support the overall ambition of the QAAF and the QOC in hosting the WIC in 2010, encouraging young people to adopt sport in every aspect of their lives. Areas of development during the Ambassador Programme were:

- Promoting Qatar's advanced sporting facilities
- Reinforcing the campaign objective of 'Challenging the Limits'
- Representing Doha 2010 on the global stage
- Generating primary and follow-on media coverage
- Ambassadors secured included: IAAF president Lamine Diack, IAAF Vice Presidents Sergei Bubka and Lord Sebastian Coe, as well as top athletes such as Usain Bolt, Elena Isinbayeva, Daryon Robles, Blank Vlasic and David Oliver, among others

Results

There were several success points and factors during the event. Some of the most important keys issues that determined the success of this event were that:

- The event was recognized as one of the most successful branding and communication campaigns in the history of IAAF indoor events (see Table 17.5).
- The management allowed enough time to develop the overall marketing plan.
- The support of Q-media was obtained for outdoor advertising.
- Diverse channels of communication with the public were used.

Branding and look

Outdoor advertising was utilized to develop the three phases of the advertising campaigns:

- Build brand awareness
- Generate information about the event
- Generate calls for action for ticket sales and attendance

Table 17.5 *IAAF WIC 2010 TV viewing figures at May 2010*

IAAF World Indoor Championships – Doha 2010

Territory	TV Stations/ Channels		Total Broadcast (Minutes)	Cumulative Audience (000>$)	Friday 12 Broadcast Minutes	Friday 12 Audiences 000>	Saturday 13 Broadcast Minutes	Saturday 13 Audiences 000>	Sunday 14 Broadcast Minutes	Sunday 14 Audiences 000>
EUROPE										
Croatia	HRT2	live/delayed	341	925	79	99	151	274	110	551
Cyprus	LTV Sports HD	live/repeat	3735	40	570	8	510	8	210	4
Czech Rep	CT4 Sport	live/repeat	1254	633	454	165	616	274	182	194
Finland	YLE TV 2	delayed	159	727	58	195	54	270	47	262
France	Direct 8	live/highlights	570	327	270	140	210	140	90	47
Great Britain	ESPN	live/highlights	939	56			28	1	203	1
Greece	ERT1	live	495	239	314	100	181	139		
Hungary	Digi Sport	live/delayed	1000	200	460	84	360	95	180	46
Ireland	Setanta	live	1015	170	275	54	470	81	140	35
Italy	RAI Sport Piu	live/delayed	622	194	372	78	55	64	194	52
Poland	Orange	live/highlights	1223	32	528	16	534	17	164	0
Portugal	RTP2	live	978	409	475	55	313	186	180	169
Romania	TVR 2	live/repeat	1983	102	546	37	642	42	735	23
Russia	NTV	live/repeat	3190	60	1070	23	1190	23	1220	22
Serbia	ArenaSport1	live/repeat	802	8	292	2	650	1	156	4
Slovenia	RTV2	delayed	372	141	161	41			211	101
Sweden	SVT 1 & 2	live/highlights	1253	646	594	211	409	107	250	327
TOTAL EUROPE	**17 Territories/18 CH**		**19931**	**4,909**	**6,518**	**1,308**	**6,373**	**1,722**	**4,272**	**1,838**
AFRICA										
Pan Africa (40 countries)	Supersport	live	1465	135	650	52	570	45	245	39
TOTAL AFRICA	**40 Territories/1 CH**		**1465**	**135**	**650**	**52**	**570**	**45**	**245**	**39**

(Continued)

Table 17.5 (Continued)

IAAF World Indoor Championships – Doha 2010

Territory	TV Stations/Channels		Total Broadcast (Minutes)	Cumulative Audience (000>$)	Friday 12 Broadcast Minutes	Friday 12 Audiences 000>	Saturday 13 Broadcast Minutes	Saturday 13 Audiences 000>	Sunday 14 Broadcast Minutes	Sunday 14 Audiences 000>
ASIA										
China	CCTVS-Beijing Sp-Shang	live/repeat	1719	12,217	385	4344	314	312	428	365
Hong Kong	CH631	live/repeat	5820	676	480	57	945	79	645	68
Japan	TBS	highlights	120	511					120	511
Middle East	Al Jazeera	tbc	tbc	6,060	tbc	600	tbc	935	tbc	245
India	ESPN	live/repeat	1380	3,807	450	1902	210	634		
Malaysia	ASTRO Super Sports	live	1190	207	530	82	120	41	540	82
Philippines	ESPN	live/repeat	2215	152	450	17	390	51		7
TOTAL ASIA	**26 Territories/8 CH**		**12444**	**23,630**	**2,295**	**7,002**	**1,979**	**2,052**	**1,733**	**4,564**
OCEANIA										
New Zealand	Sky TV	highlights	172	2						
Australia	SBS One	highlights	59	83					59	83
TOTAL OCEANIA	**2 Territories/2 CH**		**231**	**85**	**0**	**0**	**0**	**0**	**59**	**83**
AMERICAS										
Argentina	TYC Sports	live/repeat	900	159	420	48	180	23	180	65
Brazil	Sport TV	live	713	377	529	51	179	18	105	309
Canada	CBC	live	60	144			60	144		
Chile	TVN – C13	highlights	421	2,367	64	668	158	867	211	732
Mexico	Televisa	delayed	180	2,700			120	1530	60	1170
Panama	TVMAX – RPC	delayed	390	81	150	38	60	17	180	26
Peru	Canal 9	delayed	98	252	28	48	35	95	35	110
USA	Universal	live/repeat	2640	18,923			120	1958	360	3260
TOTAL AMERICAS	**8 Territories/8 CH**		**5402**	**25,003**	**771**	**805**	**732**	**4,629**	**951**	**5,607**
TOTAL WORLD	**93 Territories/37 CH**		**39473**	**53,762**	**10,234**	**9,167**	**9,654**	**8,448**	**7,260**	**12,131**

The outdoor advertising channels below were used to execute the advertising campaign, in addition to other advertising channels:

- Number of flags produced and installed inside venue: 150
- Number of flags produced and installed around city: 850
- Number of mupies (static, doubled-sided displays): 560
- Number of bridges and scaffoldings: 5
- Number of look elements and applications: 50
- Number of lamp post banners: 200

Signage

Way-finding and other signage are an important part of the event branding. We develop way-finding throughout the city to direct spectators and potential spectators to the event site and Fan Zone. The site is large and directions are needed to park and how to reach the venue or the Fan Zone. Once inside, the spectator needs to know where to go. Thus, uniformed signage is a key branding element. Below is a summary of the number of signs produced for the event:

- Number of way-finding signs produced/used: 606
- How many days in advance of event signage was installed: 15 days

Merchandise

Merchandising is a way to promote the event and leave a memory of it. The marketing department developed 12 types of merchandise items related to the event. Merchandise can also generate brand awareness and ticket sales.

- Number of items produced: 49,500
- Number of stores at Aspire: 3
- Number of stores throughout the city: 3

Public relations

This data shows information on the main aspects of the marketing awareness campaign of the IAAF WIC Doha 2010:

- Number of publications distributed: 10
- Number of hits on website: 418, 391
- Number of fans on the Fan Page: 2130

Ticketing

The following numbers represent the ticket sales outlets distribution:

- Number of tickets sold overall: 25,775
- Total number of tickets sold at Virgin MegaStores: 13,748
- Number of online tickets: 12,027

Table 17.6   *IAAF WIC 2010 ticket sales*

Ticket Sales

	Session 1	Session 2	Session 3	Session 4	Session 5	Total/Attendance
Virgin Villaggio	1,150	2,786	1,551	3,195	2,930	11,612
Virgin Landmark	336	524	342	496	438	2,136
Online						12,027
Total Sales						**25,775**

Aspire Dome Ticket Sales

	Session 1	Session 2	Session 3	Session 4	Session 5	Total/Attendance
12-Mar-10	215	880		62		1157
13-Mar-10			418	1306		1724
14-Mar-10					1185	1185

Table 17.6 represents the overall ticket sales information for the IAAF WIC Doha 2010 event.

Sponsorship

The sponsorship programme was developed as an opportunity for national companies to be associated with the IAAF World Indoor Championships that took place for the first time in the Middle East. It was a way for local businesses to show their support and commitment to the Vision of Qatar as a 'Global Sport Capital'. Sponsors gained national and international awareness through high-profile television coverage with Al Jazeera Sports, and had the chance to be linked with the superstars from the world of athletics competing in the event. These sponsors are presented in Figure 17.4. The sponsorship categories were:

- Official IAAF partner: 6
- Official IAAF supplier: 1
- National partner of the DLOC: 2
- National supplier of the DLOC: 7
- Public institute of the DLOC: 1

Fan Zone

The Fan Zone was developed to create excitement about the event and at the same time to give the sponsors a chance to activate their sponsorship programme during the event. The Fan Zone is also a way to generate impulse ticket and merchandise sales for potential spectators.

- Number of outlets at Fan Zone: 33
- Number of sponsors present at Fan Zone: 4
- Number of cultural activities: 11
- Number of fans at the Fan Zone: 8000

Figure 17.4   *WIC Doha 2010 IAAF sponsors and broadcasters*

Case Analysis

The marketing strategy of the 13th IAAF Indoor World Championships 2010 in Doha illustrated some key considerations for the organizing committee and their stakeholders. This section will address some key points in the creation of a value constellation.

The DLOC promoted specific values such as integrity, inspiration, leadership, collaboration and camaraderie for the IAAF WIC 2010 in Doha. However, the intrinsic characteristics of their services and products are filtered by the subjective perception of the stakeholders for which they are intended. Normann and Ramirez (1993: 66) stressed the fact that the 'focus should be on the value-creating system itself, within which different economic actors – suppliers, business partners, allies, customers – work together to co-produce value'. Consequently the DLOC and its stakeholders must create the conditions to create a sustainable value constellation. It must be achieved through the management of five important areas:

- The strategic stakeholders to be involved;
- The convergences between their respective goals and objectives;
- The characteristics of the collaborative programme(s) that will enable these goals to be achieved;
- The resources (finance, human, technology, facilities …) engaged by each partner and their aggregation;
- The management and the governance of the programme.

The DLOC is part of a large network made up of various kinds of stakeholders which provide resources and skills that will be used to structure and implement the event organization. A sport event should be considered and managed as a collaborative programme aiming to co-create the value with the stakeholders involved. As bidding and organizing committees are parts of networks, competition is between networks, rather than between individual organizations.

Relationship marketing based on collaborative programmes

The approach to relationship marketing taken by the DLOC enabled them to manage this major event as a collaborative programme involving key partners, and as such provided a greater value to their stakeholders. Parvatiyar and Sheth (2000) proposed a four-stage process for companies engaging in cooperative and collaborative relationships with stakeholders. Figure 17.5 presents the four phases that aim to create competitive advantage based on collaborative relationships: (1) the relationship building based on a marketing programme; (2) the management and the governance of the programme; (3) the assessment of the programme outcomes; (4) the relationship value enhancement.

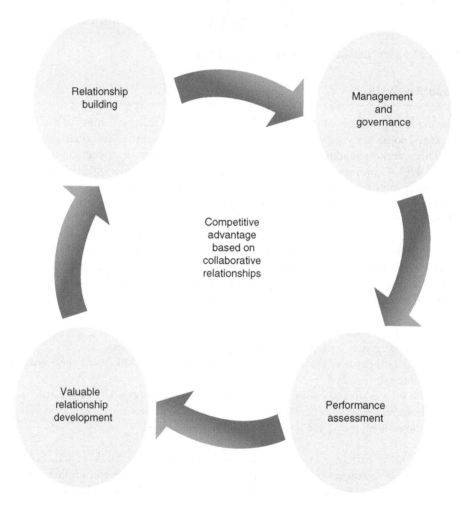

Figure 17.5   *The four-stage process model for engaging in cooperative and collaborative relationships with stakeholders (adapted from Parvatiyar and Sheh, 2000)*

Relationship-marketing strategy based on internal, network and market systems

The DLOC adopted a relationship-marketing strategy based on the internal, network and market system. This strategy is efficient because organizing committees are network based. They operate in a system formed by numerous stakeholders providing the necessary resources for the event organization. Importantly for future events, the relationship-marketing strategy that focuses on the market and network sub-sectors can only be designed and implemented if the organizing committee manages its internal relationships effectively. Many event managers underestimate the important supporting role marketing can play in increasing the success of events. Internal marketing builds the foundations for the implementation of marketing actions in the market and network sub-sectors. It is an ongoing process that occurs within organizing committees that have developed functional processes that recruit, align, motivate and empower employees and volunteers at all levels.

The principles of relationship marketing should be applied step by step. Ferrand and McCarthy (2008) suggest a three-step process. The first step concerns the organizing committee itself, within which the foundations of the marketing action must be built. It requires modifying relations with stakeholders, behaviour, skills, resources and the internal organization of the organizing committee. Internal marketing is the major issue allowing management of the resistance to change. The second step concerns the creation and development of relationships with targeted end-users, which involves a second challenge – that of improving loyalty. The third step is to introduce the changes needed to allow the implementation of a network-oriented relationship marketing approach, as it is more difficult to manage the relationships within a network than to manage a one-to-one relationship. It is only when an organizing committee has developed the skills to manage market-based relationships that it will be able to develop collaborative relationships with its stakeholders.

Major sport events have a large number of stakeholders and the organizing committee must prioritize them in order to select those to engage in collaborative programmes. Clarkson (1995: 96) suggests that the primary stakeholder group 'is one without whose continuing participation the corporation cannot survive as a going concern' and the secondary groups 'are defined as those who influence or affect, or are influenced or affected by, the corporation, but they are not engaged in transactions with the corporation and are not essential for its survival'. This categorization allows an organizing committee to focus its collaborative strategy on the most important stakeholders.

Branding strategy and linkage with the stakeholders' experience

Usually brands are registered (trademarked) with a regulatory authority and so cannot be used freely by other parties. Technically, a brand helps to differentiate the goods and services of one organization from those of another. In reality, brands are much more than that: they create a relationship with their customers based on their experiential value (Ferrand et al., 2005). According to Smith and Wheeler (2002) there are two strategies for creating a branded customer experience. The first strategy aims at 'experiencing the brand', which was a 'pull strategy' used by the IAAF WIC 2010. In collaboration with its stakeholders, the DLOC increased the appeal of the brand event through this process. This strategy 'begins with the brand and its desired values, turns these into a promise for target customers, and delivers the promise in a way which brings the brand alive'(Smith and Wheeler, 2002: 10). Nevertheless, fulfilling promises requires involving and managing relevant resources, effective teamwork, strong communication and quality management. The second strategy is aiming to create a unique experience for targeted customers and then branding it accordingly. This 'push strategy' is important for events with less international appeal. When this works successfully it is common for stakeholders to spread news of the unique and valuable experience using word of mouth and social media. Many major sport events with a high level of international appeal are combining these two strategies in order to link the brand with the experience and to relate this experience to its friends.

Case Review Questions

1   Who are the primary and secondary stakeholders for the IAAF WIC 2010? Do you think this distinction is useful? What risks does such an approach imply?
2   Why is the IAAF WIC 2010 valuable for the primary stakeholders?
3   Which primary stakeholders are involved in collaborative strategies? What benefits do they receive through this collaboration?
4   How could the collaborative strategy between primary stakeholders be improved in order to create value constellation?

References

Clarkson, M.B.E. (1995) 'A stakeholder framework for analyzing and evaluating corporate social performance', *Academy of Management Review*, 20(1): 92–117.

Ferrand, A., Torrigiani, L. and Povill, A.-C. (2005) *Routledge Handbook of Sports Sponsorship: Successful Strategies*. Abingdon: Routledge.

Ferrand, A. and McCarthy, S. (2008) *Marketing Sports Organizations: Building Networks and Relationships*. Abingdon: Routledge.

Gerrard, B. (2005) 'A resource-utilisation model of organizational efficiency in professional sports teams', *Journal of Sport Management*, 19(2): 143–169.

Normann, R. and Ramirez, R. (1993) 'From value chain to value constellation: Designing interactive strategy', *Harvard Business Review*, 71 (July/August): 65–77.

Parvatiyar, A. and Sheth, J.N. (2000) *The Handbook of Relationship Marketing*. Thousand Oaks, CA: Sage.

Smith, S. and Wheeler, J. (2002) *Managing the Customer Experience*. London: Prentice Hall.

18

Event Operations: The London City Airport's Fundraising Day

Polly Larner

Introduction

The organization

Opened in 1987, London City Airport (LCA) is an inner-city airport in private ownership (not part of BAA or the local authority) and was created to serve a niche business travel market. Located in London's Docklands with its runway along a disused quay and surrounded by water on three sides, the airport has faced a wide range of operational challenges in its (to date) 25 years of existence, requiring specially modified aircraft and specially trained pilots to cope with its steep glide path on take-off and landing as well as a relatively short runway. Aircraft must also carry out noise abatement procedures in order to comply with the airport's planning and operational regulations. It has dense housing and schools within 100m of its perimeter, industry with tall chimneys within 500m and the skyscrapers of Canary Wharf in line with its flight path a mere 3km away. Until December 2005, when the Docklands Light Railway extension was opened, it was only served by buses and a dilapidated suburban surface rail line.

The LCA experienced steep growth, supported by the local council (Newham) and business associations, and required several amendments to its planning permission to enable this in terms of more aircraft movements a year, physical developments to the terminal, offices and runway. Other measures included limited operational hours, continual pollution monitoring and sound insulation for local homes in order to minimize local resistance and a consultative committee of industry, local authority and community representatives.

Currently (April 2011) LCA has 13 partner airlines, plus executive air charter, and serves 31 destinations in 12 countries including the USA. LCA itself employs 130 people, with a total of approximately 750 working at the airport for airlines and in concessions, ground handling, duty free shopping, catering and car hire.

The event

This event was created as part of a Corporate Social Responsibility (CSR – see Cavagnaro et al., this volume) and advocacy strategy to endear the airport to local residents. The annual Fun Day began as a tenth birthday party for those in the borough who had applied for tickets through the local newspaper. These entitled them to free entry, a free birthday tea with birthday cake, free attractions including an air show, entertainment and a raffle for valuable prizes. Approximately 5000 people attended on a Saturday afternoon, the only possible time for such an event as the airport is closed overnight in accordance with its planning permission. Funds generated from sales of food and drink beyond the birthday tea, plus some specific activities, for example pony rides and general raffles and tombolas, were donated to LCA's chosen charity, Richard House – then London's only hospice for life-limited children located within 2 kilometres of the airport's runway. This was deemed a success by local attendees and the airport and became an annual event with the aim of increasing the fundraising potential and numbers attending as well as forming an important part of a stakeholder relationship management strategy.

By 2009, the event had grown to accommodate 26,000 visitors (LCA estimate, 2009) with sponsorship accounting for the operating costs, including LCA staff time and necessary fees for the air show and other attractions such as a flight simulator, and with a surplus from this and income on the day to donate to Richard House. Each year required a novel approach, from a carnival theme to the Wild West, and other draws including celebrity involvement. Operationally the event became more complex and with more organizations involved the stakeholder list grew. Operating costs exceeded £120,000 in 2008. In recent years a consultant was employed to obtain sponsorship, and in some years an external event organizer to plan and book the programme of entertainment and activities, excluding the air show which has always been managed by LCA.

The brief

Key objectives each year include:

- Raising more money for Richard House than in previous years.
- Involving more partner organizations in activities and sponsorship.
- Cementing relationships with the local authorities of Newham and Tower Hamlets.
- Having the widest range of activities and entertainments available in recognition of the very diverse population of Newham, where more than 100 languages are regularly spoken and many different ethnic communities and cultures co-exist in a densely populated and rather underprivileged borough.
- Being inclusive and being green.
- Involving more local associations in displays and fundraising activities.
- Involving more of LCA's staff in developing, operating and managing the Fun Day.

Outcomes

The event achieved its objectives notably in terms of CSR, building relationships and enhancing stakeholder relationships. Attendance at the event has grown in line with aspirations, though on occasion income has not reached the target, when the financial outcome was met by additional donations from sponsors and input from the airport from its own budgets to the benefit of the charity. In 2009 nearly £42,000 was donated.

Case Elements

Operating the event – July 2008: LCA's Circus Fun Day

The pre-event timeline

July 2007
The LCA announces the amount raised from the event and the date of the 2008 event to the public, stakeholders, airport partners and participating organizations, individuals and attractions and ensures all involved are thanked appropriately.

September 2007
The first meeting of the working group comprised of selected airport staff (PR, operational, financial) and generally no more than eight in number, to examine the deconstruction and evaluation of the 2007 event and determine actions to be carried forward.

At this point, key decisions are made:

- Whether to appoint an external fundraiser, event organizer or publicist. It decides to use in-house staff but to appoint a sponsorship consultant to raise funds.
- The preferred ideas for themes: a circus is decided on.
- Who are to be the lead managers from LCA to ensure legal and health and safety requirements are met, community and stakeholder relationships are managed effectively and objectives remain SMART (Sustainable, Manageable, Achievable, Realistic, Timely).
- That an initial risk assessment should be conducted and a matrix drawn up.
- The charging policy: it is reconfirmed that the event aims to provide a range of free attractions for those attending, as part of the CSR and Customer Relationship Management (CRM) strategy given the low-income profile of the local community. Stalls managed by community groups and LCA-based experiences will be free as will the circus. The fun fair will be managed on an hour-slot wristband basis, colour-coded, at £5 for unlimited use per adult or per child. Based on previous years' experience, it will be essential to monitor the funfair gate as sales have been made in excess of the cash returned. Other attractions including food stands will be charging the public, with income to the Fun Day either on a pitch-fee basis or with a percentage returning to LCA, varying according to contract.

October 2007

The LCA's working group nominates lead executives for operational matters who will report to the working party at regular monthly meetings and in more frequent one-to-one conversations as appropriate. These executives, along with the external fundraising consultant appointed from a shortlist of three, are introduced to LCA stakeholders and partners including Newham Borough Council's planning and licensing team in order to progress plans. LCA must manage and implement the air show element scrupulously in liaison with the private pilots involved and air traffic control as this is highly specialized and complex given LCA's specific environment. Ongoing risk assessment revisions are undertaken.

October 2007 to June 2008

LCA staff develop the Fun Day product. *Part A*: Licensing and legal requirements are checked. These differ from place to place and are largely determined by the local government authority. They may also change from year to year so it is essential to review requirements annually. For LCA's Fun Day these generally include:

- Obtaining a TEN (Temporary Event Notice) – under the Licensing Act 2003 (Permitted Temporary Activities) from Newham Borough Council – to permit the event to take place in an environment not generally used for events and so not licensed. This will require consultation with the local residents and the submission of a developed event plan including information on noise levels, especially as the Fun Day takes place in what is a closed period for the airport (Saturday midday–Sunday late morning) as stipulated in its planning permission. Conditions may be imposed in granting this which the authorities will check before the event: failure to comply may result in the event being prevented from taking place. Currently there is no requirement for a TEN, as the airport is on privately owned land.
- Planning permission from the local authority for any temporary structures such as staging and marquees, depending on the event product content. These are generally not required if erected for less than 28 days.
- An entertainment licence for live music, dancing and performances (under the Licensing Act 2003). Currently there is no requirement for an entertainment licence as the airport is on privately owned land, though performing rights issues and royalties must be addressed.
- Local authority registration to enable raffles and prize draws. Requires compliance in how these are administered and differs depending on purpose and area of the country.
- A Civil Aviation Authority (CAA) licence, which is required for the air show, including conditions relating to Public Safety Zones. These zones are areas outside the airport perimeter over which the participating aircraft may fly and so may potentially create an incident (technical failure, or, as a worst-case scenario, a crash into a housing area), and raise noise and pollution concerns.
- Food handling regulation. Those organizations offering food and prepared drinks in the food court must demonstrate their compliance with the Food Handling and Hygiene Regulations (Food Safety [General Food Hygiene] Regulations 1995 and the Food Standards Authority's Food Handling Regulations [England] 2006).

- An alcohol licence. LCA has a licence for its terminal bars. These will not be available to the public on Fun Day though VIPs will be offered complimentary alcoholic drinks in the Departure Lounge set aside for them. Security staff at the entrance gates will check visually for any alcohol being brought on site.
- Copyright issues and performing rights issues being checked with performers. This includes costuming and look-alikes as attempted prosecutions for infringement have been recorded recently.
- Staff working at airports being routinely cleared through Criminal Record Bureau (CRB) checks and being trusted with cash and lost property. In some cases staff have undergone CRB Enhanced Disclosure which, if clear, permits them to work with minors – these staff will be allocated to look after 'Lost Children' and youth groups performing.
- Compliance with the requirements of the Disability Discrimination Act (2005). This affects access and general facilities at the airport, which are already compliant, but the Fun Day attractions and extra services must also comply. Exceptions are possible: for example some of the aircraft are not wheelchair-accessible so to visit them would require a physical lift on board by specially trained staff. If this is explained on a sign and/or announced in the programme, for example, there is no problem. In most cases the disabled visitor can enjoy the full experience.
- Compliance with the provisions of the Health and Safety Act 1974 and later amendments and additions, addressed through the risk matrix. Staff are briefed by LCA's health and safety (H&S) specialists throughout the development and operational phases to report potential hazards and infringements. Security staff in particular and all staff will be briefed to be vigilant for any evidence of weapons and drugs among the crowd.

Other activities continue. The look and the logo are created. Publicity is generated, sponsorship packages are developed and community engagement sought. Ongoing risk assessment revisions are undertaken as elements of the product content are committed and any external circumstances affecting the event change. Contingency and emergency plans are developed. Where these may differ from standard airport operating procedures, these elements are rehearsed. Local signage is agreed as to detail and location/installation with the Automobile Association (AA) for directional signage from access routes and public transport (DLR – Docklands Light Railway) and buses. The Airport Chaplain is briefed – he offers non-denominational worship opportunities, and is available to help and counsel in a crisis. He advises on the provision of prayer rooms equipped for and available to members of the different faiths represented in the airport staff 'family' and, as a serving clergyman in the hugely diverse Borough of Newham, is able to take into account the needs of other faith groups likely to come to the Fun Day.

Part B: The Fun Day end-product is decided on and will include:

- Opening parade with celebrities.
- Circus – ethical, no performing animals.
- Fun fair – game stalls with prizes, haunted house, cakewalk, children's rides, miniature train rides around the site, bouncy castles, 'gladiator' games.

- Birds of prey – static display of live birds from a local sanctuary.
- Pearly Kings and Queens from local East End of London boroughs (a nineteenth century Cockney tradition – a role handed down within families. 'Pearlies' wear costumes decorated with pearl buttons and feathers).
- Raffle and tombola stalls with prizes donated by the LCA and on-site partners which include airlines, duty-free shops, car hire companies and other concessions.
- Community information, association and club stands. These include a wide range of ethnic groups, literacy schemes, sports, music and games clubs.
- An entertainment strand to include the Ascension Eagles (local youth cheerleaders), local ethnic music and dance groups, including West African, Irish and capoeira troupes and a local Air Force Cadet marching band.
- Look-alikes, magicians, stilt-walkers – professional, entertaining the queue before gates open and in the Fun Day area.
- Costumed characters – representatives of local community groups as cartoon characters.
- An air show, a key feature of the event, lasting approximately an hour (split into three sessions) including static aircraft, some of which may be visited by those attending (for example, a British Airways [BA] Avro RJ-85 120-seater), a descent by the British Army sky-diving team, a wing-walking display, aerobatics by light aircraft and classic aircraft (for example, Spitfire, P51 Mustang, Antonovs, Yak) either as a fly-past or landing – some may be boarded by visitors.
- Displays of classic cars, motor bikes and model aircraft including motor-bike trails along the runway and demonstration flights by powered model planes.
- Food court – British and ethnic specialities including Asian, Afro-Caribbean, Tex-Mex, a hog-roast, vegetarian, juice and ice cream.
- VIP/Sponsors lounge – in the airport departure lounge, providing a panoramic view of runway and activities, with complimentary catering sponsored 'in-kind' by one of LCA's catering franchises.
- Goody bags of small gifts and vouchers, along with the day's edition of the London *Evening Standard* newspaper and airport and sponsor/partner information, which are distributed as people leave – number calculated as average of one per family so approximately 10,000. Team of staff needed to collate contents for the day.
- Temporary facilitates such as toilets and crowd-control barriers lining the runway, containing crowd access to static aircraft, marking safety lanes for emergency access and barring public access to specific operational areas.
- The public address system (PA) and commentators, including a professional master-of-ceremonies and an LCA aviation expert.
- First Aid/lost children/lost property provision.
- Security to be provided by LCA's own company and local police.
- The marshalling of free car parking in LCA's on-site car parks by teams from local Scout troupes.
- Many other event experiences, such as: fortune-teller and palmist; British Airways run a 'be a steward' experience for children (where they dress up, deliver the safety announcements, put on life-jackets and serve meals from the trolley); volunteers of the Territorial Army with equipment including armoured car, tents, assault course;

the LCA airport fire crews (fire-rescue-boat rides on the dock, squirt the hose, go up on the telescopic escape ladder); adult learning and other educational activities; HM Revenue and Customs (HMRC) showing prohibited imports and sniffer-dog demonstrations; tethered balloon ascents; and many more.

June 2008

Once the licences are in place and sponsorship agreements are concluded with income largely assured, the event product is finalized and site plans are drawn up. Locating each event component within the event area is a logistical challenge. The area consists of the gate-rooms, apron (where aircraft draw up to the gate-rooms) and runways/taxiways. The public area covers approximately 5000m^2 and is around 1km long.

Site plans also identify specific services/locations required, for example power sources, water, shade for animals. The programme can now be timed and the schedule developed to ensure no conflicts and that all safety aspects are addressed – for example, no model aircraft flying or balloon ascents when the air show is taking place. Dressing/waiting areas for performers, First Aid post, lost property and lost children points and a rest area are allocated using some of the 13 gate-rooms at ground level. Access to the VIP/Sponsor area is marked, the list of guests nominated by LCA and stakeholders/sponsors is checked and access control (by special ticket) agreed. The LCA staff/event management company 'uniform' of Fun Day branded T-shirts is ordered in a range of sizes based on those staff working at the event unless officially uniformed, for example security and fire crews.

Internal communications plans are developed and tested, for example staff participating to use either walkie-talkies or mobile phones depending on their roles, with spare batteries/chargers available. Crisis plans are revisited and the decision-making chain of command established for each area of Fun Day activity working with the LCA event co-ordinator in consultation with the team. Signage is finalized and produced for the Fun Day area, including marshalling points for attractions to await their individual set-up access time-slot, organized according to their individual number – early numbers first. These are adjacent to the western RVP (Rendez-Vous Point – special perimeter gates kept clear and signed to allow access in to the airport for emergency services).

Importantly, at this stage LCA issues an Airport Director Information (ADI) notice to its partner airlines and their ground handling agents and other concessions and to NATS. The ADI states that under no circumstances except notified emergency will aircraft be permitted to land after 12 noon or take off after 12.30pm on the day of the event. This means that any aircraft unable to leave by that time will be grounded until the airport re-opens the next day and any aircraft running late in landing, even if for a night-stop (scheduled parking at LCA until the next day), must divert to an alternative airport. This of course excludes air-show aircraft.

30 June–4 July 2008

The final checks take place. Staffing rotas and positions are established. Specific staff are allocated to 'host' each VIP and sponsor to ensure that the terms of the sponsorship agreement are met, to assist attending media and in particular to escort celebrities and ensure they are in the right place at the right time for photo opportunities, meeting-and-greeting and participating in prize draws and similar activities. Staff are also allocated to 'chugging' – collecting cash donations from among those attending by rattling a box or bucket – to benefit Richard House, beneficiary of the Fun Day, as well as collecting cash takings from attractions as agreed in individual contractual terms of participation: they will carry copies to minimize dispute. LCA's photographer is briefed on specific shots needed for PR use and sponsors and otherwise given a roving commission including video footage. Programmes are printed for the public attending, each with an individual stamped number to enable participation in a free prize draw.

London Fire Brigade controllers, local police superintendents, LCA security and LCA's fire chief meet to consider the current status of possible threats and hazards. Final details of the air show are confirmed to NATS, attending pilots and organizations and long-range weather forecasts considered – these may require a rescheduling of air show components in case of, for example, high winds or thunderstorms as well as possible adaptation of layout, structures or staging. Wet-weather contingencies are readied if significant rain is likely.

The operations team reconfirms set-up slot timings and other details with each attraction, service provider and participant. Communications plans are revisited including checking radio frequencies to avoid interference, especially regarding air show activity. The risk assessment is finalized and any remaining mitigating activity put in place where necessary and where possible in advance. This becomes increasingly important as the day of the event approaches. Local internal and external circumstances are discussed and on the evening of 4 July the decision to stage the Fun Day is confirmed in the knowledge that every precaution possible has been taken to ensure that the event can operate safely and within the law.

5 July 2008: The day arrives

Scheduling and operational constraints

A numbers of factors affecting the timing of the event and its programme constituents from set-up to break-down and site clearance are not negotiable; others require consideration and accommodating in the day's operating schedule:

- The event opens at 2pm and closes at 6pm.
- Set-up and break-down can only take place from 6am on the day of the event and the airport must remain operational until 12.30pm on Saturdays, reopening on Sundays at 9am with flights resuming at 10.30am. This means that the event area will not be wholly free for set-up until after 12.30pm and everything must be cleared before 9am the next day.
- Security, HMRC and other control authorities, fire crews and air traffic control must remain operational throughout given the nature of the event and airport operational directives.

- Two access routes are broken by swing bridges within 1km of LCA. These may be required to open for shipping accessing the dock at times which would impede set-up and break-down in particular and could lead to congestion and delays for those members of the public arriving and leaving. These bridge movements are generally known a minimum of 24 hours in advance.
- Large-scale attractions require several hours to set up and test-run, including the circus tent which in addition needs artiste practice time.
- Health and safety checks and other final approval inspections must be conducted before the OK to open the gates can be given.
- The runway and taxiways must be cleaned and checked for FOD (Foreign Objects and Debris – oil leakages, plastic food wrappers, nuts and bolts or anything likely to damage an aircraft or cause it to swerve while taxiing or on take-off or landing, no matter how tiny or apparently harmless in appearance to the non-specialist) before the airport can be notified to NATS as reopening and able to receive aircraft.

Scheduling is therefore crucial, and an understanding of how long elements take is important in order to plan access slots and location of attractions.

The first element allowed on-site must be the crowd-control barriers, one stretch of which will be moved along the Fun Day area from the western RVP gate as airport operations draw to a close. LCA's Ground Operations team will direct incoming flights to use stands/gates progressively nearer the terminal's arrivals entrance as time goes on to free more of the apron area for setting up.

The apron has a number of inset power points from which cabling can be run to feed catering equipment, the PA system and rides. LCA technicians must check all set-ups as cabling is installed to ensure there is no overload or other hazard, including loose cabling, poor connections and untested or poorly maintained equipment. All electrical equipment should carry a current PAT-test sticker (Portable Appliance Testing is a requirement under the H&S Act 1974 and is valid for 12 months from date of test).

Public access for the Fun Day is through the eastern RVP, about 1km distant from the western RVP, at the end of the terminal complex where there is a covered walkway from the car park, taxi-rank and bus stops. The DLR station is integrated into the terminal and remains open with a normal service. Buses also run according to their normal schedule at the time of the Fun Day.

Box 18.1   Event Operations: A view from the coal-face*

5.30am Arrive at airport to see a snake of lorries and vans queuing up at the western RVP – looks as if some have been there overnight. Security are already making sure they are lined up in slot order and getting some to reverse around into their rightful positions! Make it to the boardroom for the bacon sandwich

(Continued)

(Continued)

breakfast briefing in good time, so collect my T-shirt to be sure to get the right size: the rush starts around 8am and last year saw one of the big guys with it tied round his shoulders as the biggest size didn't fit. The Managing Director went mad when he saw it; as always he's got an eagle eye for detail. The goody-bag-stuffers are only waiting for the *Evening Standard* to be delivered – they've worked all night!

6.00am There are enough key workers present so the briefing gets under way. We watch PowerPoint slides of the layout, with changes highlighted. There's a pack for us all along with our communications gear so no need to take notes. LCA's airfield operations director explains the air show elements and we talk about the weather: looks as if it'll be dry but gusty with low cloud. That means some of the aerobatics may not happen and there may not be as many balloon ascents as planned. No matter that the programme says 'subject to weather and other circumstances beyond our control' there will always be someone to complain. We go over team rotas, checking who's confirmed they will be working and who will deputize for key roles such as money matters and timings in case of absentees. The final arbiter on timings and operational details is our Assistant Managing Director (AMD) who's already here to give the briefing. I seem to be trouble-shooter-in-chief: I know that'll mean no voice and sore feet by the end of the day! 'Mission Control' is at Gate 5, next to the PA set-up and commentary point, half-way along the stretch of Fun Day activity. Must refill my water bottle.

6.30am Out on the apron, wearing my yellow high-visibility jacket and ear-defenders because of proximity to the readying aircraft, I'm watching the barrier team slot them together so quickly that already the runway is enclosed with two access points free for the taxiways and the first dividing line is in place. In front of that the first flight of the day is already taxiing for take-off: once that is gone the dividing line can move up 100m or so. Beyond it, lorries are off-loading brightly coloured funfair rides, the first batch of portable toilets are in place and one of the bouncy castles is inflating slowly. I check that it is properly anchored even at this early stage. The fire crew on duty wave, taking a break from checking the no.2 and no.3 engines which will be used for rides and display, while no.1 remains on the alert. The fire chief is at the eastern end going over arrangements for rides on the dock in the fire-boats: the water is choppy and so these too may be curtailed.

The walkie-talkie buzzes: there's a query at the western RVP. The guy bringing the flight simulator – always popular despite costing £5 a go – reckons he's in the wrong spot as he needs power and there is no outlet in easy reach. I check the plan: he didn't tell us he wasn't bringing his own generator as in previous years. Discuss with the technicians and manage to move him near an outlet with spare capacity. He's pleased, as this is nearer the air show static display. So now we juggle some other attractions by a few yards to take up the space and improve visitor flows.

(Continued)

(Continued)

10.30am More flights have now cleared without any delays or technical problems and so we have moved the dividing barrier more than half-way along the apron. The PA centre is in place and being connected though testing must wait until the last flight has gone. Signage is being put up where set-up is finalized, and I can see a thick sprinkling of Fun Day T-shirts busy all across the apron – the walkie-talkie is crackling non-stop now. Fortunately for a moment nothing needs my attention. I come across a group of people limbering up – circus acrobats and jugglers getting ready to move into the big top (well, small top!) once it is up and rigged safely. I'm told it takes 45 minutes from start to finish – I'll believe it when I see it. They should be able to start in 30 minutes or so, after the next flight leaves. It's refuelling now so should complete its turn-around in time and then we can move the dividing barrier to free up the circus space.

11.15am Grab a cup of coffee with our PR officer: she's really stressed. Calls have been coming in from the main celebrity saying he's running late. He's needed for the Opening Parade, of course. The sponsorship consultant has also been asking for changes to the VIP guest list – fortunately that's achievable: we decide to leave the special tickets for them by name at the entrance to the Departure Lounge – renamed 'VIP area' for the day: the sign looks good. Last year we had complaints about that – they said everyone was a VIP and should be allowed in. We couldn't think of a suitable alternative, so we'll see what the reaction is this year. A TV crew has turned up with no warning and so is being briefed on what's happening when and where on the site. They seemed to think it would all be in full swing now, so maybe they won't wait. As a holding operation we put them together with our media-savvy Managing Director who's just arrived.

12.00 noon I go out to the front of the terminal in response to a call from the Information Desk – they have a bus-load of Scouts who aren't sure what they are meant to be doing. I quickly print off a copy of their activity sheet which explains timings, locations and tasks and go over it with their leader, along with reference copies of the programme. They will be manning the approach road from the roundabout to the terminal front, waving on cars and explaining parking and any other points to people as they arrive. Other groups will be at the car park entrances marshalling cars towards empty zones and later to empty spaces and finally to overflow parking by the cargo and engineering sheds. We've laid on refreshments for them at 2.45pm when we can assume most people will have arrived. The Scouts can then join in the fun. The leader asks if there is the chance to meet our main celebrity. I promise to try and arrange this.

The 'welcome' banner is up over the eastern RVP gate, through which the Opening Parade will pass followed by the queuing public at 2pm sharp – if all goes well. I go back airside to the event area. The hot-air balloon is being readied, crowd-control barriers are almost complete, just leaving room for the last aircraft to pass on to the taxiway, and classic cars and motorbikes are being revved up

(Continued)

(Continued)

ready to get into position. The Ground Operations team is laying out fluorescent flight lines on the ground for the air-show planes to indicate their performance area. They also must land and taxi at specific distances from the public for safety reasons; these distances are specified by the CAA as part of the permission to hold the air show and so we've put in special double barrier lanes for safety.

12.30pm The last plane departs. The terminal closes to the public and there is a mad rush of activity to finish set-up. The community stands are looking good though I have had to persuade one stand to dispose of balloons they've brought ready to decorate their stand: if a balloon broke lose it could be sucked into an aircraft engine and cause an accident – they see reason. HMRC are ready with their exhibition and dog display – the dogs are inside in the cool. The tarmac and concrete are now radiating heat from a bright though clouded sky.

There are some heavy clouds on the horizon and quite a strong wind. Airport partners are readying their stands – ranks of raffle and tombola prizes and pricing information. Troupes of dancers and entertainers begin to arrive – I get a call from a harassed-sounding colleague with a teenage group who have not requested changing facilities but arrived with racks of costumes. I speak to their director and we arrange a shared gate-room on a timed basis with a dancing-school ballet group. Fortunately nobody objects to mixed changing – the racks can act as screens.

The Food Court is coming alive with enticing cooking smells. I walk down to see a chef slicing up a whole roast pig for his hog-roast open sandwiches, there's jerk chicken, gumbo simmering, Thai and Chinese food being prepared. Makes me hungry – I grab a quick sample.

1.00pm I am scheduled to meet our AMD and fundraising consultant to catch up on any problem areas before we walk the course with the local police superintendent, Fire Brigade leader and Newham H&S and licensing representatives. If they don't like what they see, we may not have a Fun Day! It seems we're on target and as far as we can tell there is nothing likely to upset them.

They arrive on time and we set out from the eastern VIP gate. Their eyes are everywhere, but they seem to be ticking all the boxes on their forms. They do ask for certain guy-ropes on the circus tent to be flagged with bunting to draw the eyes of passers-by who might walk into them – not difficult to deal with. They check the readiness of the fire crews and the public safety zones surrounding the air show and static aircraft – all well. I leave them to it as I get a call reminding me I should be marshalling the Opening Parade.

1.40pm The Marching Band has arrived and is down by the long-term car park tuning up. The Territorial Army open jeep, festooned with LCA colours – bright blue and green ribbons and rosettes – is also there ready to head the Opening Parade. No sign of the main celebrity yet: the Managing Director is pacing the front of the terminal. People have been arriving for some time and have parked and are queuing along the walkway and way down the road.

(Continued)

(Continued)

I call the entertainment team leader and ask him to hurry up the entertainers scheduled to amuse the crowd: he promises to dispatch them immediately. I see the stacks of programmes inside the RVP gate and staff are gathering ready to hand them out as people come in. There's a big notice informing them about their 'lucky number' and the Grand Prize Draw. It seems we are almost ready.

2.00pm Our celebrity has arrived and is instantly catapulted into the jeep ready for the parade. Just waiting for the green light from the operations team to start the parade which will pass the queuing people and have the gate swung open ceremoniously as they approach. After five minutes there is still no 'all clear' call. I check – and they can't find the key for the gate!

This has happened before – so no lesson learnt there, then. I gather a runner is rushing for the security control-room's master key. I ginger up the entertainers to keep the crowd's attention.

2.08pm The queue is getting restless. Finally the call comes and I signal the band to start. The fanfare is a bit wobbly, but they get into the swing and step out bravely, the jeep following. There are cheers and whistles – the gate swings open to reveal an honour-guard of cheerleaders and staff waving and applauding, ready to hand out programmes. This mammoth event is finally under way.

From here on in it will have a momentum of its own. Decisions will be made on the spot, things will happen and be dealt with, and we'll all find time rushing by until the PA announces 'Goodbye until next year' and we can start clearing up and the great break-down.

3.15pm I get a call to help one of the teams of cash-collectors: they have to be in pairs for security. This pair has so much in weight of coins that their bag has broken. I find some spares and take them around with me, reminding teams it's better to trek back to the financial manager's office more frequently than spill the money. It looks as if people are being generous as the chuggers too have heavy buckets.

The air show is under way at this point and there's a lull for the attractions and stalls as people gaze skywards. I help a family to the First Aid point as the mother has some grit in her eye and the children are howling. The sniffer-dogs look hot as the sun has come out on their display area and their carry-cages don't look cool either. I borrow a light gazebo from the Samaritans who now are in the shade and get it over to the dogs' area.

A colleague on Information Point duty calls me over. She is talking to an irate elderly man, trying to explain why he keeps hearing what he takes to be gun-shots. He believes we are killing birds on the airport and is threatening to prosecute LCA. I take him to a nearby gate-room; we sit down and I explain that what he hears are maroons – blank, noisy shells fired into the air from a special pistol by our trained operational staff. This is standard airport operating practice, necessary to deter flocks of birds from settling on the runway and surrounding grassland or dock – Canada geese are a particular problem. If we don't scare birds away they could collide with an aircraft and cause a crash. He seems to understand, thank goodness.

(Continued)

(Continued)

There seems to be a mass of people round the fortune-teller: she's very popular. I get one of our team to set up a timed-ticket operation as some people tell me they've been waiting half an hour. Aiming for 10-minute slots at £3 a go, we ought to manage around another 18–20 appointments. Maybe next year have several clairvoyants?

I pick up a conversation between the control tower and our AMD. It seems there's a light aircraft in the vicinity running out of fuel. The pilot's in touch with NATS and is suggesting he land here, as he's seen planes on approach. It's decided he won't be permitted to try, given all our activity, especially as there is another suitable airfield not too far away – we all hope he makes it!

4.20pm Just spotted a really fun interaction – there's a woman dressed as Father Christmas from the Richard House stand chatting to a colourful group of people wearing all kinds of bright ethnic clothes – saris, shalwar kameez, burkas, ghandi jackets and those wonderfully wound Nigerian turbans matched to their gowns ... that says it all: what a multi-cultural area we live and work in, and how good to get everyone together enjoying a day out. Already the tombola stalls are looking as if a swarm of locusts has descended – few prizes left, so takings will be good. A Moslem lady wins a bottle of wine – the stall organizer immediately substitutes it with a basket of toiletries.

I see one of our team charged with getting feedback from the public who seems to be struggling. We've planned an informal chat rather than a hard questionnaire. The family being engaged in this seem to be angry. They are black, of all ages, and I wonder whether they are suspicious of our motives. It seems they are: they are worried by our asking whereabouts they live and how they travelled to the Fun Day. Once I explain again, reassuring them that we only want to plan an even better event for next year and that they won't be identified in any way by talking to us, they relax. I hand back to my colleague and leave him to carry on.

4.40pm Panic call from the portable toilet company: they've got to close one bank of loos as they are running low on supplies – chemical as well as disposables. We decide the set nearest the eastern RVP would be best as people will be on their way out more than in at this stage and could probably wait until they get home.

5.30pm It's time for the Grand Prize-giving. Our celebrity has been busy entertaining, shaking hands, giving autographs and being photographed with loads of people: he's very good-tempered about it and hasn't whinged once. Makes a change from last year's prima donna! Now he joins LCA's Managing Director on the big stage, flanked by those of the team who can be spared. There are funny speeches, the list of prizes is read out to 'oohs' and 'ahs' – flights, weekend breaks, luxury hire car for a week, and more. The draw takes ages as not everyone whose lucky number is drawn is apparently present, but eventually the top prize goes to a young man in a wheelchair, who's been in the front row for the different shows all afternoon. He's quite overwhelmed. A first-time flyer, he and a friend will be off to Paris with Air France, who'll look after him well. Good result!

(Continued)

(Continued)

5.50pm The end is in sight. Already the funfair is packing up and some of the stalls are deserted. The PA announces the end of the Fun Day, though there are still some 4000 people around out of the 25,000 estimated to have attended. As the celebrity leaves, I realize I didn't match him up with the Scout troupe for a photo as I'd promised – I'll have to apologize to the Scout leader and think of another way to say thank you and mark the event or they may not be so ready to help next year.

6.00pm Barriers are being collected, the last of the air-show planes takes off and Ground Services are out with their machines sweeping the runway. Cars and lorries stream away. We all help, by taking down signage, picking up litter, carrying stuff, generally talking to everyone who's participated and picking up their thoughts on how it all went from their perspective. Generally positive. We'll undertake formal feedback from participants, sponsors and stakeholders in the coming days, but it's nice to get a sense of it. Certainly I don't think there were many complaints from the public attending – even the wind dropped a bit and the sun stayed out most of the time. Our Managing Director comes by to say thank you – he always does, though we'll hear later if anything wasn't quite right in his view.

9.30pm Looks as if the last attraction is on its way and only LCA's team are left to finish readying the airport for the next day. The crowd-control barriers are still here – neatly stacked for collection at 6am tomorrow to be off to the next event. One classic car refused to start and has been pushed into the car park. The owner has summoned mechanics so hopefully he'll be on his way soon. I take a call about some lost property: a man is missing his signet ring – he's not sure when he last noticed it, but it might have fallen into the toilet or slipped off his finger while he was doing gladiator games. We don't have it recorded as handed in, but I take details and will circulate a request for information. Doubt it will turn up.

10.00pm On my way home!

*'From the coal-face' is a British colloquial term referring to workers who are stationed at the front line of the workplace. Essentially it derives from those who scraped the coal of the face of the mine; in events this could be seen as the event-day interface between the event's management and the stakeholders.

Case Analysis: Wash-up and Evaluation

Given the overriding informal atmosphere of the event, LCA decided that formalized evaluation input from the public would not be appropriate. The debriefing of all staff took place on the following Monday morning and all points, good and bad, were recorded for assistance in planning the next Fun Day.

The sponsorship consultant e-mailed in a detailed report which read positively with, in her view, nothing significant likely to affect the sponsorship monies pledged. The financial manager reported estimated income net of expenditure in line with the target of £45,000 and confirms a best estimate of 24,500 attending. A date was decided for the ceremonial cheque presentation to Richard House.

Key team members met with stakeholders on a one-to-one basis during July to discuss the event, again recording points for future reference. Those providing attractions were contacted similarly for their views within three working days and asked whether they would be interested in attending next year.

Case Review Questions

1 Consider the stakeholders for this event and outline the particular aspects in which they would have an interest. Do you see any areas of conflict? What might they be and how would you overcome this? How would you keep stakeholders informed and engaged?

2 Do any of the aspects of health and safety related to the Fun Day product give you cause for concern? What would you wish to discover more about? Do you see any points where practice could be improved?

3 Who could be approached to sponsor the event and what would you consider as the benefits for them? What ingredients would you suggest as part of a tailored sponsorship package for each organization?

4 How could the airport maintain the freshness and appeal of the event for the future, helping to assure it reaches its objectives of more people attending and more income for charity – given the site constraints and increasingly challenging social and economic conditions? Critique ideas and range in order of likely success and practicality.

5 In small groups, sketch out a *crisis management scenario* based on the plane low on fuel crash-landing on the airport – consider who would be involved in controlling this and what practical actions would be involved in implementing it, basing your suggestions on a timeline. Following peer critique decide whether your crisis management plan would result in a positive or negative impact on the airport's image and core business.

Index

Page references to Boxes, Figures or Tables will be in *italics*